Private Myths

Private Myths

Dreams and Dreaming

ANTHONY STEVENS

Harvard University Press
Cambridge, Massachusetts

First Published in Great Britain by Hamish Hamilton Ltd
The moral right of the author has been asserted

Library of Congress Cataloging-in-Publication Data

Stevens, Anthony.
Private myths : dreams and dreaming / Anthony Stevens.
p.   cm.
Originally published: London : Hamish Hamilton Ltd., 1995.
Includes bibliographical references and index.
ISBN 0-674-21638-5 (alk. paper)
ISBN 0-674-21639-3 (pbk.)
1. Dream interpretation—History. 2. Dreams. I. Title.
BF1091.S724   1996
154.6'3—dc20   95-45926
                                                              CIP

A myth is a public dream, a dream is a private myth.
JOSEPH CAMPBELL

Contents

Acknowledgements

I should like to express my thanks to the following publishers for permission to quote from previously published material: to Routledge and the Princeton University Press to quote from *The Collected Works of C. G. Jung*; to Random House, Inc., for permission to quote from *Memories, Dreams, Reflections* by C. G. Jung, recorded and edited by Aniela Jaffé; to the Oxford University Press to reproduce the analysis of Jung's dream of the customs inspector, on pages 55–62, from my *Jung* in the Past Masters Series; to the Hogarth Press to quote from *The Interpretation of Dreams* by Sigmund Freud and from *The Freud/Jung Letters* edited by William McGuire; to Penguin to quote from *The Dreaming Brain* by J. Allan Hobson; to the Yale University Press to quote from *The Multiplicity of Dreams* by Harry T. Hunt; to Faber & Faber to quote from *W. H. Auden: The Collected Poems* and from *Four Quartets* by T. S. Eliot; to the J. B. Priestley Estate to reproduce Priestley's great 'Dream of the Birds' from *Rain Upon Godshill*; to William Morrow & Co. to quote from 'Big Dream, Little Dream' by Louis Simpson; to James MacGibbon to quote from 'Thoughts About the Person from Porlock' by Stevie Smith; to Sony Publishers to quote from 'Mr Jones' by Bob Dylan; to the Toronto University Press to reproduce Paul D. MacLean's diagram of the triune brain; and to Edward F. Edinger to reproduce and adapt his diagram on page 323.

Among those who read early drafts of this book I am grateful to the following for their comments and suggestions: Julian David, Neil Phelps, Salley Boatswain, Norman Curtis, and Andrew Franklin.

Warmest thanks of all go to Norma Luscombe for the unfailing care, skill and generosity of spirit with which she word-processed all stages of the book and for producing an immaculate final draft for my copy-editor, Annie Lee, to attack with a rare combination of precision and tact.

I

THE POETRY MACHINE

*The vast majority die without realizing more than a
fraction of their powers. Born millionaires, they live and
die in poverty.*

A. R. ORAGE

In the final stages of planning this book, *I had a dream in which
Carolus Oldfield, John Bowlby, and a man in a white coat (whom I took to
be some sort of scientist or laboratory technician) were arguing over a piece of
apparatus. From the look of it, I gathered that it must be an EEG machine,
as it had electrodes for attachment to a subject's scalp, and wires leading to
pens which squiggled spiky lines on a revolving drum of paper; but Carolus
referred to it as a 'poetry machine'. In the next room a young woman was
singing, and I awoke moved by the simple beauty of her song.* What did
this mean? Why should these characters appear to me just as I was
about to begin writing? And why should one of them refer to an
electro-encephalograph as a poetry machine? Who, you may wonder,
were these people anyway?

Carolus Oldfield had been Professor in two university Departments
of Psychology at which I studied in the 1950s, first at Reading and
later at Oxford. A kind and generous teacher, he taught me most of
what I know about the use of scientific method in the study of
psychological phenomena. Later on, when my medical training was
complete, he encouraged me to do a doctorate (an MD) based on
research into the attachment behaviour of infants at the Metera
Babies Centre in Athens, and asked John Bowlby to act as my
supervisor. To my great satisfaction, Bowlby agreed.

For a budding analyst, as I then was, this was a stroke of immense
good fortune. Through his internationally acclaimed work on the
mother–child attachment bond, John Bowlby had already revolution-
ized psychoanalytic theory and he was to prove a wonderfully
stimulating mentor to have at that time in my life. John's chief

distinction in my eyes was his success in working towards Freud's ambition to bring psychoanalysis into the mainstream of biological science. Unfortunately, not many analysts were enthused by his example, and continued to base their belief systems not on research but on the hallowed, though tainted, texts of the master. The result is that psychoanalysis has remained more like a sect than a science.

Though I was to differ from John in my espousal of the Jungian cause (his own training had been in the Kleinian school of analysis), he nevertheless gave his support to my efforts to link Jungian theory with his own 'Attachment Theory' and with the findings of ethology (the branch of biology that studies animal behaviour in the wild), and the warmth of his response to my first book on these matters (*Archetype: A Natural History of the Self*), published in 1982, had meant a lot to me.

As I thought about the dream, I recognized that it had been evoked by the preparation of this book. What was its message? I felt it was stressing the need for me to take account of the scientific tradition that Carolus Oldfield and John Bowlby represented; but, at the same time, it was reminding me that the creator of dreams is a poet. The young woman in the next room is the familiar of any male Jungian analyst – his anima, the feminine complex in himself, mediatrix of unconscious communications, she who is on the side of Eros, music, poetry, and life. 'The anima,' Jung once observed, 'is the archetype of life itself.' Her song serves to emphasize the message that Carolus is giving me.

The man in the white coat was concerned in my dream with operating the 'poetry machine' and ensuring that it kept accurate records. Much of the scientific research on dreams conducted during the last forty years has depended on the use of the electro-encephalograph, as we shall see in Chapter 4. Information of the greatest importance has come out of this. Unfortunately, few books that deal with the interpretation of dreams give much attention to these research findings, while the majority of books on the scientific study of dreams focus on neurophysiology and have little to say about their psychological content, which, as often as not, is dismissed as possessing no significance or meaning. This is short-sighted and no longer acceptable.

We have reached a point in the history of oneirology (the study of dreams) where it is simply not good enough to discuss dreams as if they were purely psychological or entirely neurophysiological phenomena. Clearly they are both. Any useful contribution to the subject of dreams must attempt to integrate what is known about them from both psychological *and* neurological points of view. Dreams are psychobiological events, and, as I hope to show, they owe their origins as much to our evolutionary history as a species as to our personal history as individuals.

That dreams should be a focus of systematic study is particularly significant at the present time, when psychoanalysis has come increasingly under attack for its shaky foundations in science. The serious decline in Freud's scientific reputation in recent years has effectively diminished respect for all schools of psychotherapy, since, in the public mind, they are all tarred with the Freudian brush. As a result it has become a matter of urgency for those of us who have the future of psychotherapy at heart to frame our hypotheses in testable forms and to describe our practices so that their validity can be publicly assessed. At the same time it is vital that we do not forget, in the interests of science, that the dreaming brain is more than an electrochemical system responsible for 'information processing', and that, if it is a machine, then it is, as Carolus says of the electro-encephalograph in my dream, a *poetry* machine. Psychotherapy and dream analysis are, and always will be, arts rather than sciences, and in putting our work on a verifiable footing we need not surrender the capacities for insight, compassion, and wisdom which personal commitment and long experience bring.

One ambition that has inspired me throughout my professional life is the wish to contribute to the development of a coherent theory of human nature. Under Bowlby's influence, I came to see that use of the comparative method – bringing together the data of depth psychology, evolutionary biology, social science, and anthropology – is indispensable to formulating such a theory. The comparative study of dreams is of central importance to this objective, because, as I hope to show, dreams relate us directly to the age-old concerns of humanity. The findings of psychology, analysis, ethology, and neuroscience are now sufficiently advanced for their synthesis to start what could prove to be the most exciting and creative period in the whole history of oneirology.

Of all developments in the latter half of the present century, it is the ethological revolution, combined with EEG research, that has transformed our understanding of the nature and function of dreams. It has also gone a long way towards confirming the clinical intuition of C. G. Jung, in the first decade of the century, that the fundamental consanguinity of our species is apparent not only in our bodies and our genes but in our myths, dreams, psychoses, and cultural artefacts. The fundamental structures upon which human development proceeds – which Jung was to call the *archetypes* of the *collective unconscious* – are apparent in the play and linguistic abilities of children, the stories and narrative poems that peoples of all cultures delight in, the ritual practices, songs, chants, and dances that human beings have always felt a need to perform. Anthropology, psychiatry, neurology, and depth psychology all provide valuable insights into the ways in which our personal realities are influenced by a deeper archetypal reality. Jung referred to this deeper reality as 'the two million-year-old Self' and saw it as implicated in everything we do, say, or think. Nowhere does this primordial survivor reveal itself more vividly than in our dreams, which link us, as the neuroscientists have demonstrated, with the most ancient structures in our brains. Every night we enter a mythic realm, a dark, primordial labyrinth, inhabited by the gods and ghosts of our ancestors, and glean from them some of the ancient wisdom of our kind. Such figures commonly take on contemporary guises, but the new myths that our dreams fashion out of them are the old myths of humanity presented in modern dress. The primordial Self, so fundamental to the life of our dreams, is the very embodiment of our evolutionary inheritance.

Of the three figures in my dream, I could identify two (Carolus and John) as guru figures, personifications of Jung's 'wise old man'. What of the third, the man in the white coat? Working on my associations to him, it became clear to me that he was a modern 'hero' figure – a pure scientist determined to advance the frontiers of knowledge through a single-minded application of experimental method and the use of logical deduction based on reproducible and verifiable facts. A good practice when encountering an unknown figure in a dream is to hold an imaginary conversation with him. When I did this, I learned that my scientist considered dreams to be meaningless charades, entirely explicable in terms of neurochemistry. I put it to him that he held this view because he had never engaged with his dreams as real psychological events, and had failed to make a personal connection to them. If he would only do this, I argued, he would soon discover how rich with meanings they were. He replied, rather irritably, that he had better things to do with his time.

Researchers who focus on the neurophysiology of dreams, while denying them psychological meaning, are not unusual. They are like engineers who concern themselves with the technology of a television set while taking no interest in the programmes being transmitted. Few laypersons, I imagine, are as blinkered as this, but many may treat their dreams like a television set, left on, unattended, in the corner of a room, so that the programme conveys little to them except at an unconscious level. Since they have no clear understanding of what the programme is about they cannot be bothered to give it the attention necessary to find out. Like my scientist, they feel they have better things to do with their time. But in this they throw away a valuable asset, for in dreams we possess a resource which we neglect at considerable personal cost. By granting access to the deepest levels of human experience, dreams can contribute to our health and personal development, as well as making us more acutely conscious of what it *means* to be alive. Dreams are not esoteric phenomena that only highly qualified analysts can understand. As I intend to demonstrate, the art of working profitably with dreams is something that anyone can learn should they really wish to do so.

Because the dream state contributes to creative efficiency in a huge range of human activities, the scope of this book is necessarily wide. Beginning with the earliest dream records known to history, Chapters 2 and 3 will discuss the development of theories relating to dreams, and the techniques which have been devised for discovering their meaning, from hunter-gatherer times up to the present. Chapter 4 reviews the findings of dream science, relating them to the analytic theories of Freud and Jung, to Paul MacLean's neurological model of the triune brain, and to Edelman's 'neural-Darwinist' theories of memory and consciousness. Chapter 5 outlines Jung's concepts of the archetype and the complex and examines their role in dream formation in the light of biological theory. The actual processes of dream formation are considered in Chapter 6, where the 'dream work' is compared and contrasted with other creative capacities such as language, poetry, story-telling, memory, play, symptom-formation, magic and ritual. The genius possessed by the human psyche for fabricating images loaded with meaning is examined in Chapter 7, on Symbolism. Chapter 8 describes the use of dreamwork in analytic therapy, while Chapter 9 provides detailed advice on how to work on dreams on one's own. A number of dreams which typically occur in the course of analytic practice are analysed in Chapter 10. The extraordinarily rich contributions that dreams have made to the arts and sciences are examined in Chapter 11, while the capacity of dreams to change the course of history is discussed in Chapter 12. Finally, the role of dreams in the development of individual consciousness is examined both in relation to the survival of the species (Chapter 13) and the well-being of the soul (Chapter 14).

In producing such an all-embracing book, I realize that I may be accused of getting out of my ghetto and tackling matters best left to my betters; but I am prepared to take that risk, for I feel that the time for such a book is ripe. Because of the profound significance of dreams for each of us personally, as well as for the future of our civilization, I should like to think that what I have to say in these pages will be of interest to laypersons and to professionals on both sides of the epistemological divide – making the principles of dream interpretation accessible to scientists, the findings of dream science accessible to practising analysts, and the principles and the findings of both camps available to anyone who is intrigued by the subject of dreams.

The overriding purpose that has guided me throughout this book is to give my readers a *feel* for dreams, by initiating them into the secrets of dream language and syntax, so that they may begin to appreciate the messages contained in these rich and inspiring communications for themselves. The presentation of historical, hermeneutic and scientific information, though important, is subsidiary to this aim.

The full analysis of a dream demands time and space. Many examples used to illustrate arguments in the text are necessarily brief and to the point. However, in order to provide readers with some experience of the extraordinarily rich web of meanings, inferences, and objectives implicit in these 'documents of the soul', I shall devote more space to the analysis of certain key dreams than is usual in a book of this kind. If one is to appreciate the incredible subtlety and ingenuity of the dreaming Self, there can be no substitute for a lengthy and detailed examination of specimen dreams, setting them in their personal, cultural, and archetypal contexts. For this expository purpose, I have selected examples that have played a crucial part in the history both of analysis and of our culture – e.g. Freud's dream of Irma's injection (pp. 42–6), Jung's dreams of the customs inspector (pp. 55–62) and of killing Siegfried (pp. 115–24), Hitler's dream of being buried alive (pp. 293–7), and the Great Dream of René Descartes (pp. 297–318).

These examples all have the advantage of being in the public domain and of being derived from persons now dead. The public analysis of the dreams of persons still living gives rise to problems of confidentiality and professional ethics. Dreams are the most private of all things, and it can be an unnerving experience for people to see such personal items in print, even when, as is the case in this book, their identity is disguised and the material published with their full knowledge and consent. I want to express my warmest thanks, therefore, to those who have granted me this privilege, because it is true to say that without their co-operation it would not have been possible to write this book.

In addition, I have allowed myself to follow the example, set by Freud and Jung, of using my own dreams, where appropriate, to illustrate the points I wish to make. It is inevitable when writing a book of this kind that one should dream about the work in progress. Some of these book-related dreams have, in fact, proved so apposite as to warrant their incorporation as integral parts of the text. These are included, not out of a desire for self-advertisement, but because they provide fresh and instructive instances of how the unconscious comes to the aid of the conscious ego when it is grappling with a task beyond its capacity.

2

FROM GILGAMESH TO FREUD

For the King of Ramparted Uruk
Has altered the unalterable way,
Abused, changed the practices.
The Epic of Gilgamesh

No sooner had people discovered the art of literacy, it seems, than
they began to record dreams. In the second century AD, a Roman
soothsayer called Artemidorus travelled throughout the civilized
world collecting material for his magnum opus *Oneirocritica* (*The
Interpretation of Dreams*). In the library of King Ashurbanipal at
Nineveh he found records of dreams inscribed on clay tablets which
dated back, we now know, to approximately 3000 BC and even
earlier. When the remains of Ashurbanipal's library were excavated
in the mid nineteenth century, among the many collections of
dreams were found fragments recounting the Babylonian epic of
Gilgamesh, King of Uruk. Other tablets, similarly incised with
cuneiform characters, were unearthed in the ruined temple of Nabu,
Sumerian god of wisdom. From these sources, carefully assembled
and transcribed, we learn how Gilgamesh, at the beginning of the
epic, had grown overweening and was troubled by bad dreams.
These he took to his mother, Ninsun, who told him what they
meant: someone, no less powerful than Gilgamesh, was about to
enter his life. Gilgamesh would struggle with the newcomer to gain
supremacy over him but would fail, for they were destined to
become bosom companions and together they would achieve great
feats.

This is the first dream interpretation in history and, like many
subsequent interpretations, it takes the form of a prophecy. But with
hindsight we can understand the dreams of Gilgamesh as a psychological attempt to compensate for his manic grandiosity. As Ninsun
knew only too well, power had gone to his head: he was amassing

8

great wealth, forcing his people to build higher and ever higher the great ramparts of Uruk, and systematically ravishing every virgin in the kingdom. The arrival of his new companion, in fulfilment of the dream prophecy, brings hope of a transformation in Gilgamesh. Enkidu, for such is his name, turns out to be a 'wild man', a creature of nature, who grew up with the animals of the forest, counting himself one of their number. He is the embodiment of humanity's primordial self and Gilgamesh needs him to ground his inflated ego, which has cast off the ancient modesty of the hunter-gatherer in order to seek its own aggrandisement at whatever cost to the natural order of things. In so doing, he has 'altered the unalterable way, abused, changed the practices'.

In Gilgamesh's dreams, and his subsequent relationship with Enkidu, we find the earliest expression of the conflict still raging in us between our civilized consciousness and the 'wild man' whom Jung referred to as 'the two-million-year-old man in us all'. As Ninsun advised Gilgamesh, so Jung predicted that each of us must struggle with this powerful character in ourselves, and turn him (or her) into a willing companion if we are to achieve anything of value in our lives. 'Together the patient and I address ourselves to the two-million-year-old man that is in all of us,' wrote Jung. 'In the last analysis, most of our difficulties come from losing contact with our instincts, with the age-old unforgotten wisdom stored up within us. And where do we make contact with this old man in us? In our dreams' (Jacobi, 1953, p. 76).

Every society known to anthropology has had theories about dreams and techniques for interpreting them. We cannot know at what stage in our evolutionary history these began to be formulated but we can be sure that they are very ancient, going back to times long before the dawn of history. The huge literature which has accumulated in all parts of the world since Gilgamesh consulted Ninsun not only demonstrates the perennial human fascination with dreams but reveals a remarkable consistency of hermeneutic understanding.

Dream Theories

Without theory facts are dumb.
LORD HAYEK

Broadly speaking, three theoretical orientations can be discerned:

(1) Dreams are caused by supernatural agencies such as gods or demons and are to be understood as messages. Dreams caused by gods are 'good' dreams sent to guide us; dreams caused by demons are 'bad' dreams sent to destroy us. The task of the dream interpreter is to differentiate 'good' and 'true' dreams from 'bad' or 'false' ones. Interestingly, ideas that dreams come from 'outside' or from God are still entertained by young children in our own culture – until they are taught to believe otherwise.

(2) Dreams are actual experiences due to the external wanderings of the soul during sleep. They are important, potentially dangerous excursions which may have a profound influence on the destiny of the dreamer: on one hand they enable us to do and see things beyond our waking capacities, but on the other they are perilous, for if one is wakened before a dream is over the soul may not have time to return to its abode and one may be deprived, as a consequence, of one's sanity. The function of the interpreter is to understand what the soul has experienced and, when necessary, to locate and recover it if it has become lost. Although this explanation has long been discounted in the West, the feeling that we actually leave our bodies in dreams is reported by contemporary dreamers who have had 'out of body' experiences: they sometimes have a problem 'getting back' into their bodies, or may be aware of a disinclination to do so.

(3) Dreams are natural phenomena, the results of normal mental activity during sleep. Those subscribing to this theoretical orientation disagree whether dreams are meaningful and whether they are susceptible to interpretation.

Of the three orientations the first two have by far the oldest and most hallowed provenance. Only in two civilizations and during two relatively brief periods of history has the third found any degree of acceptance: in ancient Greece between the third and first centuries BC and in Western society since the nineteenth century AD. While folk interest in dreams has always been apparent, especially in their necromantic implications, Western intellectuals since Roman times have tended to distance themselves from the views held by common people; and when academics embarked on the serious study of 'savages' in the eighteenth and nineteenth centuries, they were typically disdainful of the universal patterns of dream lore and interpretation that they discovered. Although this contempt for dreams has persisted in certain quarters right up to the present, the influence of Freudian theories, particularly in America during the first part of this century, resulted in a resurgence of ethnographic studies of primitive oneirology – though these observations suffered the distortion of being forced through a psychoanalytic sieve and squeezed into the cognitive stereotypes so popular at the time.

By the 1950s, dream ethnography had become part of the 'culture and personality' industry. This coincided with a decline in Freudian influence and the abandonment of cross-cultural surveys in favour of close scrutiny of individual cultures conceived as discrete entities. As a result, ethnographic interpretations became far more constrained, in line with the environmental determinism and doctrinaire behaviourism which have blighted the social sciences, with few exceptions, for the greater part of this century.

It is not possible in one chapter to present a comprehensive account of oneirology from primordial times to *fin-de-siècle* Vienna but only to select certain moments when crucial insights into the nature of dreams entered the mainstream of history. These will be examined chronologically.

Primordial Societies

The human mind tends always and everywhere to think alike.
J. S. LINCOLN

Although anthropologists, toeing their party line, have persistently emphasized cultural differences, they have nevertheless succeeded in establishing the existence of dream interpretation as a 'cultural universal'. Not even the most dedicated cultural relativist denies that in all societies studied there exists a body of lore about dreams (*oneirology*), a set of assumptions about interpreting them (*oneirocriticism*), and practical ways of using them (*oneiromancy*).

No less universal are beliefs that dreams result from night journeys of the soul and from visitations by disembodied spirits. All pre-literate peoples believe dreams to be important and attribute special value to individuals whose dream life is rich or who possess a special gift for dream interpretation. Anthropologists are in no doubt about the contribution that dreaming makes to cultural stability and innovation in all primordial societies. And as J. S. Lincoln concluded in his hugely influential book *The Dream in Primitive Society*, published in 1935, the dreams of primitive people are amenable to the same principles of interpretation as those of contemporary Westerners.

Generalizing from the anthropological data, it would appear that four basic types of dream can be distinguished: (1) 'big' dreams possessing cultural significance; (2) prophetic dreams that foretell or give advance warning of future events; (3) medical dreams that promote healing; and (4) 'little' dreams which are of purely personal relevance to the dreamer.

Though primitive people value all dreams, the ones they value most are 'big' in character. These powerful dreams, which anthropologists call 'culture pattern dreams' (Lincoln) or 'official dreams' (Malinowski), were considered by Jung to be archetypal expressions of the human collective unconscious, and, as he noted, they commonly coincide with a subjective and sometimes overpowering sense of awe, dread, fascination and wonder, which Rudolf Otto described as *numinous* – the very essence of genuine religious experience (1950). That numinous dreams should have been so widely revered is not only because of their shattering impact but because of the universal belief that they granted access to supernatural wisdom and guidance. For this reason, they were indispensable to shamans and medicine men, conferring on them the power to heal, to divine the future, and to recover souls. Numinous dreams were also sought before assuming a special role or identity, as in the initiation of young men as warriors or shamans, and in the 'vision quest' so prevalent among North American Indian tribes. By contrast, the sort of dreams investigated by contemporary researchers and psychoanalysts seem insignificant and primitive peoples would have judged them too trivial to bother about.

The discovery that archetypal dreams have occurred abundantly in so many different cultures comes as something of a shock to us, since in our society they are rare and misunderstood. It seems that as human societies have developed from the primitive through the nomadic, agricultural and early urban stages to the elaborately complex societies of modern times, there has been a decline in the incidence and power of archetypal dreams, which have been replaced by 'little' personal dreams. This truth was brought home to Jung in the mid 1920s when he visited the Elgonyi people of Kenya. He never forgot a conversation he had with an Elgonyi medicine man, who told him that his people had always paid great attention to their 'big' dreams, which guided them in all the important decisions of their lives. But now, the old man added sadly, the Elgonyi no longer needed their dreams because the white man, who ruled the earth, knew everything, and, as a consequence, big dreams were no longer needed.

Why hunter–gatherers should be particularly favoured by the experience of archetypal dreams can be explained on the basis of their closeness to the gods, their preoccupation with the life of spirits, and the animistic vitality with which they imbue all natural phenomena. It is a world view which many of us share, even in our highly urbanized society, when we are young children, identifying ourselves imaginatively with animals, birds, wind, fire, earth, and water – a propensity which the romantic poets carried into adult life and elevated into the cult of 'nature mysticism'. Moreover, children, like pre-literate peoples, often believe their dreams to have been real experiences, that the events occurring in them actually happened. These childhood propensities and beliefs would doubtless have persisted in us had our parents not persuaded us that our sleeping adventures and waking fantasies were 'only dreams'. If we but crack the civilized veneer, the primitive stands revealed in us all.

Early Civilizations

And the goddess Ishtar appeared to each man in a dream, saying: 'I will march before Ashurbanipal, the king whom I have created.'

SOLDIERS OF ASHURBANIPAL'S ARMY

The main developments in primordial theories and practices seen in the earliest civilizations are: (1) the incorporation of dream interpretation into institutionalized religion; (2) the deliberate induction of dreams (*incubation*) in the interests of healing in specially constructed *temeni*, or sacred precincts; (3) the inscription of dreams and their interpretation on clay tablets and papyri; and (4) the development of techniques for distinguishing between 'good' and 'bad' dreams and of rules for discovering what they mean.

The earliest records of dreams are the Assyrian and Babylonian dream books, which, as we have seen, were found at Nineveh in the library of the Assyrian King Ashurbanipal, who reigned between 669 and 626 BC. Many of them betray a concern with the dangerous character of dreams sent by demons and spirits of the dead. It was in order to protect themselves from these baleful influences that the Babylonians erected temples to Mamu, goddess of dreams, and practised propitiatory rites in her name. The primary interest in dreams at the time seems to have been in the salutary warnings they could provide about the future. Many of the interpretations recorded strike us as outlandish, savouring of what Freud was to call 'wild analysis', but some of them still make sense: to dream of drinking water, for example, meant long life, while drinking wine meant a short one – an early warning of the dangers of alcoholism, perhaps. To dream of flying was to alert one to the possibility of impending disaster – a warning that pride goeth before a fall, a lesson that Icarus was to teach the Greeks.

The Egyptians, like the Assyrians and Babylonians, also regarded dreams as warnings, though they believed they came directly from the gods rather than from demons or spirits. Although the gods demanded penances and sacrifices in order to avert disaster, they would also oblige by answering questions put to them by dreamers.

14

On the whole, the Egyptians regarded dreams to be beneficent, though they could be malevolent as well, and were the first civilized people known to have practised dream incubation, in order to evoke dreams concerned with particular issues or needs, such as sickness and healing.

The Egyptian god of dreams, Serapis, had a number of temples (serapeums) throughout Egypt, the most famous being at Memphis, built about 3000 BC. The earliest account of Egyptian dream interpretation is the Chester Beatty papyrus in the British Museum. Inscribed about 1350 BC, it came from Thebes in Upper Egypt and records some 200 dreams, many of them dating from much earlier. The mode of interpretation used is particularly interesting to us because it anticipates three principles employed by Freud, namely, the elucidation of visual or verbal puns, the detection of hidden associations, and the use of contraries, whereby a dream is interpreted as meaning the opposite of what it represents (as, for example, when a sick man dreams of dying it means that he will get well).

Dream interpreters from Egypt and other cultures from the distant past remarked on the delight that dreams take in punning. Although these punning interpretations made good sense at the time, subsequent generations have made little of them. But this has not stopped them from reappearing again and again in crude dream dictionaries. In the Chester Beatty papyrus, for example, we learn that to dream of uncovering one's behind means one is about to lose one's parents. This is incomprehensible unless one knows that the Egyptian word for buttocks closely resembled the word for orphan. Many arbitrary and apparently absurd interpretations listed in dream books probably owe their origins to once vivid puns in languages long dead. Examples of puns that still work will be given in later chapters.

Although distinct traditions of dream interpretation developed in Babylonia, Persia, Egypt, and Greece, many ideas gained general currency throughout the Near and Middle East as a result of travel, conquest, and trade. Thus the practice of dream incubation, which was highly developed in Egypt in the name of Imhotep, god of healing, was taken over by the Greeks and conducted in the service of Asklepios. But, in all probability, the Egyptians had themselves borrowed the practice, as they borrowed much besides, from earlier, less complex societies. The same must be true of the ancient Chinese who also developed an elaborate tradition of dream interpretation and incubation.

Whereas peoples of the Near and Middle East attributed dreams to external agents such as gods and demons, orientals took up the primordial notion that they had an inner source – the dreamer's wandering soul. For the Chinese there existed two kinds of soul: a *material* soul, or *p'o*, implicit in the physical essence of the individual which died with him, and a *spiritual* soul, or *hun*, which could leave the body every night during sleep and finally departed at the moment of death. Like innumerable peoples before them, the Chinese believed it dangerous to waken a dreamer from sleep lest the soul be lost and the sleeper deprived thereby of his reason. This ancient belief resurfaced in the 1960s in the laboratory finding (now largely discredited) that subjects, deprived of their dreams by being wakened every time a phase of REM sleep occurred, became hallucinated, deluded, and paranoid.

Separation of the *hun* from the body was held to be responsible not only for dreams and madness but also for visions, trances, and fits. As among Siberian shamans, once free of the body the *hun* could communicate with the spirits of the dead and with the gods. Such experiences were held in high esteem, and this is doubtless why the Chinese practised dream incubation in the same manner as the Egyptians and the Greeks.

In the struggle to achieve some orientation to the awesome power of dreams, the human ego everywhere resorted, as always when confronted with complex phenomena, to *taxonomy* – differentiation and classification into groups. One of the most elementary forms of classification assorts phenomena into opposite categories: hence the ubiquitous preoccupation with distinguishing good dreams from bad, true from false, divine from demonic, and big from little. In India, the classification of dreams favoured by the *Vedas*, the sacred books written between 1500 and 1000 BC, was between lucky and unlucky dreams, interest being focused on their predictive power. The most sophisticated Indian ideas about dreams occur in the *Atharva Veda*, which teaches that the last dream of a series has the greatest significance for the dreamer and that the later in the night that a dream occurs the more likely it is to come true. This *Veda* also relates the contents of dreams to the temperament of the dreamer, an observation confirmed by my own clinical experience that depressed people tend to have depressed dreams while manic people have manic dreams, a finding which, it must be acknowledged, does not sit well with Jung's theory of compensation (i.e. that dreams seek to balance conscious imbalances).

The *Vedas* also reveal an understanding of the idea that dreams emerge from liminal regions between different levels of consciousness. The *Brihadarmyaka-Upanishad* declares that there are essentially two states: one in this world and one in the other world. A third state, intermediate between them, is the state of sleep. Then follows a crucial statement: in the intermediate state one possesses the capacity to perceive both other states simultaneously, 'the one here in this world, and the other in the other world'. This corresponds to the Jungian insight that dream contents are the products of interaction between events proceeding in the dreamer's personal waking life ('this world') and the archetypal programme of the collective unconscious ('the other world'). The waking state was considered to be less 'real' than the dream state, precisely because the latter has access to both realms of knowledge and experience. The highest state is that of dreamless sleep, where one is in tune with the other world, untroubled by mundane preoccupations, and united with the infinities of time and space. Trance-inducing techniques were devised in the East (yoga for example) for the inducement of this blissful condition.

Vedantic understanding of trance, dream and reverie as representing liminal states intermediate between consciousness and unconsciousness reveals a degree of psychological sophistication unattained in the West till the twentieth century. It was Jung's discovery that *active imagination* occurs in the form of a waking dream (a dreamlike state proceeding in the absence of sleep) – a condition very like that produced by hallucinogenic drugs – in which one can observe one's conscious thoughts and actions while at the same time enjoying access to images, fantasies, and emotions normally inaccessible to consciousness.

Classical Oneirology

'Dreams, sir,' said the cautious Penelope, 'are awkward and confusing things: not all that people see in them comes true. For there are two gates through which these insubstantial visions reach us; one is of horn and the other of ivory. Those that come through the ivory gate cheat us with empty promises that never see fulfilment; while those that issue from the gate of burnished horn inform the dreamer what will really happen.'

HOMER, *The Odyssey*

As in so many other areas of life, the Greeks had extremely sophisticated ideas about dreams, though these took several centuries to emerge. In Homeric times the Greeks were convinced of the divine origin of numinous dreams and were no less preoccupied with the question of how to distinguish between those which were true or false. Homer's own distinction, namely that true dreams came through 'the gate of horn' and false dreams through 'the gate of ivory' is itself based on a Greek pun. In the mentality of those times, such distinctions were a matter of life and death. To act on a false dream as if it were true could end in unmitigated disaster, as Xerxes discovered when he led his army to destruction because his dreams had falsely convinced him that an attack on Greece would result in victory.

First on record as having proposed a purely rational explanation of dreams was Heraclitus (450–375 BC), who observed that when we sleep we inhabit an entirely private world peculiar to ourselves: far from being communications from the gods, Heraclitus maintained, dreams are the ordinary accompaniments of the sleeping mind, and, in his view, had less significance than experiences which we share in waking consciousness with others. This view, expressed by Heraclitus 400 years before Christ, is shared by the majority of educated people in the West at the present time.

Other Greek writers who have exercised a profound influence over our contemporary ideas about dreams were the great physician Hippocrates (460–377 BC) and the philosophers Aristotle (384–322 BC) and Plato (426–348/7 BC). Hippocrates, like the Assyrians and Egyptians, was interested in the prophetic nature of dreams, but he tried to put this capacity to scientific use in diagnosing the onset of disease. Such dreams were referred to as 'prodromal' (from the Greek word *prodromos*, 'running before'). Symbolic representation of symptoms indicating the onset of a mental or physical illness, before it has become evident to the patient or his physician, is a possibility that continues to stimulate much interest. To dream of springs or rivers, Hippocrates suggested, raises the possibility of impending urogenital problems, while floods and inundations indicate the presence of too much blood and the need to bleed the patient.

Like the ancient Chinese, Hippocrates also emphasized the importance of astrological influences on dream content. How is it that people of such outstanding intelligence could make an emphatic association between the heavens and their dreams? To understand this curious equivalence one must appreciate the extent to which people living before the advent of watches, compasses, portable sextants, reliable maps, and meteorological predictions depended on their own observations of the heavens to navigate their ships, traverse plains and deserts, tell the time of day, the season of the year, the occasion for planting crops, the best moment for harvesting them, and so on. It is reasonable to assume, therefore, that celestial changes should not only feature in dreams but also be thought to possess the power to produce them. Moreover, at a time when the gods were considered responsible for regulating all aspects of life, it was not extravagant to believe that their influence might extend to the actual content of dreams. Thus, although Hippocrates insisted on their medical implications, he also accepted that some dreams were divinely inspired.

Aristotle, on the other hand, denied both astrological and divine origins to dreams, because the observation of sleeping animals showed that they dreamed as well. This is a crucial observation, for it makes nonsense of many dream theories, including Freud's idea that dreams result from censored sexual wishes. The theories which Aristotle outlined in three books, *On Dreams*, *On Sleep and Waking*, and *On Prophecy in Sleep*, come closer to modern views than any writers before him and than most who have come since. Aristotle concurred with the position adopted by Hippocrates that dreams reflect bodily changes, reasoning that subjective sensations must be heightened during sleep since all external sensations are then reduced or absent, but he went on to maintain that dream images have an influence on subsequent behaviour in that they are carried over into the waking state and act as starting points for our conscious thoughts. People made the mistake of believing such dreams to be prophetic of subsequent events when in fact they were directly responsible for bringing them about.

Aristotle's philosophical works have been among the most influential writings in the history of Western civilization, yet his views on dreams went largely disregarded for over 2,000 years. One of his most extraordinary insights anticipated Jung's discovery of the collective unconscious, for, like Jung, Aristotle observed that the hallucinations of the mentally ill, the illusions of ordinary people, and the content of fantasies and dreams all had a great deal in common, and he concluded that this might indicate that they shared a common origin.

Plato's ideas are also strikingly modern and, indeed, his most important formulations directly anticipate those proposed by Sigmund Freud. Since we no longer exercise rational control over our passions while asleep, argued Plato, we find ourselves doing things in dreams that we should be ashamed to do in reality: 'The virtuous man is content to *dream* what a wicked man really *does*' (quoted by Freud, 1900, p. 782). Lust, rage, sacrilege, all can achieve full expression in our sleeping fantasies, where they take on the guise of subjective reality. 'In all of us,' he wrote, 'even in good men, there is a lawless wild-beast nature, which peers out in sleep.' In this statement we encounter for the first time in history a description of that psychic daimon that Freud was to call the *Id* and Jung the *Shadow* – and also more than a hint of the psychodynamic mechanism that Freud termed *repression*.

Prophetic Dreams

Calpurnia, here, my wife, stays me at home.
She dreamt tonight she saw my statue,
Which like a fountain with an hundred spouts
Did run pure blood; and many lusty Romans
Came smiling, and did bathe their hands in it.
And these does she apply for warnings and portents

And evils imminent; and on her knee
Hath begg'd that I will stay at home today.
WILLIAM SHAKESPEARE, *Julius Caesar*

Despite the influence of Aristotle and Plato, belief in the prophetic power of dreams persisted. The Romans were particularly fascinated by this phenomenon and some impressive examples are preserved in their literature. Although Calpurnia's dream warning Julius Caesar of his assassination went unheeded, the life of his successor, Augustus, was saved as the result of the warning dream of a friend. Augustus came, as a result, to grant such importance to dreams that he decreed that any citizen who dreamt of the Commonwealth must tell his dream in the market place. He would often act on his own dreams without subjecting them to question: Suetonius Tranquillus reports in his *Lives of the Caesars* (second century AD) that Augustus risked making a great fool of himself by going about Rome begging for alms because it had been predicted he would do so in a dream.

Of all premonitory dreams it seems that the most common are those foretelling the death of the dreamer or someone known to him, and well-attested examples have continued to be recorded right up to modern times. One celebrated instance is that of the French actor Champmeslé, who died in 1701. Two days before his death, his mother and wife (both dead) appeared to him in a dream and beckoned him towards them. Convinced that the dream foretold his end, he collected all his friends about him, paid for a funeral mass, heard it sung, and then, on leaving the church, expired. It is possible, of course, that Champmeslé's unconscious had processed information which indicated a terminal illness.

No such explanation would, however, account for Calpurnia's dream of Brutus's assassination of her lord or for the dream that Abraham Lincoln told his wife a few days before he was murdered. In Lincoln's dream, he saw a coffin guarded by soldiers in the White House and on inquiring who had died was told, 'The President, killed by an assassin.' Nor can the prodromal hypothesis of Hippocrates account for the extraordinary dream of Bishop Joseph Lanyi, tutor to the Archduke Franz Ferdinand, who dreamt a day beforehand of the Archduke's assassination at Sarajevo in June 1914. So disturbed was the Bishop by his dream that he wrote it down, drew sketches of the incident, and even attempted to warn the Archduke in time. When he discovered that the message had failed to get through to the Archduke, Lanyi celebrated a mass for him. Afterwards he learned that the dream's prophecy had been fulfilled.

Such accounts have a powerful impact on our contemporary imagination, no less than on the minds of our more credulous forebears, and they have inevitably given rise to much speculation and theorymongering. In *The Unknown Guest*, Henri de Maeterlinck suggested that 'every event, past, present or future, in any point of space, exists now somewhere, in an eternal present, and being exist-ent, it is possible for us in certain states to become conscious of events in which we discern the future, that is to say, which we in our pas-sage through time have not yet arrived at'. He concluded: 'According to the theory, every dream is a partial consciousness of some scenes or events in this eternal present, events, that is, which may be past, present or future.' J. W. Dunne expressed similar ideas in his book *An Experiment with Time*, published in 1927, while Jung developed his theory of *synchronicity* to account for such phenomena.

Aristotle's explanation was altogether more down to earth: he proposed not only that dreams could anticipate future actions on the part of the dreamer, by inventing ideas which later governed his waking actions, but he also made the valid point that so many dreams are dreamt that it would be surprising if at least some of them did not resemble later events. As with faith healing, so it is with prophetic dreams: one success can outweigh a thousand failures. Aristotle's view was endorsed by Cicero, who said: 'For what person who aims at a mark all day will not hit it? We sleep every night, and there are very few on which we do not dream; can we wonder then that what we dream sometimes comes to pass?' (*On Divination*).

Religious Dreams

When I say, My bed shall comfort me, my couch shall ease my complaint; then thou scarest me with dreams, and terrifiest me through visions; so that my soul chooseth strangling and death rather than my life.

JOB 7

For rationalists, the report of prophetic dreams inevitably throws doubt on the dreamer's veracity, and to those unwilling to believe in them no amount of 'well-attested examples' will bring conviction. No such scepticism seems to have afflicted traditional Christians, Moslems and Jews, however. The sacred texts of these great world religions, as well as those of Buddhists and Hindus, are full of dreams and visions, it being universally accepted that it is in such experiences that divinity is most likely to reveal itself. In the Bible there are more than seventy such references; the Babylonian Talmud, written between 600 and 200 BC, has four chapters devoted to dreams, and much of the Koran was revealed to Mohammed in dreams. Prophetic dreams abound in both the Old and New Testaments. For example, the flight into Egypt is determined by three dreams: in the first, the wise men are warned not to return to Herod; in the second, an angel warns the Holy Family to flee into Egypt in order to escape the massacre of the innocents; and in the third, Joseph dreams of an angel informing him of Herod's death and telling him that all will be well if he returns to Israel.

Jewish scholars enjoyed a celebrated reputation as dream interpreters, and when a Pharaoh had an important dream it was to these luminaries that he turned in order to understand its meaning. Joseph's interpretation of Pharaoh's dream of seven fat and seven lean kine as representing seven good years followed by seven years of famine is a famous example. The sophistication of Jewish oneirocritics may be judged from Daniel's shrewd interpretation of Nebuchadnezzar's dream as warning of the imminent onset of a mental breakdown. The best known of the Talmudic dream interpreters is Rabbi Hisda, who declared that 'a dream uninterpreted is like a letter unread'. He also understood the warning and transformative functions of dreams, maintaining that disturbing dreams were more significant than pleasant dreams because the distress they caused motivated us to do something to prevent their fulfilment and to mend our ways. Another important figure, Rabbi Bizna, recognized the many levels of meaning that could be contained in one dream or one dream image, recording that once he took a dream to two dozen different interpreters in Jerusalem: each gave him a different interpretation, and, he adds wryly, all of them were right! This could be understood as an early insight into the phenomenon that Freud was to call *condensation*, when a single dream image has contained within it a number of meanings.

Islamic dream interpreters were even more numerous, and also more systematic in their methods, than the Jews, presumably because Mohammed himself attributed great importance to dreams. He was in the habit of asking his disciples to retell their dreams, interpreting those which he thought to be significant. Particular importance was attached to a truthful recital of the dream and, interestingly, it was thought to be essential that the dream be recounted immediately on waking, advice commonly given to contemporary patients by their analysts. The personal characteristics of the dreamer were carefully taken into account.

Dream Incubation and Healing

When being twice admonished in his sleep, to cut the artery that lies between the fore finger and the thumb, and doing it accordingly, [Galen] was afreed from a continual daily pain with which he was afflicted in that part, where the liver is joined to the midriff.

CLAUDIUS GALENUS

Interest in the healing power of dreams reached its peak in classical times in the Asklepia (temples sacred to Asklepios, the Greek god of healing), over 300 of which were scattered throughout Greece. These sanctuaries were places of great beauty, surrounded by hills, woods and sacred streams, situated close to the sea. Here the importance of ritual for healing and the incubation of dreams was clearly understood. Having completed a long and perilous journey by ship and donkey, the patient underwent ritual purification: his clothing was removed, he drank and bathed in the sacred waters, and was dressed in clean robes. At the altar he made sacrifice and paid homage to Asklepios before entering the *abaton*, the sacred abode of the gods, which was inhabited by snakes. There a sleeping draught was administered and the patient left to sleep, on the ground in earliest times (*incubation* means 'lying on the ground') but later on a couch, the *kline*, forerunner of the analytic couch and the clinical couch used for medical examination. Asklepios usually appeared to the patient in a dream, conveying a message of healing which could itself be instrumental in producing a cure. It required no interpretation: the dream experience was itself the instrument of healing.

There can be little doubt that these practices often had a beneficent outcome. In the temples sacred to Imhotep and to Asklepios, it was understood that rituals, architecture, sounds, smells, and a holy atmosphere had a profound influence on the kind of dream experienced by the patient. Modern dream researchers, working on subjects in their laboratories, have sometimes lacked this understanding.

Although numinous dreams are universal, their imagery and the figures appearing in them are related to the commonly held beliefs and ideals of the culture in which they occur. For example, it would be unlikely for a devout Catholic to dream of Shiva performing his cosmic dance, or a Hasidic Jew to be selected for a visitation by the Virgin Mary. This is, and always has been, true. Thus, Egyptians dreamt of Imhotep, Greeks of Asklepios, and Christians of angels, just as Freudian patients have tended to have 'Freudian' dreams, and Jungian patients to have 'Jungian' ones, and so on. All dreams are influenced by suggestion and by cultural factors, not just incubation dreams, but their inherent power has been apparent to human communities at all times throughout history, and they have been understood as performing similar functions wherever they have occurred. Yet before Roman times, no one devoted his life to the systematic study of dreams.

Early Dream Research

A man dreamt that he slipped out of his flesh just as a snake sheds its old skin. He died the following day. For his soul, which was about to depart from his body, provided him with these images.

ARTEMIDORUS

The first to do this was Artemidorus, who wrote his *Oneirocritica* only after he had completed years of painstaking field work, visiting libraries and centres of healing throughout Italy, Greece and the Near

East, interviewing dream interpreters, buying old manuscripts and papyri, until he had made himself familiar with all that was known or believed about dreams up to that time.

His approach to individual dream interpretation was no less methodical or, one might say, 'scientific'. First, he required a detailed account of the dream. Then he needed six essential pieces of information, which he called *natura, lex, consuetudo, tempus, ars,* and *nomen* (i.e. whether the events in the dream were natural, lawful, and customary for the dreamer, what was happening at the time of the dream, and the dreamer's occupation and name). These facts established, Artemidorus proceeded, like Freud seventeen centuries later, to consider every component of the dream, its imagery and associations, before providing an interpretation of the dream as a whole.

Although many of his interpretations seem quaint to us, influenced as they were by the superstitions current at his time (to dream of snakes, for example, means one will suffer a long illness; large pots mean the dreamer will enjoy a long life; if a sailor dreams of having his head shaved it forewarns him of a shipwreck, etc.), he nevertheless consistently warned against looking up standard interpretations in dream books, pointing out that symbolic meanings could change with time, across cultures, and from person to person. The dreamer's personal circumstances were of great importance and one should always be on the lookout for puns. Artemidorus was one of the very first to employ an empirical approach to dreams, reporting that his own understanding had been improved by investigating the outcome of no less than 3,000 dreams.

In Artemidorus, therefore, we find a worthy forerunner of Freud and Jung. Not only did he advocate a serious, considered approach to each dream but he also laid emphasis on the principle of *association* – the special significance of the ideas a dream image evokes in consciousness. Association, Freud believed, was the key to successful dream interpretation. But whereas Freud was at pains to elicit associations from the dreamer, Artemidorus's main interest was in the associations evoked by the dream image in the mind of the interpreter. For his part, Jung was concerned with the associated ideas evoked in the minds of both dreamer and interpreter, and he used these, as we shall see, in his practice of *dream amplification*. Moreover, Artemidorus distinguished between two classes of dream: the *insomnium*, which arose from the present state of the body and mind and related to the activities and experiences of ordinary life, and the *somnium*, which invariably carried a deeper allegorical or mythic significance and could foretell future events. This distinction has evident parallels with that made in pre-literate societies between 'little' and 'big' dreams and Jung's distinction between dreams of personal and dreams of collective, transpersonal significance.

Artemidorus stands as a salient figure linking modern with ancient traditions of dream interpretation. For all the naïvety of many of his pronouncements, he was an early devotee of the empirical method, adopting a commendably flexible approach to every dream and establishing the existence of certain basic types of dream as well as the ubiquitous recurrence of particular dream symbols. Freud was to proclaim his debt to him by giving his own great work the same title as Artemidorus gave to his: *The Interpretation of Dreams*.

The Early Church Fathers

In dreams the thirsty man seems to be among springs, the man who is in need of food to be at a feast, and the young man in the heat of youthful vigour is beset by fancies corresponding to his passion.

GREGORY OF NYSSA

The writings of the early church fathers need not detain us long for, with the exception of four of them, they had little original to add to what had already been written by the classical philosophers and physicians. The exceptions are Tertullian, St Augustine, Gregory of Nyssa and Synesius of Cyrene.

In his *Treatise on the Soul*, written about 203 AD, Tertullian equated sleep with a form of self-limiting death experience during which the soul, as at the termination of mortal existence, leaves the body: as he put it, 'the soul disdaining a repose which is not natural to it, never rests'. Tertullian's idea of the never resting soul has persisted into modern oneirology, as in Jung's statement that throughout our waking life 'we continue to dream below the threshold of consciousness' (*CW*16, para. 125). However, it was not Tertullian's purpose to suggest that the soul is responsible for the production of dreams: that responsibility lay with God, with demons, or with Nature. The soul was a spectator, as at a circus or the Colosseum, and had no power to influence the course of dream events as they unfolded. This opinion has also found modern advocates, who see the dream's most striking characteristic as its capacity for spontaneous self-creation, quite independently of the dreamer's will or intention. As Jung put it, 'I do not dream: I am dreamt.'

One of the first to appreciate that parts of the psyche must remain unconscious was St Augustine (354–430 AD): 'I cannot grasp all that I am,' he confessed. This worried him, for he feared that God might hold him responsible for the contents of his dreams, and he knew these to be beyond his control.

Closest in spirit to both classical authors and modern analysts was Gregory of Nyssa, who held that dreams were natural phenomena susceptible to a purely psychological explanation. As a Christian he accepted that God had it within His power to inspire prophetic dreams in certain especially worthy individuals, but he regarded these as miraculous communications which were not dreams in the ordinary sense of the word. In his treatise, *On the Making of Man* (380 AD), Gregory maintained that dreams occur because in sleep the senses and the intellect are at rest, which accounts for the absurdity of many dreams. The actual content of dreams is determined by memories of one's daily activities and one's physical state at the time of the dream. In this he comes very close to Freud's formulation that dreams are wish fulfilments: for in Gregory's view dreams were most commonly motivated by the passions, and the most powerful of these was sex. Passions were expressions of man's 'brute nature' which must forever be held in check by the intellect if he is not to fall into sin. In sleep alas, the intellect ceases to be vigilant and our passions can therefore achieve expression in our dreams. The anticipation of Freudian theory is very striking.

Writing at about the same time as Gregory of Nyssa, Synesius of Cyrene described a model of the psyche which made an interesting distinction between *mind* and *soul* and proposed *fantasy* as the means of communication between them. *Mind* relates consciously to things as they are, *soul* is concerned with things that are coming into being, while *fantasy* provides the means by which the soul represents to consciousness its knowledge of things which will come to pass. This approximates to Jung's insight that dreams and fantasies reveal new character formations that are attempts at a future, more mature personality, to break through into consciousness.

Thus, whereas Gregory of Nyssa manifests a somewhat 'Freudian' emphasis on the importance of basic drives, and especially of the sex drive, seeking fulfilment in dreams, Synesius of Cyrene shows a more 'Jungian' emphasis on the creative, teleological propensities of the soul.

The Unconscious

The key to the knowledge of the nature of the soul's conscious life lies in the realm of the unconscious . . . The first task of a science of the soul is to state how the spirit of Man is able to descend into these depths.

CARL GUSTAV CARUS

The unconscious is not something that was 'discovered' by Sigmund Freud as some of his popularizers have suggested, but a hypothesis that emerged erratically between the seventeenth and nineteenth centuries. Though the ancient Egyptians and Hindus were aware that they could experience different degrees of consciousness ('this world' and 'the other world') and St Augustine was worried by his inability to control what he dreamt, the first clear formulation of the idea that something goes on in the soul that we know nothing about was that of Gottfried von Leibniz (1646–1716). Leibniz compared this activity to the circulation of the blood in that it sustains our conscious existence without our realizing it 'just as those who live near a water mill do not perceive the noise it makes' (*New Essays Concerning Human Understanding*). Some put the origins of the idea even earlier than Leibniz, attributing it to an English Platonist, John Norris (1632–1704), who maintained that 'there are infinitely more ideas impressed on our minds than we can possibly attend to or perceive'.

From thence forward the hypothesis arose by a gradual process of accretion, first bursting into public awareness with the Romantic

Movement in Germany and the *Naturphilosophie* of Friedrich Wilhelm von Schelling (1775–1854). The history of this theoretical epiphany has been catalogued by L. L. Whyte in *The Unconscious Before Freud* (1979) and by Henri Ellenberger in his dazzling treatise *The Discovery of the Unconscious* (1970). As these invaluable researches reveal, the first to make a link between unconscious activity and dreaming was a physicist, G. C. Lichtenberg (1742–99), who gave careful attention to his own dreams because he found in them wonderful ideas which lay sleeping in his soul. As the eighteenth century drew to a close, the idea gained currency that the unconscious was an expression of Nature and, as a consequence, the mystic source of all imagination and creativity. Poets like Friedrich Schiller (1759–1805) held not only that 'poetry sets out from the unconscious' but actually advocated the use of a form of free association to liberate the creative faculties from the critical restraint of reason, while Johann Wolfgang von Goethe (1749–1832) described the imagination as 'pure nature' and declared that he wrote his phenomenally influential *Werther* 'practically unconsciously'. By the time these statements were made the Romantic Movement was in full flood.

Schelling's philosophy of nature, an offshoot of Romanticism, insisted that nature and spirit were one: 'Nature is visible Spirit. Spirit is invisible Nature.' Consciousness and matter both evolved out of a common principle – the 'World Soul'. The vital link between man and nature was the unconscious, and by granting it our reverential attention we became a conduit for the *All-Sinn* – the 'Universal Sense' – which declared itself in art and poetry, in madness and mystical ecstasy, in myths and in dreams. Schelling's ideas were later to sustain Jung as he felt his way towards the formulation of his own hypothesis of a collective unconscious, as did another concept of Romantic philosophy – that of primordial phenomena (*Urphänomene*). Goethe, in many ways the godfather of *Naturphilosophie*, believed, for example, in the existence of a primordial plant (an *Urpflanze*) from which all other plants were derived by metamorphosis. One can detect this idea behind Jung's theory of archetypes and Rupert Sheldrake's concept of morphogenic resonances. Among other *Urphänomene* was the *androgyne* – the romantic belief in the fundamental bisexuality of human nature, an idea taken up in the late

30

nineteenth century by Wilhelm Fliess and Sigmund Freud, and in the early twentieth by Carl Gustav Jung in his archetypes of the *anima* and *animus*.

More specifically, the dream theories of Freud and Jung were anticipated by Gotthilf Heinrich von Schubert (1780–1860) in his book *The Symbolism of Dreams*, in which he contrasted the picture language of dreams with the verbal language of waking life, maintaining that dream language is 'hieroglyphic' and manages to pack many meanings into one image (the phenomenon which struck Freud as one of the main functions of the *dream work* and which he termed *condensation*). Schubert argued that dreams draw on a universal language of symbols, which is common to peoples throughout the world, and to peoples of the past as well those of the present. Here we have a clear forerunner of Jung's archetypal symbols arising from the collective unconscious. Schubert believed that at night the human mind may sometimes perceive visions of events to come, but that dreams more often have an amoral and demonic character because neglected and repressed aspects of the personality come to the fore during sleep. Here, as with Plato and Gregory of Nyssa, we have a prefiguration of the Freudian view of dreams.

The nineteenth-century writer who was to have perhaps most influence on Jung's thinking was Carl Gustav Carus (1789–1869). In his book *Psyche*, he defined psychology as the science of the soul's development from the unconscious to the conscious state; he described the unconscious as indefatigable (in that it did not require periods of rest like the conscious mind), as essentially healthy (it is imbued with 'the healing power of nature'), and as possessing its own innate wisdom. Carus considered that it was through the unconscious that we remain in communication with the rest of the world. He also proposed that the unconscious exercised a *compensatory* function in relation to consciousness – a notion which Jung was to develop as a primary concept in his theory of dreams.

Another source for the ideas later developed by Freud and Jung, as well as Freud's other leading colleague with whom he eventually fell out, Alfred Adler (1870–1937), was the philosophy of Friedrich Nietzsche (1844–1900). In addition to being the seat of passions and instincts, Nietzsche held the unconscious responsible for co-ordinating the stages of life characterizing the development of individual members of the species. Dreams played an important role in this personal evolution, since Nietzsche regarded them as enactments and re-enactments of life events proceeding at both the personal and the collective level. Nietzsche believed that the basic human motivation was the will to power and this view was later developed by Adler in his own psychology, which he called *Individual Psychology*, to differentiate it from Jung's *Analytical Psychology* and Freud's *Psychoanalysis*. Adler's Nietzschean insistence on the primary compensatory importance of power was the cause of his break with Freud.

Nietzsche was also responsible for the dynamic theory of mind which was adopted in their different ways by both Freud and Jung – the idea that there exist quanta of mental energy which can be inhibited or repressed, transferred from one drive to another, or sublimated from an instinctive to a spiritual form. The source of instinctive energy Nietzsche called '*das Es*', a term which Freud borrowed on the suggestion of his exotic friend Georg Groddeck and which is translated in the English versions of Freud's works as 'the Id' ('a cauldron full of seething excitations' – Freud, 1933).

The psychoanalytic concept of psychic energy, largely derived from Nietzsche, was originally introduced by the Viennese physician Franz Anton Mesmer (1734–1815). Mesmer achieved great fame and notoriety through his success in treating a variety of nervous maladies by what is now called hypnotism but Mesmer termed 'animal magnetism'. Basing his idea on Newtonian physics (which he completely misunderstood), Mesmer claimed animal magnetism to be a physical 'fluid' pervading the whole extent of the universe. The difference between health and illness was determined by the balance, or imbalance, which existed between the animal magnetism in the patient's body and that in the outside world. Mesmer believed that he, and his chosen assistants, possessed the ability to store up 'subtle fluid' in their persons and then channel it into patients in such a way as to restore their magnetic equilibrium. In many ways, Mesmer's idea of magnetic fluid resembles the Polynesian concept of 'mana', a universal energy which can be stored in people, objects, or places and detected through its magical effects.

Most famous among the many exponents of hypnotism in the

nineteenth century were Jean-Martin Charcot (1825–93) and his pupil Pierre Janet (1859–1947), and their work was indispensable to the development of twentieth-century dream theory, Freud having studied under Charcot in 1885 and Jung under Janet during the winter semester of 1902–3. These French neurologists provided clear empirical evidence for the existence of powerful unconscious ideas and emotions which were capable of profoundly modifying the behaviour of hypnotized subjects. At public demonstrations at the Salpêtrière Hospital in Paris they induced hysterical symptoms in hypnotized subjects (e.g. paralysis, blindness, deafness, etc.) and then removed them by hypnotic suggestion. Charcot and Janet were particularly interested in the phenomenon of multiple personality, when two or more apparently separate personalities coexist in the same person. This occurred, they believed, when split-off fragments of the total personality followed an unconscious development of their own and could be revealed under hypnosis or in spontaneous clinical disturbances.

Until his encounter with Charcot Freud had been a clinical neurologist, but under the Frenchman's influence he became a dynamic psychologist, returning to Vienna in 1886 to start a practice with Joseph Breuer (1842–1925), who enjoyed a considerable reputation for curing patients by a technique which he called *abreaction*. Under hypnosis, Breuer encouraged his patients to relive traumatic experiences responsible for making them ill and to discharge the powerful emotions associated with these often forgotten (i.e. unconscious) events. Freud was greatly impressed by Breuer's results and attributed the origins of psychoanalysis to Breuer's treatment of a patient whom they called Anna O., 'whose numerous hysterical symptoms disappeared one by one, as Breuer was able to make her evoke the specific circumstances that had led to their appearance'. Thus, for example, her difficulty in swallowing food apparently disappeared when she remembered and 'abreacted' to Breuer her feelings of revulsion when a dog had lapped water from her glass.

When Freud began to practise in Vienna, therefore, appreciation of the psychodynamic importance of the unconscious was already well advanced. But where previous thinkers had conceived of the unconscious as a mere counterpart to consciousness, Freud came to understand that it constituted the very foundation of the psyche. All psychological phenomena, from slips of the tongue to the most elaborate psychiatric symptoms, were determined by events proceeding beneath the threshold of consciousness, and of no phenomena was this more true than the contents of dreams and the processes by which these contents were created. When he turned his attention to the study of dreams – a study which was to absorb him for the whole of the 1890s – it was because he saw their interpretation as '*the royal road to a knowledge of the unconscious activities of the mind*' (Freud, 1976, p. 769, his italics).

3

FREUD, JUNG AND AFTER

Theories are the very devil.

C. G. JUNG

In the early morning of 24 July 1895, Freud dreamt a famous dream that has gone down in history as 'the dream of Irma's injection'. He was staying with his family at Belle Vue, a favourite resort on the outskirts of Vienna. As he worked on the dream later that day, the thought suddenly struck him that *it was the fulfilment of a hidden wish*. This flash of illumination brought with it the conviction that he had found the key to unlock the door to the unconscious mind. 'Insights such as this,' he later declared, 'fall to one's lot once in a lifetime.' The riddle of dreams, which had preoccupied oneirologists for millennia, had at that precise moment been solved. So certain was he of the epoch-making importance of his discovery that he entertained the idea that one day a marble tablet would be affixed to the façade of the Belle Vue villa stating that *In this house on July 24th, 1895, the Secret of Dreams was Revealed to Dr Sigm. Freud* – a fantasy which has subsequently been implemented in reality.

Sustained by this absolute conviction, he wrote his magnum opus, *The Interpretation of Dreams*, completing it in 1899. This extraordinary book, which has dominated theoretical approaches to dreaming throughout the twentieth century, opens with an assertion as bold as a fanfare of trumpets: 'In the pages that follow,' declares Freud, 'I shall bring forward proof that there is a psychological technique which makes it possible to interpret dreams, and that, if that procedure is employed, every dream reveals itself as a psychical structure which has a meaning and which can be inserted at an assignable point in the mental activities of waking life' (p. 1). What was this miraculous technique? Freud called it *free association* – the procedure he learned from Joseph Breuer, who employed it so successfully, or so Freud maintained, in the treatment of Anna O. By giving free rein to her

35

thoughts this patient was able to recover memories linked with each of her phobias, and this enabled Breuer not only to make sense of her symptoms, but to remove them. We now know that this is untrue, and that the outcome in this case was far from satisfactory, but this did not discourage Freud from adopting Breuer's technique, and acclaiming its crucial contribution to the interpretation of dreams.

Free Association

A thing in a dream means what it recalls to the mind.
SIGMUND FREUD

Free associating is easy once one has acquired the knack. It is a matter of letting one's thoughts off their customary leash and allowing them to wander where they will, being careful not to censor or dismiss them, however obscene, absurd, or irrelevant they may appear. In order to derive the data necessary to interpret a dream one associates to each dream image in turn until a network of related ideas has been constructed so as to link the dream with one's present circumstances and with relevant memories from the past. Putting together all these pieces of information, according to Freud, yields the meaning of the dream.

The initial reaction to a dream on waking up is usually puzzlement ('What an extraordinary dream! Why on earth should I dream that?') because dreams do not immediately fit in with what we know about ourselves when we are awake. To appreciate the meaning of a dream we need to forge links between our waking and sleeping states of being. With his discovery that free association makes this possible, Freud, at a stroke, rendered dream dictionaries obsolete. The only dictionary we need to decode our dreams, Freud commented, is not on our bookshelves but in our heads. Free association dispenses with the services of necromancers and soothsayers and turns dream inter-pretation into a scientific procedure. We shall see how Freud used this technique when we consider his analysis of the dream of Irma's injection (pp. 42–6).

Freud's whole approach was in stark contrast to that adopted by the scientists of his day, who regarded dreams – as they regarded the delusions and hallucinations of psychotic patients – as meaningless artefacts. Both Freud and Jung were to spend their lives reacting against this sterile position. As Freud wearily observed, *les savants ne sont pas curieux.*

The Nature and Purpose of Dreams

The meaning of every dream is the fulfilment of a wish.
SIGMUND FREUD

Although he called his book *The Interpretation of Dreams,* Freud devoted less space to actual *interpretation* than to the examination of what dreams *are* (*description*) and of *why* they take the form they do (*explanation*). His work with Charcot in Paris and with Breuer in Vienna convinced him that psychiatric symptoms were derived from the psychological defences devised by patients to protect themselves from unbearable feelings. Freud's intuition told him that dreams must arise in the same way. Feelings and buried experiences which are felt to be potentially threatening or dangerous are excluded from consciousness out of self-defence. Something in the patient, unknown to him or her, keeps these disturbing feelings unconscious: it *represses* them. Freud called this repressive agent the *censor,* and, later, the *superego.* The repressed feelings do not, however, go away: they persist as dynamic unconscious potential and can outwit the censor by manifesting themselves in symptoms – and Freud now realized, in dreams. The insight gained while concentrating on the dream of Irma's injection, combined with what he had learned through working with Breuer, led Freud to conclude that a dream is, in essence, *the hallucinatory fulfilment of a forbidden wish.* Since the wish is perceived as dangerous or unacceptable by the censor, it is expressed in the dream in a disguised or symbolic form. Just as a soldier, terrified of going into battle, and no less fearful of being convicted of cowardice, might deal unconsciously with these painful emotions by developing an hysterical paralysis of his legs, thus rendering himself a casualty before the battle begins, so an office manager, wishing to have sex with his married secretary, might dream of pushing in and pulling out the drawers of her filing cabinet, without having his morals or his slumbers disturbed.

During sleep the censor is sufficiently vigilant to deny entry to dreaming consciousness of wishes of a frankly forbidden nature, but it is not so vigilant as to detect such wishes if they are decked out in some disguise. The function of the dream mechanism (which Freud called the *dream work*) is to provide disguises which are crafty enough to deceive the censor. As a result of this subterfuge, the forbidden wish appears in the *manifest content* of the dream in some form of symbolic representation. In other words, dream symbols are coded messages which possess sufficient ingenuity to slip past the censor. The function of dream interpretation, on the other hand, is to decipher the code; and this can be achieved by free association.

Why should this subversive charade be necessary? Freud's answer is, quite simply, that it is necessary *because it enables the dreamer to go on sleeping*: 'All dreams are in a sense dreams of convenience,' he wrote. 'They serve the purpose of prolonging sleep instead of waking up. *Dreams are the GUARDIANS of sleep and not its disturbers*' (Freud, 1976, p. 330; his italics and capitals). The forbidden wish forms the *latent content* of the dream: the *dream work* transforms the latent content into the *manifest content* in such a way as not to disturb the ego or wake the dreamer.

The Dream Work

A dream without condensation, distortion, dramatization, and above all, wish-fulfilment, surely hardly deserves the name.

SIGMUND FREUD

To disguise the latent content, the dream work makes use of a number of techniques which Freud describes as *displacement* (by which a potentially disturbing idea is converted into a related but less disturbing image), *condensation* (the combination of a number of ideas into a single image), *symbolization* (by which a neutral image is used to represent a potentially disturbing, usually sexual, idea), and *representation* (the conversion of dream thoughts into visual images), and

38

these account for the often bizarre or irrational nature of the manifest dream. Freud even goes so far as to make the circular argument that the bizarre nature of dreams is itself evidence for the existence and function of the censor in disguising the dream's true meaning. It is evident, however, that if the latent dream thoughts are to be represented in the dream they will have to be turned into images, or 'a thing that is *capable of being represented*' (Freud's italics). This transformation, Freud adds, offers 'the same kind of difficulties to representation in dreams as a political leading article in a newspaper would offer to an illustrator. But not only representability, but the interests of condensation and the censorship as well [under an undemocratic regime] can be the gainers from this exchange' (p. 455).

Freud gives many examples of such representation. One that he quoted in later editions of his book was the illustrated dream of a French nursemaid (though the motive for her dream seems to have been more the need to ignore a disturbing stimulus than to disguise a forbidden wish).

'The first picture (Figure 1) depicts the stimulus which should have caused the sleeper to wake: the little boy has become aware of a need and is asking for help in dealing with it. But in the dream the dreamer, instead of being in the bedroom, is taking the child for a walk. In the second picture she has already led him to a street corner where he is micturating – and she can go on sleeping. But the arousal stimulus continues; indeed, it increases. The little boy, finding he is not being attended to, screams louder and louder. The more imperiously he insists upon his nurse waking up and helping him, the more insistent becomes the dream's assurance that everything is all right and that there is no need for her to wake up. At the same time, the dream translates the increasing stimulus into the increasing dimensions of its symbols. The stream of water produced by the micturating boy becomes mightier and mightier. In the fourth picture it is already large enough to float a rowing boat; but there follows a gondola, a sailing-ship and finally a liner. The ingenious artist has in this way cleverly depicted the struggle between an obstinate craving for sleep and an inexhaustible stimulus towards waking' (p. 486).

Freud also cited in later editions the experiments of Herbert Silberer (1909) on the transformation of thoughts into pictures in

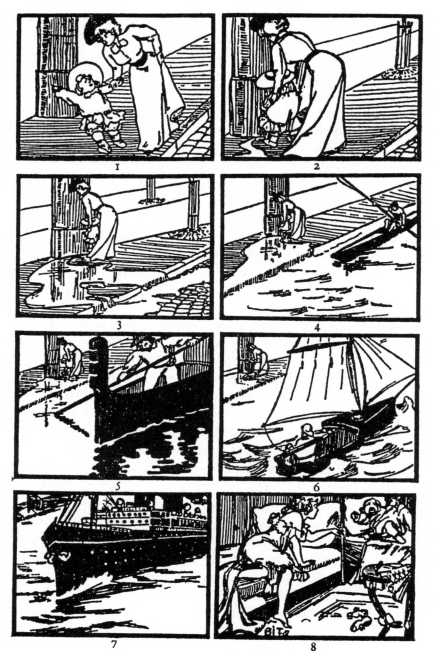

Figure 1.　A French nurse's dream.

order to demonstrate this one factor of the dream work in isolation from the others. 'If, when he was in a fatigued and sleepy condition, he set himself some intellectual task, he found that it often happened that the thought escaped him and in its place a picture appeared, which he was then able to recognize as a substitute for the thought' (p. 460). For example, when, under these circumstances, Silberer concentrated his thoughts on having to revise an uneven passage in an essay, he saw himself planing a piece of wood. Freud was particularly interested in dreams whose content was determined by sayings or catch-phrases, such as Alexander the Great's dream of a satyr. Alexander had surrounded the city of Tyre (*Tyros* in Greek) and he was uneasy about the way in which the siege was dragging on. Then he dreamt of a satyr (*satyros* in Greek) dancing on his shield. His adviser, Aristander, divided the word for satyr into *Sa* and *Tyros*, encouraging the king to press home the siege and become master of the city. *Sa Tyros* means 'Tyre is thine'. Freud notes with approval Ferenczi's observation that every tongue has its own dream-language and that it is not really possible to translate a dream from one language into another. Hence, as we have already noted, the obscurity of many dream dictionary interpretations.

An amusing example of such dreaming occurred to me in Moscow in 1985. I dreamt I was observing a bee hovering at the entrance to a hole in a tree. Sometimes it would approach and make as if to enter the hole, but then it would withdraw again. This was repeated several times, and I woke up. Thinking about the dream, I reflected that the bee was behaving in a very suspicious and 'cagey' manner. Then the meaning of the image struck me: it was a cagey bee. Before retiring the previous night, my host, a Western ambassador serving in Moscow, had been telling me how careful he had to be in view of the vigilance exercised by those members of his staff who had been planted on him by the KGB! The dream represented how 'cagey' one had to 'bee' in dealing with the 'cagey bee'. Verbal restatement of the visual imagery of a dream can often prove illuminating in this way, and plays a role in the interpretation of any dream.

Freud held that dreams fashioned their manifest content out of memory residues from two sources: the previous day's *Tagesreste* (the day's residues) and from childhood. But more fundamental to the process of transforming memories and wishes into images was the manner of their distortion: 'the kernel of my theory of dreams,' he wrote, 'lies in my derivation of dream-distortion from the censorship' (p. 418). '*Dream-displacement* and *dream-condensation* are the two governing factors to whose activity we may in essence ascribe the form assumed by dreams . . .' (p. 417). There can be no doubt that both displacement and condensation occur as, for example, in the office manager's dream of manipulating the drawers of his secretary's filing cabinet. Condensation is also apparent in the sexual pun implied by the word 'drawers' and by the notion of 'filing' – the rhythmic up and down motion being itself symbolic of sexual intercourse. As Freud says: 'each of the elements of the dream's content turns out to have been "overdetermined" – to have been represented in the dream-thoughts many times over' (pp. 388–9).

The question is whether these techniques are dependent on the process of outwitting the censor for their *modus operandi*, as Freud maintained. Freud's determination to bring his theory of dreams into line with his theory of neurosis made him refuse to consider the possibility that distortion and condensation, like symbolism and pictorialization, could more easily be ascribed to normal dream syntax – i.e. the way the brain naturally operates in dreaming sleep. It is just as likely that the manifest content *is* the dream, as Jung maintained, and that the 'latent content' does not exist, but is merely the conscious set of associations to which the dream gives rise. The 'latent content' may be no more than the intellectual superstructure which the Freudian ego builds on the 'manifest content' in the process of Freudian 'interpretation'. But before entering a debate on the validity of Freud's theories, let us examine them in the light of the dream whose analysis revealed to him 'the Secret of Dreams'.

The Dream of Irma's Injection

'If you still get pains, it's really only your own fault.'
SIGMUND FREUD

Earlier that summer of 1895, Freud had psychoanalysed Irma, a young widow and friend of the family, but with only partial success:

'the patient was relieved of her hysterical anxiety but did not lose all her somatic symptoms'. In order to bring her treatment to a successful conclusion he had 'proposed a solution to the patient which she seemed unwilling to accept'. While they were thus at variance, he had broken off the treatment for the summer vacation.

Then Freud received a visit from a colleague and friend whom he calls 'Otto', who had recently stayed with Irma and her family in the country. When Freud asked after her health, Otto replied: 'She's better, but not quite well.' Freud detected a note of reproof in Otto's voice, and this disturbed him so much that in order to justify himself he spent the whole evening writing out Irma's case history so as to present it to 'Dr M.', a leading figure in Freud's Viennese circle. 'The dream of Irma's injection' occurred the following night.

In the dream, *Irma is a guest at a party, and Freud takes her aside to reproach her for not accepting his 'solution', adding: 'If you still get pains, it's really only your own fault.' She replies: 'If only you knew what pains I've got now in my throat and stomach and abdomen — it's choking me.' Alarmed, Freud examines her, concerned that he may have missed some organic illness. His worst fears are confirmed when he finds 'extensive whitish grey scabs upon some remarkable curly structures which were evidently modelled on the turbinal bones of the nose'. He calls in Dr M., who repeats the examination, and they are joined by Otto and by another friend and colleague, 'Leopold'. Dr M. diagnoses an infection and they all agree as to its origin: not long before, when Irma was feeling unwell, Otto had given her an ill-advised injection of trimethylamin 'and probably the syringe had not been clean'* (p. 182).

It was at once clear to Freud what had triggered the dream: 'The news which Otto had given me of Irma's condition and the case history which I had been engaged in writing till far into the night continued to occupy my mental activity even after I was asleep' (p. 183). However, he had no idea what the contents meant, so he went to work painstakingly recording his associations to each part of the dream. In their published form they take up twelve pages of his book. 'I became aware of an intention which was carried into effect by the dream and which must have been my motive for dreaming it. The dream fulfilled certain wishes which were started in me by the events of the previous evening . . . The conclusion of the dream, that

43

is to say, was that I was not responsible for the persistence of Irma's pains but that Otto was. Otto had in fact annoyed me by his remarks about Irma's incomplete cure, and the dream gave me my revenge by throwing the reproach on to him. The dream acquitted me of the responsibility for Irma's condition by showing that it was due to other factors – it produced a whole series of reasons' (p. 196).

He lists these reasons: '*I* was not to blame for Irma's pains, since she herself was to blame for them by refusing to accept a solution. *I* was not concerned with Irma's pains, since they were of an organic nature and quite incurable by psychological treatment. Irma's pains could be satisfactorily explained by her widowhood . . . which *I* had no means of altering. Irma's pains had been caused by Otto giving her an incautious injection of an unsuitable drug – a thing *I* should never have done. Irma's pains were the result of an injection with a dirty needle . . .' (pp. 196–7).

Freud concludes: 'The dream represented a particular state of affairs as I should have wished it to be. *Thus its content was the fulfilment of a wish and its motive was a wish*' (p. 196; Freud's italics). The Secret of Dreams, therefore, was that they represented the fulfilment of a wish and the nature of the wish could be determined through the use of free association.

For one who insisted on the primacy of the sexual impulse in the production of neurotic symptoms and dreams, Freud is surprisingly reticent on the extent to which hidden sexual wishes were involved in the Irma dream, except in his associations to the substance 'trimethyl-amin' which Otto had been so misguided as to inject. He recalled a conversation with Wilhelm Fliess, the Berlin biologist and nose and throat specialist whose friendship was of deep importance to Freud in the years immediately preceding the publication of his book, in the course of which Fliess mentioned his belief that trimethylamin was a product of sexual metabolism. Moreover, Fliess 'had drawn scientific attention to some very remarkable connections between the turbinal bones and the female organs of sex' (p. 194). Irma was a young widow, Freud reflected, adding: 'if I wanted to find an excuse for the failure of my treatment in her case, what I could best appeal to would no doubt be this fact of her widowhood' (i.e. that she was sexually frustrated).

What Freud omits to tell us is that, at the time of his dream, his wife was again pregnant and that the prospect of an enlarging family was adding financial worries to his concern for his professional reputation. Nor does he discuss the question of Irma's *transference* to him (the unconscious recapitulation of intense feelings in relation to him which had previously been experienced in relation to salient figures in her past life, such as her father). Had Irma declined to terminate her treatment on the terms of Freud's 'solution' because her transference was unresolved and because she sustained unfulfilled longings for a much closer relationship with him? Was Freud sexually attracted to her? He gives an apparently unconscious clue that he may indeed have been seeking to control such feelings, when explaining why, in the dream, he had conducted his examination with the patient fully clothed: 'Frankly,' he ingenuously observed, 'I had no desire *to penetrate more deeply* at this point' (p. 189; my italics). The dream may well have arisen out of a conflict between his desire to possess Irma physically and the ethical code which proscribed any such transgression, or between his desire to bring her treatment to a satisfactory conclusion and his reluctance to lose regular contact with her as a patient.

Freud does not touch on these matters. Nor does he examine the evident sexual symbolism of Otto's injection of Irma (syringe in German is *Spritze* = squirt), that the syringe, being dirty, resulting in an infection and scabs on her turbinal bones (= sexual organs), could be interpreted as intercourse resulting in venereal disease. Was Freud jealous of Otto for having spent time with Irma in the country? Did he unconsciously wish to get his own back by suggesting that Otto had given Irma something worse than an iatrogenic infection?

Much more information about the background to this dream has come to light since the publication in 1985 of the full correspondence between Freud and Wilhelm Fliess. It appears that Irma was in fact a composite figure, created by Freud's unconscious, based on two young widows who were patients of Freud and known to his family: Anna Lichtheim and Emma Eckstein. In 1895, at Freud's request, Fliess operated on Eckstein for persistent pain and bloody secretions from her nose. Initially, Freud had diagnosed these symptoms as psychosomatic, saying that she was 'bleeding for love' of him. But when the symptoms persisted, he invited Fliess to examine her for fear that he could be missing an organic cause. The operation seems not only to have been unnecessary and ill-advised, but Fliess botched it, inadvertently leaving behind a gauze pack in one nasal cavity. When this was found and removed two weeks later by another surgeon, Eckstein had a severe haemorrhage, which, in less expert hands, might have proved fatal. This was an evident piece of malpractice that Freud was careful to conceal in his published associations to the dream.

For all the many pages of analysis provided by Freud, his interpretation raises more issues than it resolves. Freud's reticence is understandable, however, in view of the circumstances and the times: it is not surprising that he should confess to a 'natural hesitation about revealing so many intimate facts about one's mental life' – an inevitable drawback of the brave method he uses throughout the book of demonstrating oneiric functions by the interpretation of his own dreams. Acknowledging his reluctance 'to penetrate more deeply' into Irma's significance for him, he counters: 'If anyone should feel tempted to express a hasty condemnation of my reticence, I would advise him to make the experiment of being franker than I am. For the moment I am satisfied with the achievement of this one piece of fresh knowledge' (p. 198). But as a result of Freud's 'natural hesitation' about revealing intimate facts, the dreams he reports and analyses have more to do with his professional than his sexual life.

Criticisms of Freud

We must not be led astray by initial denials. If we keep firmly to what we have inferred, we shall in the end conquer every resistance by emphasizing the unshakeable nature of our convictions.

SIGMUND FREUD

Acceptance of Freud's theory of dreams must rest on the truth or falsehood of his basic propositions. These are as follows:

(1) All dreams are wish fulfilments.

(2) All dreams are distortions of repressed wishes.

(3) All repressed wishes are infantile in origin and usually sexual in nature.

(4) The manifest content of dreams is always related to the events of the previous day as well as to childhood memories and wishes.

(5) Symbols are disguised representations of sexual ideas, conflicts or wishes.

(6) The function of dreams is to preserve sleep.

Are these propositions true? Enough evidence exists for us to reply with relative certainty: in the categorical form that Freud states them they are not. Freud's besetting sins as a theoretician were dogmatism and over-generalization. Many of his statements illustrate these tendencies and give rise to contrary speculation in the reader's mind, viz: 'The instigation of a dream is always to be found in the events of the previous day' (Freud, 1976, p. 229. *Always?* What about anticipation of events in the day to come?). 'Our theory of dreams regards wishes originating in infancy as the indispensable motive force for the formation of dreams' (*SE* 5, 589. *Indispensable?* Can there be no other motives?). The dream is 'a substitute for an infantile scene modified by being transferred onto a recent experience' (1976, pp. 696–7. Occasionally perhaps. But is this always the case?). 'Every dream [is] linked in its manifest content with recent experiences and in its latent content with the most ancient experiences' (*SE* 4: 218. *Every* dream? What about dreams of the future? Or dreams of landscapes one has never seen? To whose 'ancient experiences' is he referring, the individual's or mankind's?). 'Dreams are the GUARDIANS of sleep' (1976, p. 330. Have they no other function?). 'It is fair to say that there is no group of ideas that is incapable of representing sexual facts and wishes' (p. 491. *No* ideas? Possibly so. But how far are you willing to press the point?). And so on.

In writing *The Interpretation of Dreams*, Freud was astute in guessing the kinds of objection that might be raised to his theories and in seeking, not always successfully, to pre-empt them. To his assertion that all dreams were wish fulfilments, for example, he realized that his readers would wonder how he could reconcile this idea with disagreeable night experiences, such as anxiety dreams and nightmares. There is no difficulty about this, counters Freud: the disagreeable experience derives from the manifest content only; analysis of the latent content will invariably reveal a wish. Because the wish expresses a forbidden impulse it generates fear to waken the dreamer

47

when the censor is not entirely efficient in keeping it repressed or disguised. And how is Freud to sustain his belief that most dreams arise from *sexual* wishes when the majority of dreams are devoid of sexual content? Simple: the censor sees to it that, through displacement, condensation, and symbolization, the latent sexual wishes are manifested in asexual forms.

The trouble with Freud, as Jung was to discover to his cost, was that if you engaged him in argument you could never win. If you put it to him that not all dreams are distorted in the way he said they were, that not all dreams are wish fulfilments, and not all symbols sexual in origin, then in Freud's view you were obviously guilty of 'resistance' (i.e. you were actively avoiding, *repressing*, or *denying* true ideas because you found them threatening or distasteful).

Freud's determination always to be in the right is nowhere better demonstrated than in his comments on patients who produced dreams apparently incompatible with his theories. For example, he tells us that the day after he had explained to one of his women patients that dreams are fulfilments of wishes, she brought him a dream in which she was travelling with her mother-in-law to a place in the country where they were to spend their holidays together. Freud goes on: 'Now I knew that she had violently rebelled against the idea of spending the summer near her mother-in-law and that a few days earlier she had successfully avoided the propinquity she dreaded by engaging rooms in a far distant resort. And now her dream had undone the solution she had wished for: was not this the sharpest possible contradiction of my theory that in dreams wishes are fulfilled? No doubt; and it was only necessary to follow the dream's logical sequence in order to arrive at its interpretation. The dream showed that I was wrong. *Thus it was her wish that I might be wrong, and her dreams showed that wish fulfilled*' (1976, p. 234; Freud's italics).

Here, as in many other instances, Freud wants to have it both ways. When people disagreed with him, he was unsympathetic to the possibility that he could be wrong. It was because his self-respect and intellectual security depended on his being right that he put all such questionings or disagreements down to the patient's 'resistance'.

Dreams like the above, Freud says, 'appear regularly in the course of my treatments when a patient is in a state of resistance to me; and I can count almost certainly on provoking one of them after I have explained to a patient for the first time my theory that dreams are fulfilments of wishes. Indeed, it is to be expected that the same thing will happen to some of the readers of the present book: they will be quite ready to have one of their wishes frustrated in a dream if only their wish that I may be wrong can be fulfilled' (1976, p. 242). In a footnote, added in 1911, he writes: 'During the last few years similar "counter-wish dreams" have repeatedly been reported to me by people who have heard me lecturing, as a reaction to first making the acquaintance of my "wishful" theory of dreams.' A Jungian, as we shall presently discover, would, on the contrary, see such dreams as instances of the Self rebelling against unnecessary and artificial constraints and expressing its natural spontaneity.

Sometimes of course he was right but certainly not always right. Such was the power of Freud's personality, however, and the strength of the transference that it encouraged, that patients were under considerable duress to conform to his theories. Should they 'resist' his interpretations as seeming apparently untrue, then Freud would threaten to discontinue the treatment. This is nicely demonstrated on p. 409 where Freud is describing a patient: 'It would have been tempting to diagnose a neurosis (which would have solved every difficulty), if only the patient had not repudiated with so much energy the sexual history *without which I refused to recognize the presence of a neurosis* . . . a few days later I informed the patient that I could do nothing for him and recommended him to seek other advice. Whereupon, to my intense astonishment, he started apologizing for having lied to me. He had been too much ashamed of himself, he said, and went on to reveal *precisely the piece of sexual aetiology which I had been expecting* and without which I had been unable to accept his illness as a neurosis' (my italics). This passage is unpleasantly reminiscent of the proceedings of the Inquisition, and one cannot read it without feeling that the unfortunate patient made precisely the confession that Freud was demanding so as to be permitted to remain his patient. But this is a possibility that Freud does not consider. This arbitrary attitude is even apparent in his own dreams, for he treats Irma in the same way that he treated all patients who 'resisted' him. In the dream, it will be recalled, he reproaches Irma for not accepting his 'solution', adding: 'If you still get pains, it's really only your own fault.' He sums up this somewhat totalitarian attitude in one sinister aphorism: 'Psychoanalysis is justly suspicious. One of its rules is that *whatever interrupts the progress of analytic work is a resistance*' (1976, pp. 661–2). Indeed, the whole dream – the most crucial in the history of psychoanalysis – is an expression of his determination to vindicate himself at the expense of others.

Freud adopted exactly the same approach to colleagues who disagreed with him. 'Don't deviate too far from me,' he wrote in a letter to Jung, 'when you are really so close to me, for if you do, we may one day be played off against one another.' Then he adds: 'My inclination is to treat those colleagues who offer resistance exactly as we would treat patients in the same situation' (*The Freud/Jung Letters*, p. 18).

This tendency to impose his theories in an arbitrary and authoritarian manner had unfortunate consequences not only for Freud's colleagues and patients but also for the development of dream science as a whole. The vigour of his arguments, backed up by the force of his personality, nipped a growing experimental tradition in the bud. The truth is that Freud was in love with his own theories and, as Jung observed early in their friendship, he seemed committed to his sexual theory to an almost fanatical degree: 'When we spoke of it his tone became urgent,' Jung noted. 'A strange, deeply moved expression came over his face' (*MDR*, p. 147). It was as if sex had assumed a *religious* meaning for Freud, who was an atheist. Jung felt it was as if he had rejected God and put sex in His place.

From the very beginning of their friendship in 1907, Jung had grave misgivings about the fundamental place granted by Freud to sexuality, but whenever he voiced his reservations Freud dismissed them as due to inexperience: consequently, Jung considered it more tactful to keep his doubts to himself. Jung was just over thirty and Freud already in his fifties when their friendship began, and the younger was considerably in awe of the older man. Reflecting on this fateful relationship towards the end of his life, Jung wrote: 'Under the impress of Freud's personality I had, as far as possible, cast aside my own judgements and repressed my criticisms. That was the prerequisite for collaborating with him. I had told myself, "Freud is far wiser and more experienced than you. For the present you must simply listen to what he says and learn from him." And then, to my own surprise, I found myself dreaming of him as a peevish official of the Imperial Austrian monarchy, as a defunct and still walking ghost of a customs inspector'! (*MDR*, p. 159).

Jung's dream of the customs inspector provides the key to his understanding of the meaning of dreams in the same way as the dream of Irma's injection provides the key to understanding Freud's. But before we examine this, and other examples of Jung's dreams, we must first turn our attention to the evolution of Jung's ideas during the period of his friendship with Freud.

Jung's Approach

I have no theory about dreams.

C. G. JUNG

Throughout the six years of their friendship (1907–13), Freud and Jung were in complete agreement in attributing a fundamental importance to unconscious processes in the genesis and treatment of mental illness and in the production of dreams. Their differences, as they emerged, and in so far as Jung dared to express them, were not confined to the central position that Freud granted to sex but also concerned the extent to which the unconscious might be structured by the evolutionary origins of the human species, and the manner in which dreams might be considered to reflect this structure. In the years immediately preceding his first encounter with Freud, Jung had made an international reputation for himself as a psychiatrist and research psychologist, working at the Burghölzli Hospital in Zürich as second-in-command to the great Eugen Bleuler, the originator of the term 'schizophrenia'. Unlike the majority of psychiatrists before or since, Jung actually attended to what his psychotic patients said. What particularly interested him was the similarity which the content of schizophrenic delusions and hallucinations bore to one another, not only in different patients but to the content of myths and fairy tales derived from peoples all over the world. These observations convinced Jung that some universal structures must exist in the mind and in the brain which underlay all human experience and behaviour. When he coined the term *collective unconscious* to describe this universal substratum it was in order to distinguish it from the purely *personal* unconscious of Freudian psychoanalysis. Although Freud accepted that some 'archaic remnants' were occasionally revealed in dreams, he attributed little significance to them, believing that most of our mental equipment is acquired individually in the course of growing up. Jung, on the other hand, asserted that all the essential psychic characteristics that distinguish us as human beings are with us from birth. These typically human attributes he first called *primordial images* and later *archetypes*.

Archetypes Jung saw as basic to all the usual phenomena of human existence. As innate structures they possessed the capacity to initiate, control and mediate the common behavioural characteristics and typical experiences of all human beings everywhere. On appropriate occasions, archetypes could be conceived as giving rise to similar thoughts, images, and feelings in people, irrespective of their class, creed, race, geographical location, or historical epoch.

Confirmation of these ideas came to Jung in a dream during the summer of 1909 when he was travelling with Freud to fulfil a lecturing engagement at Clark University in Worcester, Massachusetts:

He was on the top floor of an old house, well furnished and with fine paintings on the walls. He marvelled that this should be his house and thought 'Not bad!' But then it occurred to him that he had no idea what the lower floor was like, so he went down to see. There everything was much older. The furnishings were medieval and everything was rather dark. He thought, 'Now I really must explore the whole house.' He looked closely at the floor. It was made of stone slabs, and in one of these he discovered a ring. When he pulled it, the slab lifted, and he saw some narrow stone steps leading down into the depths. He went down and entered a low cave cut out of the rock. Bones and broken pottery were scattered about in the dust, the remains of a primitive culture, and he found two human skulls, obviously very old and half disintegrated. Then he awoke (MDR, p. 155).

When Jung reported this dream to his travelling companion, all that interested the latter was the possible identity of the skulls. Freud wanted Jung to say who they belonged to, as it seemed evident to him that Jung must harbour a death wish against their owners. Jung felt this to be irrelevant, but, as usual, he kept his doubts to himself, and, for the sake of peace, he named two people to keep Freud happy. Privately, he turned the dream over in his mind, and it dawned on him what his dream house represented: *it was an image of the psyche.* The room on the upper floor represented his conscious personality. The ground floor stood for the *personal* unconscious, while in the deepest level of all he reached the *collective* unconscious. There he discovered the world of the *primordial man* within him. To Jung, the skulls had nothing to do with death wishes: they belonged to our human ancestors, who had shaped the common psychic heritage of us all.

Another dream that was to prove of critical significance to the relationship was one of Freud's which Jung attempted to interpret on the basis of only a few guarded associations. When Jung pressed him for more information, Freud looked rather suspiciously at him and declined: 'I cannot risk my authority,' he said. At that moment, commented Jung, he lost his authority altogether. 'That sentence burned itself into my memory; and in it the end of our relationship was already foreshadowed. Freud was placing personal authority above truth' (*MDR*, p. 154).

The manner in which their friendship eventually broke up was typical of both men. To Jung, the purpose of life was to realize one's own potential, to follow one's own perception of the truth, and to become a whole person in one's own right. This was the goal of *individuation*, as he later called it. If he was to keep faith with himself, he had to go his own way. For Freud, belief in the correctness of his own theories was, as we have seen, absolute, and this made him so intolerant of dissent that he usually ended up provoking it.

The different theoretical orientations of Jung and Freud are reflections of their differences as men, being of different psychological type (Jung an introvert and Freud an extravert) and growing up in different cultural, intellectual, and religious environments. Jung, a rural Protestant, insecurely bonded to a depressed, sometimes absent mother, was a deeply introverted man, steeped in theology and

Romantic idealism while Freud, an urban Jew, doted on as a child by a young and beautiful mother, was an extravert, educated in a progressive tradition that led him naturally into science. Not surprisingly, these differences are as apparent in the dreams they dreamt as in the theories they produced to explain them. On the whole Freud's dreams were relatively fragmented and disorganized in comparison with Jung's, which tended to have more coherent symbolism and a stronger narrative structure. Freud's dreams consequently required a more elaborate use of free association to make sense of them, whereas Jung's yielded their meaning if approached in the same way as parables or myths. Moreover, Freud's censor remained almost as much on duty when he free associated in full consciousness as when he dreamt in his sleep, for he concealed from his readers, as he possibly did from himself, his powerfully ambitious strivings for professional pre-eminence as well as drawing a discreet veil over his sexual desires. 'So far as I knew,' says Freud, in the preamble to the discussion of a dream relating to his appointment as professor at Vienna University, 'I was not an ambitious man' – a statement betraying a staggering lack of insight, given the details of his biography.

The greater coherence of Jung's dreams made him more aware of the narrative structure that he considered evident in most well-remembered dreams, while the more episodic nature of Freud's dreams inclined him to attribute whatever narrative fluency they revealed to what he called *secondary elaboration* – i.e. to the organizing and rationalizing influence on the dream material exercised by the ego on waking.

Jung was struck by the resemblance he detected between the natural structure of dreams and the formal structure of Greek tragedy. He divided this into four stages:
(1) the *exposition*, which sets the place and often the time of the action, as well as the *dramatis personae* involved; (2) the *development* of the plot, in which the situation becomes complicated and 'a definite tension develops because one does not know what will happen'; (3) the *culmination* or *peripeteia*, when 'something decisive happens or something changes completely'; and (4) the *lysis*, the conclusion, the solution, or result of the dream-work (*CW*8, paras 361–4).

Jung's dream of the customs inspector, which occurred shortly before he broke off his friendship with Freud, follows this pattern. It is appropriate, therefore, to examine it at this point.

The Customs Inspector and the Knight

At the stroke of noon the descent begins.

C. G. JUNG

The dream was as follows:

'[*I was*] *in a mountainous region on the Swiss–Austrian border. It was toward evening, and I saw an elderly man in the uniform of an Imperial Austrian customs official* [stage 1: the exposition]. *He walked past, somewhat stooped, without paying any attention to me. His expression was peevish, rather than melancholic and vexed* [stage 2: the development]. *There were other persons present, and someone informed me that the old man was not really there, but was the ghost of a customs official who had died years ago* [stage 3: the peripeteia]. *"He is one of those who still couldn't die properly"'* [stage 4: the lysis].

This is not the end of the dream, however, as Jung finds himself transported to another place and a similar narrative structure is repeated: he now finds himself in a city.

'*The city was Basel, and yet it was also an Italian city, something like Bergamo. It was summertime; the blazing sun stood at the zenith, and everything was bathed in an intense light* [exposition]. *A crowd came streaming toward me, and I knew that the shops were closing and people were on their way home to dinner* [development]. *In the midst of this stream of people walked a knight in full armour. He mounted the steps toward me. He wore a helmet of the kind that is called a basinet, with eye slits, and chain armour. Over this was a white tunic into which was woven, front and back, a large red cross* [peripeteia] . . . *I asked myself what this apparition meant, and then it was as if someone answered me – but there was no one there to speak: "Yes, this is a regular apparition. The knight always passes by here between twelve and one o'clock, and has been doing so for a very long time (for centuries, I gathered) and everyone knows about it"'* [lysis].

Interpretation

My whole being was seeking for something still unknown.

C. G. JUNG

In working on a dream the starting point for Jung was not interpretation but 'amplification' – that is, to enter into the atmosphere of the dream, to establish its mood as well as the detail of its images and symbols, in such a way as to *amplify the experience of the dream itself.* Then its impact on consciousness is enhanced.

As we shall see in Chapter 7, Jung's concept of the symbol differed radically from Freud's. Because in Jung's view every symbol encompasses more than can be said about it, he insisted that it should not be 'reduced' to its origins, but that its implications should be examined in an archetypal light. Instead of breaking the dream down into a series of intellectual formulations, one should *circumambulate* its symbols (*lit.* walk round about them), allowing them to reveal their different facets to consciousness. Personal associations need to be taken into account, but a full appreciation of the dream's intention cannot stop there if one is to receive all that it has to offer.

The first thing that strikes one about the dream as a whole is the powerfully arresting quality of its mood and imagery, as well as the stark contrast apparent between the sad, ghostly customs official and the extraordinary, surreal presence of the medieval knight. That the dream opens on the Swiss–Austrian border must carry some significance, as must the dress, appearance, and manner of the customs official. Why should he not be there and why can he not die properly? Why is the knight, who should have died so long ago, seen striding through the streets of a modern city? While the former is old and worn out, a has-been, the latter is imbued with the vibrant intensity of an archetypal image – the knight in shining armour.*

In Jungian therapy, it is customary to approach a dream in three

---

* In my book, *Jung* (1994), I subject this dream to a detailed analysis in order to demonstrate the classic Jungian approach to dreams. Since this dream is so crucial to the history of dream interpretation, I have reproduced here, with the kind permission of the Oxford University Press, the salient features of the analysis.

stages. The first attempts to establish the context of the dream in the life of the dreamer, so as to understand something of its purely personal significance. Next, the cultural context has to be defined, since the dream is invariably related to the milieu and time in which it was dreamt. Finally, the archetypal content is explored so as to set the dream in the context of human life as a whole, since at the most profound level dreams link us with the age-old experience of our species.

In practice it is seldom possible to keep these stages separate because, inevitably, the personal, cultural, and archetypal components of experience, as well as perceptions of their meaning, constantly interact. However, in the interests of clarity, we will consider the elements of this dream under three headings, while tolerating the unavoidable overlap between them.

Personal Context The associations which Jung reports to the dream are brief and to the point, for he did not advocate uninhibited use of free association as did Freud. To Jung, association only facilitated dream interpretation as long as it was confined to the images in the dream. Freudian free association, in Jung's view, carried the dreamer away from the dream and served only to lead him back, time and again, to his childhood complexes, and, to Jung's mind, this defeated the object of the exercise.

With the word *customs* Jung says he at once associated the word 'censorship', and in association with *border* he thought of the border between consciousness and the unconscious on the one hand, and between his views and Freud's on the other.

Of the knight Jung says: 'One can easily imagine how I felt: suddenly to see in a modern city, during the noonday rush hour, a crusader coming toward me. What struck me as particularly odd was that none of the many persons walking about seemed to notice him . . . it was as though he were completely invisible to everyone but me . . . even in the dream, I knew that the knight belonged to the twelfth century. That was the period when alchemy was beginning and also the quest for the Holy Grail. The stories of the Grail had been of the greatest importance to me ever since I read them, at the age of fifteen, for the first time. I had an inkling that a great secret still lay hidden behind those stories. Therefore it seemed quite natural to me that the dream should conjure up the world of the Knights of the Grail and their quest – for that was, in the deepest sense, my own world, which had scarcely anything to do with Freud's. My whole being was seeking for something still unknown which might confer meaning on the banality of life' (*MDR*, pp. 158–61).

Cultural Context   A frontier is an agreed line of demarcation separating two states: in terms of dream logic, it makes little difference whether these be nation states or states of mind. What cannot be overlooked is that Freud's state is Austria and Jung's Switzerland; and Freud, in some official 'imperial' role, is patrolling the border between them. At a frontier, personal belongings are subject to scrutiny, suitcases opened and searched for contraband, and one's passport examined to ensure that one's credentials are in order, and all this is done by a customs officer. Could this be a reference to the subject matter of psychoanalysis (the borderline between consciousness and the unconscious) and to Freud as the master analyst, peevish, vexed, and sad because he suspects the dreamer is harbouring ideas that are both subversive and objectionable? In reflecting on the dream, Jung certainly made this connection. But why, he asked himself, should he dream of Freud as the ghost of a customs inspector? 'Could that be the death-wish which Freud had insinuated I had felt toward him?' He thought not, for he had no reason for wishing Freud dead. Rather he saw the dream as compensating and correcting his conscious attitude to Freud, which he now perceived as unduly deferential. The dream was recommending a more critical, more robust manner in his dealings with Freud.

The confusion between Basel and Italy in the second part of the dream is probably a reference to the achievement of Jung's fellow Baseler, Jakob Burckhardt, who linked the civilization of their home town with that of the Renaissance in Italy. This Italy is the world of Dante and Beatrice, Petrarch and Laura, of love, art and the rebirth of the human spirit. That the sun is at its zenith as the people stream home from the shops evokes the crisis of mid-life, as Jung was to describe it: 'At the stroke of noon the descent begins. And the descent means the reversal of all the ideals and values that were cherished in the morning.' The first half of life is the life of 'getting and spending', but now the shops are shut and this phase is over. What promise does the future bring? The answer appears in the extraordinary figure of the knight, dressed in armour; not a man of the future, but an archetypal figure from the past, the Christian gentleman, the chivalrous warrior. He belongs to the twelfth century, which Jung associates with the beginning of alchemy and the emergence of the legend of the Holy Grail.

Archetypal Context The archetypal images of greatest significance in this dream are the vessel (the Grail), the knight/warrior, and the cross. These in turn, and by association, bring up the archetypal themes of the old and dying king, the wounded-healer, and the shaman/magician.

According to legend, the Grail was the vessel used by Jesus at the Last Supper and later by Joseph of Arimathea to collect and preserve the Saviour's blood after the Crucifixion. It is thus the most precious object in Christendom. The theme of the miraculous vessel is much older than Christianity, however. As Freud would have been the first to agree, the Grail or vessel is a feminine symbol, a womb in which a miraculous, life-giving transformation occurs. The vessel or *vas* was central to the alchemical tradition which began in ancient China and reached Northern Europe, as Jung comments, in the twelfth century. The Gnostics, with whom Jung felt a close affinity, believed that one of the original gods had made a gift to humanity of a *krater*, a mixing vessel, in which those who sought spiritual transformation were immersed. Medieval mystics later adopted the vessel as a symbol of the soul, which exists to be filled and replenished endlessly by Divine Grace.

Association of the Grail legend with England and King Arthur's Knights of the Round Table came through the figure of Merlin, the great magician, shaman and bard of Celtic mythology. Merlin was born of an illicit union between the devil and an innocent virgin and thus emerged as a counterbalance to the figure of Christ. Early in his career, Merlin presides over a dragon fight which results in the deposition of the old usurper King Vertigier and his replacement by King Uter, to whom Merlin confides the secret of the Grail,

instructing Uter to set up a Third Table. The First Table was that of
the Last Supper; the Second was the Table on which Joseph of
Arimathea had kept the Grail, and it was *square*; the Third Table,
which King Uter will provide, must be *round*. This rounding of the
square is the very essence of the *mandala* configuration and symbolizes
the achievement of wholeness, the complete realization of the Self.
Taken in the context of Jung's thinking as a whole, the quest for the
Holy Grail can be understood as the individuation quest undertaken
sub specie aeternitatis.

The Grail legend fascinated Jung all his life. As a boy he read
Malory and Froissart and of all music he loved Wagner's *Parsifal* the
most. As far as the dream is concerned, the most interesting aspect of
the legend, apart from the vessel itself, is the theme of the 'old sick
king', Amfortas. Like Chiron in Greek mythology, Amfortas suffers
from a wound which will not heal; and the fascinating aspect of this
wound is its situation: it is in the thigh or genital region. Amfortas's
wound is a sexual wound, his problem a sexual problem. He wishes
to relinquish his kingly authority and pass it on to Parsifal, much as
Freud, in anointing Jung his 'Crown Prince' and 'Son and Heir'
made clear his wish to hand his authority over to Jung, but he cannot
do so until Parsifal questions him about the Grail.

Jung himself did not make this connection between Amfortas and
Freud, but he made it with his own psychologically weak father, a
country pastor who had lost his faith and who was the psychological
precursor of Freud in his life: 'My memory of my father is of a
sufferer stricken with an Amfortas wound, a "fisher king" whose
wound would not heal – that Christian suffering for which the
alchemists sought the panacea. I, as a "dumb" Parsifal was the witness
of this sickness during the years of my boyhood, and, like Parsifal,
speech failed me. I had only inklings' (*MDR*, p. 205).

Freud was no less a 'fisher king', and in his presence Jung was no
less incapable of speech than Parsifal, never putting Freud to the
question about his service to the god of sex. That is why their
relationship lasted as long as it did.

The solitary crusader is the Christian soldier, marching as to war.
He has a goal, a destiny which he has no choice but to fulfil. It is an
image of what Jung was to become, not as a Christian but as a man.

'If a man knows more than others, he becomes lonely,' he wrote at the end of his life. 'There was a daimon in me . . . It overpowered me . . . I could never stop at anything once attained. I had to hasten on, to catch up with my vision. Since my contemporaries could not perceive my vision, they saw only a fool rushing ahead . . . I was able to become intensely interested in people, but as soon as I had seen through them, the magic was gone. In this way I made many enemies. A creative person has little power over his own life. He is not free. He is captive and drawn by his daimon . . . This lack of freedom has been a great sorrow to me. Often I felt as if I were on a battlefield, saying "Now you have fallen, my good comrade, but I must go on"' (*MDR*, pp. 328–9).

Enough has been said for the reader to appreciate that the analysis of a dream in the manner advocated by Jung is no easy matter. It is a discursive process requiring considerable erudition as well as a gift for symbolic understanding. Much more is involved than a mere interpretation of its basic message, which, in the case of the dream of the customs inspector, might be stated simply as, 'Get rid of Freud and go your own way.'

The world of the knight, of the Grail, and of Merlin was not Freud's world but Jung's world. The trouble with modern society, like the origins of neurosis, was not so much sexual repression as 'loss of soul', a lack of perception of the sacred. Freud's contribution served only to compound the plight of our culture, for he struggled to find the sacred in one basic instinct, sex. The knightly ideal, one of the noblest expressions of the European spirit, was being ignored. The knight's holy quest was degenerating into the 'wasteland' of our post-Christian civilization.

This theme recurred in another dream in which Jung found himself surrounded by sarcophagi dating from Merovingian times. He passed by dead figures from the eighth century and went on until he came to some twelfth-century tombs, where he stopped before the corpse of a 'crusader in chain mail who lay there with clasped hands. His figure seemed carved out of wood.' For a long time Jung looked at him and thought he was really dead. But suddenly he saw that a finger of the left hand was beginning to stir gently (*MDR*, p. 167).

The knight was still alive in his unconscious, offering him a way forward out of the past, away from the moribund figure of Freud, the vexed customs officer. But it was a future and a past (red cross on the front and on the back of the crusader) that was marked by the Christian symbol for wholeness and redemption, the state of at–one-ment with God. He would have to go on like the knight, his progress ignored by the populace around him, supported only by his own 'inner light' and the few congenial souls he was able to collect at his own Round Table.

Freud and Jung Assessed

Philosophical criticism has helped me to see that every psychol-ogy — my own included — has the character of a subjective confession.

C. G. JUNG

The dream theories of both Jung and Freud are largely speculative and deeply subjective, being imbued with the personal psychology and professional ambitions of their originators. Jung acknowledged this more openly than Freud: in an article describing his differences with Freud, published in 1929, from which the above epigraph is taken, Jung wrote: 'Even when I am dealing with empirical data, I am necessarily speaking about myself' (*CW*4, para. 774).

Of the two psychodynamic approaches, Jung's was indeed the more empirically inclined: 'I do not know how dreams arise,' he wrote. 'And I am not sure that my way of handling dreams even deserves the name of a "method".' But this display of modesty did not deter him from rejecting the basic tenets of Freud's dream theory and from replacing them with suggestions of his own.

In fact, most of Freud's hypotheses have proved untenable in the light of dream research, while Jung's have stood up to the test of time. For example, the well–established observation that all mammals dream and that human infants devote much of their time to REM (rapid eye movement) dream sleep, both in the womb and post-natally, would seem to dispose of the idea that dreams are disguised expressions of repressed wishes or that their primary function is to preserve sleep. It is more likely that dreams are, as Jung maintained, natural products of the psyche, that they perform some homeostatic or self-regulatory function, and that they obey the biological imperative to promote adaptation in the interests of personal adjustment, growth, and survival.

That Jung's hypotheses should enjoy greater compatibility with recent research findings than Freud's is surprising in view of Freud's original commitment to zoology and neuroscience. From 1876 to 1882 he worked at the Physiological Institute of Ernst Brücke (1819–92) in Vienna. Brücke, who was a hero of Freud's, believed that all vital processes would eventually be reducible to physics and chemistry, thus eradicating the need for such terms as 'spirit', 'life force', 'soul', etc. This teaching had a big impact on Freud, and he remained a determinist to the end, convinced that all psychic phenomena, whether thoughts, dreams, images, or fantasies, must be completely explicable in terms of previous eventualities in accordance with the laws of cause and effect.

The reason why Freud stuck so rigidly to his Sexual Theory was because for him it was *the* link between body and mind, and because he believed, faithful to his training in Brücke's laboratory, that neurosis, like dreams, would ultimately prove to have a physical basis (a hope which he incorporated in his *Project for a Scientific Psychology*). As he wrote to Jung in April 1908: 'In the sexual process we have the indispensable organic foundation without which a medical man can only feel ill at ease in the life of the psyche' (*The Freud/Jung Letters*, pp. 140–41).

It was a shrewd position to adopt. Not only was sex indispensable to the survival of the species, but, under Darwin's influence, Freud understood sexual selection to be a primary factor in evolution. His sexual theory, therefore, could provide psychoanalysis with a sound organic basis in biology. That he was adopting an incredibly narrow perspective could not be so apparent to Freud as it is to us. Ethology, the branch of biology that studies animal behaviour in natural habitats, was a science yet to be born, and Freud knew nothing of the rich diversity of instinctive patterns of behaviour occurring in nature, for the zoology of his time confined its observations to animals in captivity, where opportunities for actualizing instinctive potential were sadly lacking. When territorial and dominance conflicts are ruled out by lack of space and competition, there is little else for bored, well-nourished animals to do than pass their time in what used to be called 'self-abuse'. Moreover, sexuality assumed an exaggerated importance in Freud's practice because the nineteenth-century bourgeoisie *was* sexually repressed. It cannot be denied that our contemporaries are much less inhibited in this respect, and this is not unconnected with the effect of Freudian ideas on our culture.

Freud gave up physiological research in order to earn enough money to marry Martha Bernays. He did not wish to become a physician: sheer necessity drove him to it. As we have noted, his primary motivation was to seek the essentially Adlerian goal of intellectual pre-eminence. When he became a physician it was essential, given his character structure, to carve out a territory in which he, and he alone, could rule. His association with Charcot and Breuer provided him with the inspiration to graft psychological ideas on to the physiological principles he had acquired from Brücke, and as he developed the theory and techniques of psychoanalysis it was inevitable that he should wish to ground them in biology. 'My dear Jung,' he said on one much quoted occasion, 'promise me never to abandon the sexual theory. That is the most essential thing of all. You see, we must make a dogma of it, an unshakeable bulwark' (*MDR*, p. 173). Dreams, neurotic symptoms, perversions, jokes, slips of the tongue, all rested on this single 'indispensable organic foundation' (i.e. sexuality).

The basic need of mental life, Freud believed, was to achieve a state of tranquillity through the complete discharge of all tensions. He was later to call this the Nirvana principle. Thus the healthy person, untroubled by dreams, was a bonded heterosexual with a regular and satisfying sex life, who could discharge his or her sexual tensions in repeated orgasms and enjoy a recurrent state of tensionless Nirvana. There is little objective evidence to support this view, and much to refute it. But such was the brilliance of Freud's rhetoric, his impressive diligence, and his powers of political persuasion, that few subsequent psychodynamic formulations have escaped his influence. As J. Allan Hobson (1988) has demonstrated, 'The seeds of almost all of Freud's important psychological ideas grew out of the soil of the neurobiology of 1890, and this is particularly true of his theory of dreams' (p. 62). As a result, Freud's assumptions about the ways in which the central nervous system functions were deeply flawed, for he believed it to be an essentially passive organization, responsive only to outer stimulation, and incapable of generating either its own energy or its own information. Thanks to the research of the last fifty years we now know that the nervous system is metabolically capable of generating (and cancelling) its own energy, and genetically capable of producing much of its own information. We also know that episodes of REM sleep and dreaming occur as a result of the spontaneous activity of the central nervous system, acting independently of stimuli arising from the environment.

However, despite Brücke's influence, Freud eventually decided to disown the relationship between neuroscience and his dream theory, and as a consequence he suppressed his *Project for a Scientific Psychology*. This was partly because he realized that neurobiology was still in its infancy and that an attempt to build a new psychology on its basis would be premature. It was also because he wished his theories to appear original and to survive any revolutionary developments that might occur in neuroscientific research. Nevertheless, his notion of repressed libido which could discharge itself in the manifest content of dreams, the symptoms of neurotic illness, perverse sexual acts, and inadvertent slips of the tongue, was the product of the now discredited teaching he received in Brücke's laboratory.

This has had dire consequences for the development of psychodynamic theory. Because it is based on the out-dated *a priori* assumptions of its founder, psychoanalysis has resisted scientific verification and has become trapped in an intellectual time warp. During the same period, however, there have been dramatic developments both in neurobiology and in dream science which have left psychoanalysis languishing in a state of self-absorbed isolation. If a dream theory is to be valid, it must take account of neuroscience as well as psychology, so that their findings can be compared and integrated with each other.

In comparison with Freud's theories, Jung's are less vulnerable to attack, for they are more in line with the modern view of the mind-brain as a self-energizing system programmed to seek specific biosocial goals. Thus, modern dream researchers agree with Jung in rejecting

Freud's view of the manifest content of the dream as representing the disguised fulfilment of a forbidden wish and accept Jung's assertion that dreams are 'transparent' natural events, occurring spontaneously, and proceeding quite independently of any personal wish or intention. 'Dreams are impartial, spontaneous products of the unconscious psyche, outside the control of the will,' wrote Jung. 'They are pure nature; they show us the unvarnished, natural truth, and are therefore, fitted, as nothing else is, to give us back an attitude that accords with our basic human nature when our consciousness has strayed too far from its foundations and run into an impasse' (*CW*10, para. 317). 'They do not deceive, they do not lie, they do not distort or disguise . . . They are invariably seeking to express something that the ego does not know and does not understand' (*CW*7, para. 189). The dream is 'a spontaneous self-portrayal, in symbolic form, of the actual situation in the unconscious' (*CW*8, para. 505).

What Freud called the manifest content, or the dream's façade, was in Jung's view merely an expression of the dream's obscurity, and this, he comments, 'is really only a projection of our own lack of understanding' (*CW*16, para. 319). Our dreams need to be interpreted not because they are *disguises* but because their meanings are formulated in a pictorial 'language' which we can construe only when the images are put into words. Jung agreed that some dreams may represent wishes or fears, but he insisted that most dreams have much wider concerns: 'Dreams may contain ineluctable truths, philosophical pronouncements, illusions, wild fantasies, memories, plans, anticipations, irrational experiences, even telepathic visions, and heaven knows what besides' (*CW*16, para. 317).

Moreover, Jung held that dreams contributed to the well-being of the whole psychic economy by performing an essentially *compensatory* function, the purpose of which was to balance one-sided or unduly constricted conscious attitudes. This compensatory view of dreams, which finds echoes in recent biological theories of REM sleep, was consistent with his concept of psychic homeostasis. Jung viewed the psyche as a self-regulating system which strives perpetually to maintain a balance between opposing propensities, while, at the same time, seeking its own growth and development. 'The psyche is a self-regulating system that maintains its equilibrium just as the body does. Every process that goes too far immediately and inevitably calls forth compensations, and without these there would be neither a normal metabolism nor a normal psyche. In this sense we can take the theory of compensation as a basic law of psychic behaviour. Too little on one side results in too much on the other. Similarly, the relation between conscious and unconscious is compensatory' (*CW*16, para. 330). Thus, in Jung's view, dreams 'add something important to our conscious knowledge', and 'a dream which fails to do so has not been properly interpreted' (*CW*16, para. 318). Dreams 'always stress the other side in order to maintain the psychic equilibrium' (*CW*7, para. 170).

In one sense, Jung's theory of compensation may be seen as an extension of Freud's theory of wish–fulfilment, for both theories conceive dreams as a means of making accessible to consciousness something previously unavailable and unconscious. But whereas Freud held the purpose of the dream to be one of deception so as to outwit the censor and enable the repressed contents to enter consciousness in disguise, Jung thought its purpose was to serve individuation by making valuable unconscious potential available to the whole personality.

Furthermore, in contrast to Freud's causal or reductive attitude, which traced dream contents back to their infantile instinctual origins, Jung advocated a constructive, forward-looking approach which sought to discover where the dream contents might be leading. Accordingly, in Jung's opinion, dreams serve the teleological imperative implicit in the psychic structure as a whole, which works unceasingly towards its own realization in life. (*Teleo* is a combination word derived from *teleos* meaning perfect, complete, and *telos*, meaning end; *teleology*, therefore, is about attaining the goal of completeness.)

Further disadvantages of psychoanalytic theory from which Jung dissociated himself were Freud's uncritical acceptance of Lamarckian ideas in biology, as well as his view of dreams which linked them to the production of neurotic symptomatology and which denied them any inherently creative, healing, or teleological role in the development of the personality. In these respects, too, psychoanalysis has been sidelined by contemporary developments. Thus, J. Allan Hobson, one of the leading pundits of modern dream research, has come to regard the dream process as 'more progressive than regressive; as more positive than negative; as more creative than destructive. In sum, as more healthy than neurotic' (1988, p. 16). This was the position that Jung had reached by 1912!

After a century of research and practical experience, it is easy to be wiser than Freud and to point out the flaws in his arguments, but one should not lose sight of the immensity of his achievement or the power of his cultural influence on the century now drawing to a close. If Jung was able to develop a hermeneutic approach to dreams more in keeping with contemporary science, it is because he learned well the lessons Freud had to teach him and was able to use them as a foundation on which to establish his own analytical psychology. When we celebrate Jung's triumph in devising new techniques for liberating the incalculable wealth of the unconscious in dreams and in the imagination, we should not fail to notice that he was sitting securely on the shoulders of Sigmund Freud.

Later Developments

'I followed you.'
'I saw no one.'
'That is what you may expect to see when I follow you.'
SHERLOCK HOLMES

Post-Freudian and post-Jungian trends in dream interpretation have thrown up a number of authors who have emphasized, supplemented, or developed certain elements of the corpus of theory and practice bequeathed by the two giants of dream psychology. Every analyst could produce a selection of favourites from among these authors: the most important, in my view, are Alfred Adler, Wilhelm Stekel, Samuel Lowy, Thomas French, Erica Fromm, Montague Ullman, Fritz Perls, Medard Boss, Charles Rycroft, and James Hillman.

Consideration for the limitations of space, to say nothing of the tolerance of my readers, must prohibit a detailed exposition of the ideas of each of these theorists. I can do no more than summarize those of their observations that are germane to the arguments I wish to advance in this book. Anyone wishing to pursue these ideas at greater length will find a key work by each author listed in the Bibliography.

Alfred Adler and Wilhelm Stekel

Dreams are a dress rehearsal for life.
ALFRED ADLER

Adler, who was fourteen years younger than Freud, was, together with Wilhelm Stekel, among the first to join Freud's circle in Vienna and was active in the psychoanalytic movement from 1902 to 1911, when Freud ejected him for 'heresy'. Having got rid of him, Freud wrote to Jung, 'I mean to be more careful from now on that heresy does not occupy too much space in the *Zentralblatt*' (the psychoanalytic journal on which Adler and Stekel were co-editors). For some time before this both Adler and Stekel had been a source of anxiety and irritation to Freud. On 25 November 1910 he wrote to Jung: 'My spirits are dampened by the irritations with Adler and Stekel, with whom it is very hard to get along. You know Stekel, he is having a manic period, he is destroying all my finer feelings and driving me to despair ... Adler is a very decent and highly intelligent man, but he is paranoid; in the *Zentralblatt* he puts so much stress on his almost unintelligible theories that the readers must be utterly confused. He is always claiming priority, putting new names on everything, complaining that he is disappearing under my shadow, and forcing me into the unwelcome role of the aging despot who prevents young men from getting ahead. They are also rude to me personally, and I'd be glad to get rid of them both ... I wouldn't mind throwing the *Zentralblatt* after them ...' (*The Freud/ Jung Letters*, p. 373). This opinion of Adler was confirmed by Freud's biographer, Ernest Jones: 'He was evidently very ambitious and constantly quarrelling with others over points of priority in his ideas' (Vol. 2, p. 130).

Adler was essentially the psychiatrist of the agonic mode: all his life, the basic plot (see p. 157) that absorbed his attention was the 'rags to riches' story; he saw human existence as a struggle to compensate for feelings of inferiority, acquired in childhood, through the achievement of a position of superiority. This Adlerian reading of human motivation has sometimes been identified with Nietzsche's 'will to power', but power was not a primary drive in Adler's view: it was merely a manifestation of the *compensatory striving* towards superiority. The particular form of striving adopted by an individual was called by Adler his or her 'life style'.

As his writings make clear, Adler was more interested in social behaviour and personal relationships than in dreams, and he never published a comprehensive account of dreaming. On the whole, he was of the opinion that dreams served to reinforce the life style and to assist the dreamer in striving towards the goal of superiority. 'In a dream the individual's goal of achievement remains the same as in waking life, but a dream impels him toward that goal with increased emotional power . . . In dreams we produce the pictures which will arouse the feelings and emotions which we need for our purposes, that is, for solving the problems confronting us at the time of the dream, in accordance with a particular style of life which is ours' (Ansbacher, 1956, pp. 360–61).

'The self draws strength from the dream fantasy to solve an imminent problem for the solution of which its social interest is inadequate . . . This seeking of a solution contains the "forward to the goal" and the "whither" of Individual Psychology in contrast to Freud's regression and fulfilment of infantile wishes. It points to the upward tendency in evolution, and shows how each individual imagines this path for himself. It shows his opinion of his own nature and of the nature and meaning of life' (p. 359).

For his part Wilhelm Stekel also rejected Freud's causal determinism and shared Adler's teleological view of dreams: 'Dreams always seek to explore the future, they show us our attitudes towards life and the ways and aims of life' (Ellenberger, p. 598).

Thus, although neither Adler nor Stekel produced a coherent dream theory worthy of the name, their insights are in line with the hypothesis that in dreams we draw on unconscious resources to promote adjustment to our present and future circumstances.

Samuel Lowy

Making up for what our conscious thinking neglected.

In some ways Lowy's view of dreams had more in common with Jung and Adler than with Freud. Like Jung, Lowy conceived the psyche to be a self-regulating system and held dreams to be indispensable to the maintenance of 'psycho-affective homeostasis'. He believed that the 'affective reverberations' of dream memories exercised a revitalizing effect on the personality by compensating for the deficiencies of consciousness and preparing the dreamer to deal with eventualities which lay ahead: 'When, for instance, we refuse to see some real difficulty, some threatening complication, and exorcize it from our conscious thoughts, and then this reality appears in our dreams, this is probably not mere exhortation, or warning, but a sign that the subconscious psyche is usefully dealing with the difficulty in question, that it is mobilizing and integrating the thought-processes relating thereto, that it is preparing itself for and against the eventuality, forming, as it were, "antibodies", and *thus making up for what our conscious thinking neglected to do because it was unable to cope with it.* If, then, the real difficulty actually occurs, the psyche, the nervous system, the personality are not unprepared, not quite without mental "antitoxins"...' (Lowy, 1942, p. 5; his italics).

That we forget most of our dreams does not nullify their psychological influence because a dream is *consciously* experienced during sleep. What the unconscious puts at the disposal of the dream ego is, in fact, conscious as long as we are dreaming. We only despise our dreaming consciousness when we are awake: 'why assume and take for granted that the world of dreams wants to be compared with, and related to, the world of reality and realistic thinking? *The contrary is much more probable. The world of dreams is a world apart*' (ibid., p. 56; Lowy's italics). The importance of the dream experience is in the dream itself. If we happen to recall it to waking consciousness, that is a bonus, a 'secondary gain', for it enhances the dream's psychological impact.

Lowy goes on to make the important point that the past and the present are synthesized by *the condensing action of dream symbolism* and that this synthesis has the essentially therapeutic consequence of promoting the unity, constancy, and balance of the psyche as a whole: 'By means of the dream-formation,' he wrote, 'details of the past are continually introduced into consciousness . . . This connecting function of the dream-formation is reinforced considerably by the formation of symbols . . . Dream-formation thus causes not only a connection of single details, but also of whole "conglomerations" of past experience. But this is not all. Through the constancy and continuity existing in the process of dreaming, there is created a connection with this dream-continuity. Which fact greatly contributes to the presentation of the cohesion and unity of mental life as a whole' (ibid., pp. 201–2).

Lowy's most significant contribution to the art of dream interpretation, however, was aesthetic and practical rather than theoretical: he emphasized that the meaning of a dream is better appreciated through intuition rather than logic, and that the analyst should 'feel himself into the dream-event', and 'let the image of its totality pass through his own psyche' so as to 'transform the verbalized dream-image into a "living context"'. He compares this mysterious and wonderful process to the manner in which an *apparently monochromatic ray of sunlight is decomposed into its individual and differently coloured components, by being passed through a prism* (ibid., p. 89; Lowy's italics).

What matters is that both dreamer and interpreter should share the emotional and cognitive impact of a dream as a living experience if its compensatory function is to be enhanced and ego-consciousness correspondingly enriched.

Calvin S. Hall

The universal constants of the human psyche.

The researcher who has done most to advance our epidemiological knowledge of dreams is Calvin S. Hall. Together with Vernon J. Nordby, Hall spent most of the 1950s and 1960s collecting and categorizing dreams and their contents from a large number of subjects from various parts of the world. Although Hall and Nordby assert that their research is uninfluenced by Freudian assumptions, these assumptions are nevertheless apparent. For example, they interpret dreams in which predatory animals with big teeth pursue the dreamer as castration dreams. They do not for one moment consider the possibility that such dreams could be phylogenetically determined. One dream that they cite as a castration dream in fact expresses the archetypes of landscape, predation, and escape. A young man reported the following: *'I dreamed that I was in a large open space and huge animals of all sorts with wide open mouths and big gnashing teeth were chasing me. I ran from side to side trying to escape. The huge animal monsters finally hemmed me in. They were going to claw and eat me. I awoke'* (Hall and Nordby, 1972, p. 26).

On the basis of their examination of over 50,000 dreams, Hall and Nordby concluded that a number of typical themes are represented over and over again. By a theme they meant the same basic plot or event. 'This is true for individual dream series as well as for sets of dreams obtained from groups of people,' they wrote. 'These *typical dreams*, as we shall call them, are experienced by virtually every dreamer, although there are differences in the frequency with which these dreams occur among individual dreamers and among groups of dreamers' (p. 19).

Like Jung, Hall came to reject Freud's distinction between latent and manifest contents, believing dreams to be transparent and undisguised. Like Jung again, he also found that the meaning of a single dream becomes more readily apparent when considered in the context of a whole series of dreams from the same dreamer. In his book *The Meaning of Dreams* (1966), Hall wrote: 'We believe there are symbols in dreams and that these symbols serve a necessary function, but it is not the function of disguise. We believe that the symbols of dreams are there to express something, not to hide it' (p. 95). 'There are symbols in dreams for the same reason that there are figures of speech in poetry and slang in everyday life. Man wants to express his thoughts as clearly as possible in objective terms . . . He wants to clothe his conceptions in the most appropriate garments . . . For these reasons, the language of sleep uses symbols' (p. 108).

Hall did more than anyone to rehabilitate the manifest content of dreams, which had hitherto suffered the consequences of Freud's neglect on account of his much greater interest in the 'latent dream thoughts'. But Hall's major contribution to dream psychology has been his demonstration that certain symbols occur again and again in dreams of people from differing cultural and linguistic backgrounds. This has done much to stimulate sympathetic interest in Jung's theory of archetypes.

Thomas French and Erika Fromm

Personal relations are the important thing for ever and ever.
E. M. FORSTER

In 1964 Thomas French and Erika Fromm published their book *Dream Interpretation*, in which they revised dream theory to accord with analytic interest in interpersonal relationships. Their central assumption was that the primary function of dreams was to work on relationship problems in the dreamer's personal life and find solutions to them. Thus a recent conflict in the family or the working environment would, by analogy, evoke memories of similar problems the dreamer had attempted to deal with in the past. These related memories constituted the dream's 'historical background'. The 'cognitive structure' responsible for the manifest dream was made up from the network of associations existing between the historical background, the focal conflict or problem, and the dreamer's present situation. The objective of dream interpretation was, in their view, to make the cognitive structure of the dream conscious so as to assist the dreamer to achieve more efficient solutions to his interpersonal problems in real life. This line of approach has proved extremely influential.

Montague Ullman

Perhaps our dreaming consciousness is primarily concerned with the survival of the species and only secondarily with the individual.

Montague Ullman was one of the first dream theorists to be inspired by the revolution that followed the discovery by Aserinsky and Kleitman that rapid eye movement sleep is reliably associated with dreaming. He took two of Freud's basic assumptions about dreams and stood them on their head: in Ullman's views, (1) the function of

74

dreams was not to protect sleep but to promote *vigilance*; and (2) far from bowdlerizing the truth, dreams possessed the capacity to express the truth even more bluntly than the conscious ego. 'The affective overtones of the dream are direct, though often subtle, clues to the objective truths involved in the problematic situation. If anything, self-deception is more difficult to effect in a dream than in waking life. This is so because the individual has to explain in depth – that is, in a more complete and historically or genetically integrated fashion – the nature of the threat or upset that besets him' (1962, p. 24).

Like French and Fromm, Ullman stressed the role of dreams in relating present problems to similar experiences from the past: 'The remarkable feature of the dream content lies in the dreamer's ability to express in symbolic or metaphorical terms the connection between a present problem or aspects of the past experience related to the problem and culled from all levels of the longitudinal history of the individual. The dream states more about the problem and the healthy and defensive reactions evoked by it than is immediately accessible to waking consciousness' (1962, p. 19). 'Asleep, we turn our attention to the reality of our interconnectedness as members of a single species. In this sense, we may regard dreaming as concerned with the issue of species interconnectedness . . . Were there any truth to this speculation it would shed a radically different light on the importance of dreams. It would make them deserving of higher priority in our culture than they are now assigned' (quoted by Taylor, 1992, p. 100). Ullman goes much further than French and Fromm, and, for that matter, further than any other theorist at that time, in attributing a biologically adaptive function to the dream and in taking account of the neurophysiological evidence available to him.

Frederick S. Perls

Every individual, every plant, every animal has only one inborn goal – to actualize itself as it is.

'Fritz' Perls, founder of the Gestalt school of therapy, is commonly credited with greater originality than he deserves. His main contribution to dream theory was his emphasis on the importance of taking

75

all characters and symbols in a dream as direct expressions of the personal psychology of the dreamer. This view has been praised as offering a radical departure from the instinctive/reductive approach of Freud, but it is little more than a rephrasing of the *subjective* technique of dream interpretation already introduced by Jung. Perls's theoretical application of the self-realization concept is also borrowed from Jung and from Abraham Maslow.

Where Perls did make a contribution was in his use of role-playing techniques to bring the part personalities apparent in dreams to greater consciousness. If, for example, you dreamt you were in a dilapidated car that kept misfiring as you drove it uphill, while in the back seat a woman muttered critical remarks to herself, Perls would get you to speak out your thoughts, not only as the driver but as the passenger and the car as well – since these are all aspects of yourself. By acting out each of these roles in turn you come to a better understanding of how they influence your life. This again was an adaptation of Jung's *active imagination*, but it provided a useful variant that many subjects found easier to use. When practised regularly, it enabled dreamers to come to a better understanding of their dreams and of themselves without the expensive services of an analyst.

Medard Boss

*I have the most impressive evidence for the inseparable belong-ingness of the things, animals and people encountered by the dreamer to the total pattern of relationships in which he moves and has his being. So much so that he exits **in** and **as** his relationship to them.*

Medard Boss was an existentialist, who, like Fritz Perls, had little that was original to contribute to dream theory. His main influence was on the manner in which dreams are received and worked on by the analyst. Like Jung, he stressed the fundamental *reality* of all psychic experiences, including dreams, insisting on the importance of con-scious participation in the dream as a basic ontological fact of experience. This, Boss maintained, was more important than mere interpretation. Although few people agreed with him, Boss's stand-

76

point was a necessary corrective to those who approached dream interpretation as an intellectual exercise. If therapeutic work with dreams is to be productive, it is essential that the dreamer should 'own' his dream and experience it as a living aspect of his psychic reality. These points had already been made more persuasively by Jung, but Boss helped to widen their currency.

Charles Rycroft

The Innocence of Dreams.

A number of analysts who trained and worked in the Freudian tradition have attempted to rectify the deficiencies, as they see them, of Freud's theoretical understanding of dreams. Erik Erikson (1954), for example, assisted in the rehabilitation of the manifest content of dreams by placing an Adlerian emphasis on the manner in which the manifest content reflects the dreamer's life style: it is a 'reflection of the individual ego's peculiar time-space, the frame of reference for all its defenses, compromises and achievements' (p. 21). Erich Fromm (1951) argued for a more creative function for dream symbolism, which he conceived in almost Jungian terms as a forgotten universal language: 'I believe that symbolic language is the one foreign language that each of us must learn. Its understanding brings us in touch with one of the most significant sources of wisdom, that of the myth, and it brings us in touch with the deeper layers of our own personalities. In fact, it helps us to understand a level of experience that is specifically human because it is that level which is common to all humanity, in content as well as in style' (p. 10).

The Freudian who has done most, in my opinion, to liberate the dream from the reductionist and pathological strait-jacket imposed on it by Freud is Charles Rycroft (1979). Following the example of the philosopher Suzanne Langer, he starts from the standpoint that 'symbolization is a natural state of mind, not a defensive manoeuvre designed to conceal meaning', and in his book *The Innocence of Dreams* he goes on to define dreams as *the activity of the imagination during sleep* – 'imagination being that function or faculty which enables us to remember what has happened, to envisage what has yet to happen, to imagine things that may or could never happen, and to use images of one set of things to make statements about something else, i.e. to use metaphor' (p. x).

As with other innovative Freudians, Rycroft has allowed himself to be influenced by Jung, as evidenced by his acceptance of the view that dreams indicate 'the existence of some mental entity which is more preoccupied with the individual's total life span and destiny than is the conscious ego with its day-to-day involvement with immediate contingencies, and which not uncommonly encounters blank incomprehension from an ego which is unprepared to admit that its conception of itself may be incomplete and misguided' (p. xi).

Dreams, for Rycroft, are innocent in the sense that they 'lack knowingness'. They display an indifference to received categories and are uncontaminated by the self-conscious will. They can be regarded as 'metaphorical messages from one part of the self to another, typically from a wider self to the conscious ego'. The art of interpreting dreams is essentially the ability to think in metaphors: it depends on 'the interpreter's intuitive capacity to perceive the similarity between things that are in other ways dissimilar' (p. x). Rycroft's main message is that 'dreams are best understood if one ceases to think of them as discrete phenomena or events but instead responds to them as momentary glimpses of the dreamer's total imaginative fabric, into which are woven all his memories, expectations, wishes and fears' (p. xi).

This position is entirely in keeping with modern neuroscientific understanding of the processes involved, and is a good example of how shrewd psychological insight can be integrated with hard scientific evidence to give a more complete and accurate picture of the complex phenomena of dreaming than when either side wanders off in pursuit of its own theories without any reference to the other.

James Hillman

Call the world if you please 'The Vale of Soul-Making'.
JOHN KEATS

Rycroft's conception of the essential *innocence* of dreams (i.e. that they are autonomous, lack guile, and are uncontaminated by the will) is one that has been current in Jungian-circles since the 1920s, and no one has been a more articulate celebrant of these unfettered gifts of the imagination than James Hillman (1975). He takes dreams as providing an actual model of the psyche 'because they show the soul apart from life, reflecting it but just as often unconcerned with the life of the human being who dreams them. Their main concern seems not to be with living but with imagining.'

Hillman draws on Lévi-Strauss's fantasy of 'the raw and the cooked' – the *raw* being pure nature, the *cooked* being what man (and his culture) make of it. Thus for Hillman, the dream is not pure nature, but elaborated nature, *natura naturata*. The dream digests bits and pieces from the day (Freud's *Tagesreste*) and converts them into images. There is a breakdown and assimilation of the dayworld: 'the dream-work cooks life events into psychic substance by means of imaginative modes – symbolization, condensation, archaization. This work takes matters out of life and makes them into soul, at the same time feeding soul each night with new material' (Hillman, 1979, p. 96). The 'dream-work' (Freud's *Traumarbeit*) is the work of the imagination set free of ego interference. 'Even the dumbest dream can astound us with its art, the range of its reference, the play of its fancy, the selection of its detail' (p. 93).

Soul-making is a term Hillman borrowed from the Romantic poets. William Blake uses it in *Vala* and John Keats in a letter to his brother: 'Call the world if you please, "the vale of Soul-making". Then you will find out the use of the world . . .' This provides Hillman with his philosophical perspective: 'the human adventure is a wandering through the vale of the world for the sake of making soul. Our life is psychological, and the purpose of life is to make psyche of it, to find connections between life and soul' (p. ix). To the achievement of this purpose the imagination, set free in dreams, is indispensable. 'The synthetic cooking operation of the dream-work . . . brings disparate ingredients together and concocts them into new things. These dream things we call symbols' (p. 134).

Dreams are the chefs preparing the nourishment that sustains the soul's existence, and this culinary expertise continues irrespective of the analytic attitude we adopt to it. 'Before an interpretation ever begins, the dream is already working on consciousness and its day-world by digesting the day residues into soul-stuff and by placing one's actions and relations into its dream fantasy . . .' (p. 123). We are such stuff as dreams are made on.

Hillman is always a richly stimulating read. Unfortunately, he is also a psychological extremist who will have no truck with the 'materialism' of all other approaches to the dream. Never must the soul be conceived of as 'an epiphenomenal vapour secreted by the brain'. The dream is 'an autochthonous image, a *sui generis* invention of the soul' (p. 70). This determination to extol the soul and denigrate the brain has involved him in a circular or, one might say, *uroboric* argument: while the dream is indispensable to soul-making, the soul is no less indispensable to dream-making. In attempting to defend this hardly defensible position Hillman declares that: 'The tradition of depth psychology is to stay at home and create its own ground as it proceeds,' asserting that Freud and Jung both 'abjured anatomy, biology, natural science, and theology for their basic premises' (p. 6). But this is not entirely true; certainly not of the first three disciplines named. Freud elected to stay at home *faute de mieux*, as we have seen, because neurophysiology was not sufficiently advanced to develop his 'Project for a Scientific Psychology' as he originally intended. Jung, like Freud, acknowledged the fundamental importance of 'the "psychic infra-red" the biological instinctual pole of the psyche', which 'gradually passes over into the physiology of the organism and thus merges with its chemical and physical conditions' (*CW*8, para. 420). It was this biological pole of the archetype that Jung compared to the ethological 'pattern of behaviour' and which he designated 'the proper concern of scientific psychology' (*CW*18, para. 1228).

Rather than stay at home, I would have us abandon psychological provincialism and intellectual agoraphobia in order to journey far into the past and way over the horizon to cultures remote from the traditions of Western psychology, and deep into the oldest regions of our brains. Only then can we gain a perspective on our dreams which is wide enough to reconcile their contemporary manifestations with the archetypal predispositions by which they are shaped.

Conclusion

Conclusions are names we give to the moments when we get
tired of thinking and take a rest.

ARTHUR BLOCH

The disdainful view of dreams adopted by rational, educated people since Roman times has in the present century been radically revised. For the first time since Artemidorus dreams have been deemed worthy of systematic investigation and considered capable of contributing significantly to the meaning and well-being of our lives. This has been due largely to the cultural stature of Freud and the intellectual achievement represented by his book *The Interpretation of Dreams*. That Jung and others were able to penetrate further into the mystery of dreams owes much to the unambiguous clarity with which Freud formulated his theories and to the uncompromising vigour with which he defended them; for, although this inhibited scientific research on dreams, it nevertheless provided his fellow analysts with a wealth of material to reflect on and a firm corpus of dogma to react against in forming their own ideas.

It is perhaps ironic that it is non-Freudians who have benefited most from Freud's discoveries. Freud and a number of his followers have, it is true, attempted to revise his original dream theories, and they may, according to their own opinion, have succeeded in doing this; but, to the non-Freudian, not an awful lot seems to have changed. (I exclude such luminaries as Rycroft, Winnicott, and Bowlby from these strictures, for they did not revise Freudian theory so much as revolutionize it to the point that they could no longer consider themselves to be Freudians.) As we have already noted, there has been something of a shift among neo-Freudians in the direction of granting greater respect to the manifest content of the dream and to the adaptive work of the ego which this content is thought to represent, but the old distinction between manifest and latent contents still prevails as does belief in the wish-fulfilling function of dreaming. Indeed, in America, traditional Freudian analysts have fervently resisted the revisions of those of their, largely European, colleagues who have declared an interest in ego psychology and object relations theory.

These controversies have coincided with a withering of Freudian interest in dreams. Already by 1937, Ella Freeman Sharpe had noticed the pendulum of psychoanalytic concern swinging away from dream interpretation and, as Sarah Flanders (1993) declares, it has never swung back. The interest that has been focused instead on object relations and the analysis of the transference has been sustained by the belief that unconscious fantasy expresses itself through every activity of life (e.g. in symptoms, speech, and gestures as well as in dreams) and, as a consequence, 'the focus of a contemporary [Freudian] analysis is emphatically on the dreamer, not the dream' (Flanders, p. 20).

In contemporary Jungian analysis the situation is very different. Here focus is still on the dream and on what the dream means for the dreamer (though some Jungians, especially some members of the 'Developmental School', have allowed themselves to be swayed by neo-Freudian trends away from the analysis of dreams to analysis of the transference). When dreams are still granted attention by Freudian analysts, they are largely understood to be 'revelatory of the object relations lived out between analyst and patient in the psychoanalytic process' (p. 21). Dreams can, of course, reflect these relations, but to confine interpretive interest to them is, in my view, to neglect most of the wealth that dreams have to offer. That Freudians have to a certain extent abandoned dreams reflects more the failure of Freud's theories to explain them than any lack of significance in the process of dreaming itself.

However, beyond the confines of traditional psychoanalytic discourse and controversy, the horizon is bright. The discovery of REM sleep, the use of neuroscientific research techniques, the accumulation of a century's experience of analytic practice, and the adoption of a biological perspective has brought us to the point where we may now develop a deeper awareness of the meaning and importance of dreams than has ever fallen to the lot of human consciousness.

4

DREAM SCIENCE

*I suspect that there are more things in heaven and earth
than are dreamed of, or can be dreamed of, in any
philosophy.*

J. B. S. HALDANE

In 1845, four brilliant pupils of Johannes Müller (1802–58), the
founder of modern physiology, signed their famous 'pact against
vitalism', which, ironically and tragically, may have helped to kill off
their illustrious chief. Müller, who was both a vitalist and a nature
philosopher, suffered bouts of severe depression throughout the latter
part of his life and committed suicide, it is thought, at the age of
fifty-six. Like all vitalists, he believed all living organisms were
driven by a life force which was not amenable to scientific measure-
ment. His pupils flatly rejected this idea and their pact against it
inaugurated a period of rapid progress in physiological research,
which was to result in the eventual establishment of a science of
dreaming.

Conflicts like that between Müller and his pupils are so common
in the history of ideas that Leon Daudet coined a special term for
them: *invidia*. One of our most ancient propensities, it seems, drives
us to seek membership of mutually antagonistic groups – resulting in
the in-group/out-group distinction so typical of human social organization. The inescapable truth is that the moment one joins a group it
becomes an in-group, and all similar groups to which one does not
belong become out-groups. In-groups mobilize loyalty and attachment, out-groups hostility and suspicion. Wars between nations,
struggles between political parties, *invidia* between rival scientific,
artistic, religious, and psychoanalytic factions, all are illustrations of
this tendency, and the scientific study of dreams is by no means
immune to its influence.

Oneirology has been riven by conflicts since Aristotle rejected the idea that dreams were omens sent by the gods. In modern times the battle between vitalism and materialism has been paralleled by tournaments between the protagonists of mentalism and epiphenomenalism, nativism and empiricism, behaviourism and psychoanalysis. Hostility between Freudian and Jungian schools of analysis is but a further instance of this human penchant for polarizing issues and taking sides. The longest and most determined war has been fought between those who believe dreams to be meaningful psychological communications on one side and those who see them as the meaningless waste products of brain metabolism on the other. Artists, writers, poets and analysts tend to belong to the first category, behaviouristic psychologists, neuroscientists, and sleep laboratory researchers to the second. It is the latter group that is represented by 'the man in the white coat' in my dream (see p. 1 above). As Freud wrote at the end of the last century: 'Dreaming has often been compared with the "ten fingers of a man who knows nothing of music wandering over the keys of a piano" . . . and this simile shows as well as anything the sort of opinion that is usually held of dreaming by representatives of the exact sciences. On this view a dream is something wholly and completely incapable of interpretation; for how could the ten fingers of an unmusical player produce a piece of music?' (1976, p.148).

This materialistic, anti–psychological attitude has persisted right up to the present time, fuelled by the current enthusiasm for computer analogies of the brain. For example, in 1977 J. Allan Hobson and his Harvard colleague Robert McCarley proposed an entirely neuro-physiological theory of dreaming which they called the 'activation-synthesis' hypothesis. According to this theory, dreams are evoked by a 'dream state generator' which is 'switched on' in the brain stem during REM sleep and bombards the forebrain with randomly synthesized misinformation. Dreams are the result of the cerebral cortex making whatever sense it can out of the nonsense with which it is presented. 'In other words, the forebrain may be making the best of a bad job in producing even partially coherent imagery from the relatively noisy signals sent up by the brain stem . . . The brain, in the dreaming sleep state, is thus likened to a computer searching its addresses for key words.' Essentially, dreams were, in their view, merely the senseless, random accompaniments of autonomous electrical activity in the sleeping central nervous system, and the question as to whether or not dreams had a meaning was a red herring.

Another computer analogy was advanced by the British psychologist, Christopher Evans, in his book *Landscapes of the Night: How and Why We Dream*, where he proposed that dreaming represents the brain-computer's 'off-line' time, when it processes information gathered during the previous day and updates its programmes in anticipation of the morrow.

Then in 1983, Francis Crick and Graeme Mitchison proposed their 'reverse learning' theory of dreaming, namely, that dreaming is merely a means of dumping redundant information, of 'removing parasitic modes which arise after the [cortical] system has been disturbed either by growth of the brain (when new connections are constantly being made) or by the modifications produced by experience'. What is happening during REM sleep, they assert, is 'an active process which is, loosely speaking, the opposite of learning. We call this "reverse learning" or "unlearning". In other words: "we dream in order to forget."'

Crick and Mitchison's hypothesis has received so much attention that one might have thought that it was something startlingly new, but if one did one would be wrong. A very similar idea was proposed as long ago as the 1880s by Robert, who described the dream as 'a somatic process of excretion'. 'A man deprived of the capacity of dreaming,' Robert wrote, 'would in course of time become mentally deranged, because a great mass of uncompleted, unworked-out thoughts and superficial impressions would accumulate in his brain and would be bound by their bulk to smother the thoughts that should be assimilated into his memory as completed wholes.' This view, as Freud commented, reduced dreams to the lowly status of mere 'scavengers of the mind'.

Similarly, two of the signatories of the anti-vitalist pact, Hermann von Helmholtz (1821–94) and Ernst Brücke (1819–91), both staunch empiricists, insisted on the primacy of physiology over all psychological considerations in accounting for dreams. Brücke's influence, as we have seen, prompted Freud to draw up his *Project*, which he subsequently renounced in favour of an entirely meaning-orientated *psychology* of dreaming. The trouble is that researchers become so attached to their own orientation, and so hostile to those who adopt another, that they forget they are all partially sighted observers examining different aspects of the same elephant in the dark, each believing that the particular bit of trunk, foot, or tail they are grasping represents the whole beast. Freud was evidently grasping its private parts.

Infinitely preferable to this groping in the dark would be a holistic attitude to dreaming, enabling the hermeneutic (interpretative) and scientific (experimental) approaches to complement and correct one another to the mutual advantage of both. The best of the contemporary dream researchers, such as J. Allan Hobson, have come to recognize this. In place of the purely physiological approach which he originally adopted, Hobson has, as noted in the last chapter, come round to the view that dreams are not without psychological meaning: 'I differ from Freud in that I think that most dreams are neither obscure nor bowdlerized, but rather that they are transparent and unedited,' Hobson declares. 'They reveal clearly meaningful, undisguised, and often highly conflictual themes worthy of note by the dreamer (and any interpretive assistant). My position echoes Jung's notion of dreams as transparently meaningful and does away with any distinction between manifest and latent content' (1988, p. 12).

Hobson even mentions with approval the Senoi-Malaysian people who discuss their dreams every morning and consider them to be guides to their current concerns and actions: 'like the Senoi,' adds Hobson, 'I regard dreaming as indicative of my internal state and take its data into account in my day-to-day self-assessment.' This is precisely the same exercise that Jung practised on a daily basis for most of his life after his break with Freud.

Another important dream researcher, Kleitman's pupil William C. Dement, to whom we owe the term 'REM sleep', also came to appreciate that dreams are rich in meaning and can carry enormous transformative power. One of his own dreams demonstrates this:

Some years ago I was a heavy cigarette smoker – up to two packs a day. Then one night I had an exceptionally vivid and realistic dream in which I had inoperable cancer of the lung. I remember as though it were yesterday looking at the ominous shadow in my chest X-ray and realizing that the entire right lung was infiltrated. The subsequent physical examination in which a colleague detected widespread metastases in my axillary and inguinal lymph nodes was equally vivid. Finally, I experienced the incredible anguish of knowing my life was soon to end, that I would never see my children grow up, and that none of this would have happened if I had quit cigarettes when I first learned of their carcinogenic potential. I will never forget the surprise, joy, and exquisite relief of waking up. I felt I was reborn. Needless to say, the experience was sufficient to induce an immediate cessation of my cigarette habit. This dream had both anticipated the problem, and solved it in a way that may be a dream's unique privilege.

Only the dream can allow us to experience a future alternative as if it were real, and thereby to provide a supremely enlightened motivation to act upon this knowledge (quoted by LaBerge, 1985, p. 192).

This is a good example of the superior wisdom that dreams can access to the dreamer as well as the therapeutic influence they can exert by correcting potentially self-destructive attitudes of ego-consciousness. To dismiss dreams of this order as mere 'activation-synthesis' or 'reverse learning' is not only inadequate, it is insulting. Nor can these reductive, neurologically based theories give a useful account of how dreaming evolved, why it has persisted, and what its psychobiological functions can be.

The Dreaming State

We are the music-makers
And we are the dreamers of dreams,
Wandering by lone sea-breakers,
And sitting by desolate streams;
World-losers and world-forsakers,
On whom the pale moon gleams:
Yet we are the movers and shakers
Of the world forever, it seems.
ARTHUR O'SHAUGHNESSY

The crucial event in dream research this century was the observation made in 1953 by Eugene Aserinsky and Nathaniel Kleitman that REM sleep is associated with dreaming. Once again, it is, on the face of it, surprising that publication of their finding caused such a stir, as it was far from being an original discovery. How many people may have reached the same conclusion since we began sharing our lives with dogs so many thousands of years ago is a matter for conjecture. However, we know for a fact that the Roman poet Lucretius did so about 44 BC, for in his *De Rerum Natura*, completed in that year, he described the twitching feet of a dog as it lay asleep on the hearth and concluded that it was dreaming about chasing a rabbit. In the seventeenth century, Lucia Fontana also noted that all animals periodically move their eyes while asleep and concluded that these movements were associated with dreaming. As the great Charles Darwin himself wrote in *The Descent of Man*: 'As dogs, cats, horses, and probably all the higher animals, even birds, have vivid dreams, and this is shown by their movements and the sounds uttered, we must admit that they possess some power of imagination' (Darwin, 1871, p. 74).

Academic purists insist that we cannot know whether animals dream or what they dream about, but it seems entirely reasonable to infer from their behaviour during the REM state that they are in fact dreaming. All of us who have received a training in academic psychology have been taught to wield Occam's razor (which states that in the interests of scientific parsimony we should not multiply entities beyond necessity) on the issue of animal awareness, but this has had the effect of divorcing human psychology from that of the rest of the animal kingdom and has provided scientists with the necessary defences and rationalizations to perform sometimes appalling experiments on animals on the grounds that 'they are not like us' and that, as a consequence, such atrocities are ethical. As Harry T. Hunt cleverly observes in his book *The Multiplicity of Dreams*, 'We need to consider the corresponding dilemma of theoretical parsimony in trying to explain how creatures with an activated cortex, organized sequences of outwardly inhibited behaviour (which can be surgically disinhibited) and scanning eye movements are not experiencing anything. All of us with pets have noted the twitches, groans, vocalizations, sexual, aggressive, and appetitive behaviours, and rapid paw movements of ostensible walking and running that occur during the animals' sleep. Parsimony calls this dreaming' (p. 49).

The inference from animals to man was but a short step, and it was made by Robert Burton, the author of *The Anatomy of Melancholy*, who wrote that 'as a dog dreams of a hare, so do men on such subjects as they thought on last', adding sagely: 'the Gods send not our dreams, we make our own' (MacKenzie, 1965, p. 81). As a Latin proverb put it: *Canis panem somniat, piscator pisces* (the dog dreams of bread, the fisherman of fish). So why should Kleitman and Aserinsky's observation work as such a stimulus to research? The answer is that it opened up a whole new world of inquiry, making it possible to study both instrumentally and objectively the relationship between the body and the mind, between consciousness and unconsciousness, and, as I shall hope to make clear, between phylogeny (development of the species) and ontogeny (development of the individual).

Another ancient observation that studies using the electro-encephalograph (EEG) have been able to confirm is the Hindu description of three states of mind: wakefulness (*vaiswanara*), dreaming sleep (*taijasa*), and dreamless sleep (*prajna*). As is now well established, the dreaming state of REM sleep is quite different from any other psychophysical state. Typically associated with a low-voltage, desynchronized pattern of electrical activity arising from the cerebral cortex, REM sleep is also characterized by rapid conjugate movements of the eyes, sporadic activity in certain groups of small muscles together with an absence of tone in the large anti-gravity muscles of the legs, back and neck. The pulse and respiration are irregular, the penis becomes erect (thus giving encouragement to the Freudians), and the blood pressure, brain temperature, and metabolic rate are all raised. When subjects are awakened from this state dreams are reliably reported on 70–90 per cent of occasions.

Periods of REM sleep regularly occur about every ninety minutes throughout the night, each episode persisting for a longer period of time, ranging from approximately five minutes to forty minutes. This cyclic regularity would suggest that dreaming is not dependent upon outside influences and this has been confirmed by the failure to induce REM periods experimentally by application of external stimuli – a finding compatible with Freud's assertion that the content of dreams is determined not by extrinsic stimulation but by programmes intrinsic to the dreamer's own mind.

A Typical Night's Sleep Sleep is initiated by the hypnagogic state, lasting several minutes, in which fragmented images and dramatic episodes are perceived in vivid clarity. The hypnagogic state is followed by slow wave NREM (non-rapid eye movement) sleep, so called because the EEG record shows waves of low frequency and large amplitude, while the eyes remain still.

This background NREM sleep persists for about ninety minutes. Then the first REM stage of the night intercedes. The EEG readings become irregular in frequency and low in amplitude – very like those observed in people when they are awake. This first REM episode usually lasts about ten minutes. The second and third REM periods are of increasing duration and follow shorter NREM episodes. The final REM interval lasts from twenty to thirty minutes and is usually followed by waking. If a dream is remembered at all, it usually arises from this last phase of REM sleep. Altogether REM occupies about 25 per cent of each night's sleep. For those interested in statistics, this means that a seventy-five-year-old person will have spent at least 50,000 hours dreaming. This amounts to 2,000 days or six years. It is not an inconsiderable activity.

Initial research findings indicated that dreams were confined to periods of REM sleep, most subjects denying that they were dreaming when awakened during NREM sleep. However, a doctoral dissertation completed in 1960 by David Foulkes threw considerable doubt on this. Foulkes woke his patients during both REM and NREM sleep, but instead of asking if they had any dreams to report he asked what thoughts were going through their minds. NREM awakenings produced reports of mental activity on 20–60 per cent of experimental trials. Foulkes concluded that it is not possible to equate dreaming with REM sleep, since there is so much mental activity proceeding outside the REM stage.

However, when reports from REM and NREM awakenings are compared, a qualitative difference is found between them. NREM reports are less 'dream-like' than REM reports, while NREM experiences are more like ordinary everyday thoughts and are usually rather banal and repetitive in content. It is rare for NREM thoughts to be associated with sensory illusions or the hallucinated dramas so typical of REM experiences. If it is true that some form of mental activity goes on throughout the whole course of a night's sleep, then for most of the time one is not dreaming but thinking. Overall, the evidence would indicate that the mind is never entirely at rest, a conclusion very much at variance with the traditional view of sleep and with Freud's insistence that dreams are the guardians of this still unexplained condition.

Dream Biology

The evolutionary stratification of the psyche is more clearly discernible in the dream than in the conscious mind. In the dream, the psyche speaks in images, and gives expression to instincts, which derive from the most primitive levels of nature.

C. G. JUNG

If sleeping and dreaming do not perform vital biological functions, then they must represent Nature's most stupid blunder and most colossal waste of time. When an animal is asleep it cannot protect itself from predators, cannot forage for food, cannot procreate, or defend its territory or its young. Yet for over 130 million years, despite enormous evolutionary changes, sleeping and dreaming have persisted in large numbers of species.

During each twenty-four-hour period, all animals display circadian rhythms of activity and rest. Some animals, such as owls, bats, and rodents, are active at night and rest in the daytime, while others, like humans, chimpanzees, and dogs, go about their business in daylight and rest when it is dark. The biological advantages of sleep are that it helps conserve energy while, at the same time, enforcing immobility and keeping the animal out of danger in its burrow, nest, or home.

Non-REM sleep evolved about 180 million years ago, when warm-blooded mammals evolved from their cold-blooded reptilian ancestors, whereas REM sleep evolved about 50 million years later. Until then, the early mammals, known as monotremes, reproduced by laying eggs in the same way as reptiles and birds. REM sleep appeared on the evolutionary scene when mammals began to reproduce *viviparously* (their offspring were born directly from the womb, not hatched out of eggs). Why should these evolutionary developments coincide, in the first instance, with quiet non-REM sleep and, secondly, with the innovation of active dreaming sleep?

The most likely explanation arises from the differing metabolic needs of reptiles and mammals and the greater immaturity (and learning capacity) of viviparous young. Being cold-blooded, reptiles have a ready source of energy in the sun, but this is not available to them at night, when they are particularly vulnerable to attack. Warm-blooded mammals, on the other hand, are less at the mercy of the weather and the time of day because they have acquired the homeostatic capacity to maintain their own constant body temperature. However, to sustain this, mammals have to seek more energy in the form of food so as to stoke the boilers of their metabolism, and, as a consequence, an efficient method of energy conservation such as that provided by longish periods of sleep is an adaptive survival mechanism of obvious significance for them.

But what of dreaming sleep? Here the explanation must have to do with the greater vulnerability of viviparous offspring. Whereas birds and lizards are reasonably well developed when they break out of their eggs, viviparous young are relatively helpless, and have to accomplish much learning and growth, particularly of the brain, before they are capable of independent survival. As we shall see, REM sleep is thought to play an important role in developing the infant brain and in activating those neural programmes responsible for basic and characteristic patterns of behaviour, such as those involved in maternal bonding, in environmental exploration, and in play.

Certainly, the presence of REM sleep in so many species and its persistence through so many millions of years can only indicate that dreams perform a crucial survival function in all mammals. This realization has stimulated intense study of mammalian sleep in the belief that it can reveal the meaning, purpose and function of dreams.

Animal Dreams   In the light of all the evidence amassed during the past forty years, no one but the most fanatically anthropocentric behaviourist would seek to deny that animals have dreams. But can we ever hope to know what it is that they dream about? The answer is that we can, and that we almost certainly do. The evidence comes from direct observations of the behaviour of intact and surgically deprived animals during REM sleep, and from inferences based on

EEG recordings taken from wide-awake animals as they perform activities essential for their survival. We owe this evidence to Michel Jouvet of the University of Lyon and to Jonathan Winson of Rockefeller University.

Jouvet has made two outstandingly important observations: (1) that dreams arise from bursts of activity in biologically ancient parts of the brain; and (2) that both animals and humans get up and act out their dreams when the brain centres responsible for inhibiting movements during sleep are incapacitated. For example, dreaming cats (whose descending neural fibres responsible for inhibiting movement during REM sleep have been cut) will, in their sleep, get up and 'stalk' hallucinated prey, 'pounce' upon it, 'kill' it, and start to 'eat' it.

Winson's research interest has been primarily focused on the relationship between REM sleep and memory. The neural basis for memory storage has been traced to a part of the limbic system called the hippocampus (the Greek word for 'seahorse', which it resembles) and to its connections with the neocortex of the brain. In 1954, John D. Green and Arnaldo A. Arduini of the University of California at Los Angeles recorded a regular signal of six cycles per second in the hippocampus of apprehensive rabbits. They named the signal *theta* rhythm.

Further observations on other awake animals, including tree shrews, moles, rats, and cats, detected theta rhythm when they were behaving in ways most crucial to their survival. Thus predatory behaviour in the cat, prey behaviour in the rabbit, and exploration in the rat were most reliably associated with theta rhythm and it is precisely these behaviours that are, respectively, most important for their survival. For example, a starving rat will always carry out a preliminary exploration of the environment before it settles down to eat the food placed in front of it.

Finally, in 1969, these observations were supplemented by a report from Case H. Vanderwolf of the University of Western Ontario that there was one behaviour during which all the animals he studied consistently revealed hippocampal theta rhythm, and that was REM sleep.

It was clear, therefore, that theta rhythm was involved in dreaming, in memory storage, and in the performance of crucial survival behaviours, and this led Winson to a highly significant conclusion – namely, that *'theta rhythm reflected a neural process whereby information essential to the survival of a species – gathered during the day – was reprocessed into memory during REM sleep'* (Winson, 1990, p. 44; my italics).

On the whole, Winson's suggestion was enthusiastically received, for it made persuasive sense of the data. Dreams, it was widely agreed, could be the means by which animals update their strategies for survival by re-evaluating current experience in the light of strategies formed and tested in the past. This is done when the animal is asleep because it is only during sleep that the brain is free of its outer preoccupations and able to perform this vital activity – rather like bank clerks doing their sums after the public is locked out and the blinds drawn down.

Most important of the brain structures thought to be crucial to memory processing and storage is the hippocampus, situated in the temporal lobes on both sides of the brain. In addition, the hippocampus, hypothalamus and thalamus are all parts of the limbic system which is involved in the experience of emotion as well as the storage of memories. The hippocampus receives information from the cerebral cortex via the cingulate gyrus. From the hippocampus it passes via the fornix to the hypothalamus and through the mammilothalamic tract to the thalamus before returning to the frontal lobe of the cortex.

The hippocampus is indispensable to short-term memory. And it is the hippocampus that is most cruelly affected in Alzheimer's disease, which accounts for the inability of patients afflicted with the condition to remember things from one moment to the next. However, their long-term memory usually remains relatively intact; at least, in the earlier stages of the disease. These patients are quite unable to tell you what they have just had for lunch, but they have no difficulty in singing hymns learned in childhood or remembering details of where they went to school. Research with patients having lesions specifically involving the hippocampus (and not other structures as in Alzheimer's disease) have demonstrated that it takes approximately three years for a short-term memory to be efficiently 'stamped in' to the long-term store. Thus, patients who have suffered severe hippocampal damage can recall nothing of what has happened during the last three years but can remember events that occurred before that. Once entered in the long-term memory, events prove extremely resistant to loss.

The remarkable process by which short-term memories are selected and transferred into the long-term memory store remains obscure. However, it seems increasingly probable that dreaming is involved – as is a mechanism which Winson has called *neuronal gating*, by which chemically active *neurotransmitters* are denied or given access to specific areas of the brain. The hippocampus is one such area. When an animal is awake, the neuronal gates protecting the hippocampus remain closed. When the animal falls asleep, the gates begin to open, permitting appropriate neurotransmitters to enter and pass their influences on to other parts of the limbic system. With the onset of REM sleep all gates are wide open and theta rhythm appears.

Winson believes that what is true of lower mammals could also apply to primates, including humans: 'Dreams may reflect a memory-processing mechanism inherited from lower species, in which information important for survival is reprocessed during REM sleep. *This information may constitute the core of the unconscious*' (p. 47; my italics). The association between dreaming and remembering is apparent in experiments on both animal and human subjects: REM sleep deprivation impairs the capacity to remember tasks from one day to the next.

For a short-term memory to be transferred to the long-term memory store, therefore, it has to be *dreamed into the memory circuit* for three years. Animal studies have demonstrated that, in the process, the neurones and their synaptic junctions making up the circuit actually grow into well-established routes of communication, like well-trodden paths through a wood. Hence the notion that for a memory to become permanent it must be 'stamped in' to the limbic circuit while key references are stored in the neocortex.

However, for all its billions of cells, the neocortex is of finite size, and if all events and experiences were placed on permanent record in the long-term memory, the brain would need to be much bigger than it is. Winson conjectures that it would be so large that we should need a wheelbarrow to carry it about in. Clearly some sorting process must be at work, selecting what is important and 'memorable' from what is insignificant and to be discarded. Could dreams be implicated in this procedure? Crick and Mitchison are not the only researchers to think they are, though these authors have chosen to emphasize the discarding 'unlearning' aspect of the dream rather than the aspect concerned with selecting and recording. In fact, most dream researchers are now of the opinion that dreams are involved in the selection and retention of memories significant to the individual. The crucial question concerns the criteria on which the selection is based: what decides whether an experience is sufficiently important to be built into the permanent repertoire of memories available to a mammal as it goes about its daily life? Winson's answer is that it is the collective 'phyletic memory' of the species. In other words, dreaming is a *selective processing device* which constantly monitors and evaluates recent memories against a store of coded information in the central nervous system which has been painstakingly assembled during millions of years of evolution and which provides an indispensable set of rules for determining what is significant for a member of a given species and what is not.

In support of his argument about brain size, memory storage, and the function of dreaming, Winson cites the example of one of the last surviving monotremes, an anteater known as the echidna – an egg-laying mammal that emerged from the reptiles about 180 million years ago. From our point of view the most important facts about the echidna are that, although a small animal, it has a relatively enormous neocortex (as large as ours, in fact) and it does not have REM sleep. Since it does not dream, the echidna needs a much larger cerebral cortex to hold all the information it gathers in a lifetime of monotreme existence.

For millions of years it would seem that evolution stopped right there. But then, with the emergence of viviparous mammals, an extraordinary innovation occurred. This happened because there was a limit to the size to which heads could expand (to accommodate an ever-increasing cerebral cortex) if the newborn infant could hope to pass through its mother's pelvis and survive. The problem of how to reconcile restricted head size with cerebral efficiency was one that took Nature a long time to solve, but the solution she came up with was one of startling originality: REM sleep.

A comparison of what we know about animal dreams with what we know of our own yields one important difference, and that concerns the nature and complexity of what is dreamt, for animal dreams appear to be linked more directly to phyletic considerations than our own. While it is true that our dreams can present us with the great archetypal themes of human life, this is by no means invariably the case. When animals get up and act out dreams for us, however, they seem always to involve the major survival issues of the species concerned. This must reflect evolutionary developments that have occurred since we parted company with our mammalian ancestors – our acquisition of language and the use of symbols, for example. As a result of these developments, human consciousness is less tightly strapped down to the archetypal bandwagon on which it rides, and we are able to assess present information in the light of past personal experience, without having constantly to refer back to ancient phyletic programmes in the collective unconscious. This has enabled ontogenetic learning to proceed with greater efficiency in humans than in other primates and mammals, and it is not unreasonable to expect such an advantage to be reflected as much in our dreams as in our cultural behaviour.

Identifying his 'memory processing device' with the unconscious, Winson concluded that Freud was right in viewing dreams as meaningful and as constituting the Royal Road to the unconscious, but that he was wrong in considering the unconscious to be a seething cauldron of various lusts, and wrong again in interpreting dreams as disguised versions of these lusts. However, Winson made little reference to Jung, and this was a grave omission. For what is so fascinating about the hypotheses of both Winson and Jouvet is that they exactly parallel Jung's idea that dreams compensate for one-sided attitudes of the conscious ego by mobilizing archetypal components from the collective unconscious in order to promote the individual's better adaptation to life. In fact, *their hypotheses are Jungian theory in modern biological dress.* Yet the irony is that while Winson praises Freud for having got it partially right, neither he nor Jouvet gives much credit to Jung, who seems to have got it wholly right.

The truth of this assertion becomes more evident the deeper we delve into the primordial history of our psyches and our brains.

97

Dream Amnesia

'I've a grand memory for forgetting, David.'
ROBERT LOUIS STEVENSON

One intriguing paradox needs to be addressed: if dreams are so important, and if they are so intimately involved in memory storage, why do most people have difficulty in remembering them? There are two possibilities:

(1) If Crick and Mitchison's 'reverse learning' model is correct, then remembering dreams would be counter-productive, because we should be remembering what dreams are designed to make us forget. However, there is little to be said in favour of this hypothesis. People who make a practice of remembering their dreams do not suffer the mental impairment that it would predict. On the contrary, they seem to benefit.

(2) Since we have to learn the ability to distinguish between what happens to us in dreams and what happens in waking reality, it could be that nature has conveniently arranged things so that dreams are usually forgotten. This would help to protect those not capable of learning the distinction – namely, animals and young children. If, for example, a rabbit dreamt on successive nights that a pack of hounds was lying in wait for it outside its burrow, and if it then remembered the dream on waking and considered it represented reality, it could well starve to death through an appropriate fear of making sorties in search of food. It is, therefore, better for the rabbit that it should forget the dream while at the same time benefiting from the increased vigilance that the dream may have induced. Since dreaming is an ancient adaptive mechanism with a very long evolutionary history, it is not implausible that dream amnesia is built into the system. Dreams perform the same functions in ourselves as in all other mammals, and it would not be surprising if we forgot our dreams for similar reasons. If an animal remembered its dreams and behaved as if they were real, it would defeat the whole purpose of dreaming, for its behaviour would become not more

adaptive but less, and its conduct would probably give rise to the suspicion that the unfortunate creature was psychotic. That remembering dreams does not on the whole render human adults psychotic is precisely because they are able to make a clear distinction between dreaming and waking reality.

Of the two theoretical possibilities, therefore, the second is more persuasive.

Archetypal Priorities in the Brain

We may hope to gain the same understanding of the development and structure of the human psyche as comparative anatomy has given us concerning the human body.

C. G. JUNG

The first thing to say about the human brain is that it is a hierarchical system: this is a reflection of its architecture, its evolution, and its enormous functional complexity. Dominating the entire apparatus are the two massive cerebral hemispheres, with their convoluted cortical covering, which contain no less than 75 per cent of the approximately 20,000 million neurones in the brain. Beneath these relatively recent additions much older parts of the brain exist which still possess their full functional integrity. A crude distinction between these older and newer components was made many years ago by James Olds (1922–76), who called them the 'hot' and 'cold' brains respectively. By the 'hot' brain Olds was referring to the mid-brain, which can in many ways be identified with the Freudian 'Id': it appears to function in accordance with the 'pleasure principle', in that it is impulsive, incautious, and unashamedly appetitive. The hot brain wants its own way, and it wants it *now*. The 'cold' brain, or cerebral cortex, on the other hand, is more rational and more susceptible to social conditioning: like Freud's 'reality principle' it mediates the passions of the hot brain to the environment, and causes them to heed the constraints of outer necessity.

A far more sophisticated and empirically productive distinction

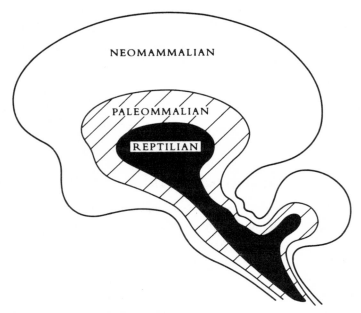

Figure 2. MacLean's three brains (from MacLean, 1973).

than that of James Olds was made in the 1960s by the American neuroscientist Paul MacLean, who conceived of the brain not as a unity but as *three brains in one*, each with a different phylogenetic history, each with 'its own special intelligence, its own special memory, its own sense of time and space, and its own motor functions' (MacLean, 1976). MacLean's famous diagram of the three brains, which together make up what he calls the *triune* brain, is reproduced in Figure 2. Another American neuroscientist, Jim Henry of Los Angeles, has argued that the dominant left cerebral hemisphere represents a fourth and phylogenetically most recent system which is peculiar to our species.

In line with these suggestions, it is likely that the brain evolved in four stages:

1. The Reptilian Brain   This is the brain stem, an upward growth of the spinal cord, and the most primitive part of the brain. We share it with all other vertebrates and it has remained remarkably unchanged by the march of evolution. It contains nuclei which are vital to the maintenance of life, such as those controlling the cardiovascular and respiratory systems. In addition, the reptilian brain contains the *reticular activating system*, which is responsible for alertness and the maintenance of consciousness, and is also responsible for initiating REM sleep. Millions of neuronal projections radiate from here to the forebrain as well as the hippocampal and amygdala structures known to be involved in memory consolidation and dreaming. Moreover, the reticular activating system mediates the *orientation response* displayed by all vertebrate animals when they fix their attention on novel stimuli in the environment and cease all physical movement as they do so.

At the early evolutionary stage represented by the reptilian brain emotions had not yet emerged, nor had cognitive appreciation of future or past events. Behavioural responses at this level are largely governed by instinct and appear to be relatively automatic. The typically reptilian behaviours of territorial acquisition and defence, as well as dominance striving and agonistic threat displays, are manifested at this stage of development. As Bailey (1987) says: 'Our drives, inner subjective feelings, fantasies and thoughts are thoroughly conditioned by emanations from the R-complex [i.e. the reptilian brain]. The reptilian carry-overs provide the automatic, compulsive urgency to much of human behaviour, where free will steps aside and persons act as they have to act, often despising themselves in the process for their hatreds, prejudices, compulsions, conformity, deceptiveness and guile' (p. 63).

2. The Paleomammalian Brain   This is made up of those subcortical structures collectively known as the mid-brain. The most important components of these from our point of view are the limbic system, including not only the hippocampus, the hypothalamus and the thalamus, but the pituitary gland as well (which controls the activities of all the endocrine glands in the body). The limbic system is a homeostatic mechanism *par excellence*: it not only maintains a sensitive control of hormone levels but also balances hunger against satiation, sexual desire against gratification, thirst against fluid retention, sleep against wakefulness. As we have already noted, it also plays an indispensable role in memory storage.

By this evolutionary stage, the major emotions of fear and anger have emerged, as well as those of love and attachment together with their associated behavioural response patterns of flight or fight, bonding and mating. Conscious awareness is more in evidence and behaviour is less rigidly determined by instincts, though these are still very apparent. The limbic system, which is deeply implicated in these emotions and behaviours, includes the oldest and most primitive part of the evolving cerebral cortex – the so-called *paleocortex*.

In all mammals, including man, the mid-brain is, therefore, a structure of the utmost complexity, controlling basic psycho-physical responses and attitudes to the environment. An animal, deprived of its cerebral cortex, can still find its way about, eat, drink, and avoid painful stimuli, but it has difficulty in attributing *meaning* to things: a natural predator will be noticed, for example, but not apparently perceived as a threat. Thus, accurate attribution of meaning evidently requires the presence of the cerebral hemispheres. That the mid-brain should be so intimately implicated in all the basic behavioural patterns which serve survival and adaptation points to this region as being the locus of those neuronal complexes most critically involved in archetypal functioning.

3. The Neomammalian Brain   This is the *neocortex*. It is responsible for cognition and sophisticated perceptual processes as opposed to instinctive and affective behaviour.

4. The Human Brain   By this stage lateralization of function between the two hemispheres has occurred, with the development of the left dominant hemisphere responsible for rational, empirical thinking, as well as the use of language and speech.

Attempts to integrate the two disciplines of neurophysiology and ethology have resulted in the focus of intense research interest on the mid-brain as the region subserving species-specific patterns of behaviour. MacLean (1975), in particular, demonstrated that such fundamental behaviours as maternal attachment, courting and erotic behaviour, together with the emotions which accompany them, are dependent on the activation of neuronal systems in the mid-brain, especially in the limbic system.

MacLean's conclusions were derived largely from animal studies, but the work of Flor-Henry (1976) and Schwartz *et al.* (1975) indicated that they were no less applicable to man. These researchers demonstrated that human emotional responses are dependent on neuronal pathways linking the limbic system with parietal and frontal areas of the right cerebral cortex. It appears, moreover, that this whole complicated right hemispheric/limbic affectional system is under the control of the left frontal cortex, which suggests that the 'cold' dominant hemisphere has a role in repressing or inhibiting the emotionally toned activities of the 'hot' paleo-mammalian brain.

It begins to look, therefore, as if Jung was right when he guessed that the archetypal systems of the collective unconscious, if they could be given a local habitation and a name, must have their neuronal substrate in phylogenetically old parts of the brain. It is not, of course, possible to designate any precise neurological location for any of the archetypes. The mid-brain structures involved in archetypal functioning must have an extremely complex and widely ramifying neurological basis involving millions of neurones in the brain stem and limbic system (the instinctive or biological pole of the archetype) and both cerebral hemispheres (the psychic or spiritual pole).

Archetypal Priorities in Dreams

We may expect to find in dreams everything that has ever been of significance in the life of humanity.

C. G. JUNG

More interesting still, the hierarchical structure of the brain is also reflected in the way it builds behaviour patterns out of what ethologists call *fixed acts*: these are stereotyped motor sequences which are the building blocks of behaviours necessary for survival and reproduction, and they are as apparent in typical dream sequences as they are in patterns of behaviour. For example, defensive behaviour, such as fleeing from threat, is apparent in the classic chase dream, attack behaviour in dreams of physical combat, and appetitive behaviour in dreams of a frankly erotic nature. The basic four Fs of fixed action are feeding, fighting, fleeing and fornication. If REM is indeed a 'genetically determined behavioural rehearsal', then the vital significance of dreams is that they enable the animal to respond appropriately to eating, aggressive, attacking, or sexual opportunities even before the gustatory, threatening, or erotic stimuli have been encountered in reality: the neural programme for behavioural acts must be in place before any particular behaviour is demanded.

In his invaluable book *The Dreaming Brain*, J. Allan Hobson maintains that this is as true of humans as of other mammals. 'Since any form of behaviour is a complex sequence of reflex acts, the difference between this and the previous level of organization is only one of degree. Even in the fully developed human animal, when behaviour is (more or less) under voluntary control, particular behaviour has the quality of a fixed act when adequately triggered and permitted to run its course. He concludes: 'Our dreams tell us clearly that the repertoires for these "instinctual" acts are indeed represented within the central nervous system. The extraordinary plasticity of the dream experience includes a rich over-representation of significant behaviours: fear, aggression, defence, and attack; approach-avoidance; and sex. At the level of our psychological experience, we find evidence of the whole repertoire.'

Hobson's conclusion is in line with Hall and Nordby's demonstration of the universal occurrence of typical dreams involving aggression, being pursued, sex, and so on. That phylogenetically ancient structures must play an important role in human dreams may be deduced from one study of the common dreams reported by college students in which the following themes were reported in descending order of frequency: falling, being pursued or attacked, repeated attempts at performing a task, experiences connected with academic work, and sex (Sagan, 1977). All these types of dreams, with the exception of those concerned with academic work, have fairly evident phylogenetic links. It is not surprising, for example, that a creature which in earlier stages of its evolution spent much of its life in trees should experience anxiety dreams of falling. Similarly, nightmares of being pursued or attacked are to be expected in a species whose primordial conflicts have involved hunting, fighting and striving for dominance. Furthermore, the vital need to master changes in the environment, to acquire physical skills, to perform religious and social rituals, requires repeated attempts to learn and perform such tasks. Finally, the contribution of sexual behaviour to the survival of the species requires no comment.

Two Basic Archetypal Modes:
Smiling and Frowning at the Angels

Many attempts have been made to classify dreams in terms of the kinds of events, particularly social events, occurring in them. These taxonomic efforts usually end up with long lists of categories in which it is hard to discern any unifying or coherent thread. There are, however, two major and contrasting groups of behavioural response patterns about which there is an increasing measure of agreement – those which involve bonding or attachment behaviour on the one hand and those which involve conflict and dominance striving on the other. It would appear that, like other primates – and all other mammals for that matter – we are both affiliative and hostile, we want both attachments and status (i.e. we are both Freudian *and* Adlerian by nature), as has been shown by Michael Chance of the Social Systems Institute in Birmingham. Chance has described two different and antithetical types of social systems which he calls the *hedonic* and *agonic* modes respectively. The hedonic mode is characterized by affiliative behaviour in groups in which members offer mutual support. The agonic mode typically occurs in hierarchically organized groups, where members are concerned with their status and with warding off threats to it.

In confirmation of Chance's claim to have defined two basic archetypal modes, cross-cultural evidence indicates that certain facial expressions involved in hedonic and agonic relations, such as smiling, frowning, and disdain, are genetically determined. From our point of view, what is so fascinating about these behaviours is that their early ontological development seems to be linked with the REM state. Thus, REM-state smiling, sometimes referred to as 'smiling at the angels', appears in human infants before the development of social smiling in wakefulness. Similarly, complex expressions normally associated with anger, perplexity, and disdain also first appear in the REM state. In other words, these behaviours rehearse and anticipate those social capacities which will appear in wakefulness some weeks later. It was precisely such findings as these that led Michel Jouvet (1967) to conclude that the REM state plays a crucial role in the maturation of species-specific instinctual behaviour. As we shall see in Chapter 6, there is also a similar and highly instructive correlation between dreaming and playing in the development of capacities crucial to survival.

Archetypal Dreams in Early Childhood

Parents do not know what they do when they leave tender babes alone to go to sleep in the dark.

CHARLES LAMB

One question inevitably arises: if foetuses and neonates spend all or most of their time dreaming, what on earth can they be dreaming about? Presumably, these dreams must, in Jung's terminology, be entirely archetypal. As brain structures develop, the basic forms of psychological ideation and imagery associated with them are assuming their first dimly perceived forms. Support for this supposition comes from the dreams of young children, which are found on examination to be full of archetypal implications. For example, Niederland (1957) reported a young dreamer as saying, 'I had another daddy.' Then, turning to his father, the little boy added, 'the daddy was taller than you.' I recall a similar dream from my early childhood which prompted me to tell my mother about 'my other daddy' in the presence of my father, who had just returned from a long business trip! In Jung's view, all children have 'another daddy' – the *archetypal* father, which forms the basis of the child's developing father *imago*, a condensed image made up of the archetypal father and the personal father. Indeed, Jung's belief that there is an archetypal foundation to dreams came from his early realization that his childhood dreams contained transpersonal elements which could not have been derived from his own experience.

106

The common childhood fears – of the dark, of strangers, of rapidly approaching objects – are all 'archaic remnants', early warning devices put there by evolution because of the constant dangers in the ancestral environment. The dreams of childhood, as we shall see, are full of 'Things' and monsters that threaten to attack. That this seems so much worse in the dark is because humans have bad night vision and because the great cats hunt during the hours of darkness. This built-in awareness of the ever present 'Thing' that might attack makes children sensitive to cues that might naturally be associated with it. Thus, the predator archetype is evident in many childhood fears and nightmares. For example, Susan Isaacs gives an account (in Klein *et al.*, 1952) of a one-and-a-half-year-old child who was so terrified by the broken and flapping sole of her mother's shoe that the shoe had to be hidden away. When she saw it again fifteen months later she was able to say, 'I thought that it could eat me right up.'

Archetypes and Neuroscience

The psyche is a self-regulating system that maintains its equilibrium just as the body does.

C. G. JUNG

We are left with the conclusion that modern neuroscientific findings, together with the theoretical constructs placed upon them, are all remarkably compatible with Jung's theory of archetypes, originally formulated in the early part of this century. Although Paul MacLean proposed his concept of the triune brain several years after Jung's death, Jung had already suggested that dreams about mammals or reptiles could relate to phylogenetically ancient mammalian and reptilian structures in the brain and that they were to be understood as expressions of the deeper intentions of nature itself. 'The evolutionary stratification of the psyche,' wrote Jung, 'is more clearly discernible in the dream than in the conscious mind. In the dream the psyche speaks in images, and gives expression to instincts, which derive from the most primitive levels of nature. Therefore, through the assimilation of unconscious contents, the momentary life of consciousness can once more be brought into harmony with the law of nature from which it all too easily departs, and the patient can be led back to the natural law of his own being' (*CW*16, para. 351). At the time, this was little more than a hunch, but he had the courage to back it. On its basis, he built his understanding of human psychopathology and devised a treatment for its cure. In Jung's view, our major difficulties, whether neurotic, psychotic, psychopathic, or political, come from losing contact with 'the age old unforgotten wisdom stored up in us'. If we wished to re-establish contact with this great reservoir of human potential then there was only one way open to us: we must pay close attention to our dreams.

Animal dreams abound in analytic practice. For example, *a rather timid woman, who was scared of her difficult and demanding boss, dreamt of a large black dog that stood in its kennel staring at her. A voice said: 'He's stubborn but he's as good as gold if you treat him right.'* Working on the dream herself, she thought at first that the dog represented her boss, but, at her next analytic session, she realized that it was a stubborn, potentially aggressive part of herself that she wasn't using. The value of this insight was apparent in the weeks that followed, for she was able to make good use of the dog image in her working life: it gave her the courage to be stubborn and aggressive herself when her boss failed to 'treat her right'. This is an example of a compensatory dream making available to the dreamer potential that she did not realize she possessed. That she discovered her own stubbornness and aggression in mammalian form indicates that it was still not sufficiently assimilated into her conscious personality to appear in her dream as human.

Remembering the Present: Bartlett and Edelman

I cannot but remember such things were,
That were most precious to me.
WILLIAM SHAKESPEARE

Contemporary neuroscience is confirming the findings of another pioneer, the Cambridge psychologist Sir Frederic Bartlett, who in 1932 published his classic work *Remembering*: 'Remembering is not the re-excitation of innumerable fixed, lifeless and fragmentary traces,' he wrote. 'It is an imaginative reconstruction or construction, built out of the relation of our attitude toward a whole mass of organized past reactions or experience.' Remembering is an active, dynamic process which, like perceiving, recognizing, and imaging, is based on past experience but takes account of the current situation and current needs.

Bartlett rejected the atomistic-associationist psychology that preceded him with its over-mechanical notion of 'memory traces' and introduced the far more flexible concept of *schemas*, which he borrowed from the neurophysiologist Henry Head. By schema Bartlett implied a mental structure, built up over time, which is responsible for the active organization of past experiences in the light of current events. This idea has been taken up and greatly extended by Gerald Edelman of the Neurosciences Institute at Rockefeller University, whose biological theory of mind, which he calls Neural Darwinism, or the Theory of Neuronal Group Selections (TNGS), has caused much excitement. The title of one of his books, *The Remembered Present* (1989), gives a clue to what his theory is about.

From the moment of birth a growing animal has to recognize, classify, and categorize incoming sensory information so as to build up, by degrees, an adequate model of the world. This it does through a personal evolutionary process which Edelman calls '*somatic* selection', analogous to the transpersonal evolutionary process which Darwin called '*natural* selection'. Whereas natural selection results in the genetic survival of specific physical or behavioural characteristics with the subsequent emergence of new species in nature, somatic selection results in the favouring of specific cells, or groups of cells, in the brain.

Unique neuronal configurations established in the foetus are acted on by *experience* so that certain cell groups are selected rather than others and the connections between them strengthened. There are estimated to be about 100 million such groups in the brain, each group consisting of between 50 and 10,000 neurones. Whole series of neuronal groups become interconnected and respond selectively to specific elemental categories such as 'movement' or 'colour'. These series Edelman calls 'maps'. The construction of maps makes it

possible for us to create our own perceptions. It is here that somatic
selection intervenes, resulting in survival of the fittest maps: maps that
correspond to successful perceptions – i.e. they approximate most
closely to 'reality' – are strengthened, while less successful maps are
weakened or cease to be active.

The incessant interaction that proceeds throughout specific maps
and between various series of maps permits what Edelman calls 're-
entrant signalling' – a continuous communication between maps
which enables the brain to construct a percept such, for example, as
'dog'. Stroking a dog will activate one set of maps, seeing it run after
a ball another set, and hearing it bark another, and so on. Re-entrant
signalling between these various sets of maps is responsible for
synthesizing the percept 'dog at play'.

The capacity, which we all share, for making generalizations about
complex sensory information derived from different sources, made
possible by re-entrant signalling, is, in Edelman's view, the basis of
psychic development. It can achieve a remarkable degree of effectiveness even in relatively primitive animals like birds. Both generalization
and categorization are indispensable to learning in all animals, and
these activities go on all the time. Like Bartlett, Edelman insists that
these are dynamic processes involving not merely the filing of
sensory messages into already existent categories but an active recategorization of them into new percepts which are continually being
formed. It is this never-ending recategorization that Edelman identi-
fies with memory and believes to be the basis of consciousness.
Through an elaborate series of steps Edelman has extended his theory
of neuronal group selection to accommodate all the 'higher' aspects
of mind, including concept formation, language, and consciousness
itself.

A fundamental distinction made by Edelman is between 'primary'
consciousness and 'higher-order' consciousness. He defines primary
consciousness as 'the state of being mentally aware of things in the
world – of having mental images in the present, but it is not
accompanied by any sense of [being] a person with a past and a
future'. Primary consciousness results from the capacity of re-entrant
signalling to accumulate a number of categorizations into a 'scene'.
This means that *events that may have had significance to an animal's past*

learning can be related to new events' (my italics). This assimilation of past events to the present, Edelman stresses, is profoundly *subjective* and based not on objectively established 'facts' in the real world but on what had 'value' or 'meaning' for the animal in the past. This, I would suggest, is precisely what is happening in the very private and subjective experiences occurring in dreams.

From Dreams to Consciousness

The highest activities of consciousness have their origins in physical occurrences of the brain just as the loveliest melodies are not too sublime to be expressed by notes.

W. SOMERSET MAUGHAM

Edelman believes that mammals, birds, and some reptiles possess such a scene-creating primary consciousness, and that it enables these creatures to adapt efficiently to highly complex environments. Reptilian, mammalian, or avian consciousness is to be contrasted with higher-order consciousness which, according to Edelman, 'involves the recognition by a thinking subject of his or her own acts and affections. It embodies a model of the personal, and of the past and future as well as the present.' Only in humans, and to some extent in other apes, does higher-order consciousness emerge. It depends on the evolutionary development of language and symbolization, the capacities for generalization, reflection, and self-consciousness, all of which are associated with the development of the left cerebral hemisphere in man. For consciousness to become conscious of itself, the 'scenes' of primary consciousness have themselves to be subject to re-categorization.

How, then, does consciousness emerge? And what role may dreaming play in the process? To account for consciousness Edelman postulates two re-entrant processes:

(1) The linking of primary memory ('value-category' memory) with current perception through a process which Edelman calls 'perceptual "bootstrapping"'. This he holds responsible for the creation of primary consciousness.

(2) The linking of centres responsible for 'symbolic' memory and for concept formation through a process which Edelman calls 'semantic "bootstrapping"'. This he holds responsible for higher-order consciousness.

Thus, consciousness became an evolutionary possibility when a genetic variant emerged providing an animal with a re-entrant circuit capable of linking 'value-category' memory to current perception. At that moment in evolutionary time, Edelman comments, 'memory became the substrate and servant of consciousness'. I would hypothesize that that was also the moment when dreaming emerged and became the servant of both consciousness and memory.

Edelman's work gives rise to a new way of conceiving the unconscious as a blanket term describing the continuous pandemonium of re-entrant signalling between inter-related complexes of maps. Consciousness intervenes when vast numbers of these complexes are playing in concert. Individual players in the orchestra are all connected: each interprets the music individually; but at the same time each modulates the others and is modulated by them. The music is *collectively* created. There is no final or 'master' interpretation. Here modern theory differs from classical theory, which held that there must be some kind of homunculus in the brain, a small person who 'viewed' percepts and 'received' images and ideas as the brain presented them. The notion of re-entrant signalling, with all groups and maps playing their individual parts in a great orchestral symphony of meaningful sounds, has now replaced this.

The crucial point about Edelman's theory is that an exploring organism is always seeking and imposing *meaning* on events. The maps which are selected out of a great variety of neuronal groups are *maps of meaning*. If higher consciousness is present, the symbolic systems on which it depends are constructed out of meanings. This represents a conceptual revolution of the very highest significance, and it is part of a wider scientific movement to 'put the mind back into nature'. (See Jerome Bruner, 1990.) Hitherto, workers in neuroscience and in artificial intelligence have sustained the fantasy that forms of intelligence and language could be devised on the basis of pure logic without having to postulate anything so messy as 'meaning'. The realization has now dawned that this cannot be the case and it has compelled scientists to accept meaning as a fundamental concept in biology. Meaning, it seems, is something that Nature cannot do without. And that is why dreaming, remembering, and consciousness emerged as massive biological achievements.

Summary and Conclusions

Dreaming itself is the workshop of evolution.
SANDOR FERENCZI

The findings of dream science are compatible with the insight expressed by the British sexologist Havelock Ellis (1899) that dreams represent 'an archaic world of vast emotions and imperfect thoughts', the study of which might reveal to us primitive stages in the evolution of mental life (Freud, 1976, p. 126). At night, it seems, we enter an archetypal world where we participate in the phylogenetic programme of our species and share with it our mite of the day's experiences. Let us summarize the evidence:

(1) The emergence of dream sleep 130 million years ago and its persistence across a wide range of species demonstrates that it is a neuropsychic activity of the greatest biological significance.

(2) EEG records in sleeping decorticate cats and in humans with gross cerebral lesions reveal that the low voltage fast waves of REM sleep originate in evolutionarily ancient centres in the brain stem.

(3) In addition, the paleomammalian structures of the mid-brain are active in REM sleep, as may be deduced from the associated changes which occur in pulse and respiratory rates, blood pressure, penile dimensions, vaginal blood flow, emotional state, temperature regulation, and so on.

(4) When brain centres responsible for maintaining the relatively immobile state of REM sleep are removed or inhibited, animals 'act out' patterns of behaviour which are typical of their species and crucial for their survival.

(5) These observations, which clearly demonstrate that brain structures possessing an extremely long evolutionary pedigree are involved in dreaming, give impressive support for two hypotheses: (a) that neuronal complexes crucial to the human ethogram (the Jungian 'archetypes') are located in these regions, and (b) that a phylogenetic continuity exists for essential archetypal patterns which extends from reptilian through mammalian to human forms of behaviour and experience.

(6) The findings that EEG theta rhythm, originating from a specific part of the paleomammalian brain, namely, the hippocampus, is associated with the performance of crucial survival behaviours and with memory storage as well as with REM sleep, lends weight to the additional hypothesis that in dreaming sleep an animal, including the human animal, is updating strategies for survival in the light of its own experience and in the light of all the potential for experience specific to the species.

The Freudian theory of dreams is thus discredited: dreams are not instigated by wishes, whether they be sexual, repressed or otherwise. Dreams are predictable episodic phenomena, associated with cyclic functions in the central nervous system, and have their basis in biology. As Hobson (1988) has put it, dreams are the product of a 'genetically determined, functionally dynamic blue-print' in the brain, whose function is '*to construct* and *to test* the brain circuits that underlie our behavior – including cognition and meaning attribution'. While he believes this test programme to be essential to normal brain-mind functioning, Hobson does not consider that one has necessarily to remember its products in order to reap its benefits. On his own admission, however, he has found these benefits to be enhanced when he makes the effort to remember them. One can only endorse Ernest Rossi's succinct conclusions that dreaming is 'an endogenous process of psychological growth, change and transformation', and that dreams themselves constitute 'a laboratory for experimenting with changes in our psychic life' (Rossi, 1972, p. 142).

5

CONSCIOUS AND UNCONSCIOUS, COLLECTIVE AND PERSONAL

'Now you have fallen, my good comrade, but I must go on.'
C. G. JUNG

On 18 December 1913, Jung awoke from a fateful dream which made him wonder if he should shoot himself:

I was with an unknown, brown-skinned man, a savage, in a lonely, rocky mountain landscape. It was before dawn; the eastern sky was already bright, and the stars fading. Then I heard Siegfried's horn sounding over the mountains and I knew that we had to kill him. We were armed with rifles and lay in wait for him on a narrow path over the rocks.

Then Siegfried appeared high up on the crest of the mountain, in the first ray of the rising sun. On a chariot made of the bones of the dead he drove at furious speed down the precipitous slope. When he turned a corner, we shot at him, and he plunged down, struck dead.

Filled with disgust and remorse for having destroyed something so great and beautiful, I turned to flee, impelled by the fear that the murder might be discovered. But a tremendous downfall of rain began, and I knew that it would wipe out all traces of the deed. I had escaped the danger of discovery; life could go on, but an unbearable feeling of guilt remained (MDR, p. 173).

As with Jung's customs inspector dream, we shall approach this in the three contextual stages of classical Jungian analysis, establishing its personal, cultural, and archetypal associations so as to 'amplify' its meaning.

Personal Context The dream occurred a year to the day after Jung had written his most furious and offensive letter to Freud in a correspondence increasingly marked by acrimony. The gist of the letter was as follows:

Dear Professor Freud,
May I say a few words to you in earnest? I admit the ambivalence of my feelings towards you . . . I would, however, point out that your technique of treating your pupils like patients is a *blunder* . . . You go around sniffing out all the symptomatic actions in your vicinity, thus reducing everyone to the level of sons and daughters who blushingly admit the existence of their faults. Meanwhile, you remain on top as the father, sitting pretty . . . You see, my dear Professor, so long as you hand out this stuff I don't give a damn for my symptomatic actions; they shrink to nothing in comparison with the formidable beam in my brother Freud's eye . . . If ever you should rid yourself entirely of your complexes and stop playing the father to your sons and instead of aiming continually at their weak spots took a good look at your own for a change, then I will mend my ways . . . No doubt you will be outraged by this particular token of friendship, but it may do you good all the same' (*The Freud/Jung Letters*, pp. 534–5).

This was the end. A fortnight later Freud replied: 'I propose that we abandon our personal relations entirely. I shall lose nothing by it, for my only emotional tie with you has long been a thin thread – the lingering effect of past disappointments . . . I therefore say, take your full freedom and spare me your supposed "tokens of friendship"' (p. 539). Three days later Jung responded, 'I accede to your wish that we abandon our personal relations, for I never thrust my friendship on anyone. You yourself are the best judge of what this moment means to you. "The rest is silence"' (p. 540). So ended for Jung his first and only great friendship with a man, and, according to his son, Franz Jung, he never entirely got over it.

The year which had elapsed between the end of the relationship and the occurrence of the Siegfried dream had been one of appalling stress and disturbance for Jung, and for a time he teetered on the brink of a psychotic collapse. He had horrifying visions in which he saw Northern Europe flooded by a sea of blood. These were followed by dreams in which the whole continent was frozen by an arctic wave. Then a stream of fantasies was released: 'I was living in a constant state of tension; often I felt as if gigantic blocks of stone were tumbling down upon me. One thunderstorm followed another. My enduring these storms was a question of brute strength. Others have been shattered by them – Nietzsche, and Hölderlin, and many others. But there was a demonic strength in me, and from the beginning there was no doubt in my mind that I must find the meaning of what I was experiencing in these fantasies. When I endured these assaults of the unconscious I had an unswerving conviction that I was obeying a higher will, and that feeling continued to uphold me until I had mastered the task.'

All this had been released by the break with Freud, and he was still in the grip of these storms when he had his dream of killing Siegfried. 'When I awoke from the dream,' recorded Jung, 'I turned it over in my mind, but was unable to understand it. I tried therefore to fall asleep again, but a voice within me said, "You *must* understand the dream, and must do so at once!" The inner urgency mounted until the terrible moment came when the voice said, "If you do not understand the dream, you must shoot yourself!" In the drawer of my night table lay a loaded revolver, and I became frightened. Then I began pondering once again, and suddenly the meaning of the dream dawned on me . . . [it] showed that the attitude embodied by Siegfried, the hero, no longer suited me. Therefore it had to be killed.'

Given the character of Freud and Jung, it was inevitable that a row would eventually break out between them. It was heralded in 1911 by the publication of the first part of Jung's *Transformations and Symbols of the Libido* ('It is a risky business for an egg to be cleverer than the hen,' Jung wrote to Freud. 'Still what is in the egg must find the courage to creep out'), and finally erupted in 1912 with publication of part two (in a letter to Freud Jung quoted Zarathustra: 'One repays a teacher badly if one remains only a pupil'). In this work, and in a series of lectures given in New York in September 1912, Jung spelt out his heretical view that libido was a much wider concept than Freud allowed and that it could appear in 'crystallized' form in the universal symbols or 'primordial images' apparent in the myths of humanity. Jung drew special attention to the archetype of the hero, interpreting the recurrent mythic theme of the hero's fight with a dragon-monster as the struggle of the adolescent ego for deliverance from the mother. This led him to interpretations of the Oedipus complex and the incest taboo which were very different from

those proposed by Freud. (In Jung's view, a child became attached
to his mother not because she was the object of incestuous passion,
as Freud maintained, but because she was the provider of love and
care – a view which anticipated the theoretical revolution wrought
some forty years later by John Bowlby.)

The Siegfried legend had an intense personal significance for Jung.
In March 1909, he had written to Freud admitting that 'a complex is
playing Old Harry with me: a woman patient, whom years ago I
pulled out of a very sticky neurosis with unstinting effort, has
violated my confidence and my friendship in the most mortifying
way imaginable. She has kicked up a vile scandal solely because I
denied myself the pleasure of giving her a child' (*The Freud/Jung
Letters*, p. 207).

The patient was Sabina Spielrein. She had been admitted under
Jung's care at the Burghölzli in 1904. The 'sticky neurosis' out of
which he pulled her, 'with unstinting effort' (Bruno Bettelheim has
suggested that 'with greatest devotion' more accurately renders Jung's
words *mit grösster Hingabe*), was the first such condition Jung had
treated along Freudian lines and the outcome was dramatically successful. However, in the course of the intense analytic relationship, they
fell in love with one another, and Spielrein developed the fantasy that
she was destined to have a son by Jung. He would be called Siegfried.

A Miraculous Child, Siegfried would reconcile the differences
between Jung and Freud and between gentile and Jewish psychology
in one glorious epiphany. Jung was to be his physical father and
Freud his spiritual father. There was almost a major scandal about
this which could have ruined Jung's career, but Freud helped to
resolve the problem. Encouraged by Jung, Spielrein became a medical
student and qualified as a doctor, then left Zürich for Vienna in order
to train as an analyst. She proved to be a brilliant pupil, devoted to
both Freud and Jung, as well as to the psychoanalytic movement, and
she worked hard, after the two men had fallen out, to bring about a
reconciliation between them (Carotenuto, 1984).

By killing Siegfried in his dream, Jung was finally destroying this
fantasy of reconciliation: the Jewish Freud and Protestant Jung could
never be reunited in one transpersonal cause, but must forever go
their separate ways. It was a case of what David Rosen of Texas

A&M University calls 'egocide' (Rosen, 1993), which marked the beginning of the end of Jung's 'creative illness' (Ellenberger, 1970).

'After the deed I felt an overpowering compassion, as though I myself had been shot: a sign of my secret identity with Siegfried, as well as of the grief a man feels when he is forced to sacrifice his ideal and his conscious attitudes. This identity and my heroic idealism had to be abandoned, for there are higher things than the ego's will and to these one must bow' (*MDR*, p. 174).

Cultural Context Freud and Jung had conducted their friendship largely by correspondence and Freud was constantly reproving Jung for not writing more promptly and more often. Many of Jung's letters begin with an apology for tardiness, excusing himself on the grounds of work. The work on which he was engaged was less to do with the advancement of the psychoanalytic movement than Freud would have liked and more to do with Jung's own research into mythology, comparative religion, and literature. Privately, he was working out his differences from Freud and preparing the manuscript of *Transformations and Symbols of the Libido*. Freud at first encouraged him in his research because he wanted Jung to reduce the unconscious motives behind religious and mythic expressions to sex and the Oedipus complex, but, in actual fact, Jung was using myth as a basis on which to understand his patients' dreams, hallucinations, and fantasies.

In his book Jung devoted over 400 pages to analysing and amplifying the fantasies of a young American woman, pseudonymously called 'Miss Frank Miller', who had created poems and dramas while dreaming or in a hypnagogic state. One of the poems was called *The Moth and the Sun*, and a 'hypnagogic drama' called *Chiwantopel* was about the adventures of an Inca or Aztec hero. These were spontaneous productions of the unconscious which presaged the onset of a schizophrenic breakdown. In the course of Miss Miller's drama, Chiwantopel cries out: 'Alas! Not one who understands me, not one who resembles me or has a soul that is sister to mine.' Jung comments: 'Miss Miller declares that the sentiments expressed in this passage have the greatest analogy to Siegfried's feeling for Brünhilde.' They also have the greatest analogy to Jung's feelings for Freud.

In Wagner's opera, which Jung and Sabina Spielrein both knew and loved, Siegfried is the product of an incestuous union between the brother–sister pair Siegmund and Sieglinde, and Brünhilde looks with favour on this union. If Spielrein were to have fulfilled her fantasy and produced a son called Siegfried, it would have necessitated the commission of 'psychic incest' (i.e. sex between analyst and patient) and the infringement of the professional 'incest taboo' which forbids all such relationships. It would also have required Freud's tacit collusion and assistance if the affair was not to cause a scandal or an instant breach in the relationship between the two men.

Jung's commentary on Miss Miller's drama continued: 'whereas Sieglinde is the human mother, Brünhilde acts the part of the "spirit-mother"'. It will be recalled that Sabina Spielrein had told Jung that he was to be the human father of Siegfried and Freud his spirit-father. 'Siegfried's birth from the sister-wife,' states Jung, 'characterizes him as a Horus [sky god son of the brother–sister pair Osiris and Isis], the reborn sun, *a reincarnation of the aging sun-god*. The birth of the young sun, the god-man, stems from human partners, but they are really only vehicles for cosmic symbols. The spirit-mother therefore lends it her protection; she sends Sieglinde forth with the child in her womb, on the night sea journey to the East . . .' (*CW*5, para. 555; italics added). This provides something of the unconscious background to Spielrein's fantasy of giving birth to a son who would reconcile all differences between Freud and Jung and carry the torch of psychoanalysis into the future (and to the East – she was to found a psychoanalytic clinic in Russia). It also gives something of the cultural background to Jung's dream.

Archetypal Context   In his introduction to *Transformations and Symbols of the Libido* Jung expresses his admiration for Freud's *Interpretation of Dreams* and argues that anyone who can 'let this extraordinary book work upon his imagination calmly and without prejudice, will not fail to be deeply impressed at that point where Freud reminds us that an individual conflict, which he calls the incest fantasy, lies at the root of that monumental drama of the ancient world, the Oedipus legend. The impression made by this simple remark may be likened to the uncanny feeling which would steal over us if, amid the noise and bustle of a modern city street, we were suddenly to come upon an ancient relic – say the Corinthian capital of a long-immured column, or a fragment of an inscription. A moment ago, and we were completely absorbed in the hectic, ephemeral life of the present then, the next moment, something very remote and strange flashes upon us, which directs our gaze to a different order of things. We turn away from the vast confusion of the present to glimpse the higher continuity of history. Suddenly we remember that on this spot where we now hasten to and fro about our business a similar scene of life and activity prevailed two thousand years ago in slightly different forms; similar passions moved mankind, and people were just as convinced as we are of the uniqueness of their lives . . . it seems to me that Freud's reference to the Oedipus legend is in every way comparable. While still struggling with the confusing impressions of the infinite variability of the individual psyche, we suddenly catch a glimpse of the simplicity and grandeur of the Oedipus tragedy, that perennial highlight of the Greek theatre. This broadening of our vision has about it something of a revelation' (*CW*5, para. 1).

This passage, which carries clear unconscious references to his Crusader dream, provides a clue to the inspiration Jung derived from Freud to embark on his own study of mythology and his lasting fascination in the archetypal dimension of all human experience. In this extraordinarily ambitious book, Jung used Miss Miller's fantasies as an Ariadne's thread to guide him through a vast labyrinth of symbolic parallels, that is to say, 'through the amplifications which are absolutely essential if we wish to establish the meaning of the archetypal context' (*CW*5, p. xxv). But as he goes on to admit: 'As soon as these parallels come to be worked out they take up an incredible amount of space, which is why expositions of case histories are such an arduous task. But that is only to be expected: the deeper you go, the broader the base becomes' (p. xxv).

In fact, as he confesses in the 1950 version of a revised edition under the title *Symbols of Transformation* (*CW*5), he never felt happy with this book: 'it was written at top speed amid the rush and press of my medical practice, without regard to time or method. I had to fling my material hastily together, just as I found it. There was no opportunity to let my thoughts mature. The whole thing came upon me like a landslide that cannot be stopped. The urgency that lay behind it became clear to me only later. It was the explosion of all those psychic contents which could find no room, no breathing-space, in the constricting atmosphere of Freudian psychology and its narrow outlook. I have no wish to denigrate Freud, or to detract from the extraordinary merits of his investigation of the individual psyche. But the conceptual framework into which he fitted the psychic phenomenon seemed to me unendurably narrow' (*CW*5, p. xxiii). Rapidity of composition would explain the difficulty encountered by most readers on tackling this text: it is a persuasive illustration of the aphorism that 'easy writing makes damned hard reading'.

To set a dream or fantasy in its archetypal context requires an extensive knowledge of archetypal symbolism, and the Siegfried dream, like most of Jung's dreams, is rich in such symbolism – e.g. ascent and descent, death and rebirth, hero, mountain, sun, rain, and primordial man. It is not practical to examine these symbols here, but the reader will find much relevant information in the dreams discussed in Chapter 10.

We shall now examine each part of the dream in sequence.

I was with an unknown, brown-skinned man, a savage: this is the *primordial man*, the two-million-year-old man within us all, the positive shadow; in other words, the Self potential as yet unactualized in Jung's life, the creative power of the unconscious.

a lonely, rocky mountain landscape: loneliness is a recurrent theme in Jung's life, and the break with Freud meant that he was on his own once more. ('After the break with Freud, all my friends and acquaintances dropped away ... But I had foreseen my isolation and harboured no illusion about the reactions of my so-called friends. That was a point I had thoroughly considered beforehand' (*MDR*, p. 162).) The mountain landscape is the terrain of ambition and spiritual aspiration, of hierarchical ascent and descent, dominance and submission. In the context of this dream the mountain is an appropriate setting for a drama in the agonic mode (see below, pp. 248–52).

It was before dawn: the eastern sky was already bright: a new phase of life is beginning. Siegfried sounds his horn, announcing that he too intends to be part of this new day. But it is not to be. His day is done. He has no place in the new order that is just beginning.

in the first ray of the rising sun: a new phase in the life of the Self; a new chapter in the individuation process.

on a chariot made of the bones of the dead: this detail makes one think of the two skulls in the cellar of Jung's dream house (mentioned above on page 52), which Jung interpreted as representing the common ancestors of humanity (and thus the collective unconscious).

he drove at furious speed down the precipitous slope: in contrast to the rising sun, Siegfried is declining, descending fast – an image that recalls Jung's own statement about the mid-life crisis which inaugurates the second half of life (see above, p. 58: 'At the stroke of noon the descent begins. And the descent means the reversal of all the ideals and values that were cherished in the morning'). The dream came six days after Jung began the regular practice of 'active imagination': 'I was sitting at my desk . . . thinking over my fears. Then I let myself drop. Suddenly it was as though the ground literally gave way beneath my feet, and I *plunged down* into dark depths.' He began to do this every day, recording and illustrating the spontaneous fantasies that came into his mind: 'In order to seize hold of the fantasies, I frequently imagined a *steep descent*. I even made several attempts to get to the very bottom. The first time I reached, as it were, a depth of about a thousand feet; next time I found myself at the edge of a cosmic abyss. It was like a voyage to the moon, or a descent into empty space. First came the image of a crater, and I had the feeling that I was in *the land of the dead*. The atmosphere was that of the other world' (*MDR*, pp. 172–4; my italics). Thus began what he was to call his 'experiment with the unconscious'.

he turned a corner: at the precise moment that he turns the corner to enter a new phase of life he is struck down.

filled with disgust and remorse: the guilt of the parricide that Freud had always perceived in Jung; Freud fainted on two occasions when it became most apparent.

I turned to flee: the flight response, an appropriate behaviour throughout nature in response to fear.

the murder might be discovered: discovered by whom? Presumably by the archetypal Father, the Law Giver, the superego, the embodiment of Logos, who would hold the murderer responsible for his action.

a tremendous downfall of rain began: the fertilizing principle becomes active, pouring from the (paternal) heaven to (maternal) earth, from (masculine) consciousness to the (feminine = anima) unconscious. Water pouring from the heavens is purifying and healing as well as generative. It helps to wipe out the past, and the guilty traces, and inaugurates a new fertile period of life.

I had escaped the danger of discovery: he had got away with it. But the *guilt remained*. It was a drastic action, and the brutal letters to Freud which provoked the final breach between them show just how ruthless Jung felt he had to be. Life could now go on, but the burden of guilt would have to be carried thereafter. Jung's initial thoughts about the dream were that it represented the problem being played out in the pre-war world of 1913. 'Siegfried, I thought, represents what the Germans want to achieve, heroically to impose their will, have their own way. "Where there is a will there is a way!" I had wanted to do the same. But now it was no longer possible' (*MDR*, p. 174). However, Jung omits to say that it also represented what Freud wanted to achieve – heroically to impose *his* will, have *his* own way. And now *that* was no longer possible. In this dream, Jung is finally sacrificing Freud as his heroic role model and replacing him by a willingness to undertake his own descent into the underworld. As a result of the dream, 'new forces were released in me which helped me to carry the experiment with the unconscious to a conclusion' (p. 174).

Siegfried was thus a complex figure in which were condensed (1) the heroic mentor, Freud; (2) the young sun-god, the aged sun-god's 'Son and Heir' and 'Crown Prince'; and (3) a transcendent symbol capable of reconciling the differences between the two men. His death meant that Jung had finally put all that behind him and committed himself to his *own* process, the discovery of his own psychological truth.

I have dwelt on this dream, not only because of its historical importance, but because *it demonstrates the transformative power a dream can carry*, intervening in the life of an individual, one might almost say, as a supreme instrument of destiny.

Emergence of the Archetypal Hypothesis

I was committing myself to a dangerous enterprise not for myself alone.

C. G. JUNG

The theme of descent into the underworld (and the return) occurs in the epic of Gilgamesh, Virgil's *Aeneid*, and Dante's *Divine Comedy*. In Miss Miller's case, Jung had also detected a 'renunciation of the world' (associated with an introversion and regression of libido) followed by an 'acceptance of the world' (associated with an extraversion of libido and a more mature adaptation to reality). But the most interesting parallel to Jung's 'experiment with the unconscious' is the neurotic breakdown suffered by Freud in the 1890s which he cured with his own self-analysis and through his intimate relationship with Wilhelm Fliess, discovering in the process the basic principles of psychoanalysis.

The disturbance which afflicted Jung between the years 1913 and 1918 was so severe as to bring him to the edge of madness. He played in his garden like a child, heard voices in his head, walked about holding conversations with imaginary figures, and, during one episode, believed his house to be crowded with the spirits of the dead. Yet it is a measure of his unusual quality that he regarded this disaster *as if it were an experiment being performed on him*: a psychiatrist was having a breakdown, thus providing a golden opportunity for research. He could study the whole experience at first hand and then use it to help his patients. 'This idea – that I was committing myself to a dangerous enterprise not for myself alone, but also for the sake of my patients – helped me over several critical phases . . . It is, of course, ironical that I, a psychiatrist, should at almost every step in my experiment have run into the same psychic material which is the stuff of psychosis and is found in the insane. This is the fund of unconscious images which fatally confuse the mental patient. But it is also the matrix of a mythopoeic imagination which has vanished from our rational age' (*MDR*, pp. 172, 181).

The experiment with the unconscious confirmed for Jung what he had already observed in his Burghölzli patients, namely, that there exists a collective substratum to the human psyche on which the personal psyche is based.

The images which arise from this universal substratum in fantasies, dreams, myths, and psychotic hallucinations, Jung first referred to as *primordial images* (1912), then as *dominants* (1917), and finally as *archetypes* (1919). Collectively, the archetypes made up 'the archaic heritage of humanity' (*CW*5, para. 259). This usage promptly landed him in difficulties, because in describing the contents of the collective unconscious as 'primordial images' derived from the past history of mankind, Jung laid himself open to the charge of Lamarckism, namely, that he subscribed to the discredited theory that characteristics acquired through individual experience could be passed on genetically to subsequent generations. Jung did not fully acquit himself of this charge until 1946, when he made a clear distinction between the deeply unconscious, and therefore unknowable, *archetype-as-such* (similar to Kant's *das Ding-an-sich*), and the archetypal images, ideas and behaviours that the archetype-as-such gives rise to. It is the archetype-as-such (the *predisposition* to have a certain image or experience) which is inherited, not the experience itself.

Archetypes and Biology

This aspect of the archetype, the purely biological one, is the proper concern of scientific psychology.

C. G. JUNG

For the greater part of the twentieth century Jung's idea of a universal psyche made up of numerous, innate, evolved, psychological adaptations proved totally unacceptable to academic psychologists, who remained wedded to a pre-Darwinian *tabula rasa* model to which behaviourism and learning theory were inextricably linked. Attacking this 'flat earth' position in my book *Archetype: A Natural History of the Self* (1982), I argued that the archetype and the collective unconscious were respectable biological hypotheses. Drawing on data from the relatively new biological science of ethology (the study of animals in their natural habitats), I proposed that the collective unconscious contains an innate repertoire of psychological adaptations (archetypes) specifically designed to be activated by environmental variables and to be responsible for guiding the individual, stage by stage, through the human life-cycle. Since then a similar position has been adopted by a new breed of evolutionary psychologists and cognitive scientists, who speak of 'life histories' dependent upon certain evolved 'strategies' and 'tactics' enabling organisms to compete successfully for resources and live out their life span (Crawford and Anderson, 1989; Walters, 1993), and of 'Darwinian algorithms' which are 'specialized learning mechanisms that organize experience into adaptively meaningful schemas or frames' (Cosmides 1985). Like archetypes, algorithms evolved through natural selection because they were reproductively relevant in the ancestral environment (known to ethology as the environment of evolutionary adaptedness). Each algorithm is conceived as specific to a certain 'domain' – such as mate selection, resource allocation to offspring and kin, predator avoidance, site selection, language acquisition, and so on.

Whether one calls these psychological adaptations archetypes or algorithms, both cognitive science and analytical psychology conceive them as built-in assumptions that certain typical figures (e.g. mother, child, stranger, mate) and features (water, shelter, edible substances) will be encountered in the social and ecological environment. Not surprisingly, these assumptions (and their fantasized fulfilment) typically feature in our dreams.

The first rumblings of the ethological revolution became audible in mid century with the publication of Niko Tinbergen's *The Study of Instinct* (1951). In it he proposed that the behavioural repertoire of every animal species is dependent upon structures built into its central nervous system by evolution. Tinbergen called these structures *innate releasing mechanisms*, or IRMs. Each IRM is primed to become active when an appropriate stimulus – called a sign stimulus – is encountered in the environment. When such a stimulus appears, the innate mechanism is released, and the animal responds with a characteristic *pattern of behaviour* which is adapted through evolution to the situation. When allowance is made for the greater adaptive flexibility of our own species, Tinbergen's position is very close to Jung's view of the nature of archetypes and their mode of activation.

The first successful and systematic attempt to apply these concepts to human psychology was that of the British analyst and psychiatrist John Bowlby, who featured in the dream reported on page 1. Bowlby maintained that just as a mallard duck becomes amorous at the sight of the handsome green head of the mallard drake, or a ewe becomes attached to her lamb as she licks the birth membranes free of its snout, so a human mother, presented with her newborn infant, perceives its helplessness, and its need for her, and is overwhelmed by feelings of love. All these patterns of response (or *behavioural systems* as Bowlby called them) have been prepared for by nature and require no Lamarckian explanation to account for them.

Archetypal Parallels

There are as many archetypes as there are common situations in life.

C. G. JUNG

The seminal nature of the archetypal hypothesis may be deduced from the number of different versions of it that have appeared. Indeed, if the significance of an idea can be measured by the number of people who later claim it as their own, then the archetypal hypothesis must be one of the most important to have emerged in the present century. Several of the more influential parallels to the archetypal hypothesis are listed in Table 1.

Table 1: Parallel concepts to Jung's archetypes.

Ethology	Tinbergen	IRMs
Psychology	Bowlby	behavioural systems
Anthropology	Lévi-Strauss	infrastructures
Psycholinguistics	Chomsky	deep structures
Sociobiology	Wilson	genetically transmitted response strategies epigenetic rules
Psychiatry	Gilbert Gardner	psychobiological response patterns deeply homologous neural structures
Cognitive science	Cosmides	Darwinian algorithms

In addition to Tinbergen's *innate releasing mechanisms* and Bowlby's *behavioural systems* there are the unconscious *infrastructures* which Claude Lévi-Strauss and the French school of structural anthropology hold responsible for all human customs and institutions. Furthermore, specialists in psycholinguistics maintain that while grammars differ from one another, their basic forms – which Noam Chomsky calls their *deep structures* – are universal (i.e. at the deepest neuropsychic level, there exists a universal (or 'archetypal') grammar on which all individual grammars are based).

An entirely new discipline, sociobiology, has grown up on the theory that the patterns of behaviour typical of all social species, the human species included, are dependent on *genetically transmitted response strategies* designed to maximize the fitness of the organism to survive in the environment in which it evolved. Sociobiology also holds that the psychosocial development in individual members of a species is dependent on what are termed *epigenetic rules* (*epi* = upon, *genesis* = development; i.e. rules upon which development proceeds).

More recently still, ethologically oriented psychiatrists have begun to study what Paul Gilbert calls *psychobiological response patterns* and Russell Gardner calls *deeply homologous neural structures*, which they hold responsible for the achievement of healthy or unhealthy patterns of adjustment in individual patients in response to variations in their social environment. Cosmides's *Darwinian algorithms* have already been mentioned. All these concepts are compatible with the archetypal hypothesis which Jung had proposed decades earlier to virtually universal indifference.

Psychology's 'Quantum Theory'

The archetypes are the great decisive forces, they bring about the real events, and not our personal reasoning and practical intellect . . . The archetypal images decide the fate of man.
C. G. JUNG

Jung's point is that we come into the world endowed with a full complement of archetypal potential and that this influences our dreams as profoundly as anything else about us. The archetypes of the collective unconscious are responsible for guiding and controlling the life-cycle of our species – being born and being mothered, exploring the environment, showing wariness of strangers, playing in the peer group, being initiated as an adult member of the community, establishing a place in the social hierarchy, bonding between males for hunting and out-group hostilities, courting, marrying, child-rearing, participating in religious rituals, assuming the social responsibilities of advanced maturity, and the preparation for death. Hence Jung's aphorism that, ultimately, every individual life is at the same time the eternal life of the species (*CW*11, para. 146).

There is much cross-cultural evidence to support this proposal. The typical characteristics of human cultures have been catalogued independently by George Murdock (1945) and Robin Fox (1975), who list a vast array of rules and behaviours implicated in relations between the sexes, religious rituals, healing practices, dream interpretation, the holding of property, the manufacture of tools and weapons, etiquette prescribing forms of greeting, hospitality, social deference, co-operating, and so on. In Jung's view all such universal patterns are evidence of archetypes at work. In other words, our lives are not determined merely by our personal history, as Freud maintained, but also by the history of the species as a whole, encoded in the collective unconscious.

What Jung proposed was nothing less than the fundamental concept on which the whole science of psychology could be built. Potentially, it is of comparable importance to quantum theory in physics. Just as the physicist investigates particles and waves, and the biologist genes, so Jung held it to be the business of the psychologist to investigate the collective unconscious and the functional units of which it is composed – the 'identical psychical structures common to us all' (*CW*5, para. 224) 'which together constitute 'the archaic heritage of humanity' (*CW*5, para. 259). The function of dreams is to integrate this 'archaic heritage' into the personal life of the dreamer.

The Archetypal Stages of Life

Thou art woman. Thou art man.
Thou art the youth and maiden too
Thou as an old man totterest with a staff,
Being born thou becomest facing in every direction.
                                        Shvetashvatara Upanishad

Every night in our dreams we are engaged in a biological ritual whereby our own personal experience of living is transfused by the 'eternal' experience of the species. How can we conceive of this extraordinary process occurring? Jung's answer is that archetypes are charged with their own energy and programmed with their own goals, which they seek to achieve in the psyche (in the form of images, symbols, and myths) in the personality (in the form of complexes) and in outer reality (in the form of behaviour). In this they fulfil the biological objectives of survival, 'inclusive fitness', adaptation, and growth, all of which he subsumed under the psychological term *individuation*. ('Individuation is an expression of that biological process – simple or complicated as the case may be – by which every living thing becomes what it was destined to become from the beginning' (*CW*11, para. 144)).

As we follow our own peculiar mode of progression from the cradle to the grave, we pass through a programmed sequence of stages, each of which is mediated by a new set of archetypal imperatives which seek fulfilment in our psychic and behavioural development. Each set of imperatives makes its own particular demands on the environment, and its activation (or 'constellation' as Jung would say) depends on those demands being met. Should the environment, for any reason, be unable to meet them, then the individual's development suffers the consequences of what I have called *the frustration of archetypal intent* (Stevens, 1982). It is the function of dreams to help redress this misfortune by mobilizing archetypal resources to overcome the frustration. 'Although the changing situations of life must appear infinitely various to our way of thinking,' wrote Jung, 'their possible number never exceeds certain natural limits; they fall into more or less typical patterns that repeat themselves over and over

131

again. The archetypal structure of the unconscious *corresponds to the average run of events*. The changes that may befall a man are not infinitely variable; they are variations of certain typical occurrences which are limited in number. When therefore a distressing situation arises, the corresponding archetype will be constellated in the unconscious. Since this archetype is *numinous*, i.e. possesses a specific energy, it will attract to itself the contents of consciousness – conscious ideas that render it perceptible and hence capable of conscious realization' (*CW*8, para. 450, my italics).

The Constellation of Archetypes

Learn to dream, gentlemen.
FRIEDRICH KEKULÉ

A famous example of an archetype being constellated when a distressing situation arose was the discovery by Friedrich Kekulé (1829–96) of the benzene ring. For years Kekulé had been grappling with the vital problem of solving the molecular structure of benzene, and his failure to find a solution was driving him to distraction. Then in 1865 he had a waking dream (or hypnagogic experience) in which he saw a chain of carbon and hydrogen atoms turning itself into a circle, like a snake biting its tail. It was a completely spontaneous manifestation of the ancient symbol of the *uroboros*. He jolted into full wakefulness, he says, 'as if struck by lightning'. He realized at once that the benzene molecule must be composed of six carbon atoms bound to one another in a ring. With this realization all the facts of organic chemistry known up to that time fell directly into place, and the foundation of modern structural theory was laid. Reporting his discovery at a scientific conference, Kekulé said: 'Let us learn to dream, gentlemen, and then we may perhaps find the truth.'

An amusing, but nonetheless awe-inspiring, instance of the compensatory constellation of an archetype occurred to me as I was working on the outline of this book. The previous evening I had attended one of those tense, rather destructive meetings which are unfortunately prone to occur from time to time among professional groups of analysts, and I went to bed feeling discouraged, depressed that I handled my side of the argument rather badly. *In my dream I was coming out of a church hall, not unlike the one in which the meeting had been held, when my father, long since dead, came up to me and said to the people around me: 'This is my son in whom I am well pleased.' I awoke from the dream feeling moved and comforted.* My personal father had spoken to me, but in the words of the archetypal father (God). In other words, it was a therapeutic dream in which my father complex had been constellated by my depressed state and had compensated for it, so that I could get up the following morning better able to meet the demands of the day. The dream also made me realize that as a result of the uncomfortable experience on the previous evening I had undergone some kind of 'baptism' and that I must be careful not to feel 'messianic' about it.

The Discovery of Complexes

The hobgoblins of folklore who go crashing about the house at night.

C. G. JUNG

Jung introduced the term *complex* into psychology as a result of his research using the word–association test while he was at the Burghölzli Hospital in Zürich. In this test, originally devised by Francis Galton (1822–1911), a series of words is read out to the subject who is asked to respond to each stimulus word with the first word that comes into his head. Galton found that the responses were automatic expressions of thoughts, feelings, and memories which the subject associated with the stimulus word. Repeating Galton's experiments, Jung realized that these thoughts, feelings, and memories group themselves into dynamic clusters or 'feeling-toned complexes'. He compared these to the 'fragmented' or 'split off personalities' which Pierre Janet (1859– 1947), under whom he studied in Paris in the winter of 1902–3, had demonstrated in hypnotized subjects and in patients exhibiting the interesting clinical condition of *multiple personality*, where two or more apparently separate personalities are revealed in the same person.

Interest in multiple personality is extremely ancient and goes back to the notion of 'possession' by devils and alien spirits. Right up to the present, the condition has been regarded as the proper domain of the exorcist. Janet linked these 'simultaneous psychological existences' with what he called 'subconscious fixed ideas'. In Jung's view, these were identical with the complexes that he had revealed with his word-association experiments. Eventually, he came to the conclusion that whereas the collective unconscious is made up of archetypes, the personal unconscious is composed of complexes which function as sub-personalities and which 'personate' in dreams and fantasies. Jung recalled that Janet had demonstrated that 'each fragment of personality had its own peculiar character and its own separate memory. These fragments exist relatively independent of one another and can take one another's place at any time, which means that each fragment possesses a high degree of autonomy. My findings in regard to complexes,' says Jung, 'corroborate this somewhat disquieting picture of the possibilities of psychic disintegration, for fundamentally there is no difference in principle between a fragmentary personality and a complex.'

The word 'complex' rapidly passed into popular usage in both German and English, and in a review of the complex theory written in 1934, Jung commented: 'Everyone knows nowadays that people "have complexes". What is not so well known, though far more important theoretically, is that complexes can *have us*' (*CW*8, para. 200; Jung's italics). The autonomous power of complexes and their capacity to influence consciousness without our being aware of them is something that both Jung and Freud drew attention to again and again in their writings: 'an active complex puts us momentarily under a state of duress, of compulsive thinking and acting, for which under certain conditions the only appropriate term would be the judicial concept of diminished responsibility . . . They slip just the wrong word into one's mouth, they make one forget the name of the person one is about to introduce, they cause a tickle in the throat just when the softest passage is being played on the piano at a concert; they make the tiptoeing latecomer trip over a chair with a resounding crash . . . They are the actors in our dreams . . . and the deeper one penetrates into their nature – I might almost say into their biology – the more clearly do they reveal their character as *splinter psyches*. Dream psychology shows us as plainly as could be wished how complexes appear in personified form when there is no inhibiting consciousness to suppress them, exactly like the hobgoblins of folklore who go crashing about the house at night. We observe the same phenomenon in certain psychoses when the complexes get "loud" and appear as "voices" having a thoroughly personal character' (*CW*8, paras. 200–203).

Complexes are not essentially pathological as is often erroneously supposed. They are as much part of the healthy psyche as they are of the neurotic or psychotic psyche. They are, as Jung makes clear in the above passage, the functional units of which the personal psyche is composed. In other words, complexes are archetypes actualized in the mind.

From Archetype to Complex: 'The Emerging Paradigm'

> *If my analysis of the magician's logic is correct, its two great principles turn out to be merely two different misapplications of the association of ideas. Homeopathic magic is founded on the association of ideas by similarity: contagious magic is founded on the association of ideas by contiguity.*

J.G. FRAZER

How does this process of actualization occur? Jung believed that complex formation proceeded in accordance with two *Laws of Association* worked out by academic psychologists at the end of the last century: the *law of similarity* and the *law of contiguity,* and that normal complexes are formed when both these laws are satisfied. By way of illustration, let us take an archetype which is of greatest significance during the early years of life: the mother archetype. As we have noted, Jung, unlike Freud, considered the mental equipment of the child to be highly adapted to the world into which it was born. As Bowlby and his colleagues demonstrated, the neurophysiological structures concerned with the perception and experience of mothering activities, as well as the behavioural repertoire necessary to relate to the figure providing them (usually the mother), gradually mature under the organizing influence of innate 'behavioural systems' (the mother archetype) functioning within the child. Jung proposed that the mother archetype is the vital nucleus of the individual's growing mother complex: originally the *archetype-as-such* is unconscious; then, as the child matures in close proximity to the mother, so all those behaviours, feelings, and perceptions determined by the mother archetype are 'released' (as the ethologists would say) with the consequent development of the mother complex within the child's psyche and the associated co-ordination of the mother–infant behavioural chain in outer reality. Thus, a normal mother complex develops when the personal mother is perceived by the child as possessing maternal qualities *similar* to the anticipations built into the maternal archetype and when she is continuously present, or *contiguous*, throughout the formative years of childhood. On the other hand, a pathological mother complex would be formed if either of these laws is inadequately satisfied, for example, if the mother's repertoire of maternal behaviours is defective in some important way, or if there should be lengthy periods of mother–child separation. The father complex develops in much the same way.

Complexes are thus the bridge between the personal (ontogenetic) psyche and the collective (phylogenetic) psyche: they are the ontogenetic 'flesh' covering the phylogenetic 'skeleton' provided by the archetypes. Pathological complexes are invariably linked with unlived and unactualized archetypal potential which, not uncommonly, leads to a life-long quest for paternal or maternal figures perceived as capable of fulfilling the longing that this unused potential invariably creates. The previously undiscovered parent is usually encountered in the dreams of those who have lacked adequate parenting in childhood.

Although multiple personality is a comparatively rare clinical condition, it is true to say that we are all multiple personalities in our dreams and in our fantasies. None of us is a unity; each of us is a crowd. All of these personalities are the product of innate predisposition interacting with experience, and every night we encounter a selection of them in our dreams.

Jung's complex theory is a further aspect of his thinking that has well tolerated the passage of time. For example, Paul Gilbert, in his outstanding book *Human Nature and Suffering* (1989), reviews recent developments in the application of evolutionary concepts to psychiatry and declares that 'the emerging paradigm is that the human mind is a fragmented organization of mixed special purpose processing capabilities, intelligences, talents and so on'. These are relatively 'encapsulated' from one another and 'are shaped by experience into emotional schemata and cognitive schemata'. Gilbert comments that 'the greater the degree of aroused affect, the more difficulty there is in using logical reasoning' (pp. 312–13).

'The emerging paradigm', therefore, is Jung's paradigm, Gilbert's 'mixed special purpose processing capabilities' are Jung's complexes and Janet's *idées fixes subconscientes*, which *personate* in dreams. That reason should be rendered defective by aroused 'emotional schemata' reminds one of Jung's quip that we don't have complexes but complexes *have us*. The growing accord that the mind–brain is composed of special-purpose units, which Ornstein (1986) calls 'small minds', Fodor (1985) 'modules', and Gardner (1985) 'special intelligences', affirms Jung's concept of complexes developed through experience on the basis of an archetypal core.

Archetypes, Complexes, and Dreams

> The **via regia** to the unconscious . . . is not the dream as [Freud] thought, but the complex, which is the architect of dreams and of symptoms.
>
> C. G. JUNG

How can such concepts as archetypes and complexes help us to understand dreams? An example may help to make this clear.

An attractive, artistically gifted woman in her early thirties consulted me on account of problems with her partner, another woman of the same age. They had lived together for three years, but stresses were developing in the relationship which my patient could not understand and which she feared, despite all her efforts, could bring it to an end. To her first session she brought the following dream:

I am sitting at a kitchen table waiting to be fed. Miss Daley [an ex-school teacher of the dreamer] *is cooking something in a large pot. I ask her how much longer it will take as I am hungry. She sighs and tells me she is doing what she can and I must learn to be patient. I am hurt and furious*

137

but say nothing. Then she turns from the cooker and brings the pot to the table and I notice some ancient, rather primitive decoration on it as she puts it down on a mat. She lifts the lid and the kitchen is filled with a delicious aroma. Then she smiles at me and says, 'All things come to she who waits.'

The dreamer had an unhappy childhood. Her parents split up when she was three and her mother, a pleasant but selfish woman with little maternal feeling, sent her off to boarding school at the age of six. Miss Daley was kind to her and became a special favourite on whom she developed a powerful crush at the age of fourteen. During her time at school, at university, and ever since, she had been involved in a number of passionate lesbian affairs, but few of these lasted for more than several months because, as she freely acknowledged, her lovers found her 'too demanding'.

The problem (and the solution) is conceptualized in her first dream. She is impatient to be nourished and feels hurt and furious when a kindly older woman fails to gratify her need immediately. This is a re-enactment of what she experienced throughout childhood in her relationship with her mother. Her mother complex is reactivated in all her close relationships with women, and because the need for the truly nourishing mother is so powerful, and the hurt, when it is not immediately gratified, so deep, she drives away the very person capable of gratifying her desire. What she is questing for is a woman capable of making good her defective mother complex by embodying the archetype of the nourishing mother, symbolized in this dream by the ancient pot yielding the delicious aroma. In her analysis she has to deal with this need in herself, accept responsibility for it, and 'learn patience' so that she does not demand of her partner more than the partner can possibly give.

The manner in which this dream put the dreamer's psychodynamic problem in a nutshell is impressive but by no means unusual; and for this reason, many analysts attach special significance to initial dreams, which are commonly dreamt the night before the patient's first analytic session. The above dream is but one of many examples collected by me over the years demonstrating the extraordinary capacity of dreams not only to take stock of the dreamer's presenting problems but to indicate ways in which they may be solved. Other examples are given in Chapters 8 and 10.

The Goals of Dreaming: Individuation and Consciousness

The unconscious contains everything that is lacking to consciousness.
C. G. JUNG

Dreaming is a means by which the life of the individual is grafted on to the life of the species. Its purpose is to promote adaptation, growth, and consciousness. Why should consciousness be necessary? Could we not function just as well without it? What if we really *were* computers as the cognitive scientists would have us? What if we were merely sophisticated robots programmed to live as we do without *knowing* that we do it? Would we be any worse off? The biological answer is that we would.

Consciousness has evolved for good reason: it confers selection advantages on individuals possessing it. That is why highly conscious organisms like humans and dolphins have the edge on dimly conscious creatures like lizards and crabs. Consciousness enables individuals to monitor what is going on, to be aware of the nature and quality of events as they occur, and to perceive their meanings. Like God at the end of the sixth day, we can see what has been happening and *know* that it is good − or bad. In the words of St Augustine, we both exist and know that we exist and rejoice in this existence and this knowledge.

For all its spiritual wealth, the psyche is a biological achievement; it is the expression of biological 'aspiration', as is the principle of individuation itself. ('Individuation is the process, simple or complex as the case may be, by which every living organism becomes what it was destined to become from the beginning.') In the case of the human organism, this destiny is consciousness; nature has willed it so.

However, there are degrees of consciousness, as we have seen, not only between species but within species and, for that matter, between individuals and within individuals. Jung maintained that a crucial factor determining *how* conscious we are is whether we attend to our dreams and the degree to which this enables us to make what is unconscious conscious. By working with dreams we 'create soul', we 'wake up' to our total situation, 'become conscious', achieve 'wholeness'. How does this Jungian view hold up in the light of findings derived from the science of consciousness? As has been noted, Gerald Edelman, one of the most important researchers in this field, believes that consciousness depends on vast numbers of inter-connected neuronal complexes playing in concert. This is now the accepted view. A human brain contains at least 20 billion individual elements – more than three times the number of people on the planet – and each and every one of them generates messages at a rate varying between 100 and 300 signals per second. As Harry Hunt describes it: 'each of the 20 billion citizens of our brain-mind is talking to at least 10,000 *at least once*, and as often as 100 times per second. With a chatterbox of such proportions, it is to me just as incredible that such a system would *not* have awareness of itself as it is incredible that it does . . . During dreaming sleep, there is just as much activity going on within the system as there is during waking. In other words, during dreams, the system is literally talking to itself' (Hunt, 1989, p. 132). Music persists as the most fashionable metaphor for this activity: 'The music of these spheres from the galaxy within our head is consciousness. Consciousness is the continuous, subjective awareness of the activity of billions of cells firing at many times a second, communicating instantaneously with tens of thousands of their neighbours' (p. 133). It is often said that most of us pass through life making minimal use of this enormous capacity.

Hunt's view of how consciousness is synthesized is similar in some ways to the holographic model of the brain postulated by Karl Pribram which suggests that any given perceptual situation is 'taken' simultaneously by different sensory modalities so as to create a cross-modal 'hologram'. In the same way, Hunt maintains that vision, hearing, touch, and kinaesthetic sensations and percepts are constantly flowing together, influencing one another, combining and recombining, so as to create consciousness. Mind, says Hunt, is 'a complex synesthesia'. The roots of this idea, as Hunt acknowledges, lie in Aristotle's idea of a *census communis*, an inner sense common to the different senses. Aristotle believed the *census communis* to be situated in the heart and that it was responsible for self-awareness, imagery, and dreaming. The idea was taken up in the eighteenth century by Addison and Hazlitt, who argued that multiple interactions of the senses gave rise to a *total impression* that was more than the sum of its parts. This is perhaps the first suggestion that consciousness is itself a Gestalt.

Interestingly, Hunt turns, like Jung before him, to mythology in order to amplify his model of the psyche and the role of dreaming. The myth that he finds most apposite to his view is that of the Egyptian corn god Osiris and his dismemberment by his brother Set. Osiris is one of the most attractive figures in mythology. He stands as a symbol of all that is creative and life-enhancing in human beings as well as the principle of generativity in nature. Osiris marks the transition of humanity from hunter-gatherer to agriculturalist, for he taught us how to produce grain and grapes, how to make bread, wine, and beer, and how to build towns, cities, and temples. He achieved this not through violence but by gentleness, songs, the playing of musical instruments, and, above all, through example. Having achieved so much, however, he became the victim of a plot organized by his jealous brother, Set, who wanted to usurp Osiris's power for his own gratification. Set and his accomplices kidnap Osiris, nail him up in a wooden coffer and cast him into the Nile. The coffer is carried out to sea and across to Byblos on the Phoenician coast, where it comes to rest at the foot of a tamarisk tree.

Osiris's wife, his sister Isis, learns of this and goes to Phoenicia and recovers the body. To deceive Set, she hides it in the swamps of the Nile Delta. But there one night it is discovered by Set when he is hunting by moonlight. Set attacks the body with his knife, dismembering it into fourteen pieces, which he scatters far and wide. Not to be outwitted, Isis seeks out the precious fragments and collects them – all except the phallus. She reassembles the pieces and, for the first time in history, performs the rights of embalmment, which restores the murdered god to eternal life. The phallus is replaced by the Djed pillar, symbol of eternal generativity.

Osiris became a god of great cosmic significance, representative of the principles of death and rebirth, the regeneration of the corn, the vine, and the trees. As god of the dead, he enjoyed his greatest popularity, giving his devotees the hope of an eternally happy life in another world, ruled over by a just and good king. In some important respects, the Christian myth is a later re-enactment of the Osiris myth. Osiris's sojourn in the coffer and his subsequent release, his association with the tree, and his capacity to guarantee eternal life, are prefigurations of Christ's incarceration and emergence from the tomb, his suffering on the cross, and his ascent into heaven. The notions of birth, incarnation, death, and rebirth are archetypal notions, and thus recur endlessly throughout the story of mankind.

In his interpretation of the myth, Hunt sees Set as exemplifying the cognitive functions of waking consciousness – 'all that is most readily modeled in artificial intelligence'. Osiris, on the other hand, represents fertility and creativity. He is the god of the underworld and of eternal resurrection. 'His dismembered and scattered body is reassembled and revived by his sister, Isis, bringing fertility and renewal to the night world of creativity and imagination. Mind without the creative synthesis of cross-modal consciousness is like the dismembered Osiris, its separate modules and frames processing autonomously and in isolation. Vivid dreaming and related states release the sense of felt significance that is always the mark of creative insight (and living), precisely by means of the integration and flowing together of the separate limbs of the senses' (p. 214).

Hunt's understanding is essentially the same as Jung's – that the psyche is made up of a multiplicity of part personalities which it is the work of individuation to bring into an integrated whole. The anima (Isis) is the mediatrix responsible for relating unconscious to consciousness. She is the catalyst making the process possible.

The Egyptian myth of Osiris and Set, like the Sumerian epic of Gilgamesh and Enkidu, provides a metaphor of the events occurring every night in our mind-brains. It is also a parable of our history since the rise of civilization. Osiris is an example of the Great Individual, the Anthropos, and can be understood as representing both humankind and the total archetypal endowment of the Self. Set, on the other hand, offers an unflattering image of the masculine ego, usurping the power of the Self for its own greedy and destructive purposes. In Western civilization, for the last 400 years, Osiris has lain slumbering in the depths of the collective unconscious, while in the collective conscious Set has increasingly assumed command. In contrast to Osiris, Set has no time for the eternal cycles of nature: he subverts everything to his ego-centred needs in the here and now, and has little concern for ecology and the morrow. What we do to the environment is a direct consequence of what we do to ourselves, and, put in psychological terms, Set represents the selfish ego working in opposition to the selfless Self. As Jung pithily expressed it: 'There is only one thing wrong with the world, and that is man' (*CW*10, para. 441).

Elsewhere I have recounted the dream of a young farmer in which he saw an uncle murder his father (Stevens, 1993). I amplified the dream with the Osiris myth because of a quarrel which existed between the two men in reality: whereas the father favoured relatively uneconomical 'organic' farming methods, his brother advocated the use of chemicals and the latest technology. In the dream, having hacked his brother to death with a sword, the dreamer's uncle proceeded (in a subsequent active imagination) to bury the body where he hoped it would not be discovered. Understanding his dream in its archetypal context transformed the farmer's understanding of the conflict which raged both inside and outside himself, and, as a result, he was able to see a way out of his impasse and develop an objective view which transcended the polar standpoints adopted by his father and his uncle. In this instance, the dreamer was able to perceive his own psychic drama as part of the greater drama being played out on a global scale and this perception enhanced his ability to deal with it. In other words, *the dream heightened his conscious awareness of the total situation*. This, in essence, is the whole point of dream amplification on the archetypal level. The effect is to enhance the function of the dream work so as to promote personal growth, individuation, and the development of consciousness.

6

THE DREAM WORK

Creative imagination is the only primordial phenomenon accessible to us, the real Ground of the psyche, the only immediate reality.

C. G. JUNG

Psychology presents us with a problem shared by no other science: in studying the system which is the object of our investigations we are obliged to use the very system we are studying; to probe the psyche we have no other instrument at our disposal than a psychic probe. We are ourselves the mystery which we are seeking to unravel. The investigation of archetypes is rendered particularly difficult in this connection because they are unknowable at the subjective level and their function may only be inferred from their objective manifestations – in the universal games of children, for example, the typical behaviour patterns of adults, in the basic syntax of language and of dreams.

Sally Walters (1993) has raised an interesting question: if archetypal structures are of such evolutionary importance, and if they provide the essential psychological adaptations for individual living in the ancestral environment, *why should their function be unconscious?* Walters argues that the answer must be because 'there is only limited "workspace" in the brain'. Ancestral hominids, overwhelmed by information to the point that their thinking became incoherent and disorganized, would be unable to function, survive, or reproduce. The probability is, however, that archetypal functioning became unconscious long before the evolution of hominids: it happened approximately 130 million years ago when monotremes gave way to mammals and REM sleep began. The significance of dreaming for archetypal functioning is thus again stressed by their shared evolutionary history.

The archetypal manifestations we shall consider in this chapter are those aspects of dreaming which find significant parallels in the activities of speech, poetry, story-telling, symptom formation, magic, ritual, and play. These fascinating similarities throw additional light on the meaning and purpose of dreams, the means by which they are created, and the benefits to be derived from attending to them.

Psychic Dualism: Dreams and Language

You will have to multiply many times your two-fold being and complicate your complexities still further. Instead of narrowing your world and simplifying your soul you will at last take the whole world into your soul, cost what it may, before you are through and come to rest.

HERMANN HESSE, *Steppenwolf*

The mystery of dreams has always revolved round the same questions: where do they come from? What creates them? What do they mean? In dreams, as in speech, intangible ideas are being put into tangible forms – images and words. One difference between speaking and dreaming is that while we have some measure of control over what we say, we have little or none over what we dream. Dreams and speech resemble one another, nevertheless, in being sensory representations of thought: thoughts which are invisible and inaudible in themselves are rendered visible and audible in images and sounds.

A central problem which psychology shares with neurology is to explain how something so essentially occult and private can become manifest and public. Each discipline conceptualizes this transformation in its own terms: *Latent content* becoming *manifest content* (Freud), *archetype-as-such* becoming *archetypal image* (Jung), IRMs manifesting themselves in patterns of behaviour (Tinbergen), deep structures finding expression in surface structures, namely words (Chomsky). Every discipline specifies basic structures and active processes functioning in accordance with certain rules to produce surface manifestations.

It is precisely because dreaming and speaking must involve fundamental structures of the mind–brain that both these activities have been the subject of energetic research. Both are indispensable forms

145

of communication – ego communication with the Self in dreams (while asleep) and with others in speech (while awake).

Dreams naturally use the basic figures of speech defined by rhetoricians: in addition to metaphor and personification, they also commonly use simile (comparing something with something else) and hyperbole (exaggeration in order to register a point). A metaphor is a figure of speech in which one thing is compared directly to another by speaking of it as if it *actually were* the other – e.g. 'He is a snake in the grass; but she is a pillar of strength.' Dream images behave metaphorically when they draw comparisons between two people or things by emphasizing certain characteristics shared between them – e.g. *a pompous, self-opinionated colleague struts about in a dream, making pecking movements at a heap of cow manure. His neck has wattles like a cock.* When I wake up and think about the dream, I recognize the strength of my personal antipathy for this colleague (shadow-projection?). He thinks he is cock of the walk, strutting about on his own dung heap, and I'd like to wring his neck! Metaphors carry greater emotional and cognitive impact than literal statements: we use them in speech when we wish to make a point effectively, and that presumably is why the Self makes use of them in dreams. The mere act of looking at a dream as a metaphor is often quite sufficient to grant an understanding of what it is about.

The moment the psyche begins to consider something, it displays a natural tendency to differentiate the parts from the whole, the most favoured differentiation being into pairs of opposites, usually conceived as *antinomies* (i.e. complementary to one another). Examples are hot and cold, left and right, peace and war. Approaches to the study of psycholinguistics are no exception. In addition to a distinction between *language* (which is stable and collective, a shared institution) and *speech* (a personal, idiosyncratic expression of the collective form), linguistics makes a distinction between two primary modes of speech: the *metonymic* and the *metaphoric*. A metonymic statement is one in which the words are chained together in a linear sequence in such a way as to form phrases and sentences. Metaphoric associations of words are by virtue of shared radical elements (such as *carn*-ation, *carn*-al, *carn*-age, and rein-*carn*-ation), by analogy (carnation, flower, violet), and similarity of sound images. The significance of these examples will become apparent when we consider the next two dreams.

The distinction between language and speech is echoed in Chomsky's distinction between *linguistic competence* (language) and *linguistic performance* (speech) and in Benjamin Lee Whorf's distinction between *cryptotype* (the deeper structures of linguistic meaning) and *phenotype* (the literal meanings of words used metonymically). As Paul Kugler points out in his remarkable book *The Alchemy of Discourse*, Whorf's cryptotypes are analogous to Jung's archetypes, Lévi-Strauss's *Infrastructures*, and Lacan's *Symbolic Laws*.

Kugler suggests that these divisions point to a necessity within the human psyche for two complementary styles of speech, which are reflections of differing personalities within the individual, which he refers to as the metonymic and the metaphoric, the rational and the irrational, the logical and the mythical, the ego and the soul. He further compares this distinction with that made by Jung between the subjective and objective psyches, between 'directed thinking' and 'fantasy thinking' in *Symbols of Transformation* and between his *No. 1* and *No. 2* personalities in *Memories, Dreams, Reflections*. Yet another parallel is to be found in Freud's distinction between two modes of psychic functioning, namely, 'primary process', which speaks metaphorically through dreams, symptom formation, and transference, and 'secondary process', which is reality-orientated and communicates through the rational logic and syntax of the ego. Freudian therapy, Kugler tellingly observes, consists of the interpretative *translation* of the metaphoric speech of the soul into the metonymic language of the ego. ('Where Id was, there shall ego be.') Jungian therapy, on the other hand, adheres closely to the metaphoric mode, since for Jung, the language of the unconscious was not primitive or infantile but represented *the voice of nature itself*.

As with all fundamentally important observations representing archetypal functioning, the distinctions made by Freud, Jung, Chomsky, and Kugler have been repeated by others using different terms. Some of these are summarized in Table 2. For example, Suzanne Langer makes a distinction between *discursive* or *representational* symbolism (language and mathematics, where meaning resides in designated words and signs) and *non-discursive* or *presentational* symbolism

Table 2: Psychic dualism: two modes of cognitive functioning.

Kugler	metonymic speech logical thinking	metaphoric speech mythical thinking
Jung	subjective psyche directed thinking No. 1 personality	objective psyche fantasy thinking No. 2 personality
Freud	secondary process rational thinking	primary process irrational thinking
Langer	discursive symbolism representational symbolism	non-discursive symbolism presentational symbolism
Deikman	active mode	receptive mode
The brain	left cerebral hemisphere	right cerebral hemisphere

(the expressive arts and dreams where meaning resides in the felt qualities of the medium).

Arthur Deikman's (1971) differentiation is also appropriate here between the 'receptive mode' which he sees as characteristic of meditation and the 'active mode' which is characteristic of volition and the use of language. These and other pairs of distinctions are linked to the different functions of the two cerebral hemispheres, the left hemisphere being associated with metonymic, discursive symbolism, the right hemisphere with metaphoric, non-discursive symbolism (Stevens, 1982).

It is important to note that the metonymic statements of directed, discursive thought tend to have a single unambiguous meaning while metaphoric statements such as dreams, and the presentational meanings of the arts, are necessarily polyvalent and multiple. This would help to explain why there can never be one 'true' interpretation of a dream.

What Kugler is anxious to establish is a discipline which he calls *archetypal linguistics*, 'a linguistics of the metaphoric mode' which is 'concerned with the language of the poetic imagination'. As if stating a manifesto, he says: 'Archetypal linguistics studies the speech of the soul.' Some agnostic readers may be deterred by Kugler's use of the term *soul*, but, when deprived of theological overtones, soul is a useful psychological term because it implies the involvement of the transcendent, the suprapersonal, the 'eternal', the phylogenetic. In fact, it represents the whole psychic equipment operating as a totality.

Freud was himself particularly interested in the symbolic implications of words and their associations, although he did not consider these to proceed on an archetypal foundation. This interest can be detected in his analysis of the following dream, which, out of considerations of space, I have shortened to essentials. It was dreamt by one of his women patients.

She was descending from a height over some strangely constructed palisades or fences . . . not intended for climbing over; she had trouble in finding a place to put her feet in and felt glad that her dress had not been caught anywhere, so that she had stayed respectable as she went along. She was holding a BIG BRANCH in her hand; actually it was like a tree, covered over with RED BLOSSOMS, branching and spreading out. There was an idea of their being cherry-BLOSSOMS; but they also looked like double CAMELLIAS . . . When she got down, the lower BLOSSOMS were already a good deal FADED . . . A young MAN . . . was standing in the garden; she went up to him to ask how BRANCHES of that kind could be TRANSPLANTED INTO HER OWN GARDEN. He embraced her; whereupon she struggled and asked him what he was thinking of and whether he thought people could embrace her like that. He said there was no harm in that: it was allowed (Freud's capitals).

In recounting the dream, Freud put in capitals those elements that he considered were to be given a sexual interpretation. Overall, he saw the dream as representing the course of the patient's life. That *she was descending from a height* he took to signify that she was 'of high descent'. He goes on: 'the dreamer saw herself climbing down over some palisades holding a blossoming branch in her hand. In connection with this image she thought of the angel holding a spray of lilies in pictures of the Annunciation – her own name was Maria – and of girls in white robes walking in Corpus Christi processions, when the streets are decorated with green branches. Thus the blossoming branch in the dream without any doubt alluded to sexual innocence. However, the branch was covered with *red* flowers, each of which was like a camellia. By the end of her walk – so the dream went on – the blossoms were already a good deal faded. There then followed some unmistakable allusions to menstruation. Accordingly, the same branch carried like a lily and as though by an innocent girl was at the same time an allusion to the *Dame aux caméllias* who, as we know, usually wore a white camellia except during her periods, when she wore a red one. The same blossoming branch (cf. "des Mädchens Blüten" ["the maiden's blossoms"] in Goethe's poem ["Der Müllerin Verrat"]) represented both sexual innocence and its contrary. And the same dream which expressed her joy at having succeeded in passing through life immaculately gave one glimpses at certain points (e.g. in the fading of the blossoms) of the contrary train of ideas – of her having been guilty of various sins against sexual purity (in her childhood that is)' (1976, pp. 430–31). As far as the branch is concerned, he notes: 'The branch has long since come to stand for the male genital organ; incidentally, it also made a plain allusion to her family name' (p. 465). Thus, the notion of *BRANCHES of that kind* being *TRANSPLANTED INTO HER OWN GARDEN* was a clear allusion to her wish to lose her innocence and have sexual relations with the young man.

Freud interpolates in the 1914 edition of *The Interpretation of Dreams* a dream recorded and analysed by a colleague, one Alfred Robitsek. It is a very short dream, but its lengthy interpretation is a nice display of classical Freudian analysis at work.

This is the dream: *I arrange the centre of a table with flowers for a birthday.*

It was dreamt, so Robitsek tells us, by a girl who was not neurotic but of a somewhat prudish and reserved character. She was engaged, but there were some difficulties in the way of her marriage which was likely to be postponed.

Robitsek says that he was able to understand the dream without help from the patient's associations merely by the use of what he calls 'popular' symbolism – by which, presumably, he meant psychoanalytic convention. 'It was an expression of her bridal wishes: the table with its floral centre-piece symbolized herself and her genitals; she represented her wishes for the future as fulfilled, for her thoughts were already occupied with the birth of a baby; so her marriage lay a long way behind her.' He avoided suggesting the meaning of the symbols to her, and merely asked what came into her head in connection with the separate parts of the dream: 'When I asked her what flowers they had been, her first reply was: "*expensive flowers! One has to pay for them*", and then that they had been "*lilies of the valley, violets and pinks or carnations*". I assumed that the word "lily" appeared in the dream in its popular sense as a symbol of chastity; she confirmed this assumption, for her association to "lily" was "purity". "*Valley*" is a frequent female symbol in dreams; so that the chance combination of the two symbols in the English name of the flower was used in the dream-symbolism to stress the preciousness of her virginity – "*expensive flowers, one has to pay for them*" – and to express her expectation that her husband would know how to appreciate its value . . .

'"*Violets*" was ostensibly quite asexual; but . . . to my surprise the dreamer gave as an association the English word "*violate*". The dream had made use of the great chance similarity between the words "*violet*" and "*violate*" . . . in order to express "in the language of flowers" the dreamer's thoughts on the violence of defloration (another term that employs flower symbolism) and possibly also a masochistic trait in her character. A pretty instance of the "verbal bridges" crossed by the paths leading to the unconscious . . .

'In connection with "*pinks*" which she went on to call "*carnations*", I thought of the connection between that word and "carnal".' But the dreamer's association to it was '*colour*' and then '*incarnation*'. Robitsek comments that '*colour*' was determined by the meaning of '*carnation*' (flesh colour) – 'determined, that is, by the same complex'. The dreamer told him that her fiancé frequently gave her carnations and this, to his mind, confirmed their phallic meaning.

'Thus,' concludes Robitsek, 'the flower symbolism in this dream included virginal femininity, masculinity and an allusion to defloration by violence. It is worth pointing out in this connection that sexual flower symbolism, which, indeed, occurs very commonly in other connections, symbolizes the human organs of sex by blossoms, which are the sexual organs of plants. It may perhaps be true in general that gifts of flowers between lovers have this unconscious meaning' (pp. 493–6).

Robitsek's account is both straightforward and persuasive. Has the archetypal perspective anything to add? Kugler convincingly demonstrates that it has. He comments that both dreams reveal the tendency of the unconscious to construct images in accordance with phonetic associations. As Freud himself noted: 'For the purpose of representation in dreams, the spelling of words is far less important than their sound.'

Kugler quotes another dream in which a female student goes to a ball in a 'beautiful white evening dress'. Her boyfriend gives her a carnation, which, to her great embarrassment, starts to bleed. Clearly, says Kugler, some 'invariant or synchretic fantasy' must lie behind the idea of flowers as female symbols and as symbols of violation. 'It belongs to a *complex of associations which all phonetically refer to the same archetypal fantasy*' (Kugler, 1982, p. 21).

Drawing on the Burghölzli word-association research, Kugler reaffirms Jung's finding that the unconscious is a system of manifold cross-references connected through similarities of image and sound: 'Therefore, when different aspects of the archetypal image are realized in language they tend to seek similar sound patterns and form a complex of phonetically affiliated words' (p. 22). How then does he explain the curious imagistic sequence *flower→blood*? His suggestion is both ingenious and convincing. If we examine other words sharing the same phonemic patterns as *carnation* (a white or red flower) and *violet* (a bluish-purple flower), we are led inexorably to violence, rape, sex, bloodshed, and rebirth: *viol*-et→*viol*-ent→*viol*-ate; *carn*-ation→*carn*-al→*carn*-age→rein-*carn*-ation. Both sequences reveal the same complex of associations centring on a fantasy of *flowers, deflora-tion* (the same association again!) and rape from entirely different roots.

This phonemic linkage is impressive enough in English, but Kugler's argument that an archetypal image is at its core is confirmed by his demonstration that it also exists in German, French, and

Hungarian. In German *Blüten* means blossom, *Blut* means blood, and *bluten* to bleed. In French *violette* is the bluish-purple flower, *viol* means rape, and *violer* means to violate. But what clinches it is the fact that the same complex of association also exists in non-Indo-European languages: thus, the Hungarian *verág* means bloom, flower, *vér* means blood, and *véres* means bloody.

Kugler stresses that these fascinating associations are not lexical, syntactical, or etymological: they are phonemic and imagistic — a finding completely in line with Jung's conclusion at the beginning of the century that 'autonomous groups of associations' (*complexes*) are held together by phonetic links centred round a psychic image and bound together by a shared emotional tone or affect.

If Jung's theory of archetypes and Kugler's linguistic deductions are both valid then we would expect to find confirmation of this particular complex of associations in mythology. Does any example exist? Most certainly it does: the rape of Demeter's daughter, Persephone, by Hades. Persephone is picking violets, roses, and other flowers with the daughters of Okeanos. Gaia, the Earth Goddess, lures her on by showing her a beautiful flower she has never seen before. It is a rare and wonderful narcissus. As Persephone reaches out to pick it, the earth opens violently to reveal Hades in his chariot galloping towards her. He seizes her and takes her back to the underworld, a ravished bride. Eventually Zeus arranges a compromise between Hades and Demeter whereby Persephone comes to her mother in the upper world with the first growth of spring and returns to Hades in the underworld in autumn once the seed has been sown. The myth therefore links the ideas of flowers, rape, the reproductive cycles of nature, death, and reincarnation.

From a Freudian preoccupation with the purely sexual and personal implications of the flower symbol we have uncovered the collective archetypal roots of a complex (defloration, death, and rebirth) represented in the dreams of two women towards the end of the last century. That the same symbolism occurs in the dreams of our contemporaries should come as no surprise, since the archetypes at the core of our personal complexes do not change. The associations between flowers, violence, death and rebirth are everywhere apparent – in the blood-red poppies commemorating the dead of two world wars, the wreaths we place on the graves of the departed, the bouquet carried by brides to the altar, the flowers presented to soldiers by the 'love and peace' hippies of the sixties, 'Where have all the flowers gone?' as sung by Marlene Dietrich and so on. All such instances, either in dreams or in waking reality, unconsciously reinvoke the drama of Persephone and Hades, and the associations in words and images that relate us all to them. By tracing symbols to their archetypal origins in this way we are brought face to face with the unchanging psychic nature and spiritual consanguinity of our species.

The same archetypes are at work in the poems and stories that human beings in all cultures create and delight in recounting. These also provide clues to the nature and function of dreams.

Dreams and Poetry: Oneiropoiesis

The dream is an involuntary kind of poetry.
JEAN PAUL RICHTER

Oneiropoiesis is the process of dream creation (from Greek *oneiros* = dream and *poiesis* = to create). *Poiesis* is also the word from which poetry is derived. As was brought home to me in the dream I recounted at the beginning of this book, theories of dreaming that concentrate on information processing too easily overlook the fact that it is a highly creative, imaginative act. 'Dreams are inspirations,' said Jung. Some dreams are less inspired than others, it is true, but all of them have the capacity to transform reality into something more. 'Poetry proper,' wrote Martin Heidegger, 'is never merely a higher mode of everyday language. It is rather the reverse: everyday language is a forgotten and therefore used-up poem, from which there hardly resounds a call any longer.'

One major characteristic that poems and dreams have in common is the way in which they use ambiguity in order to create webs of associative meaning in the evocation of feeling and atmosphere:

154

I'll love you, dear, I'll love you
Till China and Africa meet,
And the river jumps over the mountain
And the salmon sing in the street,

I'll love you till the ocean
Is folded and hung up to dry
And the seven stars go squawking
Like geese about the sky.

The years shall run like rabbits,
For in my arms I hold
The Flower of the Ages,
And the first love of the world.

(From 'As I Walked Out One Evening',
by W. H. Auden)

These stanzas are full of archetypal images – the mountain, fish, river, ocean, sky, geese, flower – which could as easily have been dreamt as turned into poetry. Jung liked to quote an aphorism by Gerhardt Hauptmann that 'Poetry is the art of letting the primordial word resound through the common word.'

The metre indispensable to poetry has its origins in the ritual chanting of religious ceremonies. This, like REM sleep, has a 're-cruiting' or 'driving' function on the neuronal systems of the brain. Analysing the metre used in the poetic canons of many different languages, Frederick Turner and Ernest Poppel (1983) detected a rhythm which they called the *metric pulse*: in all the languages studied this had a beat between 2 and 4 seconds, with most lines averaging between 2.5 and 3.5 seconds in duration. By combining semantic meaning with an acoustic, felt rhythm, the recital of poetry brings into synchrony the activities of both left and right cerebral hemispheres and the deeper, older structures of the brain. It is likely that narrative poetry is particularly effective in bringing this about, and in this it resembles the cerebral events associated with dreaming.

This leads us to a further dualistic conclusion: dreams are poetry; consciousness is prose.

Dreams and Stories

*Myths are fragments of the soul-life of Early Man . . . The
Hero Cycle, wherever found, is a story of 'fitness' in the
Darwinian sense: a blueprint for genetic 'success' . . . whereby
a man must first prove 'fitness' and then must 'marry far'.*
BRUCE CHATWIN, *The Songlines*

For centuries writers have been fascinated by the idea that there exist
'archetypal stories' incorporating a finite number of basic plots.
Certainly, the myths, fairy tales, and legends that have held the rapt
attention of audiences round camp fires since time immemorial have
all been concerned with the Great Themes of human existence. Since
dreams too are narratives based on the same themes, the similarities
between the two genres are self-evident. Hence Joseph Campbell's
aphorism that forms the epigraph to this book.

In searching for the deep structures in the basic syntax of stories,
we can begin to examine them in terms of setting, dramatis personae, plot, Jung's *exposition, development, peripeteia, and lysis.* It
should be possible, in the manner of Kugler, to break these
narratives down into the word-images of which both dreams
and stories are composed so as to demonstrate their common
archetypal roots, but this is not the place for such a vast undertaking. As we have already seen, there are two kinds of sleep
mentation: the story-like narratives of REM sleep which unfold
like a film, and the thought-ruminations of NREM sleep that
follow no narrative pattern. It is relatively easy for independent
judges to tell whether a night report has been derived from a
subject woken from REM or NREM sleep. REM dreams alone
seem to be rated as 'proper' dreams, in that they take a dramatic
narrative form. In other words, REM reports are fiction, NREM
reports non-fiction.

Because we are social animals living in a social context, the whole
of human life is a drama: we all live out our own particular 'soap'.
How is the drama created? Jung's answer – and no one has produced
a better one – is by the Self. It contains the whole programme for life
which unfolds in response to whoever or whatever is present in the

environment and it expresses itself in our behaviour, thoughts, feelings, stories, and dreams. Both dreams and stories are special in that they act as bridges between two realms of being – inner and outer, Self and environment – integrating them into more up-to-the-minute and better adapted patterns of responsiveness.

Many have suggested possible classifications for the basic plots of stories. The system of classification I favour would attempt to link each plot to a stage in the life-cycle, each being celebrated in drama and myth, and each having become the particular concern of one or more schools of therapy. We will confine ourselves to five basic plots: (1) *the miraculous birth and childhood of the hero*, in which his special powers are detected, tried and tested; (2) *rags to riches*, in which the hero triumphs over adversity (the dragon fight) and wins the kingdom; (3) *boy meets girl* and lives happily ever after; (4) *the struggle between light and darkness*, good and evil, life and death; and (5) *riches to rags*: loss and failure, evil triumphs over good, boy loses girl, the dragon wins.

All these plots are also the stuff of dreams. They are listed in Table 3, together with the *genres* in which they most commonly feature, and the schools of analysis (or psychiatry) for which they are the primary focus of interest.

The first four of these plots are to be found in the hero myths which have been recorded in all parts of the world and form the subject of Joseph Campbell's book *The Hero with a Thousand Faces*. Hero myths symbolize the archetypal tasks of childhood and adolescence. They tell how the hero leaves home and is subjected to a number of tests and trials, culminating in the 'supreme ordeal' of a fight with a dragon or sea monster. The hero's triumph is rewarded with the 'treasure hard to attain', i.e. the throne of a kingdom and a beautiful princess as a bride. So it is in actuality: to embark on the adventure of life, a boy has to free himself of his bonds to home, parents, and siblings, survive the ordeals of initiation (which virtually all traditional societies imposed), and win a place for himself in the world (the kingdom). To achieve all this and to win a bride, he must overcome the power of the mother complex still operative in his unconscious (the fight with the dragon). This amounts to a second parturition from the mother, a final severing of the psychic umbilical

Table 3:   Basic plots, their genres and their schools of therapy.

Plot	Genres	Therapy
(1) miraculous birth and childhood of the hero	myth religion	Bowlby Freud
(2) rags to riches: the hero triumphs over adversity	myth religion literature	Adler Jung
(3) boy meets girl and lives happily ever after	fairy tale romance comedy	Freud
(4) the struggle between light and darkness, good and evil	saga myth religion	Jung
(5) riches to rags, loss and failure	tragedy	orthodox psychiatry

cord (victory over the dragon-monster often involves the hero being swallowed into its belly, from which he cuts his way out in a kind of auto-Caesarian section: as a result, he 'dies' as his mother's son and is 'reborn' as a man worthy of the princess and the kingdom). The ritual of masculine initiation at puberty facilitates this necessary transition. Failure to pass the ordeals of initiation, or to overcome the monster, signifies failure to get free of the mother: then the princess (the anima) is never liberated from the monster's clutches. And then we are into plot number five.

In girls, the transition to womanhood is more readily accomplished since feminine gender consciousness does not demand a radical shift of identification from mother's world to father's world as it does in boys. As a result, female initiation, where it occurs, is (with the exception of the appalling rite of female circumcision) a less demanding and protracted process than for boys, consisting essentially of a ceremonial recognition that a young woman has now entered the reproductive phase of her life. It is as if the ritual were designed to heighten her introverted awareness of herself as a woman *creative on the plane of life itself*, with access to a sacred realm of experience that man can never know.

In many cultures there are no female initiation rites, and the task of bringing this new feminine consciousness into being falls to the initiated male. Hence the myths and fairy tales in which the heroine lies sleeping till a prince comes to awaken her with a kiss (awakening his own anima in the process). She is the Sleeping Beauty surrounded by a thicket, or the slumbering Brünhilde awaiting the arrival of her Siegfried within the circle of Wotan's fire.

Rites of passage evolved in primitive societies in order to assist individuals through the critical periods of crisis that mark transition from one stage of the life-cycle to the next. In addition to puberty initiation rites, there are rites of incorporation into the hunter, warrior, or shamanic role, marriage rites, rites on the birth of children and the death of relations. These all possessed great value because they provided public affirmation of the fact that a significant transition had occurred and, through the powerful symbolism of the ritual, activated archetypal components in the collective unconscious appropriate to the life stage that had been reached. This archetypal potential was then incorporated into the personal psyche of the initiate.

Stories, fairy tales, and myths similarly emerged in order to facilitate this purpose. Dreams perform the same function.

Although our culture no longer provides rites of initiation, except in training members of the armed forces and providing examinations for students, there persists in all of us, regardless of gender, *an archetypal need to be initiated*. The truth of this statement can be deduced from patients in analysis whose dreams become rich in initiatory symbolism at critical periods of their lives – for example, at puberty, betrothal, marriage, childbirth, at divorce or separation, at the death of a parent or a spouse, or when confronting some new challenge. Arrival at such a moment of crisis, or attainment of a new stage of life, seems to demand that symbols of initiation should be experienced. If society fails to provide them, then the Self compensates for this deficiency by producing them in dreams. Elsewhere, I have published several examples (Stevens, 1982). A further example occurred to me shortly before I began work on the present book.

I was in a strange, rather primitive place. A boy was about to undergo an initiation. He was terrified that he would not be able to bear the pain (of circumcision, I subsequently gathered) without betraying his manhood and crying out. I felt sorry for him, and in order to console him I taught him a mantra, telling him that he must keep repeating it when the time for his initiation came and that he would be all right.

Then the master of initiation arrived, a large powerful man in a loincloth with a heavily tattooed face. In his hand he carried something sinister, which I took to be the circumcision knife. Ignoring the boy, he approached me, indicating that I too was to be initiated. There was something both familiar and frightening about him. Sensing my agitation, he held out to me the object in his hand. It was a weird kind of cross, each branch of which consisted of a baby's arm holding an apple in its hand.

The image shifted and I saw a fountain overflowing into four conduits radiating from it. I awoke feeling anxious but knowing that something important had happened.

The dream occurred the night after I had been watching a TV film about tribal initiation rites, but this would not in itself explain the development in the story and the symbolism of the dream. At the time I was 'blocked' writing a play about the Freud–Jung relationship and I had begun to feel that I should abandon the whole project. I felt the dream must be connected with this and was naturally intrigued that the Self had represented the problem as one of initiation. I at once realized that part of my blockage was *fear* – fear of failure, fear of what the critics and my peers would say of my presumption in becoming a playwright late in life and in writing dialogue for two such eminent men. To complete the play and have it produced would clearly be an initiation and I, like most initiates, was fearful that I might not pass the test.

But why should the basic drama be worked out in such a primitive form? I, a late-twentieth-century psychiatrist, find myself being initiated in the manner traditional to most human societies for tens of thousands of years. What was the mantra? And what about the curious cross? Clearly they represented some kind of helpful magic. This too was strange and alien for a man of my cultural and educational background.

Many times during the course of the ensuing day I tried to remember the mantra. I was on the point of giving up when suddenly it popped into my head: 'Oh, Negrid, Negrid!' I promptly sat down and worked out my associations. Essentially, there were three: (1) *nigredo* – a stage in the alchemical *opus*, 'the darkening of the work', which carries the psychological connotation of depression and the need to encounter the shadow (the dark, negative side of the personality that one would rather disown); (2) *Negro* – the black man, who, in the dream of a European, appears as the living embodiment of the primordial man, the positive and negative shadow; (3) 'Ah Gertrude, Gertrude, When sorrows come, they come not single spies, but in battalions' (William Shakespeare, *Hamlet*, Act 4, Scene 5).

What light did these associations throw on my dream and my situation? In the play I had been concentrating on the positive value of the friendship of Freud and Jung, all the good qualities they carried for each other. I now realized that I was holding back on the unspoken hostility which was accumulating between them and which would finally erupt towards the end of the play, each resentment piling on the next, until their comradeship perished under an avalanche of acrimony and misunderstanding. In representing this on the stage, I should stir up old Freudian and Jungian loyalties and mutual projections of the shadow. Could I handle this? The dream suggested that I could and must.

And what of the cross? There came into my mind the boastful cliché of the phallic man that his penis is like a baby's arm with an orange in its fist. In my dream the orange is replaced by an apple, which I take to be a reference to the Garden of Eden, as is the fountain with its four rivers radiating out from the centre. A Freudian would see the fountain also as phallic with the waters of life, the seminal substance of masculine generativity. But it did not escape me that both garden and cross are mandalas, emblems of wholeness. Suddenly, I saw that this represented the Jungian resolution of the Freudian problem, namely, Freud's narrow insistence that the Sexual

Theory was the key to psychic life. Sexuality was not the key but an essential portion of the whole. The lysis of my play, like the lysis of my dream, was the importance of the Freudian episode for Jung's own individuation and the development of his psychology. The same must be true for the role of sexuality in my own psychological development and individuation. As Freud said, all symbolism in dreams is 'over-determined'. Soon after this dream I was able to resume work on the play and bring it to a satisfactory conclusion.

Stories, like dreams, make patterns out of events and people and order them into sequences of activity. The psyche seems to have a natural tendency to behave in this way. It is as if we carry a number of plots round with us as an integrated system of complexes and that these function as categories into which we feed events as they occur. Such plots or typical patterns become readily apparent when one examines a large number of dreams produced over a period of several years by the same dreamer. They can also emerge when one asks someone to focus on the story-line of a dream they have just had and see whether any associated plots occur to them.

Thus, *a man dreamt that his brakes failed as he was driving his car down-hill.* When asked what he associated with this, he remembered an event from childhood when his bicycle brake cable broke as he was cycling down-hill to school. That, in turn, was associated with a memory of a skiing accident on a mountain slope when he temporarily lost control. All these linked sequences are variations on the theme of risking danger through loss of control while travelling at speed down a gradient. The dream, together with the associations that it gave rise to, could be seen as a warning to the dreamer to take care when he found himself in similar circumstances. But it was also a metaphor for how he was living his life: he was in danger of 'going down-hill' out of control.

Dreams of this kind are very important in analysis, not only for what they may tell us about the dreamer's present circumstances, but because they give us the clue to the hidden patterns which are recurrently operative in his life. They also illustrate how dreams constantly reiterate important memory traces and update them. The fact that these traces often carry with them a powerful emotional charge means that they can exercise enormous psychic clout: hence Jung's comment that we don't have complexes, our complexes have us. This important issue is addressed by Don Kuiken in his essay on 'Dreams and Self-Knowledge' in which he refers to these emotionally laden memory traces as 'affective scripts'.

Dreams and Memory

For yesterday is but a memory
And tomorrow is only a vision,
But today well lived
Makes every yesterday a memory of happiness
And every tomorrow a vision of hope.
Look well therefore to this day.

From a Sanskrit poem

Just as Jung saw that the essential element binding associations and memories into a complex was an emotionally charged image, so Freud stressed that the memories employed in the construction of the dream had a similar motivational and affective 'tenor'. Motives and feelings released by events occurring before the dreamer goes to bed persist during sleep and activate a whole family of similar memories in order to create the dream. Thus, Freud's associations to his own dream of Irma's injection revealed a cluster of memories that converged on the themes of self-justification and revenge. Such a family of motivationally and affectively similar memories, concludes Kuiken, are instances of a class of memories organized by *an affective script* (Gachenbach, 1987, p. 232).

Had one had Freud in analysis one would have been tempted to ask him if he needed to persist in his self-justificatory and revengeful behaviour. Is this not a persistent pattern that needed to be changed? Such conjecture brings up one of the dangers of analysis, however. To intervene in this way could conceivably have deprived Freud of the ambitious drive motivating his life's work; and, ironically enough, it might have deprived the world of psychoanalysis altogether! One undertakes grave responsibilities when one sits in the analyst's chair.

In developing the theory of affective scripts, Kuiken draws on the

Freudian dream mechanism of *condensation*: 'Condensation is a process by which memory elements are compared and matched. More specifically, when the compared elements are similar in some respect, they are fused into a single image or jointly represented by a collective image' (p. 234). As already noted, Freud demonstrated how the use of free association could tease out the memory strands which are drawn together to form a specific dream image or sequence. In other words, free association permits one to unravel one's complexes and reveal the skeins from which they are woven.

That the activation of relevant memory structures by pre-sleep events has effects which linger for hours would explain how it is that several dreams recorded in the course of one night commonly manifest thematic continuity. Moreover, feelings stirred in the course of these dreams may persist well into the following day. In this way, pre-sleep events (Freud's *Tagesreste*) can revive memories, stimulate complexes, and bring to consciousness archetypal elements, images and affects which would otherwise remain unconscious. This has a subtle but significant effect on ego-consciousness and the development of self-knowledge, whether an individual is in analysis or not.

As we saw in Chapter 4, the EEG theta rhythm implicates the hippocampus as a special area of focus for memory storage, archetypal patterning, and dreams. Here, and in other limbic structures, the archetypal programme resides, to be activated by relevant events (together with their associated motives and affects) to construct complexes and affective scripts. Each night the *Tagesreste* constellate these archetypally based elements in order to inform, consolidate, and modify them in such a way as to sustain their biological efficiency. This intricate and crucial process is experienced by us psychically and subjectively as 'dreaming'.

With hindsight we can see that others had similar ideas about memories providing the building blocks of dreams before Freudian psychology, theta rhythm, or the functions of the hippocampus were known about. The pioneer dream researcher, Hervey de Saint-Denis (1822–92), believed that his dreams were created out of *clichés-souvenirs* (stereotyped memories) stored in the memory and called up by related events in his daily life. *Clichés-souvenirs* bear a close resemblance to complexes, which do, indeed, have a stereotyped quality about them – the same old ideas and images bound together by the same old feeling. This stereotypy could become entrenched and maladaptive were it not for the dynamic activity so apparent in REM sleep. Past response patterns and experiences, whether individual or collective, are not merely being added to; they are being changed to make them more responsive to the demands of the present. Macbeth's 'sleep that knits up the ravell'd sleeve of care' is using wool stored up in the past to make a serviceable garment for the day to come: out of 'all our yesterdays' our dreams prepare the wardrobe of tomorrow.

Or, to change the analogy, at night a form of clerical work is in progress. Recent experiences are being put into their appropriate files on the criterion of resemblance or similarity. This is the necessary preliminary to the work of condensation, so that all relevant information can be built into an appropriate image. It is the reverse of free association. (Free association is taking the separate leaves out of the file and spreading them out all over the table.) The actual dream work of the clerical dreamer is to amend standing orders with new directives received in the previous day's mail. Whatever else we may say about it, REM sleep is not a time of rest; the brain is as busy as at any time during the day.

The dream work proceeds by analogy. Dreams recall things that happened in the past that are analogous to what is going on in the present. They do not confine themselves to putting new documents in old files: they integrate and collate them with what is on file already. Moreover, such is the dreaming brain's capacity for lateral or non-discursive thinking, that it can see resemblances to the contents of other records filed under different headings – files that it would never have occurred to the waking ego to think of consulting.

Highly practised in the skill of transposition, the dreaming brain can move whole memory systems into another key, or take two apparently different systems and detect hidden harmonies between them. Such is its virtuosity, that it can hear old themes in new variations and improvise original motifs upon them. This helps to explain how it is that in dreams we are all artists, musicians, playwrights, actors, *metteurs-en-scène*. The day residues selected by the dream as materials for the inspired *collages* of the night are gathered on the basis of experience gained in working with such materials in the past. Thus dreaming is not merely a storage process whereby short-term memories are transferred into the long-term repository, as many contemporary dream scientists suppose. It is also a process by which memories are revised and reorganized. Here again, we can see the limitations of Freud's theoretical understanding. His pessimistic and reductive cast of mind encouraged him to insist that dreams never bring up anything new: in his view they merely reworked material that had been recorded in the past. This blinded him to the dream's most extraordinary capacity – the ability to invent, to take memories, turn them round, play with them, and go beyond them. As we dream, archetypal structures are quickened by the events we dream about, their ancient wisdom and energies mobilized, and our personality subtly transformed.

Dreams and Play

Man is only truly himself when he is at play.
SCHILLER

The playful element in dreams has not passed unnoticed. For example, Freud quoted the poet Novalis to the effect that 'Dreams are a shield against the humdrum monotony of life; they set imagination free from its chains so that it may throw into confusion all the pictures of everyday existence and break into the unceasing gravity of grown men with the joyful play of a child' (1976, p. 153). Bert O. States has suggested that dreaming could be something the brain does for pleasure while the body is asleep, just as jazz musicians play the real music after the customers have gone home. This may seem fanciful, until one reflects that play is a serious business in all mammals and that nature makes all activity essential for survival intrinsically enjoyable – hence the pleasures of eating, hunting, and sex, as well as all forms of play. Play is its own reward. By ensuring that young creatures play, nature provides the means of activating unconscious potential and training behavioural systems that are vital to life: social co-operation and conflict, intimacy with peers, sexuality, physical combat, the control of aggression, hunting, ritual, marital relations,

166

child-rearing and creativity. The truth is that all the archetypal activities of human life are filled with possibilities for play. One might adapt Schiller's famous aphorism and say that man is even more truly himself when he dreams, for in our dreams we are editing and reshaping our personal version of humanity.

In his great book on man as a playing animal, *Homo Ludens*, John Huizinga remarks: 'In play there is something "at play" which transcends the immediate needs of life' – a superabundance of joyful exuberance that would seem to go beyond the bounds of necessity. This is the way of nature: for in the great evolutionary process itself there is always something 'at play', constantly trying out new possibilities, not only in dreams but in the mutation of genetic material. Just as dreams rehearse new scenarios in the light of past performances, so mutations serve up new recipes on which natural selection can exercise its choice. Dreams are microcosmic manifestations of the evolutionary macrocosm: they are symbolic representations in the psyche of natural evolutionary principles at work.

Mutation is a reckless form of gambling. More often than not nature loses. But when she wins she promotes adaptation and the generation of new forms of life by providing specific organismic solutions to specific environmental challenges, so as to work out a more successful accommodation between what the organism needs and what the environment has to offer. This, I believe, is the *paradigm on which the dreaming brain operates*.

Dreams and Mental Illness

Symptoms are always justified and serve a purpose.

C. G. JUNG

Many authorities have compared the phenomena of dreaming with the signs and symptoms of psychotic illnesses. Emmanuel Kant's observation that 'the madman is a waking dreamer' was echoed by Krauss's (1859) statement, quoted by Freud, that 'insanity is a dream dreamt while the senses are awake'. Schopenhauer (1862) described dreams as a brief madness and madness as a long dream, while Wilhelm Wundt (1874) wrote: 'We ourselves, in fact, can experience in dreams almost all the phenomena to be met with in insane asylums' (Freud, 1976, p. 162). Contemporary researchers, such as Hobson (1988), have reaffirmed that dreams and psychoses are closely related.

Hobson describes five cardinal characteristics of dreams and shows how they are mimicked in mental illness. These are: (1) the illogical content and organization of dreams which defy natural laws as well as the unities of time, place, and person; (2) the intense emotions which are capable of disturbing the mental state of the dreamer (e.g. nightmares and anxiety dreams); (3) the experience of fully formed sensory impressions in the absence of outer stimuli; (4) the uncritical acceptance of the curious and bizarre things which are seen, heard, and felt; and (5) the difficulty of remembering the dream when it is over. Hobson draws clear parallels between these characteristics and the disorientation, bizarre thought patterns, powerful affective states, delusions, hallucinations, and amnesias experienced by psychotic patients.

Viewed from the standpoint of normal consciousness, the most striking feature of both psychosis and dreaming is *loss of insight*: fantastic events seem absolutely real – so much so that awakening from a dream is like recovering from a psychotic episode at the moment the realization dawns that one has been deluded and hallucinated: 'Thank God! It was only a dream!' The discontinuities, incongruities, improbabilities, illogicalities, uncertainties, mythical constructions, and non-sequiturs so typical of dreams are very like the 'thought disorder' regularly observed in schizophrenic patients since the time of Emil Kraepelin (1856–1926), while schizophrenic 'loss of volition' resembles the common dream experience of lethargy, dragging feet, not being able to get done what has to be done. The ghastly sense of helplessness or paralysis suffered in nightmares and night terrors has parallels in the rigidity of catatonic schizophrenia and the 'tonic immobility', or 'freezing in horror' seen across the evolutionary spectrum as an extreme response to severe stress. The powerful emotions of excitement and fear which can influence the mental state in dreams are also apparent in the clinical conditions of mania and phobic anxiety. In dreams we also experience amnesia (we remember little or nothing about our waking state) and we confabulate – facts which have persuaded some researchers to compare dreaming with Korsakoff's psychosis, in which memory loss is associated with confabulation (the invention of events in considerable detail in order to compensate and disguise the memory loss). In addition, dreaming closely resembles clinical delirium; and, interestingly enough, the EEG pattern characteristic of delirium (the superimposition of fast and slow waves) is the same as that recorded from subjects in REM sleep.

Thus, it is not far-fetched to consider dreaming to be a form of licensed madness occurring in the asylum of sleep, and this conclusion has highly significant implications for psychopathology. No less an authority than Aristotle suggested that the hallucinations and delusions of the insane, the illusions of normal waking life, and the fantastic experiences of the dream world are not merely similar, but may actually share a common origin. Similarly, Hobson argues that dreaming could well be the mental product of the same *kind* of psychobiological process that appears to be deranged in mental illness. 'This conclusion gives the scientific study of the dream process implications beyond the realm of dreaming itself: since all the major signs of mental illness can be imitated by normal minds in the normal state of dreaming. The study of dreams is the study of a model of mental illness' (p. 9).

If this is so, how is it possible to maintain that dreams have an adaptive or creative function? If dreams are a form of temporary madness, how on earth can they be thought to enhance our lives? The answer is that it depends on the attitude one adopts to mental illness. If one regards all psychiatric symptoms as simply the tragic and meaningless consequences of psychopathology then it is hard to see how dreams, inasmuch as they resemble such symptoms, can have a beneficial influence. But if, on the other hand, one regards psychiatric symptoms as meaningful responses to major problems encountered by individuals in their lives, and as attempts to adapt to these problems, then the parallel with symptom formation becomes less dire in its implications for dreaming.

This was the position adopted by Jung. 'At bottom we discover nothing new and unknown in the mentally ill,' he wrote, 'rather we encounter the substratum of our own natures' (*MDR*, p. 127). His view that psychiatric symptoms are persistent exaggerations of natural psychophysiological responses was not only shared by Freud but has been reaffirmed by contemporary psychiatrists who use ethological concepts in their approach to mental illness. For example, Dr Brant Wenegrat of the Stanford University Medical Center in California sees all psychopathological syndromes, whether psychotic, neurotic, or psychopathic, as statistically abnormal manifestations of *innate response strategies* (his term for archetypes), shared by all individuals whether they are mentally healthy or ill.

Jung carried this insight one very important stage further, arguing that *symptom formation is itself a product of the individuation process*, that illness is an autonomously creative act, a function of the psyche's imperative to grow and develop having to proceed in abnormal circumstances. Neurosis is thus a form of adaptation, albeit 'inferior adaptation', of a potentially healthy organism responding to the demands of life. 'Because of some obstacle – a constitutional weakness or defect, wrong education, bad experiences, an unsuitable attitude, etc. – one shrinks from the difficulties which life brings . . .' (*CW*13, para. 472). Individuation is distorted or goes awry when one experiences difficulty in achieving mature adjustment because certain archetypal needs essential to the programme of development have not been met at the appropriate time.

Mental illness, like dreaming, can therefore be conceived as a meaningful response to the total life situation. Instead of stigmatizing psychiatric symptoms as pathological entities, they can be approached, like dreams, as symbolic communications from the unconscious, indicating where the patient has become embroiled in the fundamental problems of life and showing how he is attempting to achieve some kind of resolution of them. Thus, the discovery of parallels between dreams and the symptoms of mental illness does not require one to adopt a pessimistic or pathological view of dreaming. Freud was correct in seeing a relationship between dreams and psychiatric symptoms, not because dreams are pathological phenomena, but because dreams and symptoms are similar attempts at adaptive adjustment and derived from the same intrapsychic source.

Magic, Ritual, and Transformation

GLENDOWER: *I can call spirits from the vasty deep.*
HOTSPUR: *Why, so can I, or so can any man;*
But will they come when you do call for them?
WILLIAM SHAKESPEARE, *Henry IV*, Part I

When we dream we enter a realm which may be legitimately described as magical in the sense that literally anything can happen without any reference to the normal constraints of nature: we can fly, travel to far-off places, hold conversations with animals and with the dead, and witness extraordinary transformations. Moreover, dreams are not infrequently experienced as miraculous in their effects in that we are both animated and transformed by them. On waking from such dreams it is not unusual for us to feel ourselves and our world to be different. Nothing will ever be quite the same as it was.

It is on waking from dreams of this intensity that we receive the distinct impression that something is at work within us coming from beyond our finite selves. It is as if we are the channels through which some suprapersonal force is flowing. At such moments we experience our lives and our world as revitalized, as if reanimated by nature herself, and we touch extremes of awareness reminiscent of the intoxicating excitements of childhood.

Young children in our own culture, like all preliterate people, are entirely at home in the world of magic and they make constant use of it. An interesting example of this comes in Jung's autobiographical account of his own childhood. The unhappiness of his external circumstances drove him into a secret world of magic and ritual – e.g. the manikin he made and kept in a pencil box in the attic of his father's vicarage, his fire rituals, and so on. He had a favourite day-dream in which he was the ruler of a medieval town. He lived in a fortified castle where he guarded a Great Secret from the world. This was a thick copper column. At the top was a network of tiny capillaries through which a special spiritual substance was drawn in from the air. Once in the column this was condensed and transformed into the most wonderful gold coins, which the column then discharged below.

What is one to make of such a fantasy? A Freudian would doubtless point to the sexual symbolism of the column and see it as a metaphor for spermatogenesis, tumescence and ejaculation. Jung, however, took it as a metaphor for the transformative power of the psyche and, retrospectively, as a prefiguration of his adult absorption in Alchemy. This fantasy tower with its secret column was later implemented in reality at his tower home at Bollingen with its inner sanctum, the room forbidden to everyone but himself. It was in this room that he pursued his alchemical researches.

In his castle fantasy Jung experienced himself as the ecstatic discoverer of what he called 'a venerable and vital secret of nature'. This enhanced his understanding that the inner world of the psyche is our most precious possession and strengthened his conviction that he was born to make the unknown knowable. His intense introversion made him more aware than anyone before or since of the extent to which our personal existence is dependent upon the animal past that lives through us. 'I do not live, I am lived,' said Jung, 'I do not dream, I am dreamt.' He believed that his powers were not his own but derived from another, transcendent source. This source revealed itself most transparently in his dreams, and if he were to 'know' it, it could only be through careful examination of the night revelations which were so plentifully granted to him.

If Freud believed the language of the unconscious to be essentially primitive and infantile, to Jung it was the word of Nature itself. Nature speaks to us directly in myths and dreams. The 'transcendent' function of symbols is also a function of nature, part of the autonomous developmental process active throughout life which Jung called 'individuation', Erich Neumann 'centroversion' and Abraham Maslow 'self-realization'. Characteristically, Jung set the whole process within a cosmic context. We are the instruments of Nature's quest for self-awareness and she speaks to us most clearly in our dreams. Individuation is the creative principle animating the universe through which the universe becomes conscious of itself.

The idea that we are each of us *animated* by nature is one that our scientific world deplores. Yet children, like all primal people, are natural animists. Not only do they experience animals, plants, trees, streams, wind as alive but also as self-aware, and they feel this awareness through a *participation mystique*, using the unconscious mechanism, so well recognized by clinical psychology, of *projective identification*. The 'nature mysticism' of the romantic poets made deliberate aesthetic use of this natural imaginative technique, and it greatly influenced Jung's understanding of psychic purpose and functioning.

Whether or not one accepts Jung's romantic view of the relationship between psyche and nature, there is no doubt that all of us can experience dreams, if we open ourselves up to them, as inner springs, teeming with those archetypal energies that have inspired the human spirit since we emerged from the primeval forests and began to walk on two legs. These vital waters flow through an ancient labyrinth. The modern world blinds us to their beauty, deafens us to their sound. Dreaming the dream in sleep and dreaming it onwards in wakefulness is to enter once more this eternal labyrinth and know it for the first time. Then the animated world begins to break through into consciousness − as it did all the time when we were children − the sense, for example, that certain places are miraculous, others sombre and terrifying − the sense of *genius loci*.

Landscape is every bit as numinous to us in dreams as in waking reality, presumably because it is, to use Jung's phrase, inborn in us as a virtual image − an archetypal *given*, so to speak. The emotions roused by dream landscapes can possess a *religious* intensity, often being associated with archetypal figures and rituals which relate to the seasons, bearing a fertility or cosmic meaning linking us with our mythic past. What is the purpose of such dreams? Why have we always created fertility gods like Osiris and surrounded them with ritual and lavished worship upon them? Could it be for the same reasons that we dream? Are theologies, mythologies, and rituals the extensions of our dreams into our waking cultural life? Is dreaming an Ur-phenomenon from which these activities are derived? It is quite possible that they are. Neumann makes the observation that man's magico-religious behaviour is 'the fountain head of all culture', that by taking natural processes as models for his rituals, man produces in his own soul the same creative powers as he observes outside himself in nature. This would help to explain why it is that peoples all over the earth from time immemorial have performed religious rites designed to ensure that the crops grow and the sun courses through the heavens to return every morning after its disappearance in the night, and how it is that they could ignore the truth that the crops would continue to grow and the sun proceed on its inexorable cycle whether they did these rituals or not.

This takes us to the very heart of the mystery of magic. In his great but misguided book *The Origins and History of Consciousness*,* Neumann draws fascinating parallels between fertility or solar rituals and the ritual painting of hunting scenes in paleolithic art. He argues that the ritual representation of killing a stag in a cave painting heightened the probability that the stag would actually be killed on the hunt. Primitive man experienced this as a real connection. As adult members of Western society we no longer consider such a connection could exist, but as children we understood it perfectly. As a schoolboy in England during the last world war I made a vital contribution to the war effort by filling exercise books with drawings of Messerschmitts being shot down by Spitfires. Neumann's point is that magical rites, like religious rites, work by *acting on the person who performs them*. The outcome, whether it be in hunting or in war, is *objectively* dependent on *the powerful subjective effect of the magic ritual*. Our modern scientific view makes us assume that the paleolithic ritual of painting the death of a stag was unlikely to have had any objective effect on the animal concerned, but, in fact, Neumann argues, 'the magical effect of the rite is factual enough, and in no sense illusory'. It results, just as primitive man anticipated it would, in actual success on the hunt. However, the effect proceeds via the subject (the hunter) not via the object (the hunted) (Neumann, 1954, p. 209). The outcome is 'in the highest degree objectively dependent on the effect of the magic ritual'. Enlightened rationalism is wrong to reject such practices as illusory or futile, for 'an effect that proceeds from an alteration in the subject is objective and real' (ibid.). Here

---

* Neumann made several fallacious assumptions – namely, that ontogeny (individual development) recapitulates phylogeny (evolutionary development), that preliterate human beings were 'unconscious', and that Western consciousness has been subjected to different selection pressures to that of other civilized populations. None of these assumptions is biologically tenable.

we may detect a close parallel between ritual and dreams, for both act by increasing the power and efficiency of the subject. Dreams are the involuntary rituals of the night.

7
SYMBOLISM

In looking at objects of nature . . . as at yonder moon, dim-glimmering through the dewy windowpane, I seem rather to be seeking . . . a symbolical language for something within me that forever and already exists, than observing anything new. Even when that latter is the case, yet still I have always an obscure feeling, as if that new phenomenon were a dim awakening of a forgotten or hidden truth of my inner nature.

SAMUEL TAYLOR COLERIDGE

From the standpoint of dream psychology the most extraordinary capacity of the human psyche is its genius for fabricating images. When does an image become a symbol? *When it is endowed with meaning.* This is apparent in the German word for symbol, *Sinnbild* (*Sinn* = sense, meaning; *Bild* = image). The etymology of the word *symbol* is itself instructive. The Greek noun *symbolon* referred to a token or tally which could be used as a verification of identity. An object, such as a bone, would be broken into two halves and each given separately to two people (e.g. members of the same sect or secret society) who could then identify each other by producing both halves and checking that they fitted together. Each tally-holder knew his own half to be genuine; when contact was made, 'goodness of fit' between the two halves of the *symbolon* was the criterion which satisfied the other's *bona fides*. If perfect fit occurred a *Gestalt* was suddenly created out of the familiar (known) and the strange (unknown) parts. The conjunction of *sym* (= together) and *bolon* (from *ballo* = I throw) emphasizes the idea that the strange must be 'thrown together' with the familiar in order to construct a bridge connecting the known with the unknown, or in psychological terms the conscious with the unconscious.

Symbol formation thus requires a marriage between conscious and unconscious halves of the psyche: it is what the alchemists called a *coniunctio oppositorum.* To each half the other is indispensable: without conscious formulation the flow of unconscious images would go unrecognized; and if cut off from the unconscious flow, consciousness would be starved of nourishment. It is not extravagant, therefore, to place a high value on symbols as providing the nutrients indispensable to psychic health and vitality.

This bridge-building capacity of the psyche, uniting incompatible processes in one symbolic form, is what Jung called its *transcendent function.* The transcendent function itself frequently appears as a symbol: one of the most evocative is the caduceus, the magic staff of the Greek god Hermes (the Roman god Mercury) with its two intertwined snakes. Hermes, the psychopomp, messenger of the gods, conveyer of souls, was the mediator between the upper world and the underworld, the conscious and unconscious realms. When Hermes touched men with his caduceus they fell asleep and entered the world of dreams.

Jung's understanding of dream symbols was radically different from Freud's. Indeed, no area of disagreement more clearly reflects the temperamental differences between them than their respective attitudes to symbols. To Freud, a symbol was a figurative representation of an unconscious idea, conflict, or wish. It was a substitute-formation which effectively disguised the true meaning of the idea it represented: a sword was a symbol of the penis, the sheath a symbol of the vagina, and pushing the sword into its sheath a symbol of sexual intercourse. In Jung's view the Freudian symbol was not a symbol at all but a *sign*: 'an abbreviated designation of a known thing'. It regularly referred to something already known and embodied a meaning that was fixed. Jung's understanding of symbols was quite different. To him a symbol was 'the best possible formulation of a relatively unknown thing' which could not be more clearly represented: it was 'the expression of an intuitive idea that cannot be formulated in any other or better way' (*CW*6, paras. 814–29). For Jung the symbol never stood for something else (as it did for Freud): it was itself the best possible expression of its own meaning.

Freud regarded the unconscious as an unhealthy mire to be drained, or at least reduced in size: where id was there shall ego be. To Jung it was an ever-flowing stream, fertilizing the psychic landscape through which it flowed: the ego was constantly renewed and revitalized by its life-enhancing influence. The kind of interpretation that breaks a symbol down into its component meanings is, in the Jungian view, a form of vivisection – dissecting something living that ought to remain whole.

Symbols, Dead or Alive

A symbol remains a perpetual challenge to our thoughts and feelings.

C. G. JUNG

The essential thing about symbols, Jung insisted, is that they are autonomous: they are living entities with a life cycle all their own; they are born, they flourish, they dwindle, and they die. 'The symbol is alive only so long as it is pregnant with meaning. But once its meaning has been born out of it, once that expression is found which formulates the thing sought, expected, or divined better than the hitherto accepted symbol, then the symbol is dead.' A dead symbol is merely a conventional sign. 'It is, therefore, quite impossible to create [that is, voluntarily invent in ego-consciousness] a living symbol, i.e. one that is pregnant with meaning, from known associations. For what is thus produced never contains more than was put into it.' Symbols are both living and dead for individuals and for cultures, according to their chronological age and historical epoch. Symbols which possess great vitality in childhood often lose their magic as we grow older. So it is with cultural symbols: the crucifix, for example, once the quintessential symbol of Christendom, has lost its power to inspire piety in the majority of our contemporaries. 'A symbol really lives only when it is the best and highest expression for something divined but not yet known to the observer. It then compels his unconscious participation and has a life-giving and life-enhancing effect' (*CW*6, para. 819).

Analytic experience confirms Jung's assertion that living symbols have a life-giving and life-enhancing effect. How does this come about? Jung spelled out his answer in *Transformations and Symbols of the Libido*, where he maintained that symbols provide the means by which psychic energy can be transformed from a lower to a higher mode of application: 'the psychological mechanism that transforms energy is the symbol', he wrote (*On Psychic Energy*). In other words, *symbolism is thinking in energized images*, and this encapsulated energy-with-meaning gives the symbol its capacity to influence ego-consciousness, to redirect its orientation, and to grant access to a new pathway leading the dreamer beyond his present circumstances. Such transformations of energy underlie the 'aha' experience of analytic insight, when a previously unknown truth is symbolized, focused, and understood. This is particularly likely to occur, Jung maintained, when the symbol is 'amplified' and not analysed reductively or attributed to already experienced events.

Whether the vitality of a symbol is appreciated or not depends on the conscious attitude with which it is received. In themselves, images, like objects, are meaningless; they acquire value only when we grant it to them. In this resides the *sine qua non* of mental health and personal happiness. People who live in a meaningless, valueless world are ill: they are depressed. They are in need of a symbol transfusion. Every culture has a symbol bank. The art of therapy is to render its resources accessible to the patient so as to provide a symbol transfusion compatible with his needs. The secret is to discover that the bank is located not on Main Street but in the Self.

Symbolic Origins

*The soul has its own **logos**, which grows according to its needs.*
HERACLITUS

The traditional psychoanalytic approach as well as much contemporary psychotherapy is, alas, hostile to the symbol, for it is conceptualized, broken down, reduced. Such an attitude would be more appropriate in science and technology. Reductive analysis of things into their components makes possible the realization of great achievements, it cannot be denied, but in the process we quickly lose touch with the life-enhancement that symbolic awareness can bring. Thus through the advance of science we have lost the medieval image of a unitary cosmic order with the earth at the centre of a moral universe presided over by God, and we have found no equally satisfying image to put in its place. Yet we have always been ones for inventing theories and constructing systems of belief in order to make sense of the world and it is this propensity which gave rise to the great symbolist traditions.

Many would agree with J. E. Cirlot (1971) that this symbolic reservoir has been filled from one common source. But, like him, they are unwilling to affirm whether it originated in one human community at a certain time and place – 'a primeval focal point' in prehistory – or whether it emerged from the common structures and common propensities built by evolution into our brains. The most plausible explanation is that both archetypal structures and cultural influences have been involved. The symbolic traditions and mythologies most likely to endure are, in all probability, the most closely assimilated to archetypal needs.

That the human psyche everywhere functions in broadly similar ways is now beyond dispute: the universal themes of folklore, legend, and superstition provide overwhelming evidence in support of this assertion, as do the painstaking studies of Orientalists, cultural anthropologists, Jungian analysts, art historians, mythologists, and those versed in the arcane ramifications of comparative religion. All testify to the essential 'oneness' underlying the multiplicity of symbolic forms. The study of body-language, gestures, and facial expressions, as well as the 'deep structures' responsible for verbal communication, also point to the same archetypal origins of all cultural phenomena. What culture does is provide a *tradition* to which archetypal patterns are assimilated in the course of ontological development. Thus the kind of figures occurring in myths relate to specific cultural traditions, yet their forms are universal (e.g. dragon-like monsters, fabulous creatures that are half human and half beast, shafts of dazzling light, geometric forms such as mandalas, etc.).

As Otto Rank put it, 'the myth is the collective dream of the people', an idea developed by Joseph Campbell in his aphorism: 'A myth is a public dream, a dream is a private myth.' If people everywhere tend to dream the same themes and produce common symbols, then cultural traditions help shape these symbols and give them their particular ethnic quality, and the archetypal propensity to produce symbols of this generic type will go on as long as human beings survive, whatever their cultural circumstances. All symbols are the product of interaction between collective propensities and personal experiences: the universal transcends history; the personal relates to the here and now. The symbol is the link between the two. The more archaic the symbol, the more phylogenetically ancient its origins, the more 'collective' or 'universal' it will be. The more differentiated the symbol, the more coloured it is by the ontological peculiarities of the individual producing it.

The symbolic canons of myth and religion began when people started to reflect on their circumstances in the natural world instead of blindly existing through them, and it is clear that something of great importance occurred to us about 60,000 years ago – the time when our astrobiological preoccupations began in earnest. From being purely animistic and totemistic, our cultures passed through megalithic, lunar, and solar stages, until, with the discovery of the principles of agriculture and animal husbandry 10,000 years ago, we formed the idea that the heavenly bodies, numbers, plants, and animals, all obeyed certain laws, predictable regularities, and recurring rhythms that could be known, studied, and *recorded* for the benefit of future generations. This went along with the development of poly-theism, monotheism, and, eventually, alchemy, moral philosophy, and natural science. All these developments were dependent upon the use of symbols as regulating principles capable of imposing order on chaos, and the basic symbols which arose during the progress of human cultures and civilizations have persisted right up to the present day.

Archetypal Symbols

Every psychological expression is a symbol if we assume that it states or signifies something more and other than itself which eludes our present knowledge.

C. G. JUNG

In reconciling the general with the particular, the symbol betrays its archetypal origins. Just as a fingerprint is unique to its owner yet at the same time possesses general characteristics enabling us to recognize it for what it is, so a single archetypal pattern may achieve expression in a myriad of symbolic forms. It is for this reason that the comparative study of symbols is so important. For only when one has collected and studied large numbers of them can one begin to detect the archetype responsible for them. As Darwin demonstrated, the study of physical morphology reveals that within an apparent multiplicity of structures a small number of basic forms exists. The same is true of plots in literature and symbols in dreams.

Accordingly, symbolism works through analogy: just as the sunrise banishes darkness, so the hero emerges from the stomach of the whale, the ego gets free of the unconscious, and the boy liberates himself from his mother. Just as the sun reaches its zenith, so the hero wins the princess and the kingdom, the young man marries and finds his role in life. These analogies are experienced as meaningful because they represent parallel ideas: they satisfy what Cirlot calls 'the principle of sufficient identity'. The different images coincide and 'reveal their allegiance in one essence'. Though different existentially they unite symbolically: what is objectively a *distinctio* becomes subjectively a *coniunctio*, and the union releases a rush of psychic energy: 'aha!' Hence Aristotle's observation that the best interpreter of dreams is the man who can best perceive similarities (Freud, 1900, p. 171n).

In its endlessly repeated encounters with contemporary reality, the collective unconscious is forever bringing new symbols into being. The symbol is the flesh in which the archetypal skeleton incarnates itself. In this way the most abstract archetypal imperatives are rendered visible, either in the animate form of a human or animal figure, or in the inanimate configuration of a square, a circle, or a bridge. Thus the archetypal relationship between masculine and feminine principles, the Yang and the Yin, can be symbolized by the frank image of a man and woman in the sexual act, by a sword fitting into its scabbard, or the illumination of the moon by the sun. The archetypal conflict between good and evil and between light and darkness is dramatized in the ubiquitous motif of the hero's tournament with the dragon, which he either slays or turns into a tame beast. The general course of the human life cycle is represented in the rising, the zenith, and the setting of the sun, and the ordeals and tribulations of life by negotiating a maze or a labyrinth.

These images abound not only in the myths, legends, and fairy tales recorded by ethnographers but also in the dreams of modern men, women, and children. Particularly children. Symbols are thus parables or metaphors for archetypal intentions and needs. Every individual, family, community, nation will produce symbols appropriate to its circumstances, but, for all their apparent variety, they are based on identical structural configurations. The archetype of the masculine, for example, is charged with all the potentials and characteristics through which masculinity can manifest itself (e.g. general propensities such as penetration, aggression, competitiveness, assertiveness, generativity, protectiveness) as well as characteristically masculine patterns of behaviour (such as courting, mating, tool- and weapon-making, territorial defence, law-enforcing, dominance striving, hunting, and warfare). All these propensities and behaviour patterns have their symbolic correlates through which the masculine archetype is expressed in myths, dreams, and legends: they will be collective symbols such as the lingam, Djed pillar, lance, bull, plough, knight, king, Jehovah, as well as the personal symbols a man may have, such as his knife, pen, football boots, or qualities associated with his brothers, father, headmaster, or sergeant major. In the course of growing up a boy works his own symbolic alchemy from these personal and collective sources to synthesize his own identity with the masculine, while a girl develops her animus (her masculine complex in the personal psyche) in a similar manner.

Symbols are thus the means by which we codify meanings and incarnate them in the world of visible reality. They are perceptible formulations behind which meaningful intentions are concealed. The art of interpretation is to divine the meaning behind the formulation and transform it into words. But words can only circumscribe the meaning, never pin it down. Words *explain*, but symbols arouse intimations, possibilities, emotions, beyond the reach of verbal expression. That is why symbols have to be played with in the imagination, painted, modelled, danced, paid their due, not exhausted by wordy exploitation. Only then can their revivifying power be experienced.

The Archetypal Serpent

No country abounds in a greater degree with dangerous beasts than . . . Africa.

CHARLES DARWIN

That the serpent, for example, is an archetypal image can be deduced from its ubiquity and its power to release the emotions of awe, fascination, and dread. Why is it that modern town dwellers, who have no cause to fear snakes and who have had no previous contact with them, should not only experience a sharp frisson on observing snakes in a zoo but also have dreams and nightmares about them? Such sensitivity would be understandable among hunter-gatherers living in a snake-infested swamp, but in a Manhattan bank clerk? Clearly something phyletic is involved.

Why should we have inherited a susceptibility to serpent imagery? Presumably because many dangerous snakes inhabited, and still inhabit, those regions of Africa in which our species evolved. Having become established in the human genome at that time, some sense of the danger implicit in serpentine imagery has apparently persisted as archetypal potential in the unconscious of us all, which explains why we are still fearful of snakes (which are of no danger to us) while experiencing no corresponding fear of motor cars (which most certainly are). How could this archetypal propensity have been acquired and passed down to us? Not by being 'engraved' on the psyche by repetition through the millennia of human existence, as Jung proposed (*CW*9i, para. 99), but through the time-hallowed biological rituals of natural selection. What is inherited is not an archetypal image of the snake *per se*, but an archetypal *predisposition* to perceive danger in a configuration of snake-like characteristics – something long, sinuous and slithery, with fangs, and forked and flicking tongue.

Every species evolves in its typical environment and, in the course of its life-cycle, encounters typical situations. As a result of genetic mutations, which occur spontaneously and at random, an individual member of a species will acquire a characteristic which makes it better adapted than its fellows to respond appropriately to a certain typical situation – such as, for example, greater awareness to the danger of serpentine forms. This individual will tend to survive and pass its new genetic material to members of subsequent generations, who, possessing the desirable characteristic, will compete more effectively in the struggle for existence, and enjoy greater reproductive success. As a result, the new attribute eventually becomes established as a standard component in the genetic structure of the species.

In this manner, our archetypal propensities have become adapted to the typical situations encountered in the ancestral environment. The repeated selection of fortuitous mutations, occurring through thousands of generations and over hundreds of thousands of years, has resulted in the present genotype or *archetypal structure* of the human species. And this expresses itself as surely in the structure of the psyche as it does in the anatomy of the human physique.

Accordingly, we are predisposed and prepared to encounter archetypal figures (e.g. mother, child, father, mate), archetypal events (e.g. birth, death, separation from parents, courting) and archetypal objects (e.g. water, sun, fish, predatory animals, and snakes). Each is part of the total endowment granted us by evolution in order to equip us for life in the ancestral environment. Each finds expression in the psyche in dreams, in behaviour, and in myths. Jung summed it up, with his customary lack of biological precision, as follows: 'The collective unconscious is an image of the world that has taken aeons to form. In this image certain features, the archetypes or dominants, have crystallized out in the course of time. They are the ruling powers' (*CW*7, para. 151).

That we all inherit a propensity to respond emotionally to snake-like configurations and to create snake-like images in our dreams suggests that some capacity for generic recognition is built in to our brains. Thus the inherent propensity to recognize the category 'snake', which is apparently shared by all primates, is paralleled by other propensities, such as the human infant's capacity to recognize the generic category 'face' long before it can recognize the particular configuration of a face belonging to a special person to whom it is attached. Indeed, there is now evidence for 'face-detecting' cells in the cerebral cortex. These must in some way be involved in creating the extraordinarily detailed and character-filled faces one can observe in hypnagogic images as one falls asleep. It is not unlikely that there are 'snake-detecting' cells as well.

How is it, then, that a simple alarm system designed to protect our ancestors from dangerous reptiles has become generalized into a symbolic canon so rich as that surrounding the serpent? That one symbol can express so many different meanings must be because the sinuous, slithery schema is susceptible to contamination by other archetypal schemata – e.g. those concerned with sex, evil, healing, etc. The Self constructs its images by mixing the schemata at its disposal as the artist mixes paints of different colour. For example, on 9 March 1868, John Ruskin, who was prone to recurrent sexual nightmares, dreamt *he was showing a snake to his young cousin Joan and making her feel its scales: 'Then she made me feel it, and it became a fat thing, like a leech, and adhered to my hands, so that I could hardly pull it off'* (Rosenberg, 1963, p. 168). In this dream the snake is clearly a phallic symbol expressing guilt, disgust, and horror as well as sexuality. In Kekulé's dream cavorting snakes offered a playful uroboric solution to a scientific conundrum, while in the Garden of Eden the snake symbolized sexual temptation, evil, and rebellion against the will of God. In all these instances, length and sinuosity were basic characteristics to which other meanings were added.

Essentially, the serpent symbolizes the chthonic, most primitive form of energy and power both inside and outside ourselves. The characteristic morphology of the snake, corresponding as it does to the human brain stem and spinal cord, represents the reptilian stage of our evolution. The uroboric snake slumbering in the unconscious, coiled up in the lowest chakra of Kundalini ascent, is the reptilian life still lurking in the nuclei of the nervous system. By the practice of spiritual disciplines, so the yogis believe, the serpent can be induced to uncoil itself and move upwards via the six chakras (wheels of life) until it reaches the seventh, unnamed chakra situated in the forehead (Shiva's third eye). This is yet another metaphor of the individuation process, the elevation of psychic energies and potentials from their lowest origins to their highest modes of expression. Interestingly, the stages are commonly held to be seven in number – the seven terraces of the ziggurat, the seven rungs of the ladder in Mesopotamian tombs, the seven metals of the Mithraic ritual, the seven steps to the alchemical bath, etc. The symbolism of seven links up with the seven planets and the seven deadly sins (together with the seven virtues which compensate for them). Not infrequently, the monsters of myth and legend have seven heads, and to vanquish them is to conquer the evil aspects of planetary influence. Seven seems to owe its particular importance to the fact that it is a *ternary* plus a *quaternary*, but the phyletic significance of this has yet to be determined.

Closely associated with the snake is another symbol of individuation, the Cosmic Tree. That the tree should represent individuation and the heightening of consciousness cannot be unconnected with our ancestors' practice of climbing trees in order to use them as look-out points. But here the symbolism is again complex. In one sense the tree is phallic, erect, and masculine, while the serpent entwined about it is sinuous, dependent, and feminine. In this instance the serpent is Lilith, the temptress of Adam and Eve, Eve herself being related to an archaic Phoenician goddess of the underworld. Like all symbols, these are ordered in the imagination by the archetypal propensity to dichotomize phenomena into opposites: the tree is the Good Tree of Life encircled by the serpent principle of Evil. The serpent is itself similarly dichotomized: the Asklepian staff is encircled by the principle of sickness *and* healing, while the two intertwining snakes of the caduceus of Hermes/Mercury symbolize good and evil, health and sickness. The snake is sacred to many different healing traditions: it can kill *and* cure. The same principle is evident in the practice of homeopathy: administration of the agent that caused the disease is believed to produce the cure.

As with all archetypal symbols, different cultures relate to the serpent in their own characteristic ways. While it represented evil, temptation, and sexual passion to the Hebrews, to the Hindus it was *Shakti*, cosmic power, Nature. However, the capacity of the serpent to inspire awe, dread, and wariness is common to all human communities, and its ability to shed its old skin and replace it with a new one has led to its universal association with the ideas of resurrection, immortality, and the continuance of life.

Finally, the serpent-dragon and the half-human predator are present in so many mythic traditions that they must have been among the earliest creatures to haunt the human imagination: Humbaba (slain by

Gilgamesh and Enkidu), the Minotaur (who required a diet of seven youths and seven maidens to be served up to him every seven years), the Python (overwhelmed by Apollo at Delphi), the Medusa (whose hair is a macabre coiffure of writhing serpents), Cerberus (a three-headed dog with serpents in his throat, the guardian of Hades) all relate us to our primeval origins. 'They allude', as Cirlot says, 'to the base powers which constitute the deepest strata of spiritual geology.' Their natural adversary is the hero and, from the phylogenetic perspective, the struggle between them represents the actual struggle between our hominid ancestors and the dangerous predatory beasts with whom they were forced to compete for the earth's resources. The evolution of intelligence and speech, together with our capacity to make and use weapons, provided us with the necessary 'magic powers' to win the contest.

The battle with the monster is re-fought in our dreams, for, from the psychological perspective, the monster is the 'monster within', the greedy, destructive predator and rampant violator of innocents at the core of the shadow complex in man. The hero's victory over the monster has to be accomplished anew in every generation, for this victory alone can guarantee the maintenance and continuation of the group. As a result, each generation produces its own monsters: Shakespeare's Caliban, the Marquis de Sade's debauchees in *120 Day's of Sodom*, Mary Shelley's monstrous creation in *Frankenstein*, Bram Stoker's *Dracula*, Norman Harris's *Silence of the Lambs*, all play on the archetypal keys of predation, fear, and heroic struggle which are still as responsive in us as they were in our ancestors on the primeval savannahs. Films like *Jaws* and *Jurassic Park* likewise play games with the archetype of the monster-predator and his conquest (Cawson, 1995).

The serpent is thus a symbol of great interest, for it links phylogeny with symbology in a way that not only lends support to Jung's archetypal hypothesis but makes its mode of functioning both comprehensible and hermeneutically useful in the study of dreams. From the neurological standpoint, symbolism, such as that associated with the serpent, keeps open and live the lines of communication between the neocortex and the limbic system, enabling the dialogue between conscious and unconscious functions to occur. Not possessing the gift of speech, the old brain has no recourse but to phrase its communication in symbols, which provide a kind of 'Esperanto' that both brains can understand. The symbol is the medium which is the message. The forebrain, which has speech as well as a gift for telling stories, collaborates, transforming these symbolic messages into narrative form. The result is what we call a dream.

8

DREAMS IN THERAPY

All consciousness separates; but in dreams we put on the likeness of that more universal, truer, more eternal man dwelling in the darkness of primordial night. There he is still whole, and the whole is in him, indistinguishable from nature and bare of all egohood. It is from these all-uniting depths that the dream arises, be it never so childish, grotesque, and immoral.

C. G. JUNG

Dream interpretation, like psychotherapy, is an art and not a science. There is no right or wrong way of doing it. Each school inculcates its own doctrines into its trainees, but, with time and experience, every therapist evolves a personal style. Ultimately, there are as many ways of understanding dreams as there are therapists and clients working on them.

My own approach to dream analysis is essentially that of the 'Classical Jungian School' (Samuels, 1985), but, in what follows, I shall, inevitably, be describing how *I* analyse dreams. So the reader should be warned that I am presenting what must necessarily be a partial view. I am not claiming that my way is the right way, or even the best. It is merely what seems to work most successfully for me and for my patients in achieving what we feel to be a therapeutic outcome.

Not all therapists agree that dream analysis is an indispensable part of therapy: some treat the dream as a side issue, or even a defence against the 'real' issue, which they see as the unconscious relationship between therapist and client – the so-called transference and counter-transference relationship. These practitioners are entitled to their opinion. For my part, I do regard dreams to be of the greatest importance: more than two decades of professional work have taught me that dream analysis leads to the root of a psychological problem (as well as to its possible solution) more surely and more quickly than any other therapeutic method. Dreams always tell more than the ego can know. However careful a history I take, however penetrating my questions, and however honest the replies, I seldom feel that I have got to know somebody until I have listened to their dreams. Then I begin to understand. At the conscious level we may think we know what our problems are, but I have learned that only the unconscious *really* knows. That is why Jung would reply, when people asked him what they should do about their lives, that he had no idea, but he would be willing to listen to their dreams. To him, a dream was 'an expression of an involuntary, unconscious psychic process beyond the control of the conscious mind. It shows the inner truth and reality of the patient as it really is; not as I conjecture it to be, and not as he would like it to be, but *as it is* . . .' (*CW*16, para. 304).

That the dream provides valuable data both about the problem and its history would be important enough, but, as Jung discovered, it does much more: 'The dream rectifies the situation. It contributes the material that was lacking . . .' (*CW*16, para. 482). In other words, it works towards a creative solution. This, in a nutshell, is why the dream is indispensable: it provides the data necessary to establish the history, the diagnosis, the treatment, and not infrequently the cure.

That the unconscious has access to wisdom unavailable to the conscious mind is expressed abundantly in myth and legend. One Jewish story tells how, before we are born, an angel reveals to the soul all things that are in heaven and earth, and everything that our human destiny will bring. Then, at the moment of birth, the angel administers a flip on the nose, and we promptly forget all that we have seen and learned. Only at night does the soul escape from the body, ascend once more to heaven, and return with new life and wisdom to guide us on the morrow. As Edward Whitmont (1990) suggests, this points to 'a dynamic of dreaming that symbolically is akin to "remembering" of smaller or larger pieces of what the soul has "known" prior to birth about its life on earth . . . [These are the] basic existential patterns or archetypal motives that underlie its individual life' (p. 8).

The purpose of analysis in the Jungian view is to mobilize the transcendent function by using dreams and active imagination to grant the ego access to the archetypal world. The relationship between the ego world and the archetypal world is expressed by the belief of many West African peoples in a prenatal contract made by every individual with a heavenly double. Before you enter the world, according to this West African view, you draw up a contract with your double which prescribes what you will do with your life – how long you will live, how you will serve the community, whom you will marry, how many children you will have, and so on. Then, just before you are born, you are led to the Tree of Forgetfulness, which you embrace, and from that moment you lose all conscious recollection of your contract. Nevertheless, you must live up to all your contractual obligations. If you do not, you will become ill, and you will need the help of a diviner, who will use all his skill to make contact with your heavenly double and discover what articles of the contract you are failing to fulfil (Horton, 1961). In our Western society, the role of the diviner is taken over by the analyst.

What the soul in fact 'remembers' in the course of each night's adventure is derived not from heaven but from the Self, that compendium of human know-how wrapped up in the collective unconscious of every man, woman, and child. The Self has its own agenda and, gavel in hand, is ever ready to call the ego to order with a symptom, an emotion, or a dream. The Self's dynamic is towards incarnation: the realization of its eternal humanity in personal actuality, here and now – a purpose that Christians symbolized as God's incarnation in man, Freud caricatured as man's infantile longing for paternal guidance, and Jung identified with the individuation quest.

Psychic Defences

Courage was mine, and I had mystery,
Wisdom was mine, and I had mastery;
To miss the march of the retreating world
Into vain citadels that are not walled.

WILFRED OWEN

The psyche can be compared to a house, in which most of us inhabit the attic, leaving the rest of the building unexplored. Accordingly, our lives are more constrained than they need to be and much of our capacity lies fallow and unused. From time to time, we may feel that we could make more of our lives, attributing our failure to external circumstances – lack of money or opportunity – not realizing that the necessary resources are available in ourselves. Dreams, if we follow them, lead down to the ground floor and the basement, as well as to the landscape beyond. We might not always like what we find there, but, once the exploration is embarked upon, adventures, discoveries and surprises quickly follow. In practice it is seldom a simple process, for dreams do not yield their wisdom in language the ego can easily understand. Only with experience can one learn to appreciate the metaphors, allegories, and dramas through which their messages are conveyed and come to admire their inspired variations on the eternal themes of human existence. For this reason, analysis can be conceived as an educational procedure through which the analysand acquires the art of by-passing the Tree of Forgetfulness and countermanding the angel's flip on the nose.

For some, this can be a hard and painful experience, for the apartment in which they live is not so much an attic as a fortress, a heavily defended citadel, whose commanding officers are called Repression and Denial. Defended from the unconscious as much as from the outer world, these besieged fugitives from life potter round the safe confines of their battlements, filling up their days with little routines. Only at night dare they stray into the world beyond the walls. Dreams, in the early stages of an analysis, can put this graphically: *the dreamer is in a prison or a concentration camp; suddenly the realization dawns that the gates have been standing open and unguarded for years.* It is the analyst's duty to provide a secure enough environment for the patient to risk coming out of her* defensive prison and begin to live in the world.

It would be a mistake to assume that dreams always yield such clear messages, however. Even to the most experienced interpreter

---

* In designating a patient of unspecified sex I shall use 'she', by which I wish to make it clearly understood that I mean not only 'her' but 'him' as well. There is a statistical justification for this, in that, over the years, I have tended to have more women patients than men (the proportion is about 60 per cent to 40 per cent) and I believe my practice is not exceptional in this regard.

some will remain an enigma. This is usually not because they are meaningless but because his understanding does not go deep enough to do them justice. Analysis is an educational process for the analyst no less than for the patient.★

Reporting and Receiving the Dream

For a long time I have made it a rule, when someone tells me a dream and asks my opinion, to say first of all to myself: 'I have no idea what this dream means.' After that I can begin to examine the dream.

C. G. JUNG

Essentially, my approach is, as I say, that shared by other therapists working in the classical Jungian tradition. This means that every appointment is regarded as a social occasion as well as a professional interview, and every patient is treated with the same courtesy and warmth that one usually displays towards people for whom one has a personal regard. Jung laid great stress on this point: 'If the person has a neurosis, that is something extra,' he said, 'but people should be regarded as normal and met socially' (Bennet, p. 32). The consulting room in which patients are received is homely and pleasant, with no 'clinical' feel to it. There is no couch, and both analyst and patient sit in comfortable proximity to one another in similar easy chairs. This arrangement was advocated by Jung as a reaction against the stereo-type of the classical Freudian analyst, sitting silent and aloof, out of sight at one end of the couch, occasionally emitting *ex cathedra* pronouncements, while remaining uninvolved in what the patient is

---

★ Many psychotherapists have dropped the term 'patient', preferring 'client' or 'analysand'. This is because the majority of psychotherapists are not medically qualified and consequently feel uncomfortable about having 'patients'. As a doctor, I feel no such constraint, nor do I regard the status of 'patient' as being in any sense 'inferior' to my own. On the contrary, I regard it as privileged, and I believe that people who consult me should have the *right* to be patients. The healer–patient relationship is, after all, an archetypal relationship, and when it is constellated a healing process is already begun. To inhibit this constellation is, in my view, a therapeutic error of considerable magnitude.

going through. Instead, Jung held analysis to be a *dialectical* procedure, a two-way exchange between two people, who are equally involved.

Normal though the consulting-room may be, it is, nevertheless, a *temenos* which must not be violated, and the hour spent working there is always sacrosanct. No interruptions or disturbances are allowed: no telephone calls, no dogs, no cats, no fish, no taps on the door, only flowers, paintings and books, in a relaxed and comfortable setting, with minimal extraneous noise.

As far as the analyst's attitude is concerned, *openness* is the key. Each patient is unique. General rules, dogmatic ideas, and universal procedures are never to be applied. 'Learn your theories,' Jung taught his students, 'and when the patient walks in through the door forget them.' The analyst needs to be an attentive listener, letting his imagination play with whatever emerges as the session proceeds.

It is not unusual to plunge immediately into dreams. Generally, outer events take precedence for the first ten or fifteen minutes of the hour. Unless this brings up some major issue that the patient wants to work on, we then proceed to the dreams, which, in any case, often have more to say about a particular issue than anything the ego can produce.

If the patient comes with a number of dreams then she is asked to select one and read it out. I like to jot down my own paraphrase of the dream as she does so because it helps me to concentrate on the details of the dream: then I have the salient facts before me as an *aide-mémoire* both for the present and the future. The question of concentration is important, for the imagery of dreams is seductive, and, instead of attending to the patient's dream, one can find oneself flying off on imaginary excursions of one's own.

As the patient reads and I write, I usually find that flickers of light begin to illuminate my understanding: these are kindled as the dream draws together fragments of knowledge I already possess and breathes new life into them. However, I keep these nascent insights to myself and dutifully ask for the patient's associations and the result of any active imagination she may have done. I am not there to tell her about herself but to help her find out. Just as I ask her to choose which dream she wants to work on, so I encourage her to select which parts of the dream seem important to her, before I express any opinion about what seems important to me. This usually brings further illumination. Then the work of amplification begins, as we share the personal, cultural, and archetypal background to the dream. In this manner, without making any specific interpretations of the dream, its meanings begin to emerge as a form of consensus between us both.

Sometimes people bring me a typed or word-processed copy of their dreams, which is helpful, but I still like them to *tell* me the dream, because the manner of the telling can provide important clues to what it is all about. Since the typed copy relieves me of the necessity of writing notes, I go through the text, as the patient reads it out, using a high-lighter to emphasize important details as they strike me. This again helps focus my attention and discipline my imagination in the service of the dream.

When is it appropriate for the analyst to add his contributions to the mix? Again, there are no rules. One learns by experience when the time is right and when the hunch that is forming is the genuine article. If you are wrong, the patient usually lets you know, either then and there or later on, either directly by telling you so or indirectly by means of another dream.

Only when we both feel we have adequately dealt with a dream do we consider passing on to another one. Depending on the length and content of the dreams the patient has brought, we may work on as many as three or four in one session. A particularly significant dream can easily take the whole session, while a 'big dream' may take up a number of sessions. How long is spent on a dream has to be a matter of agreement between analyst and patient.

People vary with regard to the number and quality of the dreams they produce. Usually, once they are engaged in the process, the dreams flow copiously enough, but occasionally they dry up. It is not that the patient has stopped having dreams, she just has difficulty in remembering them. Why should this be? A number of factors may be involved. It can be a defence: the patient wishes to censor or hold back important material that is beginning to emerge but which she would rather not face up to. She may find the burden of being responsible for herself too much to carry, preferring to retreat into passivity and let the analyst do the work for her. ('What am I paying him for, anyway?') It may reflect a lack of commitment, a failure to experience the powerful significance of dreams. It may also be an expression of the transference – a projection on to the analyst, of the demanding, unloving father, for example, and a rebellion against playing the dutiful daughter role. However, dream famine in analysis is by no means always the fault of the patient. The analyst may have been insensitive or inappropriate in his handling of previous dreams and caused the patient to become disenchanted as a consequence.

When patients fail to bring dreams, one has to be particularly careful not to make them feel guilty for 'letting the side down'. It is their session, and they must feel free to use it as they wish, to bring to it and deal with whatever feels important to them. I usually wait until they raise the question about why they are not dreaming before I suggest that we might analyse the possible reasons involved.

At the beginning of treatment, there may be no hidden motive for failing to bring dreams. Dream amnesia is, after all, a natural phenomenon that has to be overcome. Possible ways of doing this are discussed in the next chapter. Perseverance usually brings memorable dreams as its reward.

At the first session, it is my practice to explain to new patients the importance of keeping an accurate record of their dreams, and I ask them to buy a capacious and attractive notebook in which to do this. I advise them to date every dream and to write it on one side of the notebook, leaving the opposite page for their associations and amplifications. I also ask them to write up what transpires in the course of each analytic session – rather like a secretary 'writing up the minutes of the last meeting' – so that the insights gained are not lost and allowed to sink back, uncherished, into the maw of the unconscious. This involves quite a lot of homework for the patient, but, as Jung discovered, the people who do best in analysis are those who work most at it on their own. My own experience confirms this. I have no doubt that time devoted to recording dreams, associations, and interpretative insights is time supremely well spent.

Complexes and Their Transformation

When in a dream I argue with someone, and he refutes me
and enlightens me, it is I who enlighten myself.
GEORG CHRISTOPH LICHTENBERG

Psychotherapy deals with mental processes which are, for the most part, irrational and emotive. Accordingly, what the analyst does and says is governed as much by intuition and feeling as by reason and 'the reality principle'. Reason has little impact on complexes, since they are essentially irrational. Once formed, they persist as emotionally loaded memories clustered round an archetypal core, reproducing their feeling patterns and their influence like an old-fashioned gramophone record, repeating over and over again in the unconscious. Psychotherapy succeeds inasmuch as the complexes are made conscious and changed. To accomplish this is not easy. It requires the formation of a good working relationship between the analyst and patient, an awareness of the transference and counter-transference interactions that are going on within that relationship, and regular work on the analysis of dreams. For dreams provide direct access to the complexes as well as mobilizing the symbolic and emotive energies necessary to change them. From the patient's point of view, successful outcome in therapy requires not only commitment, intelligence, and hard work, but also the willingness to drop self-gratifying illusions and defences and to develop the capacity to be objective about oneself.

When I say that I find dreams indispensable it is because they fulfil both the rational and the irrational goals of therapy: they put the dreamer in touch with the emotionally charged memories of which the complexes are made, they bring her face to face with how the complexes are interfering with her life, and then collaborate with her conscious personality in the work of restructuring them and liberating the archetypal potential for growth and adaptation which has been trapped within them. As this work advances, fundamental changes in perception, feeling, and behaviour become possible and the personality is transformed. To observe this fascinating process is to discover how dreams provide both the raw materials and the catalysts necessary for the transformation to occur.

But it is hard, demanding, and sometimes frightening work, because however much we might wish to get free from our complexes, and however disruptive of our happiness we may know them to be, *our complexes are us*: they are the bones and sinews of the personal psyche, the armature round which our personal identity is built. To begin dismantling these vital structures can be a threat to the security of one's very existence. As John Locke succinctly put it: 'I am what I remember myself being.' This is why self-analysis is, for most of us, an extremely difficult undertaking. One needs the introspective genius of Freud or Jung if one is to get beyond the stage of tinkering. Most of us require the presence of an experienced guide, philosopher, and friend, who, like an alchemist, is willing to devote careful attention to the transformation as it occurs.

Provided the inevitable tensions and anxieties can be tolerated within the context of the analytic relationship, progress begins to be apparent: the emotive memories bonded into a complex gradually lose their crippling intensity, the glue holding them together starts to dissolve, and the archetype at the heart of the complex quickens into life, re-energized by the prospect of more appropriate expression. New symbols emerge and with them new feelings and new perceptions. It is at these moments that the transcendent function comes into its own.

An example will illustrate this extraordinary phenomenon. Early in his analysis, a fifty-five-year-old family doctor brought his first coherent dream. It was as follows: *I am a farmer driving my cattle to market. I'm very irritated with them because they keep stopping or going down the wrong lane. The more furious I get with them, the more hopeless the situation becomes, until an elderly policeman takes over and sorts out the mess. I awake feeling angry, depressed, and close to tears.*

The dreamer was a conscientious and idealistic GP, who came into analysis because he was unhappy in his work and his marriage. He had high blood pressure, drank too much, and was prone to fly off the handle when things went wrong, as they did with increasing frequency. At first, he had little insight as to what was his problem, and had difficulty in remembering his dreams. This was the first example he brought that gave any clear indication of a powerful complex that was influencing his feelings and behaviour.

Initially, he could make no sense of it, until I asked him where in his life he experienced feelings like those released by his dream: then the penny dropped. He felt frustrated and furious, he said, when his patients or his family declined to behave in the way he thought they should. I encouraged him to go into these feelings, and when he did so, a great deal of emotion was generated. When I judged the moment right, I said: 'It's not surprising they rebel and cause you trouble when you drive them like cattle to market.' Suddenly furious, he shouted: 'I DON'T drive them like cattle!' 'Are you sure?' I asked. 'Dreams present things as they are: no one else made you into a farmer.' His anger ebbed away as he took this on board, and then the tears began.

The dream, and the emotions it released, led us back to his father complex. As a child he was greatly in awe of his father, an energetic, charismatic, extremely successful businessman, with a gift for manipulating everyone into carrying out his wishes. My patient modelled himself on his father, hoping to win his love and approval by complying with his wishes and trying to be like him. The dream image of the farmer driving his cattle to market was a perfect allegory of this pattern of dominance, control, and manipulation that the patient had thus acquired.

This realization hit him with the force of genuine insight, and he was able to face the fact that the dream expressed exactly how he was treating his patients and his family. It was also an allegory of how he was treating himself, for he drove and manipulated himself every bit as much as anyone else.

That was not all, however. What were we to make of the elderly policeman? This figure provides the lysis of the dream and the solution to the patient's problem. He is an embodiment of the transcendent function at work. We had therefore to take him very seriously. As we worked on him, we came to see that he represented two things: (1) the father he always wanted, but never had, and (2) the sort of father that he himself would like to be – kindly, understanding, capable, able to deal appropriately and without fuss with any situation that might arise. In other words, the elderly policeman carried all those attributes of the father archetype that the personal father lacked. These attributes had persisted as unconscious potential in the Self. The task of the analysis was to integrate this archetypal dynamic in the personal life of the dreamer. I believe we succeeded. But it took three years of extremely hard work.

If such work is to be fruitful, it demands regular encounters with the unconscious. Persisted in over months and years, this labour results in development of the personality and a raised level of consciousness. Recurrent acts of compensation of the ego by the Self serve the adaptive function of dreams: the ego experiences a problem or a conflict; the unconscious counters by presenting material necessary to bring about an adaptive resolution; this, in turn, enables the individual to confront further problems; these elicit yet another compensatory response from the unconscious, and so on. These are the recurrent cycles through which individuation proceeds.

But before any major transformation can occur, there has to be an awakening to one's true condition. Many traditions teach this. The Zen *koan* was designed to awaken students from their intellectual torpor – their tired, conventional way of seeing things. The programme for spiritual development devised by Gurdjieff prescribed that the neophyte needed to be shocked and provoked into awareness. Dreams can certainly perform this function, because they stir up powerful emotions which act as catalysts to change. That is why they are so crucial to the practice of psychotherapy. For it is not possible to induce radical change in basic personality structures through discussions at the ego level, or through deliberate exertion of the will. It demands the engagement of feeling and the courage to throw oneself and one's complexes into the melting pot. In dreams, thinking is more flexible and emotions are more dynamic than in wakefulness, and this increased fluidity makes it possible to try out more innovative possibilities than can occur in waking life. To engage the symbols arising from the unconscious, therefore, becomes a matter of great therapeutic relevance, for symbols are energized thoughts, they provide the necessary drive to transform psychic structures from a dysfunctional to an adaptive mode of application. Without such engagement, emotions remain untouched, and little of lasting importance can be changed. Through the medium of the dream, the conscious *thesis* and unconscious *antithesis* yield the *synthesis* of the transcendent function and the process of individuation is advanced. The product of this symbolic *dialectic* is usually increased security, sometimes personal enrichment, and, occasionally, happiness. Life has taught me that one is more likely to find these precious gifts in oneself than by questing for them in the outer world. It is the old story of the rabbi who scoured the world for the Greatest Good only to find it on returning home in his own humble abode.

The Personal Myth

Myth is more individual and expresses life more precisely than does science.

C. G. JUNG

In the course of growing up, each of us tends to develop a personal mythology, which is created out of the myths current in our culture in such a way as to meet our personal psychodynamic needs (Feinstein, 1979; Ullman and Zimmerman, 1983). These personal myths are belief systems which perform much the same function for an individual as a collective myth does for a society. They can be either effective or dysfunctional, appropriate to present circumstances or hopelessly out of date. A good personal myth is an adaptive one: it affords an emotionally satisfying synthesis of one's personality structure with one's life circumstances, and promotes effective adjustment to reality. A dysfunctional myth, on the other hand, is a maladapted belief system which results in the kind of unhappiness or misfortune that commonly brings people into analysis.

The analyst will often become aware of a patient's personal myth long before she is able to articulate it for herself. This is because she has been in the grip of it for so long that it seems to constitute reality for her: that is the way things are; they could not be otherwise. The myth may become apparent in the initial sessions of history-taking: certain recurrent patterns emerge which are indicative of the myth the patient is caught up in. More usually, it becomes apparent through work on the first dreams. As often as not, it can be summed

202

up in a single sentence: 'I am the sort of girl who always falls in love with the wrong man.' 'I am the sort of man who gets the show on the road, and then is let down by his colleagues.' 'I am the sort of woman who makes things happen for other people, but can never make them happen for herself.' 'People never recognize that I am a misunderstood genius, but one day I'm going to do something that will astonish them.' 'I am the sort of person who makes few demands, but people never live up to my expectations, and I am constantly disappointed in life.'

Most people, I suspect, go through life without pausing to consider what their personal myth might be. This is of no consequence when the myth is conducive to a reasonably happy and adjusted life. An unexamined dysfunctional myth, however, can effectively wreck all chances of personal fulfilment. The surest means of becoming conscious of your myth is to pay regular attention to your dreams. Failing that, you may have to await some major crisis to bring you face to face with it. Not infrequently, a crisis is a call to transform one's personal mythology: a long-held myth has become outdated or maladaptive and the psyche has to construct an alternative myth better fitted to the altered circumstances. This can involve profound inner conflict and stress, particularly when contrasting myths are held at the same time. The dialectic of myth (*thesis*) and counter-myth (*antithesis*) has to be worked through to a new *synthesis*, and without dreamwork or analytic help this can be a long and wearisome process which may never be satisfactorily achieved. People with chronic anxieties or recurring depressive states are in the unfortunate position of inhabiting a battleground between conflicting personal mythologies which have yet to be reconciled. Dreams provide invaluable intelligence into the strength and efficiency of the opposing forces, because they send nightly reports from the front line. Making the conflict conscious through dreamwork is to bring both sides to the conference table in the hope of achieving an armistice and working out the details of a lasting peace.

The Psyche, Objective and Subjective

One should never forget that one dreams in the first place, and almost to the exclusion to all else, of oneself.

C. G. JUNG

The most striking evidence that dreams speak with the voice of the species is their incorruptible objectivity: they concern themselves with the details of our lives, but they also remain true to their suprapersonal 'otherworldliness'. They tell us the sort of home truths that would be unacceptable from any other source: they lampoon our most cherished vanities, and present the facts of our mortality in a manner that shows they view personal death as a matter of little consequence. Nor are they any respecters of persons: their tactlessness about such figures as one's spouse, boss, or analyst can be quite breathtaking! They are honest to the point of ruthlessness. As the analysis proceeds, the unconscious makes it perfectly clear that it has no concern with the ego/persona of the analyst or dreamer, but only with the life issues constellated between them. This is why working with dreams can be a humbling experience, and why it is so valuable. For dreams are mirrors in which we see ourselves as we really are, warts and all: they enable us to see those spots where we are most blind; make us aware of those areas where we are most unconscious; show us up as stupid when we think we are most wise. Dreams speak with such objectivity because they have 'seen it all before'; their 'memory' is so much longer than ours: it goes back millions of years. This gives them their transpersonal perspective, which is part biological and part religious.

Jung often spoke of the collective unconscious as the *objective psyche* to distinguish it from the personal ('subjective') psyche. It is the objective psyche that speaks with the authority of the species, while the subjective psyche speaks out of the experience of the ego. Through the dream, each enters into a dialogue with the other, and their regular nocturnal communion is the crux of the individuation process.

The objective psyche conducts us through the stages of life, compensates our narrow ego limitations, and corrects the illusion that we are a simple unity. One has only to work a brief time with dreams to realize that, far from being a unitary individual, one is a crowd – a conglomeration of disparate personalities existing within one psychophysical entity, all chattering away, all with their own needs, wishes, intentions, and past history. To create some order amid such babel we tend to polarize this intrapsychic population into opposing camps – good v. bad, masculine v. feminine, familiar v. strange. Alliances and conflicts occur between these various groups, this one being favoured and developed, that one rejected and re-pressed, the former contributing to the persona (the personality we show to the world) and the latter cast into the shadow (the personality we keep hidden from view). Analysis which takes individuation as its goal makes these polarities conscious and recognizes them as parts of a total Gestalt, as individual components of a suprapersonal unity. The great world religions equate this realization with enlightenment, the sense of being at one with God, which is celebrated in primordial symbols – the mandala, the cross, and the figures of Christ, Moham-med, and the Buddha.

It is as if each of us is a boarding-house keeper with a large number of lodgers, all very different from one another, some easy-going and friendly, some difficult and demanding, others frankly impossible. Good sense dictates that we should get to know them and try to get on with them, for each one has tenure for life. To individuate requires virtuosity in the celebration of paradox; it demands wisdom, tact, honesty, and a capacity to perceive the one through the many.

The multiplicity of symbols in dreams reflects this plurality of personalities within the psyche, each of which, like Paul MacLean's three brains in one, carries its own charge of consciousness and has its own part to perform in the never-ending psychic drama on which we eavesdrop every night. For this reason, it is always a productive exercise to consider figures and symbols in dreams as representing parts of oneself. When one really gets down to them, dreams are, first and foremost, about *ourselves:* everything one does, says, or tackles in outer reality is conditioned by the complexes, the part-personalities, the myths and hidden dynamics operating in the Self. Failure to link a dream to the Self and to see it as a statement rich in subjective implications is to miss the main point.

Subjective interpretation assists the patient to acknowledge neglected and repressed parts of herself (the shadow) and to deal with the guilt invariably attached to them; it enables her to recognize and take back those psychic aspects that she unconsciously projects on to others; it heightens her sense of personal responsibility and encourages the development of confidence, making her self-esteem less dependent on the praise and approval of those around her.

A forty-year-old woman, whose opinion of herself was entirely at the mercy of how she felt people perceived her from day to day, dreamt that *she was back at school being publicly humiliated by a teacher. 'Why do I come here?' she wondered in her dream. 'I don't need this. Why do I put up with it?'* With this dream she began to see that it was *she* who made herself vulnerable to people's opinions by projecting on to them the 'schoolmarm' superego in herself. As she worked at becoming responsible for this she was able to avoid placing her self-concept at the mercy of others and to confront the critical parent in her psyche. A major development occurs in psychotherapeutic progress when people can give up their dependency on the authority of others and find their own authority in themselves. Dreamwork with inner figures is, I believe, the best way to bring this about.

Far from being a self-indulgence, as critics of analysis sometimes maintain, such work promotes the capacity to relate to others. Committed to adaptation, the Self works through dreams to promote adjustment to society and to individuals of special significance to us, and, through their objective subjectivity, dreams reveal how we typically handle relationships and help us find more appropriate ways of conducting our lives. A thirty-five-year-old teacher, who was friendless and isolated and spent much of his free time cooking solitary meals, dreamt that *a faceless man was putting youngsters through a kitchen blender.* Working on the dream brought home to him the extent to which he homogenized experience and failed to treat people (both inner figures and outer ones) as people. After eighteen months of analysis, he had a dream in which *he found himself selecting and polishing apples from a basket, taking pleasure in their individual appearance.* This dream coincided with development of an interest in a young woman on his school staff, and he felt sure these events were connected.

Are dreams invariably to be interpreted subjectively? If I dream of a friend lying on the ground for people to wipe their shoes on him, or see him trotting about among a flock of sheep wearing a black fleece, is the dream describing me as a doormat or a black sheep, or is it describing him? It could be either or both. Jung argued that a subjective interpretation was usually justified, unless the figure in the dream bore such a close resemblance to an actual person in the dreamer's life, that it could be calling attention to something about that person that the ego was not aware of. This can indeed be the case. For example, it is not uncommon for a loyal and trusting wife to dream that her husband is having an affair, or for a thoroughly honest businessman to dream that he is being cheated by a colleague, only to discover, on investigation, that both intimations are true. Experiences of this kind demonstrate that we have access to intuitive knowledge in our dreams that we overlook in waking life. But even in these instances, the subjective element is usually present, and before allowing the loyal wife or honest business-man to become too self-righteously indignant, it is important to ask them to consider whether there could also be an adulterer or a crook in themselves.

Dreams commonly condense both objective and subjective refer-ences in the same figure – as, for example, when a man dreams of his wife as a whore: it may well be that sometimes she behaves like a whore, but in this she could be conforming to his own whorish anima. If the dreamer learns to deal with the whore in himself he may be less inclined to evoke such behaviour in his spouse. In practice, I find it helpful to look at every dream from both points of view before attempting to formulate its meaning, much as a pilot checks his instruments before taking off so as to ensure that he is not missing something important. Dreams are subjective phenomena reflecting how we perceive people in our lives, but in fact they often possess similar qualities *in actuality* to those that we project on to them. It is as if they present us with a hook to hang projections on. The dream-maker in us is like a magpie or an artist in collages: it collects objects from the outer world to fulfil its own purposes. It lifts images, events, and people from the environment in order to symbolize the inner state it wishes to represent: it is a symbolic kleptomaniac.

A man whose business was on the point of bankruptcy, largely as a result of his own inefficiency, dreamt *he was visited by the headmaster of his son's school. The headmaster declared that the boy was inattentive and dreamy, did not prepare adequately for his lessons, and, if he wished to remain at the school, he would have to pull his socks up.* On waking, the dreamer resolved to give the boy a good talking to, for he had agreed with the headmaster in his dream. However, he had been in analysis for six months, and on his way down to breakfast he realized that the dream related as much to himself as to his son. He needed to heed the headmaster (his own superego) and do something about the dreamy, inattentive boy in himself. Over breakfast he had a more productive conversation with the boy than would otherwise have been possible, for he was able to admit his own contribution to his son's poor school performance. As Jung observed, when we want to change something in a child, we should first consider whether we had not better change something in ourselves.

In all these examples, the dreams have performed a compensatory function, in that they have incorporated something that was lacking from consciousness: each dream presented to the ego a parcel of under-utilized potential that it needed in order to live more effectively. What the dream brings up may be frightening, disturbing, and depressing, as well as life-enhancing and enriching, and accepting it is by no means always an agreeable task. But, however painful, the rewards of perseverance can be great. In most of us, valuable part-personalities have been repressed and rendered inaccessible in the course of growing up because they were felt to be unacceptable to our family. It is these rejected aspects of the Self that make up what Jung called the shadow complex. To suffer the guilt, shame, despair, and anxiety of restoring them to consciousness is to take the first step towards wholeness. As Jung said, 'it is apparently more important to nature that one should have consciousness, understanding, than to avoid suffering' (*Zarathustra Seminars*, p. 71).

The Shadow

*'I do not think I ever met Mr Hyde?' asked Utterson. 'Oh dear no sir. He never **dines** here,' replied the butler. 'Indeed, we see very little of him on this side of the house; he mostly comes and goes by the laboratory.'*

ROBERT LOUIS STEVENSON,
The Strange Case of Dr Jekyll and Mr Hyde

Although it can be depressing to deal with a shadow dream, the consequences of not dealing with it can be far worse – for depression is the result of feeling 'put down' about oneself, the result of refusing to face up to the unacceptable aspects of one's own personality. Dreamwork provides the opportunity to make good the deficiency. It is the very thing one feels worst about that it is most important to accept.

In the early weeks of an analysis, it is quite common for a patient to bring a dream in which she finds herself in a house, outside which there is some potentially dangerous or sinister figure who wants to get in. Alarmed, the dreamer goes around the house bolting and barring all the doors and windows but, as she does so, an uneasy feeling grows that these actions are futile and that, whatever she does, the intruder will succeed in intruding.

Presented with such a dream, the analyst encourages the dreamer to find out more about the intruder, in the hope that through free association and active imagination she will begin to come to terms with this sinister figure and recognize it as part of herself. This can be difficult to achieve, for the very good reason that the shadow possesses qualities that the superego (the internalized parental authority) loathes and despises: normally one denies these qualities in oneself, preferring to project them unconsciously outside on to those whom one perceives as socially undesirable. This is why the hostile figure in the dream lurks *outside* the house; but it is characteristic of the individuation process that the shadow should evidently wish to abandon its outsider status and *intrude* – i.e. to gain entrance to the conscious personality in order to promote wholeness.

While I reject the Freudian view of dreams as being solely the

209

expression of repressed or censored wishes, I do, nevertheless, accept that shadow dreams present issues which we normally choose to avoid because they are uncomfortable and we would rather not face them. There can be no doubt that we all make use of ego-defence mechanisms from time to time, and the more neurotic we are the more use we make of them. But when, with analytic guidance, the shadow is acknowledged and 'owned', an important change comes over the personality as a whole: not only do we stop running away from our own aggressiveness, but we take possession of it, assume responsibility for it, and use it, one hopes, *ethically*.

At the core of the shadow complex is the archetype of the Enemy. Learning to live on good terms with 'the enemy within' means that one is less likely to project it on to other people, and, as a result, one makes one's minute contribution to peace and understanding in the world. What happens to the ego's relationship with the shadow is a transformation from the agonic to the hedonic mode: instead of controlling (repressing) it or running away from it (denial), the ego initiates dialogue with the shadow, and, by confronting it and making efforts to befriend it, enters into a hedonic bond with it, thus rendering its energy available to the total personality.

Recognizing parts of the Self as personifications of complexes – such as the shadow, the animus, the anima, the father, the mother, the child – making them conscious, and relating to them as one would to *real* personalities, creates not only greater strength and harmony within, but improves one's capacity to interact with people in the outer world as well. The ability to relate to members of both sexes is enhanced. We become more comfortably at ease in the world of social relationships generally.

Although the shadow is usually experienced as disturbing, dangerous and hostile, this is not invariably the case. Only rejected parts of the personality are felt to be negative. The shadow also carries potential that is positive, for it incorporates parts of the Self that have remained unactualized in life because personal circumstances have not provided the necessary opportunities for its development. Jung told a story which nicely illustrates what I mean.

'Once, on a train journey, I found myself with two strangers in the dining car. The one was a fine-looking old gentleman, the other a middle-aged man with an intelligent face. I gathered from their conversation that they were military men, presumably an old general and his adjutant. After a long silence the old man suddenly said to his companion, "Isn't it odd what you dream sometimes? I had a remarkable dream last night. I dreamed *I was on parade with a number of young officers, and our commander-in-chief was inspecting us. Eventually he came to me, but instead of asking a technical question he demanded a definition of the beautiful. I tried in vain to find a satisfactory answer, and felt most dreadfully ashamed when he passed on to the next man, a very young major, and asked him the same question. This fellow came out with a damned good answer, just the one I would have given if only I could have found it.* This gave me such a shock that I woke up." Then, suddenly and unexpectedly addressing me, a total stranger, he asked, "D'you think dreams can have a meaning?" "Well," I said, "some dreams certainly have a meaning." "But what could be the meaning of a dream like that?" he asked sharply, with a nervous twitch of the face. I said, "Did you notice anything peculiar about this young major? What did he look like?" "He looked like me, when I was a young major." "Well, then," I said, "it looks as if you had forgotten or lost something which you were still able to do when you were a young major. Evidently, the dream was calling your attention to it." He thought for a while, and then he burst out, "That's it, you've got it! When I was a young major I was interested in art. But later this interest got swamped by routine." Thereupon he relapsed into silence, and not a word more was spoken' (*CW*17, para. 187).

Later, Jung gathered that the old gentleman was indeed a general, with a reputation for crustiness and a fussy obsession with military detail. It would have been far better for him (and his men), Jung commented, had he retained and developed his artistic interests, instead of drowning himself in routine.

Here again, we have an example of a dream attempting to compensate for a cramped conscious orientation by drawing attention to a neglected part of the Self. But it needed the intervention of an analyst to make the message available to the dreamer. The general was sufficiently impressed by his dream, however, to recount it to his companion, and it is just possible that, even without Jung's intervention, something of its compensatory significance might have dawned on him.

Are *all* dreams, then, compensatory? Jung wrote as if they were, but experience has taught me that in this respect he overgeneralized. As we have seen, dreams can indeed be compensatory, but this is not invariably the case. As a result of their extensive studies, Hall and his co-workers concluded that dreams usually reflect the dreamer's behaviour in waking life. It is a commonplace of analytic practice that depressed people tend to have depressed dreams, in which rays of sunshine are nowhere to be seen. Anxious people have more anxiety dreams than unanxious people, and so on. Dreams often seem to go along with the prevailing mood or attitude of consciousness. It is as if they were saying: this is the way things are. Dreams concern themselves with our daily activities, presumably in order to keep us up to scratch: a nurse dreams of treating patients, a policeman of outwitting criminals, an athlete of running marathons, etc. It seems that compensation is one of the important things that dreams can do, but, on the whole, compensatory dreams occur only when there is something that needs to be compensated.

The primary goals of dreams are adaptation and self-completion; compensation is one of the means employed to achieve these ends. However, the *possibility* that a dream is compensating a one-sided conscious attitude should always be kept in mind, for only if one is constantly alert to this possibility will one go beyond the narrow preoccupations of ego–consciousness to enter into communion with split-off parts of the psyche and encounter 'thoughts that were not thought and feelings that were not felt by day' (*CW*8, para. 300).

The Persona

The persona is that which in reality one is not, but which oneself as well as others think one is.

C. G. JUNG

When people are threatened by shadow dreams, it is because they do not wish to face up to their implications, preferring to keep unacceptable aspects of themselves hidden for fear of losing status or suffering rejection. The hidden shadow qualities are commonly concealed behind the persona, the actor's 'mask' of social adaptation we put on when we go out to meet the world. The more guilty or insecure we are about the shadow, the more prone we are to develop a persona whose *raison d'être* is to disguise, to camouflage, and to deceive. Dreams express this dilemma in plots and images, providing the opportunity not only to integrate the shadow but also to develop a less defensive, more honest persona.

In so far as the persona is a structure behind which we all defend ourselves from time to time, it is of great phylogenetic antiquity. The capacity to survive through deception (and, indeed, to survive by detecting deception) has existed for many millions of years. Some creatures lure others to their deaths with false colours, patterns, and scents, while others escape by assuming brilliant disguises or by feigning death. In human beings such techniques are regarded as shameful, except when used against an enemy in wartime, when they can incur the highest praise. In normal social life, however, only psychopaths seem able to practise deception as a routine without feeling guilt. Neurotics, who are driven to it out of desperation, live in constant fear of being 'unmasked'. Like psychotics, they may suffer from feelings of being transparent, have dreams in which they are naked, their deformities exposed, their smoke screen penetrated, their façade pulled down, and the full horror of their emptiness and shame exposed for all to see. The compulsion to maintain a deceptive image of oneself – a 'false self' as Winnicott called it – can also give rise to dreams of being a double agent, or a criminal on the run. It is commonly associated with a paranoid sensitivity to the actions and words of others, and with the need to check in a compulsive manner that one's cover has not been blown, in the hope that one can continue to operate undetected.

In these circumstances, the opportunity to share one's plight through dreamwork with an analyst can be life-saving. When the dreams have made the problem dramatically clear, the patient is assisted to acknowledge her 'guilty secret', and through the analyst's acceptance and affirmation, can find a way out of the impasse. This is the analytic equivalent of confession and redemption.

Jung found that confession of the guilty secret marked the most important moment in therapy. With this crucial event, the therapeutic alliance was forged and constructive treatment could begin in earnest. Dreams commonly make the confession possible by incorporating associative references to the secret, which, when worked on, bring the patient to the point where she can dare to share it. Enabling this to happen can demand great tact from the analyst, who should be guided by his intuition and not be over-zealous in bringing matters to a head. Getting the guilty secret acknowledged without loss of status or self-esteem is the fateful turning point: the success or failure of an analysis can hang on how this moment is handled. Integrity, as John Beebe (1992) has pointed out, is the key. The analyst must have it, so that the patient perceives him justly to be worthy of confidence and trust. There also has to be integrity in his theory and practice: there can be no fall back on Freudian 'resistance' theories in order to 'put one over' on the patient. Dreams which reveal conflict between shadow and persona point to a loss of integrity in the personality of the dreamer. There has to be integrity in the analytic relationship if this disintegrity is to be healed.

The Contrasexual Complex

Every man carries within him the eternal image of the woman, not the image of this or that woman, but a definite feminine image . . . Woman is compensated by a masculine element and therefore her unconscious has, so to speak, a masculine imprint . . .

C. G. JUNG

Since dreams are self-centred and are populated with representatives of our own part-personalities, it is not surprising to learn that male figures predominate in the dreams of men (Hall and Domhoff, 1963). However, representatives of the opposite sex are also commonly present in everyone's dreams – particularly in the dreams of women. Are *these* to be interpreted subjectively too? Jung's answer is that they are to be interpreted both subjectively and objectively.

Of all the archetypal systems enabling us to adapt to the typical circumstances of human life, that involved in relating to the opposite sex is the most crucial. Jung called this contrasexual archetype the *animus* in women and the *anima* in men. As the feminine aspect of man and the masculine aspect of woman, they function as a pair of opposites (the *syzygy*) in the unconscious of both, profoundly influencing the relations of all men and women with each other.

Jung also found that in practice both anima and animus act in dreams and in the imagination as mediators of the unconscious to the ego, so providing a means for inner as well as outer adaptation. He described them as 'soul-images' and the 'not-I', for they are experienced as something mysterious and numinous, possessing great power. The more unconscious the anima or animus, the more likely it is to be projected – the psychodynamic process responsible for the experience of 'falling in love'. For this reason, Jung called the contrasexual complex the 'projection-making factor'.

Bequeathed to us by our evolutionary history, the anima and animus are indispensable to the survival of the species, for they are responsible for initiating and maintaining the heterosexual bond. When performing this psychobiological function in dreams they are to be objectively interpreted. But their subjective manifestations as psychic components are no less important for personality development, especially when, as not infrequently happens, they are neglected or repressed on account of one's upbringing and, as a result, become contaminated by the shadow. When this occurs, feminine qualities which, in themselves, are morally neutral are, nevertheless, experienced as 'bad' and are repressed in the male, and masculine qualities are similarly repressed in the female, with the consequent experience of guilt if the contrasexual qualities are detected. This was more prone to happen in the patriarchal climate in which Jung was working, but men and women continue to experience guilt in contravening gender stereotypes, although to a less crippling extent than in the past.

It is precisely those negative aspects of the animus/anima, which have been actively denied or repressed in response to environmental pressures, that can vitiate relations with the opposite sex, disturb the inner balance of the psyche, and block all genuine creativity. For this reason, individuation demands that these neglected or despised parts of the contrasexual complex should be confronted and assimilated.

Figures of the opposite sex, whether erotically inspired or not, symbolize energies which are least accessible to the conscious psyche, but, with committed work in analysis, these vital resources can be mobilized in the service of the psyche as a whole. As the contrasexual attributes become available to the conscious personality, so a man's *Logos* is complemented by a refined capacity for intimacy, and a woman's *Eros* is tempered with rational purpose and intellectual understanding.

Some of the most poignant as well as the most powerful dreams encountered in analytic practice deal with the ego's relationship with the contrasexual aspect of the Self. For example, a depressed business-man in his forties dreamt that *a thin, waif-like girl was lying terminally sick in bed. He sat beside her weeping, holding her hand, and willing her to live.* The dreamer was an ex-commando, who had been decorated for bravery, and married three times. He was 'all man' and his anima had been neglected, deprived, and undernourished to the point of virtual extinction. Hence his depression and his inability to sustain a heterosexual relationship. The dream drew his attention to this deeply unconscious part of himself – his sensitivity, feeling, capacity to appreciate beauty, love, and personal commitment. He needed to give it succour, protect it, enable it to survive and to grow. The pathetic waif represented his soul image and because of his neglect of her she was at death's door.

A dream in which the animus is clearly contaminated by the shadow was dreamt by a thirty-eight-year-old single woman, a partner in a large legal practice, who suffered from agoraphobia: *I know that a tramp is lying in wait for me in a ditch beside the road I take when I drive home from work. I decide the only thing to do is drive very fast when I reach the place where he is lurking but, to my horror, as I approach, he rises up from the ditch and staggers into the road in front of me, waving his arms to make me stop. I panic. The only thing to do is to drive straight for him and make him jump out of the way. But he is too slow and with a sickening crunch I drive over him. I look in my driving mirror and see him lying in the road, convulsed in his death agony. Feeling that my life is over, and tortured with guilt, I drive to the nearest police station to summon an ambulance and give myself up on a charge of manslaughter.* The dream shows how far removed her conscious personality was from the contrasexual complex in herself, with the result that she feared men as being potentially hostile and dangerous and preferred to avoid them if she possibly could. In her analysis, she had to confront this issue, which had its origins in her childhood relationship with her alcoholic, unpredictable, and sexually promiscuous father. After nearly two years' work with a male analyst, animus figures began to appear in her dreams who were better disposed to her and to whom she was able to relate. This coincided with a gradual improvement in her personal relations with her male colleagues and clients.

The Self

The self is not only the centre, but also the whole circumference which embraces both conscious and unconscious; it is the centre of this totality, just as the ego is the centre of consciousness.

C. G. JUNG

The organizing genius at the heart of the total personality Jung called the Self, often using a capital S to distinguish it from the 'self' of everyday usage (which refers to the ego or persona). The Self embodies the entire archetypal endowment inherited by every human being. The Self is responsible for implementing the blueprint of life through each stage of the life-cycle and for bringing about the best adjustment that individual circumstances will allow. Its *raison d'être* is individuation. Though it has evident biological goals, the Self also seeks fulfilment in the spiritual achievements of art and religion as well as in the inner life of the soul and dreams. As a result it can be experienced as a profound mystery, a secret resource, or a manifestation of God within. It has been identified with the notion of deity in numerous cultures and finds symbolic expression in such universal configurations as circular or quadratic forms (the mandala – like those of Tibetan Buddhism or the Wheel of Hinduism), the jewel of great price (a great diamond, the Islamic 'Blessed Pearl', the Buddhist 'Jewelled Net of Indra'), the rose or lotus (the Golden Flower of Taoism), a sacred vessel, urn, or *vas*, a quaternity (any association of four people or any configuration stressing the figure four), the Royal Couple (representing the reconciliation of masculine and feminine opposites, the Yang and the Yin), a great mythic or historic figure (such as Krishna, Buddha, Jesus, Mohammed), and many others. In Jung's view, the Self provides the means of personal adjustment not only to the social environment but also to God, the cosmos, and the life of the spirit. Accordingly, he called it the *archetype of archetypes*.

The Self is most likely to achieve representation in dreams in a formal, highly structured form, such as a mandala, at times when the ego is in chaos or in crisis. A man whose wife had left him for another man, taking their young daughter with her, dreamt that he was watching the sunrise from a mountain resort in Switzerland. *As he watched, the sun developed the face of a huge clock with large Roman numerals and hands which revolved rapidly and steadily, like a radar scanner.* When he told me the dream, we both recognized that we had a 'big dream' on our hands, and we worked hard on it for an entire session. The message was that, although bereft, his essential humanity remained, that a new episode of life was dawning, that time would heal his grief, that his vision (consciousness) would be extended (the radar scanner), and that his individuation would continue in analysis (Switzerland = the home of Jung; the mountain = spiritual aspiration). The dream was indeed significant, for it gave him the courage and the necessary perspective to go on with his life.

Although the Self only occasionally puts in an appearance in the form of a numinous symbol, its presence is always implicit, for every dream is a potential contributor to the individuation process. This may not be apparent in dreams considered in isolation from one another, but examination of a series of dreams stretching over several months invariably gives the game away. Again and again they return to issues as yet unresolved, aspects of the Self as yet unlived. For this reason, dreamwork has to be kept up regularly and over long periods of time if Self-potential is to be realized and built into the personality as a whole. With practice, dream personalities become more accessible and one gets on more intimate terms with them. Big dreams come more frequently, intense emotions are released, and one is more prone to wake in the morning with the certainty that events of great significance have occurred in the night. The inner riches which these recurrent encounters reveal can only be appreciated when they have been experienced. From our parochial world of ego thoughts and emotions, the full range of human experience becomes accessible.

One is drawn into the powerful fields of force constellated between the archetypal opposites of love and hate, wisdom and folly, joy and despair. It is not an easy or comfortable task, but, once engaged in, one knows it to be a soul-stirring encounter far too important to be shirked. To reach this stage is to have one's neat theoretical assumptions blown to pieces. The archetypes cease to be hypothetical concepts, they become powers, suprapersonal forces like the gods and daimons of old, that seize hold of one's life and determine one's destiny. These overwhelming emotions are not personal creations that we invent anew each time round. They are pre-determined patterns of highly charged feeling that are released when archetypal energies are roused. To take on the unconscious is to realize that there is something truly greater than the little ego, that bobs about like a cork on the surface of the sea. 'The ego is to the Self,' said Jung, 'as the moved to the mover.' A truth that was confirmed for him in a dream:

I was walking along a little road through a hilly landscape; the sun was shining and I had a wide view in all directions. Then I came to a small wayside chapel. The door was ajar, and I went in. To my surprise there was no image of the Virgin on the altar, and no crucifix either, but only a wonderful flower arrangement. But then I saw that on the floor in front of the altar, facing me, sat a yogi — in lotus posture, in deep meditation. When I looked at him more closely, I realized that he had my face. I started in profound fright, and awoke with the thought: 'Aha, so he is the one who is meditating me. He has a dream, and I am it.' I knew that when he awakened, I would no longer be (MDR, p. 299).

He felt that the yogi was meditating his earthly form, an idea that was symbolized differently in another dream which came fourteen years later, when he experienced himself as the projection of a UFO, shaped like a magic lantern. He understood both dreams as parables: they revealed that the Self assumes human shape in order to enter three-dimensional existence. The unconscious is the generator of the empirical personality: 'Our unconscious existence is the real one and our conscious world a kind of illusion . . . This state of affairs resembles very closely the Oriental conception of Maya. Unconscious wholeness therefore seems to me the true *spiritus rector* of all biological and psychic events' (MDR, p. 300).

To embark on the journey of individuation is to live *sub specie aeternitatis*. This does not mean that one lives in a state of passive obedience to the Self; on the contrary, the ego must accept full responsibility for how it responds to all that occurs. The unconscious proposes; the ego disposes. To take on a symbol is to take on the intentions of the Self, to cross a bridge from the known to the unknown, but, if one is not, like Theseus and Peirithous, to become stuck forever to the rocks of Hades, one must be determined to return. What the unconscious produces the ego responds to, and out of the dialogue that ensues between them a new position is attained. Conscious and unconscious then become two poles of a homeostatic system, and it is the purpose of dreamwork to bring about a more balanced and more conscious relationship between them. Interaction between these equal and opposing poles yields a psychic state that is both richer and better informed than one based on either set of intentions. The ultimate position is neither one nor the other but a third previously unimagined possibility, which negates neither the conscious nor the unconscious position but does justice to them both. And it is this achievement that Jung attributed to the *transcendent function* of the psyche.

For his life-long concern with transcendent values, Jung has been dismissed as a 'mystic' – as if mysticism were a completely useless mode of apperception. If one works seriously with dreams for any length of time it is hard not to develop some degree of mystical awareness, for the dreams become more profound, more mythic, more 'religious', and expose one to experiences unmistakably suprapersonal and 'transcendent'. The mundane patterns of daily existence are transfused with that radiant intensity which is universally ascribed to 'the sacred'. Through serious dreaming, the *numinosum* becomes accessible. This does not lead to evangelical fundamentalism but to an intimate awareness of what it means to live within the context of eternity.

Transference and Counter-transference

The wounded surgeon plies the steel
That questions the distempered part;
Beneath the bleeding hands we feel
The sharp compassion of the healer's art
Resolving the enigma of the fever chart.

T. S. ELIOT

Patients in analysis often dream about their analyst, and it is not uncommon for analysts to dream about their patients. These dreams are important because they yield valuable insights into the unconscious anticipations that both bring with them into the analytic encounter. Freud introduced the term *transference* to describe the process by which a patient unconsciously *transfers on to* the person of the analyst feelings and attitudes that were, in fact, possessed by significant people in the past. This gives rise to the so-called *transference relationship*, which has to be distinguished from the *analytic relationship* or the *therapeutic alliance*, which refers to the total relationship between the analyst and patient as actual people.

Initially, it was assumed that the analyst would, through his own training analysis, be so aware of the unconscious luggage he brought with him from the past that he would be incapable of transferring it to his patients. With time and experience, however, many analysts acknowledged that this was by no means always the case and that it was necessary to monitor the unconscious reactions their patients released in them if they were not to distort the therapeutic alliance in unintended ways. These unconscious projections by the analyst on to the patient make up what came to be known as the *counter-transference*.

Jung greatly extended the Freudian view of these phenomena. Since the doctor–patient relationship is a primordial relationship that has been with us since the beginnings of time, it is inevitable that in the course of an analysis archetypal images are activated which, when projected on to the person of the analyst, can confer upon him great therapeutic or destructive power. In Jung's own experience such archetypal figures as the shaman, witch-doctor, magician, and wise old man were commonly projected. Similarly, powerful archetypes can be stirred in the analyst by the patient, colouring how he perceives and responds to her: the child, *femme fatale*, virgin, medium, *femme inspiratrice*, mother, any of these can be constellated, which adds a certain amount of psychic dynamite to the situation. Jung learned much about these potentially explosive dynamics from his alchemical studies, and his important essay *The Psychology of the Transference* (in *CW*16) is based on these researches.

All schools of analysis agree that therapeutic progress depends on making transference and counter-transference feelings conscious, though some maintain that this can be achieved without the assistance of dreams (i.e. by analysing and interpreting behaviour and feelings as they manifest themselves in the analytic setting). In this I believe them to be misguided, for dreams can reveal in dramatic detail the hidden assumptions and archetypal figures that are stirred in both participants as they work in the analytic relationship.

One of my patients, a woman in her fifties, had the following dream: *I am in an analytic session with my doctor. He is burly physically and confronting in manner. He says I use psychology and philosophy as a defence against the analytic process. 'Now,' he says, 'we must find out what you're **really** like!' It's as if I'm being dismissed as all a 'front', and I fear there's nothing left. Then some happy women appear. They are noisy, sexy, and heavily made up. One of them kisses me on the mouth.*

When she told me the dream we were able at once to agree that the analyst and the woman were creations of her own psyche. In reality I am not physically burly, nor is it my style to be overtly confronting with my patients (I always say honestly what I think, but not in a bullying or confronting manner). Nor did she know anyone like the lively, extraverted woman who kissed her on the lips. These figures were bit players in her own drama of which she was insufficiently aware.

Was the burly, confronting analyst how she experienced me? She thought hard about this, but, no, it wasn't. Was her father like this figure and does the dream doctor carry qualities she is transferring on to him out of her past? No again. Her father was a gentle pacifist, whom she loved dearly, a disciple of Swedenborg. So it seems that the burly, confronting man is the father/analyst she has *not* had. Why does the dream produce him? He demolishes her defences. She finds this devastating, but it does lead to an interesting development: it ushers in the extravert, sexy, lively women, one of whom kisses her.

At this point I had to consider what the dream was saying to *me*. Had I not drawn her attention to the way in which she used psychology and philosophy as a defence? I was certainly aware of her tendency to do this, but perhaps I had not put it to her forcefully enough. And what of the extraverted woman and her kiss? An erotic encounter in a dream with a member of one's own sex usually means that one is trying to possess or unite with those qualities that the dream figure represents. Since these qualities are not yet available to consciousness they contrast vividly with one's persona. Could this explain what was happening here? Indeed it could.

Her persona was very striking: rather too good to be true, in fact. Poised, ladylike, gentle, and sensitive, she was invariably considerate and reflective. There was never a hair out of place and her clothes were tailored, neat, spotlessly clean, and carefully chosen. This was entirely in accordance with how her beloved father had always wanted her to be: a perfect lady.

What had brought her into analysis was the need to compensate for this one-sided Swedenborgian persona in order to become an intact human being. To achieve this she had to be prepared to drop her defences and integrate her positive shadow (the lively, extraverted woman) into her total personality; but she would only succeed if she could assert herself and confront difficult issues through the *Logos* power of her animus (the burly, emphatic, no-nonsense analyst). Hence the dream. The burly analyst condenses five psychodynamic entities: (1) her father's shadow; (2) her analyst's shadow; (3) aspects of the masculine archetype that her father could not constellate but which the analysis is now activating and which are becoming available to (4) her animus and (5) the analyst in *her*. Furthermore, when I worked on the implications of the dream for myself, I had to acknowledge that there were times when her refined persona stirred the burly, confrontational male in myself, and that I had been shielding her from it. Perhaps in future I could be rather more 'up front' with her. In this way, dreams reveal information about the unconscious transactions between analyst and patient of vital importance for the progress of the work.

An analyst's own dreams can also provide him with objective insights into a patient's psychology that he has not previously recognized at the conscious level. One night, I dreamt of a new patient, a rather depressed woman, unhappily married, but a pillar of respectability in her local community. *I dreamt that valuable objects had disappeared from my consulting-room, and that she had stolen them.*

Was I to take this subjectively or objectively? Was she the thief in myself – my own pilfering anima? Or was it a compensatory dream?

Was I over-valuing her persona and not attending sufficiently to her shadow? Or was it objectively true? Had my unconscious picked up something about her that consciously I had missed? I decided to keep an open mind about these possibilities: time would tell. It did. Some weeks later, she was able to confess to me that for years she had been engaged in shop-lifting on a fairly regular basis.

As usually happens when a confession of this order is made, a strong therapeutic alliance is forged, and, for the time being at any rate, the analysis romps ahead. We quickly uncovered the reason for her shop-lifting: she felt cheated by her husband's lack of love and attention, and compensated for this by giving herself 'the gifts' that he never brought her.

Should I have told her my dream when it happened? I decided against it. The analytic relationship was in its early stages and I had to be careful that she felt secure and accepted. Telling her my dream could have jeopardized this by making her feel attacked or judged. As it was, she was able to develop enough trust to tell me the 'guilty secret' that she had shared with no one else in the world, knowing that I would not reject her or refuse to continue her treatment. What then was the use of my dream? It alerted me sufficiently to her shadow side for me to create the kind of atmosphere she needed in order to make her confession. It was a turning point in her treatment. Having understood what it was about, she was able to stop her shop-lifting and find more effective ways of recovering her self-esteem. So, in retrospect, I think my decision not to share the dream with her was the right one. Whether I should have felt the same about it had she been caught and prosecuted before she was able to tell me herself is another matter. In those circumstances, I may have blamed myself for not bringing things to a head sooner. Such decisions are among the most tricky that an analyst has to make.

The Ethics of Consciousness

The images of the unconscious place a great responsibility on a man.

C. G. JUNG

Early in his analysis, a man, who had received a strict Catholic upbringing and had been terrified as a child of hell fire, had a dream

224

in which *he was flying about in the rafters of the church his family had always attended. Beneath him were dangerous people who tried to grasp his legs, but in his own desperate exertions he managed to raise himself out of their reach. Just inside the North door was a huge, carved, stone receptacle, with a lid. Periodically a hand raised the lid and cast bodies down into the fire which raged below. Each time there was a pause, and then a hideous glow flared up as the body reached the flames. As he struggled to keep aloft, he thought to himself, 'I wouldn't have come into contact with all this beastliness but for my analysis. That's what's responsible. Without it everything would have been like it used to be!' Eventually, the strength in his arms would give out and he would have to 'fall' to meet his doom.*

A not unsimilar dream was brought to Jung by a sixteen-year-old boy. *He is walking along an unfamiliar street. It is dark and he hears steps coming behind him. With a feeling of fear he quickens his pace. The footsteps come nearer, and his fear increases. He begins to run. But the steps seem to be overtaking him. Finally he turns round, and there he sees the devil. In deathly terror he leaps into the air and hangs there suspended.*

The boy suffered from a severe obsessional neurosis, and, as Jung says: 'It is a notorious fact that the compulsion neuroses, by reason of their meticulousness and ceremonial punctilio, not only have the surface appearance of a moral problem but are indeed brim-full of inhuman beastliness and ruthless evil, against whose integration the otherwise very delicately organized personality puts up a desperate struggle.' Possessing an unbearably strict superego, the patient felt that he had to keep himself in an uncontaminated state of purity – a state symbolized in his dream as hanging suspended in the air. Jung comments that 'The dream showed him that if he wanted to come down to earth again there would have to be a pact with evil' (*CW*7, paras. 285–6).

In both cases, the dreamers are brought face to face with the shadow and it is made clear to them that they cannot escape the problem of evil, or the need to stand up to their crippling superegos, if they are to become whole. Courage and analysis can enable them to do that, but the problem will not go away: it will merely be shifted from the collective (religious) to the personal (ethical) plain.

The goals of analysis are the development of personality and consciousness through work with the unconscious. Achievement of these goals brings in its train a burden of ethical responsibility for the powerful capacities that are put at our disposal. It was Jung's major cosmological argument that the more conscious we become, the more we carry an awesome responsibility, not only for ourselves, but for our species, our planet, and, ultimately, our universe. Nature is neither conscious nor moral. She does not deal in such values as justice, compassion, concern for the ill-used and vulnerable. Blindly, she obeys her own laws, works out her own purposes, with no ethical concern for the consequences. 'The universe is not hostile,' wrote J. H. Holmes, 'nor yet is it friendly. It is simply indifferent.'

The motifs, themes, animals, and people that fill our dreams and nightmares are archetypal products of nature. By taking them into consciousness we become their custodians and are guilty of whatever harm they do. For this reason, Jung insisted, conscious integration of the images, powers, and personalities arising from the unconscious must 'be converted into an ethical obligation'. Integration of the shadow proceeds *pari passu* with reduction in the power of the superego. One's moral behaviour may then cease to be blind (i.e. unconscious, coerced by the moral code), and become *ethical* (i.e. informed by consciousness), and, therefore, *responsible*. Failure to accept ethical responsibility for the powers released from the unconscious, either by analysis or by life, can result in consequences of unqualified evil, as they did in the case of Adolf Hitler (pp. 293–7).

In the past the superego was a theological construct, its morality bore the stamp of divine sanction, its conscience was the voice of God. The 'death of God' removed all moral certainty: morality was rationalized, open to public debate, a matter of personal opinion. The Christian superego, its repression of sexuality and aggressive self-assertion undone by psychoanalytic subversion, can no longer defend us from our capacity for evil. To analyse is to risk the perilous journey, to encounter all the sins, the shames, cruelties, and banal evils that previous generations locked away in hell. It is the *via dolorosa* that cannot be shirked if one would become whole.

9
PRACTICAL DREAMWORK

*You cannot travel on the path before you have become
the Path itself.*

GAUTAMA BUDDHA

For those wishing to work on their dreams there is no shortage of practical advice. *Dreamwork* by Strephon Kaplan-Williams, *Inner Work* by Robert A. Johnson, *Understanding Dreams* by Mary Ann Mattoon, *Dreamlife* by David Fontana, and *A Little Course in Dreams* by Robert Bosnak are all to be highly recommended. The purpose of this chapter is to offer a brief guide to dreamwork based on the methods I have found most helpful in my own life as well as in professional practice.

Remembering and Recording Dreams

*Something is happening here
But you don't know what it is,
Do you, Mr Jones?*

BOB DYLAN

The vast majority of dreams are not remembered, and most people have difficulty in recalling more than an occasional example. Many are under the illusion that they never dream at all. So one must begin by acknowledging that dream recall is a relatively rare phenomenon and that dream amnesia is the general rule. It is as if Nature is jealous of her gifts and wants to conceal them from our daytime consciousness.

To set out deliberately to remember dreams, therefore, is an arduous task because it is an *opus contra naturam*, and you will not succeed unless well motivated to do so. First and foremost, one needs to develop the necessary psychological 'set' – the definite intention to

227

remember dreams and to record them. One has to get into the habit of thinking about dreams last thing at night while falling asleep and again first thing in the morning in the act of waking up. You may try saying to yourself as you compose yourself for sleep: 'I will have a dream tonight and I shall remember it in the morning.'

Very often these simple measures are quite enough to produce the memory of a dream the following morning. On waking, it is useful to ask oneself, 'What have I been dreaming?' If no dream seems to be available, don't give up. Don't let other thoughts enter your head. Don't think about the day that is just starting. Just lie still with your eyes shut and focus on the thoughts that are going through your mind. What were you thinking before that? And before that? Ah, yes, a dream! In this way you can use the chain of thoughts that have processed through your mind since waking as a means to haul yourself back into the dream.

Having chosen an attractive notebook as your dream journal, it is important to keep it, together with a ball-point pen, on the table beside your bed. The light switch needs to be accessible so that you can easily grope for it, should you wake up from a dream in the night. If you share your bed with a partner, this will require tact! A soft and gentle light on your side of the bed will be a help. Alternatively, pens are available incorporating a small electric torch which illuminates no more than the page on which you are writing.

If you sleep alone, you might consider investing in a voice-activated tape recorder. This obviates the need for waking up fully and switching on the light, and it has the advantage of allowing you to stay in close contact with the atmosphere and imagery of the dream. Speaking directly out of the dream, the tape automatically begins recording, enabling you to explore the events you have just been experiencing in greater depth than is possible in full consciousness with a pen in your hand. However, there are drawbacks to this method. In the first place, the machine is totally unselective about what it records: everything starts it off – coughs, sneezes, bed creaks, and snoring. As a result, transcribing the tape in the morning can be a chore, and you have to be disciplined about it. Otherwise you end up with interminable stretches of tape, collected over a number of nights, full of grunts, groans, sighs, and mumbled comments that, after time has elapsed, are hard to decodify into an intelligible account. Such recordings can, however, be very revealing, especially if you talk in your sleep. It is not uncommon for extraordinary voices to emerge reminiscent of a shaman or a medium giving tongue in a trance. These eerie communications provide additional insight into the part-personalities at work in the unconscious.

If on waking you cannot recall a dream, then it is a good practice to write down the thoughts that you woke up with. It is important to record something every morning. One should never write: 'No dream' or 'Nothing to report'. There is always something going on in there as you wake up. To formulate it clearly and write it down helps to develop the habit of inner awareness and increases one's sensitivity to dream images when they occur.

What is one to do if these measures fail? There is nothing else for it but to ensure that you wake up during an episode of REM sleep. This may be done by persuading your partner to wake you should he or she detect in the night (from your breathing or involuntary movements) that you are dreaming. Alternatively, you can set an alarm clock to go off about half an hour before you normally wake up. This should rouse you during the last REM episode of the night. It is preferable to use an alarm clock and not a radio clock, for the programme when it is switched on may grab your thoughts and carry them away from your dream.

When you do succeed in getting hold of a dream, write it down, however fragmentary it may be, in as much detail as you can. As you do so, you may well remember other parts of the dream. Write these down too, in whatever order they present themselves to your memory: the correct sequence can be established later. The crucial thing is to get into the *regular* habit of remembering and preserving dreams *every* morning. The more you do this the more successful you will become. You will have to accept, however, that a perfect dream record is not possible, since the act of dreaming and the subsequent act of writing down what has been dreamt are two distinct forms of experience. The difference between a dream and the record you make of it is like the difference between the performance of a play in the theatre and the account you give of it to a friend the following day. It requires the development of a good memory and careful attention to detail if you are to give a reasonably accurate summary of what occurred. With practice, you may become very good at it, but there will always be things that you forget, unconscious changes that you make to the story line, interpolations of extraneous detail, and so on. In fact, every dream exists in three versions: (1) the dream as you dream it; (2) the dream as you recall it; and (3) the dream as you report it to your analyst or to a friend. Versions (2) and (3) are subject to what Freud called 'secondary revision' or 'secondary elaboration'. These distortions are unavoidable, but with care much can be done to minimize their influence.

Associations and Amplifications

The psychological experiences of great suffering or joy first attain their entire fullness of expression when they are reverberated from dreams.

THOMAS DE QUINCEY

It is a good idea to record dreams on one side of the notebook and to leave the opposite page for associations to the themes and symbols of each dream. Illustrations of salient features, sketch-maps of dream locations, and anything else that seems relevant should be included here, or allowed to overflow on to subsequent pages. One should make as full a record as possible and not be mean with space: one can easily buy another notebook when it is needed. As you write, open yourself up to the mood, the atmosphere, the overriding quality of the dream, allow the feelings to express themselves on the page as they emerge.

When you have recorded your responses to the dream as a whole, return to examine its component parts – every person, animal, place, object, situation or idea occurring in the dream. Take each in turn and ask yourself, 'What thoughts, feelings, ideas, memories, reactions occur to me when I contemplate this?' In jotting down everything that goes through one's mind, one should try not to get carried off on a wild goose chase, associating to one's associations, but keep returning to the dream image, and see what further associations arise. Then, when the stream has petered out, proceed to the next part of the dream. The important thing is to be undirected in one's thinking – to think laterally and passively, allowing things to happen in a completely unguided way. Don't interfere, don't censor, don't select, just write down whatever presents itself. As will soon become apparent to you, the personal unconscious is a system of cross-references, and in a comparatively short time your associative efforts will yield a network of meanings providing the personal background to your dream. This is the indispensable first step.

Which of these associations is valid? They all are. Which of them throws most light on your dream? Your intuition will tell you. Suddenly, you will find yourself making a meaningful connection – or, rather, it will be made for you. Something clicks into place: 'aha!' Energy is liberated. Insight takes wing. We have lift-off!

Insight is a heady moment. It is easy to get intoxicated by it and forget to write it down. But it is too precious a moment to lose. It should be recorded so as to give it substance. Then it can be returned to at leisure and drawn on in times of need.

To establish the personal context of a dream one has to consult the inner library one carries in the subjective psyche. To establish the dream's cultural and archetypal context, however, one has to turn to art, history, and literature, and be willing to ransack the libraries of mythology, folklore, and comparative religion, for the objective psyche is not nearly so accessible. But myths, religions, and fairy tales are, like dreams, filled with the symbolic manifestations of archetypal intentions. They provide the bonds uniting the personal with the collective, as it is now and always has been. The archetypes use us as channels through which their energies flow towards the goal of their own completion. We incarnate them in our physical and mental lives: we are their functionaries. While each of us relates personally to the ancient symbols of mankind they, nevertheless, possess the universality that is the hallmark of archetypal influence. Each archetype, whether it be mother, trickster, predator, enemy, king, or the divine, exudes its own characteristic symbolism which, with experience, one can learn to recognize. Then one can turn to the encyclopaedias of mythology and the *Collected Works of C. G. Jung* and make use of that invaluable resource, the index. Research of this kind helps avoid the narrowness, the singleness of meaning that can be generated by purely personal associations. To allow the imagination to interact with mythic themes is to expand the context of the dream. Your horizons are broadened, and your experience grafted on to that of humanity – which, after all, is the purpose of dreaming in the first place.

As with free association, there is no obvious point at which amplification has to stop. What is selected by both analyst and patient is necessarily arbitrary and, if pursued too diligently, can drag them away from the living symbol and smother it with data. Amplification is not a scientific procedure but an allegorical one, a poetic and subjective search for collective parallels and metaphors. By amplifying a dream one is merely attempting to establish its family links with the symbolic offspring of the archetypal imagination which populate the hinterland of all psychic eventualities. As when finding relevant associations, we recognize a relevant amplification when it 'clicks' – when it seems best to serve the intention and amplify the meaning of the dream.

Interpretation

Dreams, like all other psychological structures, regularly have more than one meaning.

SIGMUND FREUD

People new to dream analysis often reveal a fantasy that interpretation is something done *ex cathedra* from a position of superior knowledge – as if the analyst were Sherlock Holmes or the Delphic oracle. In practice, it is a painstaking process of deconstruction and reconstruction. While the analyst may sometimes have an intuitive idea about the meaning of a dream when it is first recounted to him, its full significance only begins to emerge as the dreamer's associations are worked over, and its themes and symbols amplified. Gradually, the dream and its meaning come together to form a new Gestalt.

On approaching a dream, one is like an archaeologist examining an undeciphered script, or like Jung contemplating his first alchemical text. Perplexity rules, until one understands that they are forms of *symbolic* communication, whose meaning is governed by context. As one explores the contextual web through which the dream images are interconnected, the overall significance of the dream emerges as a gradual revelation, like a photographic image in a tray of developer. As a result, the question that neophytes are prone to ask – 'How do I know if an interpretation is correct?' – ceases to be an issue. It is not a question of getting the 'right' interpretation, but of allowing the dream to speak for itself and express all its meanings. In fact, there is only one wrong interpretation, and that is a single interpretation derived from a theoretical assumption. The key to understanding dreams is to respect the polysemy of their symbolism.

A word of warning is appropriate at this point. When you tackle a dream, you are taking on an autonomous force of nature. You are advised to approach it with caution and due reverence, because you never know what you are about to release. If you are feeling in a low or vulnerable condition, it is better to find some experienced helper rather than to embark single-handed on a voyage into the unknown. Working with dreams on one's own is a precarious business. In addition to the dangerous powers lurking in the unconscious, self-analysis is inevitably a hit-or-miss affair because you cannot see your blind spots, and it is easy to fall into the self-congratulatory trap of adopting only those insights that 'click' with your customary ego-position instead of those which lead to a more objective and perhaps more critical perspective. These difficulties can sometimes be overcome by discussing a problematic dream with a trusted friend. Another way is to join a dream group, where it is possible to work on your dreams with a small number of sympathetic people. However, you should always be careful who you trust with your dreams, for an insensitive response can wound and even cause lasting damage. It is important to remember that in your dreams you stand naked, unprotected, and as you really are. Be wary of exposing yourself to danger.

If you are determined to proceed, however, return to the dream text and check your responses to each of its components. These may be any of the following:

(1) The place, situation, building, or landscape in which the drama unfolds;
(2) The *dramatis personae*, all with their own qualities, history, and attitudes;

(3) The belief systems displayed by these personalities as well as by the dream-ego;

(4) The behaviour of all these characters which goes to make up the action of the drama;

(5) Animals are commonly present, each one carrying a symbolic charge and behaving in its own characteristic way;

(6) Symbolic objects – e.g. a ring, a pen, a sword, an earthenware jar, etc., and means of transport, such as a horse, a car, or a bicycle;

(7) The emotions, moods and the general atmosphere generated in the course of the dream;

(8) The numbers, colours, or geometric patterns which carry symbolic significance for the dreamer.

All these elements have to be taken into consideration if one is to reach a full understanding of the dream. Faced with such complexity, beware of jumping to conclusions. Be patient. Stay with the various components until the details are clear. They are all aspects of yourself: some will already be well known to you, others will strike you as baffling and strange. It is these unfamiliar images that will demand your special attention. To allow their significance to emerge, you will have to put up with what James Hillman calls 'hermeneutic frustration'. The image, says Hillman, is the teacher, and you have to control your interpretative zeal if you are to 'hear' the image and discover the part of yourself inside it.

Say, for example, you dream of a pig. When you have written down your associations, consider what role the pig is playing in the dream: how is it behaving? More important still, what is it feeling? You may feel tempted to turn to a bestiary and read up what pigs symbolize, but it is more revealing to stay with the pig in your dream. It is your pig, after all, and it is possible that it appears in your dream because your ego is pig-deficient. Perhaps your ego needs to learn from the pig. 'We have an entirely wrong idea of the animal,' wrote Jung, 'we must not judge from the outside. From the outside you see a pig covered with mud and wallowing in dirt . . . for you it would be dirty, but it is not for the pig. What you have to do is put yourself inside the pig' (Jung, 1930). Every animal is a representative of its species; but it is also an individual with a role to play in the present situation in your dream. It is a personal revelation of an archetypal form, a piece of phylogenetic consciousness seeking to be united with you, the ego. It is not helpful, therefore, to deny it, denigrate or evade it; one should befriend it, acknowledge it as kin, make it one's own. In this way you learn about 'undreamt of' capacities in yourself, liberate their energy, and actualize them as part of your psychic totality. Then you truly begin to belong to yourself.

But this can be difficult, for often we find ourselves behaving in dreams in ways we would be ashamed of in waking life – we may cheat a friend, lie to a colleague, rob a bank. 'I would never do a thing like that!' you think indignantly. But you deceive yourself: your dream has caught you at it. The honest and necessary response is to study the dream and discover where you are doing these things in yourself and in your life. This is a most important exercise. When working on a dream by oneself it is all too easy to collude with the ego and embrace a flattering, ego-syntonic interpretation. To grow in integrity and wisdom is to be ready to face the worst about yourself when a dream presents you in a bad light.

Not infrequently, a dream will exaggerate in order to make its point. It can grossly caricature some aspect of your behaviour, your attitudes, or your beliefs in order to bring home to you just how absurd you are being. This is why dreams are best interpreted subjectively – because they can be ruthlessly *objective* about the subject: you.

Sometimes, as you work on a dream, conflicting and ambiguous meanings will emerge. The best advice is not to choose between them. Rather tolerate the tension that ambiguity generates: live with it and see what comes. Above all, trust the Self; eventually the ego will understand, but it will have to learn humility.

Often, one has the sense of being bombarded with meanings from different parts of the dream and at different levels of inference. The problem is not to select which is the correct interpretation so much as to assess which of the discovered meanings is the most significant for self-understanding and for life.

Here again, the important thing is to write down your thoughts as they occur to you and then to summarize on paper what are for you the salient meanings to have emerged.

When you have done all this, ask yourself what the dream is really about? What is the basic theme? It is as well to answer this as you would a friend who inquired about a film you had seen or a book you had just read – e.g. 'Oh, it's a story about a girl who is ill-treated by the man she loves.' It could be the story of your life. Another good tip is to give the dream a title that sums up the action, rather like a headline for a newspaper story: FARMER'S CATTLE DISASTER: POLICEMAN SAVES THE DAY. This increases the impact of the dream and makes it all the more memorable.

Rituals of the Imagination

Phenomena come alive and carry soul through our imaginative fantasies about them.

JAMES HILLMAN

Dream analysis achieves little if it remains a purely intellectual activity. Dreams have to be felt and their message translated into life. Sometimes this happens spontaneously: the insight generated by a dream or a vision can be so dazzling that one is bowled over by it and one's life is transformed, like Dr Dement dreaming that he was dying from cancer of the lung (pp. 86–7 above). Such an experience brings about its own revolution and one can do no more than follow it through. Usually the message is less overwhelming and one needs to *do something about it* in order to enhance its influence. Action in the light of a dream is a psychological obligation one owes to the Self. It may be done either practically or in the form of a ritual, itself a symbolic act.

To make the most of a dream, therefore, it is advisable to proceed in three stages:

(1) Basic dreamwork, using association and amplification to establish the personal, cultural, and archetypal references of the dream and gain insight into its meaning;

(2) Register the essence of the dream in consciousness by writing up

what it means in terms of your life, illustrating it, working on its main symbols in clay, etc., so as to give it substantive form;

(3) Build on the dream, mobilizing its energy and ploughing its meaning into life, either practically, as in direct use in relationships, or symbolically, as in ritual, active imagination, psychodrama, Gestalt work, etc.

All three stages require development of one's powers of imagination, even the most practical application of a dream's disclosure. The secretary who was intimidated by her boss (p. 108 above) made practical use of her stubborn, aggressive dream-dog by summoning him up in her imagination whenever she felt she was being treated badly. The summoned image enabled her to stand up for herself in a way that was not possible before the dream presented her with this symbolic gift. Having understood it and registered its meaning in her mind (stages 1 and 2), she was able to make good use of it (stage 3) when the need arose. Though essentially a practical technique, it required imaginative power to make the most of it. Much of this power was generated by her dream.

To take another practical example, let us assume you dream of a male friend you have not seen or thought about for years. What is he doing in your dream? At first you work on your associations to determine what he stands for in yourself. Why should the unconscious bring up this figure now? Presumably because you need him to compensate for some deficiency in consciousness. He represents an aspect of yourself that you may need to develop. With luck, your intuition will tell you what this is, but, if you are still mystified, it could be helpful (1) to do some active imagination using your friend as a starting point, and (2) to consider him *objectively* as a real person. Do you need to do something about him? Why have you allowed the friendship to lapse? Should you get in touch to find out what has become of him and discover what significance you may still carry for one another? Life is short and few of us have so many friends that we can afford to squander them. The message in the dream might be that you need each other and should be friends again.

Another possibility is that you may dream of doing something that you have never attempted in your waking life: you may find yourself skiing down a slope with immense enjoyment, painting a picture, making a pot, planting a garden, or flying a plane. As well as working on the symbolic implications of this, should you consider taking up the activity in reality? Dreams often put us in touch with unlived parts of ourselves and can be taken as invitations to live them.

But most dreams are not susceptible to such practical application. Their influence needs to be incorporated symbolically. This is where ritual use of the imagination can be invaluable. Many people have problems with this, however. They may accept that dreams and insights derived from them can be extremely helpful, but they balk at the idea of making any *ritual* use of them. Ritual is an embarrassment to the contemporary mentality because its objectives stand in blatant contrast to those of scientific materialism. It was not ever thus. In the great majority of human societies ritual has performed a crucial role in the life of the individual and society. Ritual provides a powerfully efficient means for reasserting the basic truths and revitalizing the eternal values of the culture, for mobilizing archetypal energies in individual participants, and for facilitating the transition to a new status or role through *rites of passage*. But in our spiritually impoverished culture, which debauches its traditions and mocks its collective symbols, the sacred dimension has largely disappeared, and few of us ever know what it is to be touched by the *numinosum*. It was this state of subjective barrenness that Jung termed 'the general neurosis of our age'. He argued that, in the absence of collectively sanctioned rituals, we had to devise our own by turning inwards, liberating the resources of the Self, and channelling them imaginatively and ritualistically into life. Robert A. Johnson (1986) gives many instances of how this may be done on the basis of a dream. I will content myself with one example.

A thirty-two-year-old woman had a dream which brought home to her the extent to which she had been treating her husband as if he were her father. What could she do to differentiate these two crucially important men in her life? It was not enough to make a resolution to stop it. She needed to do something active about it, if the moment was not to pass, allowing her to fall back into her old ways. Through analysis she became conscious of the paternal characteristics she had been projecting on to her husband, as well as the daughter role she had been adopting towards him, and she wished to sacrifice the projection and the role. Here a ritual proved highly productive. She took all the dolls and woolly toys with which she had festooned the marital bedchamber since her wedding day five years previously and made a funeral pyre of them. For her this was a symbolic act charged with the greatest significance. It did not resolve her Electra complex in a single glorious blaze, but it was a first decisive step on the way towards resolving it. Moreover, when she was with her husband, she began the practice of repeating to herself, 'This man is not my father and I love him for himself alone.' This was an auto-suggestive ritual which, like the bonfire, evolved out of her understanding of her dream. (In her dream *her husband had given her a present for 'being a good girl' and told her that it was the last such present he would ever give her. It was a beautiful big doll — with breasts that secreted actual milk!*)

Rituals such as these can be potent means of extracting maximum value from a dream, but their very effectiveness can be a danger. The bonfire of the dolls could have cut off the dreamer from the creative, lively qualities of the child complex in her psyche, and she would have been emotionally and spiritually diminished thereby. Aware of this danger, we made sure that she kept intuitively in touch with her 'child', replacing her sterile attachment to her dolls by a more imaginative, playful attitude to her husband. Relations with him had become stereotyped and dull. Using her childlike inventiveness, she was able to do something creative about this instead of merely arranging her dolls on the bedspread and playing daughter to her husband's 'father'.

If dreams are symbolic dramas unconsciously created, then rituals are symbolic acts consciously performed. A ritual turns something inner and psychic into something outer and substantive, enhancing its impact on consciousness. Ritual-creation is, therefore, an entirely rational and appropriate activity. There is nothing mad or eccentric about it. It is only the madness of our society that makes it seem so.

Similar good pragmatic reasons justify the use of *active imagination* — the process of relating to different parts of oneself in conscious, unguided fantasy. Active imagination is like dreaming while you are awake. It is different from daydreaming because you remain alert to what is happening and interact with the figures who emerge, talking to them and listening to their replies. It also resembles a lucid dream (a dream in which you are conscious that you are dreaming), except that you are awake when it happens and not asleep. In normal dreaming you experience the dream like a play in which you may or may not have a role. You do not in any way influence the outcome of the action. In active imagination, however, you actively participate, focusing attention on the plot and the dramatis personae and subjecting them to critical scrutiny. You do not merely listen to the evidence the actors have to give: you cross-examine them.

To indulge in such activity can be no less embarrassing than performing rituals, for, here again, you have to be willing to disregard the prejudices against psychic phenomena peculiar to our culture, where the very verbs 'to dream' and 'to imagine' are used as put downs: 'You're living in a dream world!' (i.e. you are out of touch with reality). 'You're a dreamer!' (i.e. you are ditto). 'You're imagining all that!' For dreamwork to succeed in its objectives, we have to meet this prejudice and defeat it. Otherwise we get nowhere. We remain stuck in the belief that what is imagined is insubstantial, airy nothingness, without power, meaning or value. With such an attitude all psychic progeny are stillborn. We have to affirm that there is nothing disreputable about building castles in the air; on the contrary, they can prove more lasting than those built on more solid foundations.

The secret is to recognize that the figures emerging in dreams and active imagination are *real* parts of ourselves with an autonomous existence and power. We have to relate to them as we relate to people in outer reality, but in greater depth and with complete honesty. Inner work is not a time for polite evasion. Only when we commit ourselves with integrity to what happens in the psyche can we truly participate in the dynamics of the Self.

The no-man's-land between consciousness and unconsciousness is a territory normally inaccessible to us and it is not always easy to develop the knack of getting there. Those who take to it most readily are usually introverted people in close touch with their inner lives; practical extraverts, on the other hand, can find it so difficult that they give up in despair. For those who succeed, and practise it regularly, active imagination enhances the benefits of dreamwork more than any other psychic activity, for it mobilizes the transcendent function, granting a sense of inner unity, power, and certainty. It is, however, not to be undertaken lightly. It is potentially dangerous, because it amounts to a self-induced psychotic episode: one becomes a dreamer in a world awake. The danger of active imagination is that the 'dream' can take over and rule consciousness. Susceptible people in whom the ego is insufficiently robust and whose contact with reality is tenuous are to be discouraged from undertaking it: they can begin to mistake dreaming for reality, while remaining, to all intents and purposes, awake. On the whole, active imagination is best confined to those in formal analysis, when professional assistance will be available should they need it.

To do active imagination you need undisturbed peace, privacy, and time. The best practice is to allocate a certain time to it every day and arrange your life and your household accordingly. Early in the morning is a good time, before the world is up and about its business – or, if you prefer, late at night after the world has gone to bed. Since it is virtually impossible to enter the privacy of the imagination in the company of someone else, it is important to make sure that you will be alone until the session is over.

To get started one needs a *rite d'entrée*. Jung imagined he was descending into a cave. I have often made use of Aeschylus' notion (in the *Eumenides*) that when we pass into reverie or a dream our eyes revolve inwards and light up our souls so that we perceive truths that have been hidden from us during the day. What one needs to sustain is the 'liminal' state half-way between sleep and waking. One can only do this for a few minutes to start with, but, with practice, the period can be extended, depending on the intrinsic interest of the fantasy as it develops before one's in-turned eyes.

A good way of beginning is to summon up the image of a character from a recent dream – a woman, for example. Dwell on the image and allow it to develop in as much detail as you can. Then ask yourself questions about her. Who is she? What's she like? How old? Married? Who to? Children? What are her interests? What does she do with herself? What is her attitude to you and to the other characters in the dream? What does she want of you? As you work at this, replies will occur to you which *feel* to be right. Something in you seems to know the answers. Where do these answers come from? Presumably from the same source as the dream figure herself. After a while she may even begin to speak her thoughts. Then a dialogue is initiated.

In many ways, the process resembles what goes on in a novelist. For some writers it does not progress beyond the stage of asking detailed questions about the character and allowing the imagination to provide the answers, but, for others, the character begins to assume a life of her own, she makes her own gestures, chooses her own clothes and surroundings, and speaks her own dialogue, which the author takes down from dictation. When it reaches this stage of development, the creative process is akin to active imagination. The experience becomes all the more impressive as feelings and emotions are engaged.

Another way of beginning is to focus on a mood that is disturbing or puzzling you. The secret is to go into the mood, let it hold your imagination and express itself in images and words. Sometimes an image will form that seems to embody the mood itself. A man who felt inexpressibly sad about something, and could not understand what it was, settled down to some active imagination and at once saw a red brick wall bathed in warm sunlight. This triggered a memory of being sent away to school at the age of nine. He was desperately unhappy. He missed his mother terribly and felt deeply rejected by both his parents who had sent him to such a dreadful place. Opposite his dormitory window there was a red brick wall and it seemed unbearably poignant to him when the evening sun shone on it. It reminded him of his mother and filled him with an anguished longing for home. At the same time, it was a brick wall – a barrier to escape, which kept him prisoner. The image, together with the memory it evoked, made him realize that the sadness with which he had awakened that morning was about feeling abandoned and trapped, and he was able to bring these feelings to his analysis and work on them.

Granting free rein to the imagination eventually carries one beyond personal issues into the great archetypal themes of human existence. Often the same themes will repeat, and recurrent imaginations will start with the same character in the same situation. For many years, the active imaginations of one man began with a solitary horseman riding over a plain towards a forest. Nothing much occurred until he reached the edge of the forest, but, once in, almost anything could happen. The forest world was a timeless world, and the people he met there were timeless people, some terrible, some wise, and some extremely sexy. Sometimes it was so fascinating that he was reluctant to come out again. Therein lies the danger.

Another way to start is to go in imagination to a place which has evocative overtones for you. One of my patients used to return to the Cornish estuary where she spent a solitary childhood: there she would watch the ebbing and flowing of the tides, the boats riding at anchor and the gulls soaring overhead, and pass the hours in imaginary adventures. Returning to this memory had the effect of once more liberating her powers of imagination.

Active imagination should be recorded as it happens. Find a comfortable place to sit and arrange the pad, typewriter or recorder in a convenient position before you compose yourself to begin. Most people find it best to close their eyes until the fantasy has started to develop, then, when it has taken hold, open them so as to record what is happening. Using a tape recorder or having the ability to touch-type has the advantage of allowing one to pursue the imaginary events with one's eyes shut. What emerges is by no means always pleasant or necessarily interesting. Often you are presented with images, characters, and feelings you would rather pass over or ignore. But, once started, you have to accept what you are given and find the determination, as well as the honesty, to see it through. Remember that the weakest, murkiest, most inferior parts of yourself present you with precisely those areas which have the greatest potential for growth. To neglect them is to stunt your own development.

What do you do if nothing comes? Be patient, it will. The imagination, like Nature, abhors a vacuum. Wait and it will fill your emptiness with images, people, ideas, voices. Let them come. Start to record. If they go away, don't panic. Sit quietly and wait. They will return. It is like badger-watching.

When the images or inner personalities have established themselves in your mind, then the *active* part of the imagination begins: you engage with them, and start a dialogue. Treat the inner figures as living characters with a history, a will, and a life of their own. They are as real as you are, so treat them with respect. Question them, but listen with great attention to what they have to say. There is no knowing what you may learn from them. Don't forget to record both sides of the conversation. The key to *all* inner work is to get everything down in black and white (and, if you wish, in colour). How you do it doesn't matter. The important thing is to get it down. It is not really yours until you have done so.

Once started, what matters more than anything else is the whole-heartedness of your commitment. The more you feel for the people you encounter and the more you care about their responses to your questions the more it will all mean to you. The whole point of active imagination is that it is not an abstract exercise but a living process touching the core experiences of your soul. However, don't be so overwhelmed by what emerges that you lose touch with your own ego standpoint. What do *you* think about what has happened? What have *you* learned from the experience? Do you agree with the views expressed? Can you go along with the direction indicated? What significance does it carry for your way of life now and in the future? When a voice tells you to do something, always let the *ego* decide whether you should do it or not. One should not allow oneself to be the puppet of one's fantasies. At the same time, it is important to acknowledge the validity of the views expressed and be ready to see that they could be wise and correct – particularly when they conflict with one's most cherished values and *idées fixes*.

As you make your record, don't worry too much about punctuation, spelling, or presentation. The results are for your eyes only. What matters is to get it down quickly in as much detail as you can. A session that has brought up important or exciting material may later be worked up, with illustrations or commentaries, in a fair copy and kept in a special book or folder – as did Jung in his Red and Black Books. If you prefer to speak your active imagination as it is happening into a tape recorder, like a sports commentator describing a football match as it is being played, you can transcribe important parts of the tape into the Book later on. Collected together, these documents of the soul should be kept strictly private, and preferably secret, shut away under lock and key. If anyone is ever allowed to see them, that person should be special to you, with *your* interests very much at heart – e.g. your analyst or soul-mate – someone who is not going to abuse the confidence you have placed in them.

When people begin active imagination they often complain of a feeling that 'they are making it all up' and that it is therefore invalid. If you should get this feeling, do not despair. Even the most contrived fantasy is still coming out of *you* and will relate to your personal psychodynamics. Anything you produce in the imagination is the product of activity in the Self. The more time you give to the practice, the more spontaneous the results will be. The secret is patience and perseverance. When people feel that they are 'making it up' it is because they have become active too early. They have attempted to hurry the process along in order to make things happen. One must give the fantasy time to formulate. Only when it is clearly established should one begin to interact with it. Then, once you have begun to ask questions and receive answers to them, you are doing active imagination. A mathematician, whose chief love was geometry, once complained that there was no significance in what he was doing: it was all too easy to have any value. 'But,' I said, 'you are engaged in a dialogue with yourself. That is the whole point of the exercise. You are talking to the Self and the Self is answering back. That is active imagination.' He looked at me quizzically, so I added: 'Q.E.D.,' and he was convinced!

Dreamwork is an activity possessing *intrinsic value*, whether it is done in the service of a formal analysis or not. It is not possible always to achieve a full understanding of a dream, but at least one can grant it one's full attention, bring it bodily into the light of day, open oneself up to its mythology, and as Jung put it, *dream the myth onwards* in one's life. One can approach and cross the *limin*, where all essential transformations occur; encounter one's archetypal humanity, and enter a realm far richer than that of ordinary existence. To work towards fulfilment of the imperatives of the Self is to engender the sense of being 'meant', to recognize that something transcendent is playing through one's existential being. To devote time each day to the careful contemplation of dreams is to perform a ritual through which mundane routines are sweetened by the wishes and intentions of the soul.

10

COMMON DREAMS

All people living in Western civilization will have these dreams at some time in their lives, and many of them will be repeated again and again.

CALVIN S. HALL AND VERNON J. NORDBY

Dream classification is still in its infancy. Many researchers have attempted to produce classifications on the basis of detailed content analyses of dreams, using such categories as theme (falling, flying, being examined, missing trains, etc.), affect (anxiety dreams, depressive dreams, nightmares, sexual or aggressive dreams, etc.), and major life events (birth, initiation, marriage, death). This is dream classification at the Linnaean stage. What we are waiting for is a Darwin to provide the evolutionary–explanatory frame of reference within which all types of dreams may be articulated. It is not my intention to lay claim to that mantle, nor will I attempt to devise an exhaustive classificatory system such as that proposed by Hunt (1989). Classifying a dream is like trying to pigeon-hole mercury: each example has such a multitude of elusive references that it slides past whatever category one seeks to contain it in. In what follows, I have assayed nothing more adventurous than a discussion of certain types of dreams which typically occur in the course of analytic practice. In each instance we will examine the ways in which archetypal propensities interact with day residues to work out adaptive strategies during REM sleep.

That phylogenetically ancient structures play an important part in dreams becomes particularly apparent on examining the commonest dreams that people have. In Chapter 3 I called attention to the valuable work of Hall and Nordby in collecting over 50,000 dreams from large numbers of subjects in various parts of the world. The typical dreams reported involved aggression, predatory animals, flying, falling, being pursued by hostile strangers, landscapes, dreams of misfortune, sex, getting married and having children, taking examinations or undergoing some similar ordeal, travelling (whether on foot, horseback, car, aeroplane or ship), swimming or being in the water, watching fires, and being confined in an underground place. They concluded: 'These typical dreams express the shared concerns, preoccupations, and interests of all dreamers. They may be said to constitute the universal constants of the human psyche' (1972, p. 35). They thus provide copious evidence in support of Jung's hypothesis of a collective unconscious, although they do not themselves make this connection.

At about the time that Hall and Nordby were conducting their research, a fascinating study by Dr Richard Griffith (1958) in the United States in association with Drs O. Miyagi and A. Tago in Japan compared the dreams of 250 college students in Kentucky and 223 in Tokyo. More than 7,000 dreams were collected, and when they were examined to discover how often certain dreams recurred, it was found that remarkable similarity existed between the two groups. Moreover, the recurrent themes detected are very similar to those described by Hall and Nordby.

It seems that dreams return repeatedly to those themes – we would call them archetypal themes – which have typically concerned human beings always and everywhere.

Agonic and Hedonic Dreams

Where love rules there is no will to power: where power predominates there love is lacking. The one is the shadow of the other.

C. G. JUNG

Although I have no figures to prove it, it is my clinical impression that dreams have become more violent in recent years. This could be partly due to the increased sophistication of the news-gathering media and the constant stream of violent images that pour into our homes, but there can be little doubt that society is getting more violent as well. A decline in respect for the great reconciling symbols of church and state, the disintegration of family units, the wider availability of drugs and greater incidence of drug-related crime, the existence of a large under-class growing both in its size and the intensity of its resentments, are all factors in this sorry state of affairs. However, the situation is not improved by media emphasis on agonistic behaviour (aggressive conflicts over status, property, or sexual partners) and its trivialization of the hedonic virtues of compassion, empathy, and love. One of the commonest initial associations to a dream is: 'It's like the TV programme I was watching before I went to bed.' That TV violence works its way into our dreams must have unconscious consequences for our mood and behaviour, especially when we are young. Unfortunately, the movies that attract young people in their millions are also predominantly about agonistic struggles, usually represented in forms not conducive to dialogue and reconciliation with an opponent but rather to his defeat, destruction, and 'elimination'.

Simple content analyses reveal that agonistic dreams are more common among males of all ages and hedonic dreams more common among females, but both types of dreams occur in both sexes. A more significant variable than gender in determining the relative incidence of such dreams is the kind of family the individual grew up in. For most of this century, depth psychology has misconceived aggression as a unitary motivational force or instinct. Under the impact of ethology, this has given place to an understanding that aggressive behaviour is linked directly to the social context and the history of the person in whom it occurs. Violence in dreams, as in life, has its roots in biology (anatomy, brain structures, hormones, and neurotransmitters) as well as in evolved reproductive strategies, social status and territorial defence; but violence is also linked to ontological influences (early family history, parental modelling, etc.), characteristic personality patterns, and socio-economic factors (such as relative access to money, education, and social influence). The probability is that television and cinematographic representations of violence do not promote aggressive behaviour equally in all members of the public, but primarily in those among whom the seeds have already been sown in early life. The knock-on effects of violence in childhood go bashing on down through the generations. Images of violence, and the dreams they induce, have the effect of reinforcing unconscious propensities which have already been activated by life.

The same is true of hedonic, affiliative propensities, which are constellated in families where love, attachment, and mutual support are plentifully in evidence. Both hedonic and agonic patterns are available to us all. Because love and status are so important, our dreams render us vigilant to any signs indicating that our love is threatened with betrayal or our status under attack. People from stable, loving backgrounds can, for example, have powerfully agonistic dreams when they find themselves under threat at work, on a committee, or in their marriage. Dreams often provide the first indication that a marriage is going wrong when relations with anima or animus figures shift from the hedonic to the agonic mode. Personal associations to such dreams reveal that appreciation of the spouse's good qualities is giving way to a condemnation of his or her 'negative' attributes. Dreamwork can be extremely valuable at this stage, making the dreamer aware of the seriousness of the situation – that relations are in danger of becoming destructive, that negative anticipations are being reinforced, and that anger, disappointment, and struggles for power are taking the place of expressions of warmth, appreciation, and love. If the marriage is to be saved, effort is needed to contain the negative within the positive, and to shift the prevailing mode of the relationship back from the agonic to the hedonic. When the need for this effort is perceived by the ego, the unconscious will often play its role in suggesting creative possibilities for resolving the problem that the marriage has become.

Similarly, the objective of therapy, for those who have grown up in an agonistic environment and who are consequently plagued with agonistic dreams, must be to promote a shift in the hedonic direction. Usually such patients have been subjected to attacks on their status for so long that they suffer from low self-esteem and an inability to conceive of themselves as worthy of respect or affection. It is not a question of fathering or mothering such patients, for this serves to keep them dependent and childlike. The aim has to be to help them to appreciate their own competence and value. The positive regard of the therapist, together with the hedonic quality of the therapeutic alliance, will provide the necessary background for dreamwork and analysis to bring this about.

Unfortunately, people who have had little or no 'training' of their attachment systems through receiving love in childhood make poor analytic subjects because they are unable to form a close or trusting relationship with their analyst and have a tendency to interpret analytic insights as attacks on their status. For analysis to succeed it is essential that some hedonic experience should have been present in the past. A capacity for affiliation will then manifest itself from time to time in dreams and in the analytic relationship and this can be built on and 'amplified' with warmth and affirmation when it occurs.

The agonic mode can never be analysed away, however. Rank, status, dominance and submission are notes on the archetypal keyboard that it is not always possible to avoid playing. In all hierarchically organized societies a certain amount of self-monitoring and self-protective vigilance is inevitable if one is to avoid being displaced from one's position. In political philosophy the relationship between exploiting master and exploited slave has been a central issue since the discovery of agriculture and the accumulation of surpluses. In our own days, our political obsession with social equality has driven the conflict underground into extremist political movements and the sexual rituals of sado-masochism. The fact remains that whatever theoretical standpoint we may adopt to these matters, the dominance–submission diathesis inevitably resurfaces in our dreams, because we are dealing with an archetype – the ubiquitous tendency apparent in all social mammals for individuals to exert power and acquire dominance. The shaky self-confidence of neurotic patients, for example, is linked to chronic insecurity as to how they are being assessed by others. This is very apparent in their dreams, where a lot of self-testing goes on in an effort to anticipate social threats to their self-esteem. For whereas the hedonic mode is based on mutual attachment and reassurance, the agonic mode is based on mutual suspicion and defensiveness. Where the hedonic mode induces relaxation and friendly proximity, the agonic induces arousal and social distance. It is apparent, therefore, that the agonic mode predominates in all neurotic conditions. The hedonic mode, on the other hand, is conducive to health, happiness, and wellbeing. When it comes to selecting which of the two modes to emphasize, the analyst's duty is clear. Violent and hostile dreams have to be accepted, as do negative transferences, but it is essential that they are dealt with in the context of a warm and supporting relationship.

Dominance and submission conflicts proceed not only in social situations but also within the personality, for the superego can be exceptionally strict and repressive in dealing with aspects of the personality it regards as recalcitrant or incorrigible. This is vividly apparent in dreams as well as in the manner that depressed and intra-punitive people talk to themselves. Firestone (1986, quoted by Gilbert) describes one such inner harangue: 'Just be quiet. Shut up. Just don't say anything, O.K.? I don't want to hear anything from you.' Gilbert has made the interesting suggestion that such self-inflicted attacks are like auto-immune diseases, in which the body turns against itself. In both cases, one aspect of the self attacks another in the manner of a dominant reptile attacking a conspecific that has encroached on its territorial space.

Similar dynamics are apparent in people whose sexual orientation is predominantly sado-masochistic in character. Here the principle of compensation is also very evident both in their fantasies and their dreams. Masochists, for example, deny their own competitive and aggressive propensities for self-assertion and the acquisition of status, projecting these attributes on to their masters or mistresses. Sadists, on the other hand, deny their empathic, nurturing, and loving capacities, projecting these on to their slaves. However, in the dreams of both masochists and sadists, the denied qualities are apparent as unintegrated components in the psyche, and through dreamwork can be developed and made available to the conscious personality.

Agonic and hedonic dreams, therefore, afford extensive insight into the archetypal structures responsible for human social adjustment and provide valuable material for therapeutic intervention when this adjustment is impaired.

Anxiety Dreams and Nightmares

O, I have past a miserable night,
So full of fearefull dreames, of ugly sights
That as I am a Christian faithful man,
I would not spend another such a night
Though 'twere to buy a world of happy daies:
So full of dismal terror was the time.
WILLIAM SHAKESPEARE, *Richard III*

All mammals have been observed to manifest the signs of fear and anxiety; and, from their behaviour during the REM state, it seems likely that situations capable of releasing these emotions must feature in their dreams. The capacity for anxiety is biologically adaptive, and without it no mammal, ourselves included, could survive in the wild.

Anxiety dreams are very common in human subjects and their function is probably to alert us to danger. They warn, prepare, and motivate us – as does anxiety experienced when we are awake. People particularly prone to anxiety experience more anxiety dreams than calmer subjects, which tends to give the lie to Jung's theory that dreams compensate conscious attitudes. However, Freud's idea that anxiety occurs in dreams when the censor begins to fail, allowing forbidden desires to enter dreaming consciousness, accounts no better for the majority of anxiety dreams. They are usually about the same situations that evoke appropriate anxiety in reality. Moreover, anxiety dreams *can* be compensatory in function – as when we are living in a fool's paradise and being unduly relaxed about an issue to which we would do well to give urgent attention. You may have failed to prepare adequately for an examination, an important meeting, or a speech, thinking 'it will be all right on the day', only to have a dream in which you find yourself going into the examination, meeting, or assembly room, hopelessly unprepared. Such typical 'examination' or 'actor's nightmare' dreams are clearly motivational in function. Equally, an examination dream may be a metaphor for some other testing situation in life that one is not facing up to and that one is not sufficiently prepared to deal with. Work has to be done on such dreams for the true nature of their warning to be understood.

253

From the biological standpoint, anxiety is a form of vigilance. To survive in this dangerous world, an organism has to be alert to environmental changes so as to be prepared to meet whatever emergencies may arise. Pavlov considered this to be a reflex, and he called it the 'What is it?' reflex. Neither vigilance nor the 'What is it?' reflex necessarily gives rise to anxiety. Vigilance shifts into anxiety when a possible threat or danger is perceived. Progressive stages of alert can thus be discerned, passing from vigilance, through anxiety to fear, panic, and terror, each with its emotional and physical correlates. All the physical manifestations of fear – palpitations, laboured breathing, trembling, sweating, gastro-intestinal symptoms etc. – are caused by activation of the sympathetic nervous system and the release of adrenalin into the blood stream. These radical changes have the effect of preparing the organism to fight like a demon or run like hell – the fight or flight response. Anxiety dreams sometimes mobilize these physical responses; nightmares invariably do.

Nightmares are common, particularly among children, and their basic characteristics appear to be universal. They are dreams in which the dreamer feels helpless in the presence of danger and experiences overwhelming anxiety or fear. The Anglo-Saxon word *mare* meant demon and was derived from the Sanskrit *mara*, destroyer, which, in turn, probably came from *mar*, to crush. Nightmare, therefore, carries the connotation of an horrific dream of being crushed or mangled by a demon destroyer. Originally the term denoted an actual visitation from a 'night fiend', but recognition of the intrapsychic origin of dreams has coincided with acceptance that nightmares are states induced in and by the dreamer. Freud's explanation of them is a classic case of the triumph of dogma over reason. Because all dreams are wish-fulfilments, argued Freud, then it follows that nightmares are wish-fulfilments, although, of course, the dreamer is not conscious of the wish: nevertheless, Freud insisted, we *secretly* wish to experience the horrible things that happen to us in nightmares.

It must be acknowledged that humans do on occasion clearly wish to be frightened – otherwise they would not go to horror films or ride on big dippers – but this is a voluntary exposure to potentially terrifying situations in order to prove that one can master the feelings induced by them; and although these situations may be frightening, we also know that they are safe and that nothing catastrophic is *really* going to happen. Nightmares are very different: the threatened catastrophe is experienced as terrifyingly real and there seems to be absolutely no escape. Far from wishing to re-experience a nightmare, people can be reluctant to go to sleep for fear that it might return.

A phylogenetic explanation of nightmares is inherently more satisfactory than Freud's. There can be no doubt that these terrifying dreams are about survival issues and, whether we like it or not, they have the effect of toning up our 'flight or fight' responses, preparing us to deal with real emergencies should they occur. In the environment of evolutionary adaptedness, major sources of threat were predatory animals and hostile strangers, and these figures still predominate in contemporary nightmares – as do potentially dangerous situations, such as being exposed without cover in open spaces, being trapped in a confined area with no means of escape, being alone in the dark, or being high up and in danger of falling. In fact, the distinction that is commonly made between anxiety dreams and nightmares is an echo of the distinction made in psychiatry between 'free-floating' anxiety (which may be evoked by a variety of different situations) and phobic anxiety (which is specific to one situation). When the various phobias suffered by modern men and women are examined in detail, there is nothing modern about them. They are all exaggerated fears of objects, animals, or situations that were potentially life-threatening in the environment in which we evolved.

The tendency to react with fear to such common stimulus situations is due to genetic biases that possess survival value, in the sense that they prepare individuals to meet real dangers. The existence of these biases would explain how it is that in modern civilized environments fear can be aroused in a variety of situations that are not, in fact, dangerous. Thus, to panic in a shop full of strangers, or to react with terror when a garden hose slithers across a lawn like a snake, may seem absurd to a normally adjusted person, but viewed from a biological standpoint, these reactions are understandable as manifestations of ancient response patterns. People prone to nightmares are suffering from a similar exaggerated sensitivity to naturally occurring cues which were commonly associated with danger in the archetypal environment of our species.

Nightmares can also be associated with different psychiatric categories: the nightmares of obsessional patients, for example, are commonly about things getting hopelessly out of control, while those of schizoid, autistic, or schizophrenic patients are about being persecuted, devoured, taken over, and possessed: the schizoid individual is one who withdraws from the group, voluntarily putting himself beyond the pale; but there he becomes especially vulnerable to 'The Enemy', so that the shadow archetype is activated and a high degree of paranoid sensitivity is the result – both in reality and in dreams.

In keeping with a phylogenetic view of nightmares, their basic features are not dependent on learning through sight and hearing – as can be deduced from the dreams of people blind and deaf from birth. For example, as a small child, Helen Keller dreamt of a wolf 'which seemed to rush towards me and put his cruel teeth into my body! I could not speak (the fact was, I could only spell with my fingers), and I tried to scream; but no sound escaped from my lips'.

Although recurrent nightmares and anxiety dreams can be extremely disagreeable, they can, nevertheless, present valuable opportunities for learning and for growth. They may draw attention to potentially threatening situations that the dreamer has so far failed to confront. Analysis of such dreams can be an urgent necessity to discover what they are about and to assist the ego to develop more adaptive strategies for use when similar threats, either actual or metaphorical, are encountered in real life. Not infrequently, such dreamwork may result in dreamers becoming 'lucid' on future occasions when the dream occurs, enabling them to meet the threat head-on. Instead of trying to flee from the murderous gunman and waking in terror the dreamer turns to face him and ask him if he has a problem. As a consequence, there is a growth in self-esteem and self-reliance, and the nightmares may well cease. This is particularly true in the case of childhood nightmares.

Children's Dreams

'He wants to know what you are going to do about the snake-thing . . . He says in the morning it turned into them things like ropes in the trees and hung in the branches. He says will it come back tonight?'
WILLIAM GOLDING, *Lord of the Flies*

Children's dreams tell us in fascinating detail about the function and purpose of dreaming. Theoretically, the psyche is virtually all collective unconscious at birth and it can only be with the passing years that dreams will increasingly combine personal with archetypal material. As the child grows, the gradual unfolding of innate psychic and behavioural competencies will enable the child to interact with its environment and perform functions of increasing complexity. The emergence of language, parent and peer attachments, self-awareness, delight in both competitive and co-operative patterns of play gradually provides the skills necessary to adapt appropriately as a healthy social being. Dreams, like play, facilitate an elaborate discourse between the developing ego, the environment, and the Self. This inaugurates the individuation process, on whose foundations the fully grown adult may later choose to build.

At first, young children have difficulty in differentiating between dreams and waking reality, but most are capable of making this distinction by the age of five or six. The French developmental psychologist Jean Piaget considered three stages to be involved:

(1) Up to the age of three or four, children do not distinguish between dreams and waking life. They may wake up from a nightmare, for example, and believe the terrible witch is still under the bed. Parental attempts at reassurance that 'it was only a nasty dream' may be ineffective. Only the practical demonstration that there is indeed *nothing* under the bed will bring relative peace of mind.

(2) Between four and six they begin to distinguish between dreamt events and outer events, but they still have difficulty in understanding that what is dreamt is purely internal and not directly related to external reality.

257

(3) Between five and eight they are able to comprehend that dreams are exclusively *internal* phenomena; and the first lucid dreams often occur at this stage.

Analysis of the content of dreams reported by children reveals that they are more often disturbing than pleasurable. Brenda Mallon, who has published a valuable collection of such reports in her book *Children Dreaming* (1989), says that many children lamented to her that they had never had a happy dream. This is in flat contradiction to Freud's view that dreams in childhood are simple wish-fulfilments. Two instances, much quoted by his followers, concern Freud's nephew Hermann and daughter Anna. Hermann was only twenty-two months old when on the occasion of Freud's birthday he was deputed to present his uncle with a basket of delicious cherries. When the moment came, however, it was only with difficulty that Hermann could be induced to part with them. 'On the day after his birthday sacrifice,' reports Freud, 'he awoke with a cheerful piece of news, which could only have originated from a dream: "Hermann eaten all the chewwies!"' (1976, p. 210). In the second instance, Anna, Freud's youngest daughter, then nineteen months old, had an attack of vomiting one morning and was, as a consequence, kept without food all the following day. 'During the night after this day of starvation she was heard calling out excitedly in her sleep: "Anna Fweud, stwawbewwies, wild stwawbewwies, omblet, pudden!"' (p. 209). While some children's dreams no doubt fulfil the wishes uppermost in their minds, these seem to be a relatively small minority. More often, their dreams are full of anxieties and fears, and the truly interesting aspect of these fears is that they would be appropriate to children of their age group *living in the environment of evolutionary adaptedness* – i.e. they are of abandonment, being captured or kidnapped, being pursued by predatory animals and devouring monsters. Even more interesting, they characteristically echo the kinds of preoccupation typical of hunter-gatherer communities, namely, fears of witchcraft, ghosts, and malevolent spirits. Very young children also spontaneously attribute dreams to outside influences such as God, fairies, and spirits – as did our ancestors. The well-substantiated observation that children are particularly prone to nightmares could be accounted for on the basis that children are much closer to the archetypal fears of the species, namely, of being attacked by strangers or predators, or being left alone in the dark. Recurrent nightmares can be most reliably alleviated by parental accessibility and reassurance combined with regular provision of a night light.

As archetypal theory would predict, the proportion of mythic themes declines with age. Kluger (1975) found mythological themes in 47 per cent of the dreams reported by children up to the age of six, and 36 per cent up to the age of nine, but only 26 per cent in the dreams of adults.

Most impressive and delightful of Brenda Mallon's findings are the statements made by children about the nature and function of dreams. These strike one as wiser, and often more poetic, than the learned formulations of analysts and dream researchers. For example, Eve (aged four) described her dreams as 'pictures in my pillow'. Appreciation of the compensatory nature of dreams is shown by Erin (aged eleven) who said, 'We dream because we have a problem, then our dreams try to cheer us up.' The connection between dreams and memory is made by at least two of Mallon's subjects: 'Dreaming helps us get far-back thoughts which are remote and distant in our minds,' said Rosemary (thirteen); 'We dream to rewind our memory,' said Adam (seven). The Adlerian view of dreaming is beautifully expressed by Alvin (seven): 'When you want to do something you have to dream it first so you know how to do it.' The notion that dreams could be a form of entertainment is also expressed by Brian (thirteen): 'We dream so that we don't get fed up while we are asleep.'

Jung was particularly interested in children's dreams because his own experience as a child had taught him how powerful and influential they could be in forecasting and shaping future development. The earliest dreams we can remember sometimes have an awesome, almost adult feel to them. This may be due either to their archetypal loading or to parental influences. As Jung observed, children commonly dream about problems which are not really their own but belong to their parents.

Although children's dreams should be received with sensitive attention, Jung warned against working with them in too much detail since it might impair the child's adjustment to the social environment by focusing interest too wholeheartedly on archetypal fantasies. A similar danger can exist for adults who become exclusively enmeshed in their inner world at the expense of their outer relationships. However, the study of dreams of childhood is a fascinating area of research which can tell us much about the contribution of REM sleep to the adaptive competence of the emerging personality.

Diagnostic and Prognostic Dreams

Someone dreamt that the sky was destroyed. He died.

ARTEMIDORUS

Occasionally one comes across dreams which hint at some organic illness, and these have to be taken seriously because they may provide the first clue that actual disease is present. Hall (1991) reports the case of someone who dreamt of 'something exploding inside' before a diagnosis of aortic aneurysm was made (p. 194). A patient of mine awoke with abdominal pain after a long and frustrating dream in which she was trying by various means to unblock a drainpipe. She was subsequently found to be suffering from gallstones. Medard Boss (1957) describes a patient who had a dream on two successive nights in which '*a Balinese demon of disease would appear to her and force her to sit on an overheated central-heating pipe*'. On each occasion she had a severe burning pain between her legs, which passed off as soon as she woke up. On the third night she again had the dream, but on this occasion the pain persisted after waking and she found herself to be suffering from a fever. When her doctor was called, he diagnosed acute cystitis (p. 160).

There is some evidence that dreams can actually trigger the onset of medical conditions, and this is not altogether surprising in view of the major upheavals in autonomic and hormonal functioning which coincide with REM sleep. Cardiac arrhythmias, attacks of migraine and nocturnal asthma have been reliably reported as immediately following disturbing dreams, while patients with high blood pressure report dreams in which more hostility occurs than in the dreams of people whose blood pressure is normal (Katz and Shapiro, 1993).

One of Jung's patients provides an instructive example in this context. He was a learned and able man of forty, the headmaster of a great Swiss public school, and an authority on the psychology of Wilhelm Wundt, which, as Jung notes in a wry aside, 'has nothing to do with details of human life but moves in the stratosphere of abstract ideas'. He came to Jung complaining of mysterious episodes of vertigo, which were associated with palpitations, nausea, and feelings of weakness and exhaustion. It at once occurred to Jung that these symptoms mimicked those of mountain sickness, a common enough condition in Switzerland, which afflicts people not acclimatized to heights when they ascend a high mountain too quickly.

The patient came with a series of three dreams. In the first of these *'the patient finds himself in a small village in Switzerland. He is a very solemn black figure in a long coat; under his arm he carries several thick books. There is a group of young boys whom he recognizes as having been his classmates. They are looking at him and they say: "That fellow does not often make his appearance here." '*

'In order to understand this dream,' comments Jung, 'you have to remember that the patient is in a very fine position and has had a very good scientific education. But he started really from the bottom and is a self-made man. His parents were very poor peasants, and he worked his way up to his present position. He is very ambitious and is filled with the hope that he will rise still higher. He is like a man who has climbed in one day from sea level to a level of 6,000 feet, and there he sees peaks 12,000 feet high towering above him.' He wishes to push on without realizing that he is in no fit state to do so. 'This lack of realization is the reason for his symptoms of mountain sickness. The dream brings home to him the actual psychological situation.' Instead of remembering where he came from, he thinks only of his future career and his ambition to acquire a Chair as a university professor. The dream compensates this attitude by reminding him of his origins, for he is in danger of over-reaching himself.

In the second dream, *'He knows that he ought to go to an important conference, and he is taking his portfolio. But he notices that the hour is rather advanced and that the train will leave soon, and so he gets into that well-known state of haste and of fear of being too late. He tries to get his clothes together, his hat is nowhere, his coat is mislaid, and he runs about in search of them and shouts up and down the house, "Where are my things?" Finally, he gets everything together, and runs out of the house only to find that he has forgotten his portfolio. He rushes back for it, and looking at his watch finds how late it is getting; then he runs to the station, but the road is quite soft so that it is like walking on a bog and his feet can hardly move any more. Pantingly he arrives at the station only to see that the train is just leaving.'*

It is a long train and as he watches it winding round a curve he thinks, *'If only the engine driver . . . has sufficient intelligence not to rush full steam ahead; for if he does, the long train behind him which will still be rounding the curve will be derailed.'* At that moment the driver opens the throttle and the train rushes ahead. Inevitably a catastrophic crash ensues and the dreamer wakes up *'with the fear characteristic of a nightmare'.*

Dreams of being late and having to overcome obstacles which keep getting in the way are very common, particularly in people with an over-conscientious or obsessional disposition. 'The most irritating thing is,' notes Jung, 'that consciously you want something very much, and an unseen devil is always working against it . . .' The dreamer's ambition is driving him to leave home, but there is an unconscious resistance to doing so. He is the engine-driver, who thinks he can rush ahead without waiting for the rest of the train to round the bend. This behaviour Jung compares to the man's attempt to scale the 12,000-foot peak before he is ready. He forgets that his ego is 'the avant-garde' of his psychological existence and that he has to bring up behind him his 'long saurian's tail'.

The third dream Jung describes as his patient's 'big dream': *'I am in the country, in a simple peasant's house, with an elderly, motherly peasant woman. I talk to her about a great journey I am planning: I am going to walk from Switzerland to Leipzig. She is enormously impressed, at which I am very pleased. At this moment I look through the window at a meadow where there are peasants gathering hay. Then the scene changes. In the background appears a monstrously big crab-lizard. It moves first to the left and then to the right so that I find myself standing*

in the angle between as if in an open pair of scissors. Then I have a little
rod or a wand in my hand, and I lightly touch the monster's head with
the rod and kill it. Then for a long time I stand there contemplating that
monster.'

Once more the dreamer is back in his original surroundings and
finds himself with the peasant mother. Just as he impressed the village
boys in the first dream with his fine coat and books, now he
impresses the peasant woman with talk of his journey to Leipzig
(where he hopes to get a Chair). When Jung asks him for associations
to the 'simple peasant's house', he says: 'It is the lazar-house of St
Jacob near Basel.' Jung at once amplifies this association in terms
of its cultural context. The old leper house of St Jacob was the site
of a battle in 1444, when 1,300 Swiss soldiers defeated the 30,000-
strong Army of the Duke of Burgundy. The small Swiss force had
been ordered by their commander to wait for reinforcements before
launching the attack, but as soon as the enemy approached, they
threw themselves headlong into the assault, with the result that
they were slaughtered to the last man. However, their heroic stand
put a stop to the Burgundian advance. 'Here again,' observes Jung,
'we come to the idea of this rushing ahead without establishing a
connection with the bulk of the tail-end and again the action is
fatal . . . This attitude of the patient is the reason for his symptoms
of mountain sickness. He went too high, he is not prepared for the
altitude, he forgets where he started from.'

Turning to the archetypal implications of the dream, Jung draws
the patient's attention to the references to the hero motif that occur
throughout the series. He is in the grip of a hero fantasy – the great
man in the long coat with a brilliant future, the hero warrior who
charges to a glorious death on the field of honour at St Jacob, and the
hero challenger who overcomes the monster (crab-lizard). The
dreamer himself realizes this, for in his associations he volunteers, 'I
felt surrounded on either side like a hero who is going to fight a
dragon.' 'The hero motif is invariably accompanied by the dragon
motif,' affirms Jung, 'the dragon and the hero who fights him are
two figures of the same myth.'

That the monster in this instance is not a dragon but a mixture of a
reptile and crab leads Jung to a neuro-anatomical interpretation of its

significance: the lizard is a reference to the reptilian centres of the brain stem and the spinal cord, while the crab, in which the autonomic nervous system predominates, refers to the sympathetic and parasympathetic functions. On the basis of this, Jung warns the patient that his conscious attitude is in conflict with his psychophysical well-being, and that if he carries on as he is he will be cornered and attacked by his own central nervous system. This has already begun to happen in the form of symptoms resembling those of mountain sickness.

The dreamer does not accept Jung's interpretation, however. He has succeeded in overcoming the monster with his magic wand, says he; as a result he no longer needs to worry about the opposing power of the crab-lizard. But Jung dismisses this as wishful thinking; the magic wand is no lethal weapon, and the monster will be proof against it: 'What do you think is the reason why you contemplate the animal for such a long time?' he asks. 'Your dreams contain a warning. You behave exactly like the engine-driver, or like the Swiss who were foolhardy enough to run up against the enemy without any support behind them, and if you behave in the same way you will meet with a catastrophe.'

But the patient goes off to Leipzig regardless, and in due course comes to a sticky end. Jung does not describe what actually became of him, but the symbolism of the crab-lizard would make one fear a possible diagnosis of cancer. The dreams of this brief series were, thus, both diagnostic and prognostic. That they failed to have any therapeutic influence was not the fault of the dreams but the fault of the dreamer who failed to heed them (CW18, paras. 163–201).

Dreams of Falling and Flying

Rock-a-bye, baby, on the tree top,
When the wind blows the cradle will rock,
When the bough breaks, the cradle will fall,
And down will come baby, cradle and all.

Dreams promoting vigilance to the danger of falling may well owe their phylogenetic origins to the risks run by our distant ancestors swinging through the branches of tropical forests. But the need for vigilance has persisted into more recent times when trees continued to afford refuge from predators and vantage points from which to survey the surrounding savannah for game, camping sites, or potentially hostile strangers. In modern times, dreams continue to warn us to be careful in high places, both realistically and symbolically.

Dreams of flying have less evident phylogenetic roots, though humans have always been fascinated by birds, whether as prey, as signs, or as symbols, and, as the use of bird totems demonstrates, we have identified with their powers of flight, migration, and vision. Long before the age of aviation, myths, folklore, and fairy tales revealed man's envy of the birds and his longing to share with them the freedom of the skies. Not surprisingly, flying dreams are among the most agreeable it is possible to experience. To fly in a dream is to have a momentary and intoxicating awareness of what it is to be in the transcendent state, to be absolutely and uncompromisingly free and beyond all restriction. Such a condition can never last, but that makes it all the more agreeable.

The symbolism of ascent and descent, of 'rise' and 'fall', has both agonic and moral overtones. The danger of flying too high (*hubris*) and falling to one's doom (*nemesis*) was portrayed by the Greeks in the myth of Icarus. The higher you climb the harder you fall. To lose one's footing, or be knocked off one's perch, is to lose status and 'come a cropper' socially. Loss of moral status was once symbolized by the 'fallen' woman (men were apparently spared this catastrophe, except in the Biblical sense). Falling is also associated with the idea of losing control, as when 'falling in love'.

Recurrent dreams expressing fears of falling commonly arise from an obsessional need to control things because of neurotic anxiety about what could happen if control were abandoned by 'letting go'. Understanding the problem through dreamwork and allowing oneself to fall in subsequent dreams can mark an important transformation of one's coping strategies. The doctor, whose dream showed him he was treating his patients like cattle, had a recurrent nightmare that he was holding on to a cliff edge, terrified of falling. He could feel the strength ebbing from his arms and he knew that he could not hold on much longer. At the very last moment he would wake up in a sweat. Once he had grasped the symbolic significance of this experience, I encouraged him to risk letting go the next time he found himself cliff-hanging in a dream, but it was several months before he could manage it. When eventually he succeeded, he fell only a few feet into shallow water and awoke with an immense feeling of relief. This, together with other dreams about relinquishing the need *to control*, coincided with the development of a more easy-going attitude towards himself, his patients, and his family.

Dream Landscapes

What would the world be, once bereft
Of wet and of wildness? Let them be left,
O let them be left, wildness and wet;
Long live the weeds and the wilderness yet.
GERARD MANLEY HOPKINS

Dream landscapes can be detailed, emotive, and rich in symbolic implications. What can this have to do with archetypes and evolved strategies of adaptation? In their paper 'Evolved Responses to Landscapes' (1992), Gordon Orians and Judith Heerwagen argue that our aesthetic responses to landscape have been derived, at least in part, from the psychological structures that evolved to help hunter-gatherers, who had to make frequent changes of habitat, to arrive at better decisions about when to move, where to settle, and what activities to follow in different localities. Our ancestors had the same needs as ourselves – to find shelter, food and water, and to protect themselves from predators and hostile bands of people. Although we now live in rather different environments to those in which we evolved, far too few generations have succeeded one another for any radical genetic mutations to have occurred, such as would influence the kind of environments we select and respond to. As a result, Orians and Heerwagen argue, the response patterns which evolved under conditions quite different from those we now experience nevertheless influence our contemporary reactions in unconscious ways.

266

The probability is that in the environment of evolutionary adaptedness (the EEA), dreaming about landscapes served to emphasize important cues encountered on the previous day's march or hunt in the light of archetypal programmes designed to increase adaptive efficiency on the following day. In the modern world, we still have to negotiate the physical environment, assess threats and dangers, get ourselves to where we have to go, and find our way home again afterwards. As Stephen Kaplan (1992), another landscape researcher, has commented, we have not ceased to be 'information-based animals', continuously struggling to make sense of our surroundings. Survival today, no less than in the EEA, depends upon an archetypal imperative to explore and to construct 'cognitive maps' of the physical environment. Such behaviour is highly adaptive and it is not surprising that we should devote much time to it in our dreams. As a result of new information discovered during the daytime we update and extend our cognitive maps during the night.

Some fascinating research has been done on the kinds of landscape that people prefer. It appears that the sort of environment in which we feel most at home corresponds to the savannah of tropical Africa — the very landscape in which our species evolved. This is presumably because the savannah provides us with what we have always needed: ready supplies of nutritious food, trees that offer protection from the sun and can be climbed to avoid predators, long, unimpeded views, and the existence of hills, valleys, and plains enabling us to orient in space.

Another pair of researchers, Balling and Falk (1982), showed subjects from different age groups slides of landscapes which included tropical forest, deciduous forest, coniferous forest, East African savannah, and desert. They found that eight-year-old children consistently selected the savannah, saying that they would rather visit and live in such a landscape than in any other. From the age of fifteen onwards, the savannah, deciduous forest and coniferous forest were liked equally well, and all three of these 'biomes' were preferred over the rain forest or desert. The least appreciated environment for all age groups was the desert, while two slides representing the savannah during the dry season received lower ratings than the savannah during the green, growing season. This is completely in accord with the affect induced by similar landscapes in dreams, deserts being taken as symbols of aridity, isolation and despair, fertile landscapes as symbols of hope and renewal.

One extremely interesting finding was that none of the respondents in the Balling and Falk study had ever visited a tropical savannah. This, combined with the consistent preference of young children for this type of landscape, led Balling and Falk to postulate that a developmental pattern exists for landscape appreciation. We are innately programmed to respond to a savannah-like biome but this can be modified in the course of growing up by experience in other settings, such as the deciduous woods of the eastern United States which were familiar to all their subjects. Experience is clearly important in determining aesthetic responses, but it does not completely override the innate response patterns which are expressed so strongly in young children.

These findings are highly germane to our thesis. Choice of habitat exerts a powerful influence on survival and reproductive success, and the psychic and behavioural mechanisms involved have consequently been under heavy selection pressure for hundreds of thousands of years. Habitat selection involves emotional responses to key features of an environment, which induce the kind of positive or negative feelings that lead to rejection, exploration, or settlement.

For most animals, exploration appears to be a positive, cognitive and emotional experience, and is probably at the basis of all research, inquisitiveness, neophilia and desires for travel. However, it also brings potential hazards in its train. Danger may be indicated not only by dense undergrowth or lack of cover, but by signs of bad weather, forest fires, earthquakes, avalanches or landslides, all of which feature significantly in dreams, and are rich in emotive and symbolic overtones.

An approach to dreams which viewed them purely as means of 'information-processing' could conceive landscape dreams as a mere mechanism for updating cognitive maps. This would, however, completely overlook the symbolic power such dreams can hold by virtue of the deep emotions that they activate. A primitive animism persists in the unconscious and through its authority we attribute psychological vitality to the trees, mountains, streams and valleys of which our dream landscapes are constructed.

Lucid Dreams

For lucid dreamers nothing is impossible!
STEPHEN LABERGE

A lucid dream is a dream in which one knows one is dreaming. The term was introduced by the Dutch psychiatrist Frederik Willelms van Eeden in a paper he presented to the Society for Psychical Research in London in 1913, based on 352 lucid dreams dreamt by him between 1898 and 1912. He described the first of his lucid dreams as follows: *'I dreamt that I was floating through a landscape with bare trees, knowing that it was April, and I remarked that the perspective of the branches and twigs changed quite naturally. Then I made the reflection, during sleep, that my fancy would never be able to invent or to make an image as intricate as the perspective movement of little twigs seen in floating by.'* It seems that in dreams the brain can synthesize the kind of detailed perspective movements that are seen in computer games. What struck van Eeden was not only that he could become conscious while dreaming but that he was able to direct his attention and perform certain acts of free will.

Following the tradition already started by Hervey de Saint-Denys, he adopted an experimental approach to his dreams. *'On September 9 1904, I dreamt that I stood at a table before a window. On the table were different objects. I was perfectly aware that I was dreaming and I considered what sorts of experiments I could make . . . I took a fine claret-glass from the table and struck it with my fist, with all my might, at the same time reflecting how dangerous it would be to do this in waking life; yet the glass remained whole. But lo! when I looked at it again after some time, it was broken.'*

The fact that the glass broke later, 'like an actor who misses his cue', gave van Eeden 'a very curious impression of being in a *fake-world*, cleverly imitated, but with small failures'. In his dream he proceeded to throw the broken glass out of the window in order to discover whether he could hear it tinkling as it smashed in the street below. *'I heard the noise all right and I even saw two dogs run away from it quite naturally. I thought what a good imitation this comedy-world was.'*

As many others have found, becoming lucid in a dream can be an exhilarating experience. Hugh Calloway, whose pen name was Oliver Fox, was so enchanted by a lucid dream as a student that it stimulated him to become a lifelong dream researcher. He describes the crucial moment of lucidity as follows: *'Instantly, the vividness of life increased a hundredfold. Never had sea and sky and trees shone with such glamorous beauty; even the commonplace houses seemed alive and mystically beautiful. Never had I felt so absolutely well, so clear-brained, so inexpressibly free! The sensation was exquisite beyond words; but it lasted only a few minutes and I awoke'* (Fox, 1962).

Lucid dreamers agree with van Eeden that in this state it is possible to exercise some control over the content and course of the dream. New strategies can be tried out that one would never dare attempt in waking life — like turning and facing an attacking lion. You can recognize alien figures as aspects of yourself, meet them, converse with them, and come to terms with them. You can also stand outside the role you are playing in the dream, criticize it and change it. In other words, it becomes possible in a lucid dream to do directly what in normal dreamwork has to be done indirectly and the consequences can be more radically transformative.

There is an apparent kinship between lucid dreaming, active imagination, hypnotic and mediumistic trance, and certain forms of acute psychosis: all can bring about lasting changes in those who experience them. All are liminal states in which conscious and unconscious systems interact. Of all such states, hypnotic trance has received most research attention, and it has been established that in deep trance profound psychophysical changes can be produced — bleeding stopped, for example, allergic reactions inhibited, and anaesthesia induced. It is possible that the progress of certain cancers can also be inhibited by this means. Unfortunately, however, only 10 per cent of the population is capable of experiencing deep hypnotic trance, and this is not apparently something that can be learned. The healing potential of lucid dreaming has not been adequately researched, but since it *can* be learned it could prove to be widely effective.

Experimental investigation of lucid dreaming came of age with the researches of Stephen LaBerge at the Stanford University Sleep Laboratory in California. Not only has LaBerge succeeded in teaching himself and his students to become proficient lucid dreamers but he has also pioneered techniques enabling subjects to indicate to observers (with vertical movements of their eyes) when they become aware of dreaming in their sleep. This has led to a number of important experimental findings, such as that the length of time taken to dream of certain events is about the same as the time it would take to experience those events in waking reality.

In analytic practice, I have found that therapeutic progress is advanced in those patients who become proficient lucid dreamers. It is as if they can use active imagination in their dreams, with the consequence that the whole experience is more intensely filled with meaning.

Lucid dreaming may occur spontaneously, but these occurrences are comparatively rare. However, it can, as I say, be learned without too much difficulty. As with remembering dreams, motivation is the key. The important thing is to develop the necessary mental 'set' – to want to become aware of your dreams while you are in them. First of all, dream recall must be practised and improved: familiarity with dreams and their contents makes it easier to recognize dreams while you are having them. The German psychologist Paul Tholey advises the development of a 'critical-reflective attitude' to your state of consciousness. You should get into the habit of asking yourself 'Am I dreaming?' *while you are awake*, and you should do this at least ten times a day. In particular, you must ask yourself this question as you go off to sleep and as you wake up. Tholey says that people usually have their first lucid dream within a month of adopting this practice. Some even have one the first night. The crucial thing, as Stephen LaBerge says, is 'to let your body fall asleep while you keep your mind awake' (p. 152). He advises that you should count yourself to sleep: 'One, I'm dreaming, two, I'm dreaming,' and so on. Eventually, say at 'Forty-two, I'm dreaming,' you'll find that you actually *are* dreaming and, with luck, you will remain aware of the fact.

Both the Russian philosopher Piotr D. Ouspensky and the American psychologist Nathan Rapport advocated concentration on the hypnagogic impressions that precede sleep: you should keep recalling what has already passed through your mind, and, with practice, you will retain the capacity for conscious introspection as you pass into the first dream of the night.

However, these techniques are less likely to work at the beginning of the sleep cycle because REM sleep normally commences after a period of NREM. Success is more readily achieved if one takes an afternoon siesta, when it is possible to pass directly from waking into the REM state. It is certainly the time when I have had most lucid dreams and when I have also been able most reliably to 'incubate' dreams. On one occasion, I visited a little-known Asklepion in Attica with a Greek colleague. After a bucolic lunch of retsina, goat cheese and olives, I lay down on a *kline* in the *abaton* and informed my companion that I intended to go to sleep and have a dream of Asklepios. Within minutes I was asleep and Asklepios immediately appeared. He came bustling towards me and stood looking down at me in obvious irritation. 'Now look,' he said, 'I'll thank you not to come here wasting my time!' With that he hurried away and I awoke, ashamed of myself for having treated a sacred shrine of healing with levity.

In her popular book *Creative Dreaming*, Patricia Garfield advocates autosuggestion as an effective means for inducing lucid dreams. Before going to sleep she suggests repeating, 'Tonight, I *will* have a lucid dream.' She reports that when she used this technique it resulted in a 'classic learning curve, increasing the frequency of prolonged lucid dreams from a baseline of zero to a high of three per week' (Garfield, 1976, p. 184).

Once you have had your first lucid dream, it becomes easier to have them subsequently. It is as if a conceptual barrier has been broken. Before Roger Bannister did it, no one believed it possible to run a mile in four minutes. Then hundreds flooded through the barrier after him. So it is with lucid dreams.

Because dreams are so real, it is hard to 'wake up' to the fact that you are dreaming. You may *suspect* you are in a dream (the first step to lucidity) but not be convinced. How can you be sure? A test is necessary. You need to do something that you cannot do in waking life – taking off and flying, using nothing but your hands and feet, is a good test. The procedure goes something as follows: Am I in a dream? I think so. All right, I'll fly. Prepare for take off. Go! Has it worked? Yes! I fly, therefore I dream.

Prospective (Anticipatory) Dreams

Dreams prepare, announce, or warn about certain situations often long before they actually happen. This is not necessarily a miracle or a precognition. Most crises . . . have a long incubation.

C. G. JUNG

Prospective dreams are not to be confused with precognitive or prophetic dreams. 'It would be wrong to call them prophetic,' wrote Jung, 'because at bottom they are no more prophetic than a medical diagnosis or a weather forecast. They are merely an anticipatory combination of possibilities which may coincide with the actual behaviour of things . . .' (*CW*8, para. 493). That prospective dreams should occur is understandable, therefore, since 'everything that will be happens on the basis of what has been' (*CW*9i, para. 499).

That the initial dreams that patients bring to analysis may be prospective or anticipatory is what makes them of special interest to the analyst. Jung cites three such dreams, all from the same patient, and each dreamt at the beginning of a new course of treatment with three different analysts. The first of these was as follows: '*I have to cross the frontier into another country, but cannot find the frontier and nobody can tell me where it is.*'

The ensuing treatment proved unsuccessful and was broken off after a short time. Starting with her second analyst, she dreamt: '*I have to cross the frontier, but the night is pitch-black and I cannot find the customs-house. After a long search I see a tiny light far off in the distance, and assume that the frontier is over there. But in order to get there, I have to pass through a valley and a dark wood in which I lose my way. Then I notice that someone is near me. Suddenly he clings to me like a madman and I awake in terror.*'

This second course of treatment was also broken off prematurely, apparently because the analyst became too closely identified with the patient and lost his therapeutic objectivity in the process.

Her third dream came when she entered analysis with Jung: '*I had to cross a frontier, or rather I have already crossed it, and find myself in a*

Swiss customs-house. I have only a handbag with me and think I have nothing to declare. But the customs official dives into my bag and, to my astonishment, pulls out a pair of twin beds.'

Jung comments that to interpret these dreams on a reductive, causalistic basis would be to miss their point. 'They afford unmistakable information about the analytic situation, the correct understanding of which is the greatest therapeutic importance.' The third dream revealed that in coming to Jung she had probably 'crossed the frontier' and would have, among other things, to deal with the sexual problem in her marriage (*CW*16, paras. 307–12).

Though Jung agrees with biological theorists and with Alfred Adler that 'the dream prepares the dreamer for the events of the following day' (*CW*5, para. 5), he warns against taking apparently prospective dreams as oracular. Critical conscious assessment by the ego is always necessary, otherwise 'one might be led to suppose that the dream is a kind of psychopomp which, because of its superior knowledge, infallibly guides life in the right direction' (*CW*8, para. 494).

A neurological parallel can be made here. The forebrain is, in a sense, Promethean – the bringer of light (consciousness) and foresight (Prometheus = *he who knows in advance*), while the old brain is Epimethean (Epimetheus = *he who is wise after the event*) and, indirectly, the bringer of darkness (unconsciousness, and, through Pandora, evil). It is the Promethean power of the forebrain that gives dreams their precognitive capacity: they are both anticipatory and informed by archetypal wisdom. But they are not gospels – merely intimations as to future possibilities.

Sexual Dreams

It is fair to say that there is no group of ideas that is incapable of representing sexual facts and wishes.

SIGMUND FREUD

The archetypal systems involved in sexual behaviour and bonding between sexual partners both govern the life of individuals and guarantee the survival of the species. Dreams centred on these themes are among the most common of all dreams and, accordingly, Freud felt justified in reducing a vast number of objects to their supposed masculine or feminine sexual symbolism: 'All elongated objects, such as sticks, tree-trunks and umbrellas (the opening of these last being comparable to an erection) may stand for the male organ – as well as all long, sharp weapons, such as knives, daggers and pikes. Another frequent though not entirely intelligible symbol of the same thing is a nail file – possibly on account of the rubbing up and down. Boxes, cases, chests, cupboards and ovens represent the uterus, and also hollow objects, ships, and vessels of all kinds. Rooms in dreams are usually women; if the various ways in and out of them are represented, this interpretation is scarcely open to doubt . . . A dream of going through a suite of rooms is a brothel or harem dream . . . Steps, ladders or staircases, or, as the case may be, walking up or down them, are representations of the sexual act.

'In men's dreams a necktie often appears as a symbol for the penis . . . nor is there any doubt that all weapons and tools are used as symbols for the male organ: e.g. ploughs, hammers, rifles, revolvers, daggers, sabres, etc.' (Freud, 1976, pp. 470–73).

The banal reductiveness of such interpretations robs these symbols of all their other implications. And far from being disguised or Bowdlerized in the way that Freud maintained, sexual dreams are usually explicit in their content: their frank nature means that they usually portray their intentions in straightforward images without resorting to unduly complicated symbolism. That the sexual dreams of contemporary people should not on the whole need to have recourse to all the running up and down stairs, putting swords in sheaths, and generally thrusting long straight objects into round receptive ones, may well have something to do with Freud's liberating influence on our sexual attitudes.

While there is little doubt that all the objects listed by Freud may indeed represent the human genitals, they may also represent a lot of other things as well. As Jung once quipped, the penis is itself a phallic symbol. Nature clearly intended it to represent power and virility as well as male sex: this could explain why the human penis is proportionately three times larger than in any other primate (Diamond, 1991).

One of the oldest and most sophisticated attempts to conceptualize

275

the nature and influence of masculine and feminine principles is that of the ancient Chinese Taoists with their concepts of Yang and Yin, those fundamental forces held to permeate all reality and to be present and active in both men and women. The Yang principle is characterized as energetic and assertive, its attributes are heat and light (symbolized by the sun and its rays); its realms are heaven and the spirit; in its phallic, penetrating aspect it arouses, fructifies, and creates; in its aggressive form it combats and destroys; its orientation is essentially extroverted; it is positive and impulsive, but also disciplined and ascetic.

Whereas Yang is assertive and initiating, the Yin principle is passive and containing (symbolized by the moon and the cave); its realms are earth, nature, and the womb, for it is essentially concerned with gestation, giving form to the energy of Yang, and bringing life out of darkness; its movement is essentially introverted.

Our culture is not alone in regarding assertiveness, physical aggression, and destructiveness as male attributes, and gestation, nurturance, and life-enhancement as female. There are good biological reasons why this should be so. They are universally apparent distinctions, and their very universality betrays their archetypal origins.

Fundamental symbol of sexual union is the *coniunctio oppositorum* of the *hieros gamos* which was both the central preoccupation and the goal of the alchemists. However, this symbol does not occur as a disguised substitute for the sexual act; rather the sexual act is but one example of *coniunctio* symbolism. The *coniunctio* represents the marrying of opposites as a *psychic* process and the transformation that it gives rise to occurs within the psyche. Similarly, the child that the union produces is a symbolic child which recombines the opposing natures involved into a new constellation. The union may be celebrated by the King and Queen in the alchemical water bath, a man and woman in bed, the sun and the moon in the heavens, or a bull and a cow in a field: the same mystery is being perpetuated. What matters for the life of the dreamer is the attitude adopted to it by ego-consciousness. Only when the events have been carefully considered can their relevance be properly understood. It should be stressed, however, that the longing for union with the opposite is seldom merely for a member of the opposite sex: one longs for what is *perceived* as opposite and therefore needed if one is to be whole. The desired opposite quality may well be carried by a member of one's own sex, by an animal, by a mythic creature, or by anything longed for as necessary for one's completion. This central and recurrent desire was addressed by Plato in his myth of the original round human being, divided by the gods into two halves, both of which are constantly seeking to be reunited with one another. The union of heaven and earth in early astrobiological religions, the marriage of the prince and princess in fairy tales, the union of *Sol* and *Luna* in alchemy are all examples of *coniunctio* symbolism arising from the collective unconscious. Such symbolism is as richly apparent in the dreams of our contemporaries as it doubtless was in the dreams of our ancestors long ago.

DREAMS AND CREATIVITY

*All this inventing, this producing, takes place in a pleasing
lively dream.*

WOLFGANG AMADEUS MOZART

A major deficiency of Freudian dream theory, not shared by its
Jungian counterpart, is its failure to account for the creative potential
of dreams. Freud quoted extensively from the dream literature that
preceded him, but, as he admitted to Wilhelm Fliess, he regarded
most of it as futile; and in *The Interpretation of Dreams* he is particularly
scornful of theorists, like F. W. Hildebrandt (1875), who celebrated
the dream's creative virtuosity: ' "There are few of us who could not
affirm, from our own experience," wrote Hildebrandt, "that there
emerges from time to time in the creations and fabrics of the genius
of dreams a depth and intimacy of emotion, a tenderness of feeling, a
clarity of vision, a subtlety of observation, and brilliance of wit such
as we should never claim to have at our permanent command in our
waking lives. There lies in dreams a marvellous poetry, an apt
allegory, an incomparable humour, a rare irony. A dream looks upon
the world in a light of strange idealism and often enhances the effects
of what it sees by its deep understanding of their essential nature. It
pictures earthly beauty to our eyes in a truly heavenly splendour and
clothes dignity with the highest majesty, it shows us our everyday
fears in the ghastliest shape and turns our amusement into jokes of
indescribable pungency. And sometimes, when we are awake and
still under the full impact of an experience like one of these, we
cannot but feel that never in our life has the real world offered us its
equal" ' (quoted by Freud, 1976, p. 129).

Freud quotes this passage in order to dismiss it as dated, coming, as
he says, from a time when 'the human mind was dominated by
philosophy and not by the exact natural sciences'. He takes the early
nineteenth-century dream theorist Gotthilf von Schubert to task in

similar vein: 'Pronouncements such as that by Schubert (1814) that dreams are a liberation of the spirit from the power of external nature, a freeing of the soul from the bonds of the senses . . . which represent dreams as an elevation of mental life to a higher level, seem to us now to be scarcely intelligible; today they are repeated only by mystics and pietists' (p. 130).

Nowhere does Freud betray more clearly than here his reductionist cast of mind and his hostility to the view that the unconscious can yield anything new or original. A theory of dreams that conceives them as being the products of a closed system, the mere manifestations of latent instincts linked to infantile wishes, is quite unable to explain the extraordinarily rich contribution that dreams have made to cultural history – to philosophy and the arts and sciences as well as to politics and to sport.

Basing his conclusions on all the data available to him, J. Allan Hobson (1988) observed: 'During REM sleep, the brain and its mind seem to be engaging in a process of fantastic creation. It is obvious that our dreams are not simply the reliving of previous experience. On the contrary, we are often actually fabricating wholly novel ones. Thus new ideas and new feelings, and new views of old problems, can be expected to arise within dreams. These may be carried forward into the conscious mind or remain unconscious as part of our deeper creative repertoire. This apogee of the new positive functional theory of REM sleep is related to our recognition that the nervous system is more than a mere copying machine. While it is true that the nervous system is dependent upon external information to form its picture of the world, it also clearly uses that information to create pictures of the world against which it can test reality.

'Thus the brain of one and all is fundamentally artistic. We know this when we see the drawings of our children, but tend to discount it in our adult selves . . . Each of us is a surrealist at night during his or her dreams: each is a Picasso, a Dali, a Fellini – the delightful and the macabre mixed in full measure' (pp. 296–7).

Creativity has been a popular area for investigation in the last fifty years, but Gardner Murphy's (1958) analysis of the creative process into four stages has not been bettered. These are (1) *immersion* in the data; (2) *consolidation* (and *incubation*) of information and experience in

279

'storehouses' or memory banks which are not directly accessible to consciousness; (3) *illumination*, the *Eureka!* experience of Archimedes as he jumped out of his bath, which comes, appropriately enough, after a long period of 'immersion' (and incubation); and (4) *verification*, when the insight received in the moment of illumination is put to the test and its value assessed.

Illumination can occur either directly in a dream or subsequently as the result of working on the dream; illumination can also arise spontaneously, and apparently unbidden, in full consciousness. Whereas stages 1 and 4 depend predominantly on conscious, logical processes, stages 2 and 3 depend more on unconscious, symbolical, and even emotional processes. It is to these middle stages that dreams can contribute most. Edward de Bono's (1969) distinction between *vertical* (logical) and *lateral* (creative, associative) thinking is appropriate here. Whereas vertical thinking progresses in a linear manner, step by logical step, lateral thinking rearranges existing data into alternative patterns capable of generating a new and unexpected insight. Fashions change in attributing primary importance to one or other of these thinking modes, and while most authorities agree that there is an unconscious contribution to the creative process, some insist that this has been exaggerated (Altshuller, 1984). The probability is that both vertical and lateral thinking are used in problem-solving and creative achievements, and that neither form of thinking is used to the exclusion of the other. It must also be acknowledged that Murphy's four stages do not invariably occur separately in an ordered sequence: some degree of overlap between them is usual. But so many examples have been recorded which illustrate the processes that Murphy and de Bono have described that their contribution to our understanding of creative insights cannot be denied.

The actual moment of illumination is characteristically compared to a flash of lightning: 'I turned the chair to the fireplace and sank into a half sleep,' wrote Kekulé. 'The atoms flitted before my eyes . . . wriggling and turning like snakes. And see, what is that? One of the snakes seized its own tail and the image whirled scornfully before my eyes. *As though from a flash of lightning I awoke.* I occupied the rest of the night in working out the consequences of the [benzene ring] hypothesis' (de Becker, 1968, p. 84).

The idea for Otto Loewi's classic experiment demonstrating that chemical activity is responsible for the conduction of nervous impulses came to him in what seems to have been a NREM dream in 1920: 'The night before Easter Sunday of that year I awoke, turned on the light, and jotted down a few notes on a tiny slip of thin paper. Then I fell asleep again. It occurred to me at six o'clock in the morning that during the night I had written down something important, but I was unable to decipher the scrawl' (Loewi, 1960). An acquaintance takes up the story: 'The next day was agony – he could not read the scrawl nor recall the solution, though remembering that he had had it. That night was even worse until at three in the morning *lightning flashed again*. He took no chances this time but went to the laboratory at once and started his experiment' (Gerard, 1955, p. 227).

The mathematician Karl Gauss developed a capacity to solve complex mathematical problems in a state of hypnagogic reverie. The solutions often arrived, he said, like '*a sudden flash of lightning*' (Hadamard, 1945, p. 15). However, the illuminative *flash* does not come of its own accord. The necessary charge has to be generated by strenuous intellectual effort during Murphy's first two stages. Kekulé and Loewi had both been struggling with their different problems for many months before the sudden brilliant illumination flooded their mental landscape. Similar examples abound. After grappling unsuccessfully for days with a mathematical equation, the French philosopher Condorcet awoke with the solution from a dream. William Blake, who had been trying to develop a new engraving technique for months, dreamt that his dead brother demonstrated such a technique to him. When Blake woke up he tried out his brother's method and found that it worked.

Sudden creative insight results, therefore, from an apparently spontaneous and unwilled reorganization of information made available to the unconscious through the hard work involved in the stages of immersion and consolidation. As J. P. Guilford (1977) unarguably maintained, the value of stored information is proportional to its future usefulness. Creativity depends as much on the ability to 'search' the memory store for relevant information as on the intuitive capacity for insight. Suddenly the answer is 'produced'. Analysing how this occurs, Guilford made his useful distinction between the *convergent* production of stored information, in which a restricted requirement is satisfied in a situation where there is only one correct answer ('What is the capital of Spain?'), and *divergent* production, where a much broader search for related ideas is required ('How many capital cities can you name beginning with M?'). There are evident parallels here with de Bono's vertical and lateral thinking: while the conscious mind makes greater use of vertical thinking and depends more on the convergent production of stored information (i.e. it is more literal, logical, precise, serious, and consistent), the dreaming mind uses lateral thinking and convergent production to express its intentions (i.e. it tends to be more metaphoric, ambiguous, paradoxical, humorous, and capricious).

Crucial to the success of lateral thinking and divergent production is the capacity of the human mind-brain to recognize patterns or *Gestalts*. In confronting new configurations, we compare and contrast them with similar configurations encountered in the past in order to classify them and draw inferences from them. A physician does this when he examines a patient in order to arrive at a diagnosis: he matches the signs and symptoms he has just elicited against his stored knowledge of diseases which present in approximately the same manner. The 'aha' of insight occurs when an appropriate Gestalt is recognized – when the pattern fits.

Much of the scanning of memory stores that goes on in dreams is an attempt to find past experiences which correspond to what is being confronted in the present. This is as much a search for related emotional experiences as for cognitive ones. The correspondence, when it is found, can appear ludicrous to consciousness, for it may forge a metaphoric link between categories that are normally per-ceived as quite distinct – between snakes and benzene molecules, for example, or between chemistry and music. The nineteenth-century Russian chemist Dimitri Mendeleyev devoted immense conscious effort to an attempt to discover some ordering principle underlying the apparently random relationship between the basic chemical ele-ments which make up the physical world. One afternoon he was dozing in a chair while his family played chamber music in the next room. Suddenly, in a dream, he understood that the basic elements were related to one another in the same way as themes and phrases in music. He woke up and, seizing a piece of paper, was able to write out the entire periodic table which forms the basis of modern chemistry.

Fifty years later, the Danish physicist Niels Bohr carried Mendeleyev's insight a stage further. Bohr asked himself why the basic elements should exist in the first place. Why were they distinguished from one another and how did they maintain their stability? Why, for example, is there no transitional element between hydrogen and helium? After months of wrestling with this problem he had a dream in which he was at the races. The horses ran in lanes which were clearly marked with white dust. They were permitted to change lanes provided they maintained a distance between one another. If a horse ran along a white line and kicked up dust, however, it was immediately disqualified.

When he awoke, Bohr realized that this 'rule of the track' symbolized the answer to his questions. As they orbit round the nucleus of an atom, electrons keep to their arbitrarily assigned course in the same manner as the horses kept to the lanes in which they ran. The paths followed by the orbiting electrons are determined by 'quanta' of energy and these simple facts account for the stability of the elements. It was on the basis of this experience that Bohr formulated his quantum theory, for which he was later awarded a Nobel Prize.

A further dream of critical importance to the history of science was dreamt by Albert Einstein as a young man. He dreamt he was speeding down a steep mountainside on a sled. He went faster and faster and as he approached the speed of light he noticed that the stars above him were refracting light into spectra of colours that he had never seen before. This image impressed him so deeply that he never forgot it, maintaining that his entire scientific achievement had been the result of meditating on that dream. It provided the basis of the 'thought experiment' through which he worked out the principle of relativity.

In none of these instances would the fateful illumination have come had the prolonged intellectual effort involved in Murphy's stages of immersion and consolidation been neglected. The data have to be collected, organized, mulled over, and absorbed; all the logical possibilities have to be considered and tried out again and again.

Only then can the thrilling instant of illumination occur. This is the essence of *incubation* – or, as Jeremy Taylor aptly calls it, 'priming the pump'. 'All of us prime the dream pump each time we ask ourselves honest questions about our most important life issues,' Taylor writes. 'Being ready and open to the dream's healing and creative messages allows all of us to touch the archetypal creative impulse that is woven into our dreams every night' (1992, p. 35).

As Taylor rightly insists, the key to success lies in the *wholeheartedness* with which the problem has been tackled beforehand. Dreams are most likely to activate deep archetypal structures and to release the vitality packaged with them when we are totally focused in waking life on one pre-eminent issue. In this sense, Taylor argues, we are always 'incubating' our dreams, whether we realize it consciously or not. Wholeheartedness, he maintains, is the most important dynamic in developing consciousness, individuating, and living. 'I have come to see that wholeheartedness and genuine enthusiasm and involvement with the people and activities of one's life make the most difference in evolution and individuation – much more even than what one is wholehearted about. Enthusiastic, wholehearted involvement in even the most seemingly trivial affairs will promote authentic psycho-spiritual development, while even the most clever and superficially skilful participation in the most profoundly important activities, if undertaken with interior divisions and withheld feelings and energies, will not' (p. 121).

How compatible are these ideas with the findings of biology? The biological function of dreams is, as I have argued, to work on the issues that preoccupy us in daytime and to find creative ways of responding to them at night. In the wild these will be survival issues and the more threatening to survival they are perceived to be the more actively dreams will be involved in responding to them. Herein lies the secret of wholeheartedness. If we want to elicit the help of the unconscious in dealing with an issue that concerns us, we should commit ourselves to conscious work on the problem *as if our life depended on it*. Dreams help egos who help themselves. The unconscious has to be ploughed, sown, and fertilized with conscious diligence. Then it works for us, as no less an authority than Wilhelm Wundt said, 'like an unknown being who creates and produces for

284

us, and finally throws the ripe fruits in our lap' (Koestler, 1964, p. 153).

The mathematician Henri Poincaré discovered the existence of Fuchsian functions in this way. He believed mathematical talent to be essentially intuitive and dependent on unconscious thought processes which reassess and complement thoughts which have been proceeding in consciousness. 'When one is working on a difficult problem,' wrote Poincaré, 'it often happens that at the start of the work one makes no progress. One then allows oneself a shorter or longer break for rest and thereafter sits down again at one's desk. During the first half-hour one again finds nothing, and then suddenly the decisive idea presents itself . . . Probably unconscious work went on during the rest period, and the result of this labour is later revealed to the mathematician' (von Franz, 1968, p. 68).

As this statement testifies, unconscious activity occurs in wakefulness as well as during sleep, and this would explain the evident association between dream incubation and artistic inspiration. Creativity, it appears, depends on ready access to the unconscious. Describing his method of composition in a letter to 'Baron von P.', Mozart wrote: 'When I am, as it were, completely myself, entirely alone, and of good cheer – say, travelling in a carriage, or walking after a good meal, or during the night when I cannot sleep; it is on such occasions that my ideas flow best and most abundantly. *Whence* and *how* they come, I know not; nor can I force them. Those ideas that please me I retain in memory, and I am accustomed, as I have been told, to hum them to myself . . . All this fires my soul, and, provided I am not disturbed, my subject enlarges itself, becomes methodized, and defined, and the whole, though it be long, stands almost complete and finished in my mind, so that I can survey it, like a fine picture or a beautiful statue, at a glance. Nor do I hear in my imagination the parts *successively*, but I hear them, as it were, all at once. What a delight this is I cannot tell! All this inventing, this producing, takes place in a pleasing lively dream. Still, the actual hearing of the *tout ensemble* is after all the best. What has been thus produced I do not easily forget, and this is perhaps the best gift I have my Divine Maker to thank for.'

The authenticity of this letter has been doubted by some, but the observations contained in it are totally in accord with the dazzling brilliance, phenomenal range, and incredible productivity of this, the greatest of musical geniuses. Tchaikovsky, Wagner, and Beethoven all testified to the almost clairvoyant power of the inspiration under which their music was composed. The music of *Madame Butterfly*, Puccini claimed, 'was dictated to me by God; I was merely instrumental in putting it on paper.' *The Rite of Spring* was composed as a result of a vision in which Stravinsky saw 'sage elders seated in a circle, watching a young girl dance herself to death' as a propitiatory sacrifice. The music came to him when he was in a state of exhaustion and exaltation: 'I wrote what I heard. I am the vessel through which *Sacre* passed.'

Returning from a troop review in Washington during the American Civil War, Julia Ward Howe and her companions sang 'John Brown's Body', and one of them asked her why she did not write better words for the tune. That night she slept well but woke early the next morning. As she lay waiting for the dawn, the words came to her: 'Mine eyes have seen the glory of the coming of the Lord . . .' 'She lay perfectly still,' reports her biographer. 'Line by line, stanza by stanza the words came sweeping on with the rhythm of marching feet, pauseless, resistless. She saw the long lines swinging into place before her eyes, heard the voice of the nation speaking through her lips. She waited till the voice was silent, till the last line was ended; then sprang from bed and, groping for pen and paper, scrawled in the grey twilight "The Battle Hymn of the Republic".'

A famous example of dream composition is 'The Devil's Trill' by Tartini. In his old age, Tartini told the astronomer Lalande that he had had a dream in which he sold his soul to the devil, and in this dream he gave his violin to the devil to see what he could do with it. 'But,' said he, 'what was my astonishment when I heard him play with consummate skill a sonata of such exquisite beauty that it surpassed the most audacious dreams of my imagination. I was delighted, transported, enchanted, I was breathless and I woke up. Seizing my violin, I tried to reproduce the sounds I had heard. But in vain. The piece I composed, *The Devil's Trill*, was the best I had ever written, but how remote it was from the one I had heard in my dream!' (de Becker, 1968, p. 101).

These and many other examples have been collected and published by Brian Inglis in his invaluable resource book, *The Unknown Guest* (1987). Assisted by Ruth West, director of the Koestler Foundation, Inglis has collated episodes which 'appear to transcend everyday realities' and which 'suggest design: as if some prompter in the wings is operating through our unconscious minds'. This prompter, 'the unknown guest', is compatible with Jung's 'two million-year-old Self' or 'No. 2 personality'. This figure can personify as a familiar companion, like Jung's 'Philemon', in those who practise active imagination. Though uninstructed in this imaginative activity, it was evidently practised by Socrates: 'In the past the prophetic voice to which I have become accustomed has been my constant companion,' he said, 'opposing me even in quite trivial things if I was going to take the wrong course.' He called this his daemon and from the records that have come down to us from Xenophon and from Plato it is clear that Socrates assumed that he was divinely inspired, receiving messages from the gods through the medium of his inner ear – the experience known as *clairaudience* – he listened to these communications in precisely the same way as he listened to a normal conversation.

Socrates did not consider himself to be alone in possessing this gift; he shared it, he believed, with great poets: 'They utter their beautiful melodies of verse in a state of inspiration,' he declared, 'as if possessed by a spirit not their own.' True creativity depends on a state of possession, 'for whilst a man retains any portion of the thing called reason, he is utterly incompetent to produce poetry'. He must enter a state of 'divine insanity' (which we have called 'liminality') so that his muse may seize control of his creative faculties. Witnesses verified that Socrates would sometimes enter a state of trance in which he seemed rapt in contemplation and utterly unaware of the outside world.

As we shall see in the next chapter, people who have this sense of *guidance* are highly charismatic and have enormous influence over their followers. They become identified with the archetype of the hero-saviour. The membrane between conscious and unconscious processes seems to be unusually permeable in such cases. They live in a relatively permanent state of 'liminality' and they call out huge projections from others.

Both Winston Churchill and Adolf Hitler believed they played host to 'the unknown guest' throughout their lives. 'I sometimes have a feeling – in fact I have it very strongly – a feeling of interference,' Churchill told a gathering of miners in 1943. 'I want to stress it. I have a feeling that some guiding hand has interfered.' He believed that this protector had not only guided his political career but, on occasion, had saved his life, as during his escape from captivity in the Boer War and from a bomb during the Second World War. Churchill was also highly creative: he could come up with a variety of alternatives to any political problem that arose.

Another historical personage who bore an inspired life was Joan of Arc, who displayed remarkable intelligence and resourcefulness for a person of her age and social background. She believed she was inspired by God to liberate France from the English and she believed she received her instructions directly from St Katharine, St Margaret, and St Michael. As with the 'control' spirits, described to Jung by the medium, Hélène Preiswerk, these were entirely real to her. She could actually see and touch them, though usually they communicated with her through voices. It is hard to doubt the sincerity of Joan's reports, for she had every reason for playing them down: as she well knew, her insistence upon their veracity at her trial could only ensure her condemnation as a heretic.

The state of trance in which mediums speak for the spirits of the departed has been justly compared to the state of mind in which a poet, composer, or artist produces his work when under the influence of inspiration. When Schopenhauer refused to believe that the postulates which arose within his own mind were his own work but came from elsewhere, he was speaking just like a medium. Many have described the state as being one of 'possession'. In a sense, dreams are also a form of possession – as is active imagination. Before writing a commentary on a passage of scripture, the seventeenth-century mystic Madame Guyon declared she had no idea what she was going to write but, she went on, 'while writing I saw that I was writing things that I had never known; and during the time of the manifestation light was given to me that I had in me treasures of knowledge and understanding that I did not know myself to possess.' Describing the composition of his first book, the novelist Thomas Wolfe declared: 'I

288

cannot really say the book was written. It was something that took hold of me and possessed me, and before I was done with it – that is, before I finally emerged with the first completed part – it seemed to me that it had been done for me.' *Thus Spake Zarathustra* came to Nietzsche as a revelation – 'by which I mean that something profoundly convulsive and disturbing suddenly becomes visible and audible with indescribable definiteness and exactness. One hears – one does not seek; one takes – one does not ask who gives.' A sentiment which was echoed by Alfred de Musset: '*On ne travaille pas – on écoute – on attend.*'

Again and again, writers, composers, artists of all description testify to their surprise at what emerges in their work: they discover things they had never previously realized. 'I have been surprised at the observations made by some of my characters,' wrote Thackeray. 'It seems as if an occult power was moving my pen' (*Roundabout Papers*, 1860). In all these instances the subject is unusually open to influences arising from the unconscious.

Those who aspire to be writers, especially if they are of a lazy disposition, are attracted by the idea that composition can proceed from inspiration. However, the inspiration:perspiration ratio is much higher than they would like to imagine. Coleridge awoke from his opium-induced reverie and began writing *Kubla Khan*, as if to dictation, and I have often wondered why, when disturbed by the person from Porlock, he did not send him away. Perhaps he welcomed the interruption. Creativity can be a chore from which the most inspired artists long for escape.

> *I long for the Person from Porlock*
> *To bring my thoughts to an end,*
> *I am growing impatient to see him*
> *I think of him as a friend.*
>   STEVIE SMITH

Such inspiration is not confined to artists and intellectuals, however. In *The Psychic Side of Sports* (1978), Michael Murphy and Rhea H. White provide examples of players of various games who have felt some form of possession taking over as they play, enabling them to perform apparently superhuman feats. When Pelé first appeared in a

World Cup match in 1958, he played the entire game 'in a kind of trance, as if the future was unfolding before his own disinterested eyes'. Roger Bannister described how he ran the first four-minute mile in a trance-like state: 'I felt complete *detachment*.' Golfers have often described how when they are feeling in peak form they can settle down to make a long and difficult putt, certain in the knowledge that they are going to sink it. Musicians giving a great performance have reported much the same kind of feeling. Gamblers, too, experience the same kind of conviction when they know they are 'in luck'.

What seems to happen at these moments is that all the knowledge and experience stored up in the unconscious becomes available to the performing ego. The boundaries between conscious and unconscious dissolve. The trance-like condition that emerges is a form of dissociation, a detachment from all reality other than that concerned with the task in hand. Then the unconscious power is allowed to take over and the individual experiences an altered state of consciousness bringing in its train a sense of profound confidence and supreme ability.

The implication of all this is that the capacity for creative thought and action lies ready and available in the unconscious psyche of us all, if only we can develop the means of using it. The most successful techniques known to me for deliberately cultivating this faculty are dreamwork and active imagination. But, in fact, we commonly mobilize the unconscious creator in us when we concentrate on a problem, then lay it to one side, so as to return to it later. Or when instead of sitting up with a worrying preoccupation, we go to bed and 'sleep on it', to wake up with a much clearer idea of what we should do. The American writer Oliver Wendell Holmes drew attention to this in connection with the common experience of not being able to remember a name or the title of a book. 'No effort of the will can reach it; but we say, "Wait a minute, and it will come to me", and go on talking. Presently, perhaps some minutes later, the idea we are in search of comes all at once into the mind, delivered like a prepaid bundle, laid at the door of consciousness like a foundling in a basket. How came it there, we know not' (Inglis, 1987, p. 106).

Another well-known method of tapping the unconscious is to use it as an alarm clock. If you have to wake at six o'clock in the morning, merely knock your head six times against the headboard of your bed on retiring and you will wake up precisely at that time. I have also had the experience of waking in the morning, not knowing what time it is, and receiving a clear vision of a clock face giving the precise time. This is verified by switching on the light and looking at my watch. Writing on hallucinations in his *Principles of Psychology* (1890), William James declared: 'Every hallucination is a perception, as good and true a sensation as if there were a real object there. The object happens *not* to be there; that is all.'

Kekulé's command, 'Learn to dream, Gentlemen,' could equally be the advice to fantasize and hallucinate – an encouragement to all theoreticians to use their powers of lateral thinking and, having made diligent use of the logical, rational ego, to put it into 'receptive mode' and allow a bountiful unconscious to throw the ripe fruits in their lap.

12

Some FAMOUS DREAMS

The big dream feels significant.
The big dream is the kind the president has.
He wakes and tells it to the secretary,
together they tell it to the cabinet,
and before you know there is war.

LOUIS SIMPSON

The great events of the past, wars and revolutions, cultural and social movements, economic and political crises, are inadequately described by historians in terms of the rational causes which they see as leading up to them. This is a partial view because it leaves out the unconscious and biological factors involved. History is made by collective forces operating through individuals – some individuals, by virtue of their position, ability or charisma, being more salient than others. Particularly influential are those whose psychological constitution makes them at home in the liminal state. These are the prophets, seers, dictators and demagogues, the myth-makers who possess the magic to move millions. The winds they conjure up can be so powerful and persistent as to endure for millennia, driving huge populations in the direction of great good or greater evil. Whether they be Moses, Christ, Buddha, Mohammed, Mahatma Gandhi, or Hitler, Lenin, Mussolini or Genghis Khan, they transcend their purely personal condition and channel archetypal forces into the masses that throng about them. These are the Great Individuals of historical narrative who, aligning themselves with the contemporary *Zeitgeist*, become its spokesmen and its agents, proclaiming themselves servants of a higher purpose, executants of an historic mission, viceroys guided by the hand of fate. The mythology that springs up round them is made of visions and dreams. Unfortunately, the true significance of these manifestations is not always understood and the consequences can be dire. The destiny of millions can depend on the sagacity of the oneirocritics in the Great Man's entourage. Alexander's dream (p. 41 above) led to the capture of Tyre, but only after the necessary dreamwork had been completed. Xerxes (p. 18) and Hannibal were less fortunate, as were the armies they commanded.

Hannibal, the Carthaginian general, dreamt shortly before the Second Punic War that Jupiter Capitolinus invited him to attack Rome. He decided to accept the invitation, with the result that his troops suffered a greater calamity than that which awaited Xerxes. So intense was his loathing of Rome and so urgent his desire to destroy its huge empire that Hannibal seized on this dream as a justification for his belligerent ambitions, without pausing to reflect that Jupiter was the Guardian of Rome, and hardly carried the interests of Carthage close to his heart. Had he worked properly on his dream, Hannibal might have thought about this and, instead of launching his disastrous invasion, confronted his destructive urges and dealt with them in himself.

Of the demigods who have inflicted most suffering on the twentieth century, one stands head and shoulders above the rest, and he was patently aware of the liminality out of which he exerted his demiurgic power. Describing himself as a somnambulist whose footsteps were guided by Providence, Adolf Hitler was able to infect the German population with his liminal state, rendering them susceptible to the psychic epidemic whose terrible ravages were to afflict the entire continent of Europe.

Hitler's Dream and Vision

I go the way that Providence dictates with the assurance of a sleepwalker.
ADOLF HITLER

Hitler experienced a dream and a vision which he believed confirmed him in the exalted role that Destiny had prepared for him.

The dream occurred in 1917 when he was serving as a corporal in the Bavarian Infantry on the Somme. It was a nightmare: *he dreamt he was being buried under an avalanche of earth and molten iron.* He woke up and, feeling the need for air, went outside the dugout in which he had been sleeping. He stepped over the parapet of the trench and proceeded to advance into open country. This was extremely fool-hardy, but he felt he was not acting of his own free will: he was like a robot or a sleepwalker.

Suddenly, the enemy's big guns opened up and he threw himself to the ground. There was only one burst, but it was enough to make him wide awake and bring him to his senses. He hurried back to his comrades. The trench was unrecognizable. A mass of fallen earth blocked the approach, and where the dugout had been was an immense crater. All his comrades had disappeared. A direct hit had blown them to bits or buried them alive. From that day Hitler was convinced that he had been entrusted with a divine mission (de Becker, 1968, pp. 79–80).

The vision occurred on 13 March 1938, the day after his occupation of Austria, as Hitler stood on the balcony of the Viennese Hofburg, receiving the hysterical plaudits of a huge crowd. In a highly emotional state, he gazed skywards and received a clear visual impression of Odin, the old Germanic war god, looking down on the tumultuous scene and pointing imperiously to the East. Hitler took this apparition as an affirmation from on high of his plans to invade Russia. Like Hannibal, he failed to work on the deeper meaning of this visitation, with the result that he led his nation to an even greater disaster than awaited his Carthaginian predecessor. Had he thought about it, he might have recalled that Odin was not a particularly reliable god in whom to place one's trust: he was prone to abandon his devotees to death and defeat having initially led them to glory and to victory. This would at least have given him the opportunity to confront the origins of his own manic quest for world domination, and humanity could have been spared enormous suffering. But he lacked both the objectivity and the humility to adopt any other course than the one he felt Providence had chosen for him, leading his people to *Ragnarök*, taking millions of innocent victims with him.

The dugout dream was not the unequivocal sign that Hitler believed it to be, either, for it could be seen as prophetic of what was in fact to be his true destiny – death and destruction during a devastating bombardment in an underground bunker. However, it not only served to reinforce his faith in his special mission but confirmed his belief in his invulnerability. This, too, communicated itself to others, who, when Hitler was near, told one another 'nothing will happen' (Fest, 1983, p. 70). Henceforth, he saw the guiding hand of Providence in every stage of his career and had sublime faith in his intuitions, which, he was certain, were divinely inspired. His extraordinary military successes, often achieved in flat contradiction to the advice of his generals, further confirmed this for him, as did his apparently miraculous escapes from death, which occurred with increasing frequency. Having made a speech in the Party beer-cellar in Munich, for example, just before the outbreak of the Second World War, Hitler suddenly decided to leave, instead of staying on to chat with the Party faithful as was his custom. Within minutes of his departure a bomb exploded, killing eight of the old comrades and injuring scores of others. In March 1943 a bomb which had been placed on the plane in which Hitler flew back to Berlin from the Eastern front failed to detonate. A further attempt to assassinate him at an exhibition a few days later also failed because, once again, he decided on impulse to leave early.

In the summer of 1944 Hitler received what he took to be the most striking proof yet of destiny's protection. The bomb left by Count von Stauffenberg in a briefcase in Hitler's conference room was moved by a general to a position behind a heavy wooden plinth supporting the map table at which Hitler was standing. As a result of the general's quite unintentional interference, the Führer's life was saved when the bomb went off. Finally, when Albert Speer, Hitler's architect and armaments minister, decided to kill him by introducing poison gas through a ventilator to his underground bunker, Hitler decided to have the ventilation shaft protected just before Speer's attempt was due to be made.

These extraordinary instances are all examples of what Jung was to call *synchronicity*: when a powerful archetypal force is constellated in someone, outer events seem to alter themselves in conformity with it. Hitler's conviction that he was the divinely anointed hero-saviour of his people, together with his sense that he was engaged in an archetypal struggle between the powers of Light and Darkness, appeared to grant him the luck of a born gambler – until the combined might of his enemies overwhelmed him.

Hitler also seemed to possess the uncanny knack of putting himself in the liminal state when he addressed an audience, and this gave him his mesmeric power as an orator. He said he first recognized this capacity as a young man after attending a performance of *Rienzi*, which recounts with Wagnerian majesty the tale of Cola di Rienzi, rebel and tribune of the people, who was alienated from his fellow men and destroyed by their failure to understand him. Hitler's sole boyhood friend, August Kubizek, was there on this occasion and described what happened when they strolled on the Freinberg above Linz after the performance. 'Words burst from him like a backed-up flood breaking through crumbling dams. In grandiose, compelling images, he sketched for me his future and that of his people.' When Kubizek met the Führer thirty years later in Bayreuth, Hitler remarked: 'It began at that hour' (Fest, 1983, pp. 22–3).

Under Hitler's inspired guidance, the whole Nazi movement took on a pseudo-religious quality, with its rituals, parades, and swastikas. It was as if the German masses recognized him as a Messiah: they streamed to him 'as to a Saviour', a contemporary account declares. Kurt Luedecke, who was to become one of Hitler's entourage, only to end up in Oranienburg concentration camp, described the spell Hitler cast on him as an orator: 'Presently my critical faculty was swept away ... I do not know how to describe the emotions that swept over me as I heard this man ... the passion of his sincerity seemed to flow from him into me. I experienced an exaltation that could be likened only to religious conversion' (p. 154).

As a party, the Nazis had not so much a coherent political programme as a set of prejudices rooted in Hitler's personal myth and his denial and projection of his own shadow. A joke current in the 1930s referred to National Socialist ideology as 'the World as Will without Idea'. The quintessence of Hitler's world view was German nationalism engaged in a life-and-death sub-Darwinian struggle against the forces of Darkness (i.e. Bolshevism and the International Jewish Conspiracy). He was also obsessed with the idea of world-wide disease, spread by viruses and termites, and the spirochaetes of syphilis. He espoused Hörbinger's 'world ice theory', which proposed a perpetual struggle throughout the universe between fire and ice, and his imagination was inflamed by visions of cosmic catastrophe: 'We may perish, perhaps,' he said. 'But we shall take the world with us. Muspilli, universal conflagration.'

Already in 1936, Jung, who has been falsely accused of pro-Nazi sympathies (Stevens, 1994), foresaw this outcome. German mythology is unique in that its gods are overthrown by the powers of darkness. The whole mythic drama ends in *Ragnarök* as Valhalla is consumed with flames, like the Third Reich in 1945: 'The impressive thing about the German phenomenon,' wrote Jung, 'is that one man, who is obviously "possessed", has infected a whole nation to such an extent that everything is set in motion and has started rolling on its course towards perdition' (*CW*10, para. 388). There is no doubt that the Treaty of Versailles, the inflation of the 1920s, and the depression of the early 1930s, all contributed to Hitler's rise to power as the historians always tell us, but it is unlikely that his rise would have been as meteoric, or that his regime would have lasted as long as it did, had Hitler not possessed the terrible capacity to constellate the most awesome archetypes of the collective unconscious both in himself and in the people whose misfortune it was to follow him. The life of Adolf Hitler is a horrific example of the evil that can be inflicted on the world by one individual who combines ready access to the liminal state with a total abdication of all ethical responsibility for the enormous power placed at his disposal.

That the dreams and visions of rulers can have a colossal impact on history is readily apparent, but what is not sufficiently recognized is the social influence that the dream-life of artists and intellectuals can have. One dream that has had profound consequences for our culture was dreamt by René Descartes on the night of 10 November 1619.

The 'Great Dream' of René Descartes

Were it not for the leaping and the twinkling of the soul, man would rot away in his greatest passion, idleness.

C. G. JUNG

This dream, which was in three parts (between each of which Descartes awoke), was described by him as 'the most important

affair' of his life (Cole, 1992, p. 9). It confirmed him in the philosophical direction he was taking; and it is an ironical paradox that the most
influential philosophy to arise since the Renaissance, generally regarded as the very essence of rationality, should be so profoundly
affected by a dream. Indeed, it has always been an embarrassment to
philosophers that the revolutionary contribution made by Descartes
to their highly rational discipline should be derived from so irrational
a source.

Descartes was in the habit of recording his dreams in a little
notebook bound in parchment which he called his *Olympica*. Unfortunately, it was lost some time in the seventeenth century, but we
know about the dream of 10 November because it was published, in
paraphrase, by the Abbé Adrien Baillet in his *La Vie de M. Descartes*
in 1691. Baillet had access to the *Olympica* before it was lost.

In 1619, the first year of the catastrophic Thirty Years War,
Descartes had attended the coronation of Ferdinand II of Austria.
Afterwards he stayed in the neighbourhood of Ulm. It was the
beginning of winter: 'I was then in Germany, where I had been
called by the wars that have not yet finished,' he wrote in 1641.
'While I was returning toward the army from the coronation of the
Emperor, I was halted by the beginning of winter in a quarter where
no conversation diverted me and neither cares nor passions troubled
me. I remained the whole day shut up alone in a heated chamber,
where I had uninterrupted leisure to consider my thoughts.'

There, he seems to have reached an important conclusion and
made a vital discovery. The conclusion was that henceforth he would
take nothing on trust. With the exception of politics and religion, he
would think out everything for himself, relying exclusively on his
own thought processes; and, in defiance of the deeply ingrained
traditions of his society, accept nothing as true merely because it had
been stated by some revered 'authority'. The momentous discovery,
which he made the day immediately preceding his dream, was that
all sciences are susceptible to mathematical analysis and can be reduced
to one '*mathématique universelle*'. This, he decided, provided the basis
of a new and 'wonderful science'. Filled with enthusiasm by this
discovery, he went to bed and to sleep. At this point, the Abbé
Baillet takes up the story:

After he fell asleep he imagined he saw ghosts and was terrified by them. He felt a great weakness on his right side, and, believing he was walking through streets, was forced to lean over to his left side so as to be able to continue his journey.

Ashamed to be walking in this way, he made an effort to stand up straight, but he was foiled by a violent wind which spun him round three or four times on his left foot.

With great difficulty he managed to drag himself along, fearful of falling at every step. Then, seeing a college that was open, he entered it hoping to find some respite from his affliction. He tried to reach the college church in order to say his prayers, but on the way he realized that he had passed a man he knew without acknowledging him. He tried to retrace his steps in order to pay his compliments but was again foiled by the wind which blew him back towards the church. Then, in the middle of the college quadrangle, he saw another person who called him politely by name and told him that, if he wished to find Monsieur N., he had something for Descartes to give him. The gift appeared to be a melon that had been brought from some foreign country.

He was surprised to see that people who had gathered round the man in the quadrangle to chat with one another were able to stand firmly upright on their feet, whereas Descartes had still to walk crookedly and unsteadily, even though the wind had abated.

At this point he woke in pain, fearing that evil spirits were trying to lead him astray. Having fallen asleep on his left side, he now turned over on to his right side. He prayed to God to protect him from the evil consequences of his dream and to preserve him from all the misfortunes which might threaten him as a punishment for his sins. He recognized that his sins were grievous enough to call down on him the wrath of heaven, although in the eyes of men, he had led a relatively blameless life. He lay awake about two hours, pondering the problem of good and evil, and then, once more, fell asleep.

At once he resumed his dream. He thought he heard a violent report, which he took to be a clap of thunder. Terrified he awoke.

Opening his eyes, he became aware of a multitude of fiery sparks scattered throughout the room. This had often happened to him before, and it was not unusual for him to wake up in the middle of the night to find that his eyes were sparkling enough ['les yeux assez étincellans'] *for him to perceive the objects nearest to him. He was able to compose himself and once more go to sleep.*

He now dreamt that he found a book on his table, though he had no idea who could have put it there. He opened it and was delighted to find that it was a dictionary, which he hoped would be very useful to him. Then another book appeared, its origin equally unknown. This was a collection of poems by different authors, entitled **Corpus Poetarum**. *Curious to discover what it contained, he opened the book and his eye fell on the line 'Quod vitae sectabor iter?' At the same time, another man, whom he did not know, appeared and pointed out a poem beginning with the words 'Est et non', and he extolled its excellence. Descartes said he knew the poem, which was among the idylls of Ausonius and was included in the big collection of poems which lay on his table. Wanting to show this to the man, he began turning over the leaves of the book, boasting that he knew the order and arrangement perfectly. As he looked for the place, the man asked him where the book had come from. Descartes replied that he had no idea and that, only a second beforehand, he had had in his hands another book, which had just disappeared, without his knowing who had brought it or who had taken it away.*

Hardly had he finished speaking when the book reappeared at the other end of the table. On examining it, however, he discovered that the dictionary was no longer complete. Meanwhile, he found the poems of Ausonius in the anthology of poets, but, unable to find the poem beginning 'Est et non', he told the stranger that he knew an even more beautiful poem by the same author, beginning 'Quod vitae sectabor iter?' The man begged to see it and Descartes was diligently searching for it when he came upon a small number of portraits – copperplate engravings – which made him exclaim at the beauty of the book; but it was not the same edition as the one he knew.

At this point both the man and the books disappeared, but Descartes did not wake up. The remarkable thing is [the good Abbé observes] *that, being in doubt as to whether this experience was a dream or a vision, he not only decided, while still sleeping, that it was a dream, but he also interpreted it before waking. He concluded that the dictionary signified the connection between all the sciences and that the collection of poets entitled* **Corpus Poetarum** *pointed particularly and clearly to the intimate union of philosophy with wisdom. For he thought that one should not be surprised to discover that the poets, even those whose work seems to be a foolish pastime, produce much deeper, more sensible, and better expressed thoughts than are* *to be found in the writings of the philosophers. He attributed this wonder to the divine quality of enthusiasm and the power of imagination which enable the seed of wisdom (existing in the minds of all men as do sparks of fire in flint) to sprout with much greater ease and even brilliance than the 'reason' of the philosophers. Continuing to interpret the dream in his sleep, Descartes concluded that the poem on 'what sort of life one should choose', beginning 'Quod vitae sectabor iter?' pointed to the sound advice of a wise person or even to Moral Theology.*

Still uncertain whether he was dreaming or meditating, he awoke peacefully and with open eyes continued to interpret his dream in the same spirit. The poets represented in the collection of poems he interpreted as the revelation and enthusiasm that had been accorded to him. The poem 'Est et non' — which is the 'Yes and No' of Pythagoras — he understood as the truth and error of all human knowledge and profane science.

When he saw that all these things were so satisfactorily turning out according to his desire, he dared to believe that it was the spirit of truth that wished, through this dream, to reveal to him the treasures of all the sciences. There now remained nothing to be explained save the small copperplate portraits which he had found in the second book. These he no longer sought to elucidate after receiving a visit from an Italian painter on the following day.

To interpret the dream of someone long dead presents impressive difficulty because one cannot ask the dreamer for his associations or for the products of his active imagination. For this reason, when approached by Maxim Leroy, one of Descartes' twentieth-century biographers, for an interpretation, Freud declined, expressing no other opinion than that the melon was probably a sexual symbol.

However, the dream was clearly a 'big' dream, carrying great significance, not only for Descartes but also for our culture. The effort involved in attempting to unravel its meanings is worthwhile because, as I hope to show, it provides further insight into the extraordinary manner in which dreams perform their tasks and it demonstrates how a 'culture pattern dream' can provide the necessary inspiration for innovations in philosophy and science no less than in myth and religion.

Although Descartes appears to have interpreted the dream to his own satisfaction, there is more to it than met his sparkling eye. This becomes apparent if we approach it in the usual stages. My own understanding of the dream is heavily dependent on the valuable researches of John R. Cole (1992) and of that doyenne of dream interpreters Dr Marie-Louise von Franz (1968), to whom I acknowledge my grateful indebtedness.

Personal Context René Descartes (1596–1650) was twenty-three years old when he had his dream. He was the third living child of Joachim des Cartes, a councillor in the *Parlement* of Rennes. His mother, Jeanne Brochard, tragically died in childbirth the following year. His father remarried soon after the death of René's mother and only saw him during the six months every year when the courts at Rennes were on vacation. Although pleased by the boy's evident intelligence (he called him 'my little Philosopher'), he seems to have been irritated by his delicate health (René said that he had inherited his mother's weak chest and persistent cough) and his solitary disposition, later scornfully dismissing him as 'only fit to be bound in calf-skin'. At the age of eight he was sent to the Royal Jesuit College of La Flèche in Anjou. There, because of his health, he was given special consideration by the Fathers. He had a room to himself where he would lie for hours in bed meditating, a habit he was to keep up throughout his life. Not surprisingly, his school fellows made fun of him and called him *'le chambriste'*. At sixteen he left La Flèche to live in Paris, where he studied mathematics, music and philosophy. There he had some male acquaintances but women he carefully avoided.

Little is known about Descartes' personal life, but from what has been established it is clear that, like many people who have had the misfortune to lose or be separated from their mothers in early life, he had a schizoid personality. That is to say, he was a socially isolated, deeply introverted man, who appeared cold and affectless to his contemporaries, and lived in a private world of the intellect and the imagination, while eschewing all intimate relationships. He did not attend the marriage of his brother or sister, and when his sister and his father died he expressed only his *'déplaisir'*. He did have one liaison with a Dutch servant girl, it is true, which produced one daughter who died aged five, but he quickly escaped from this entanglement (a *'dangereux engagement dont Dieu l'a retiré'*). The one person he seems to have loved was a thirty-year-old Dutch philosopher, physicist and physician called Isaac Beeckman, whom he met on 10 November 1618, precisely one year to the day before the occasion of his Great Dream. Beeckman did not reciprocate his love, although an intellectual relationship continued between the two men for approximately twenty years.

Because the schizoid individual feels no sense of attachment to anyone or anything, he is often something of a nomad and a recluse. Both were true of Descartes. Between 1618 and 1628 he was constantly on the move throughout Europe, serving with the armies of Maurice of Nassau in Holland and the Duke of Bavaria in Germany, as well as in the Imperial Army of Hungary. He travelled widely throughout Germany, France, Poland, Italy, and the Netherlands. The most settled part of his life was between 1628 and 1649, when he lived in Holland and wrote his most important books; but even here he changed his lodgings no less than eighteen times. The motive behind this nomadic restlessness appears to have been a compulsion to keep his address as secret as possible. Invariably, he divided his accommodation into two parts: an outer reception room and an inner sanctum, a secret laboratory where he did experiments, dissected animals, and vivisected live rabbits. There was no need to pay attention to their squeals, he said, because they did not have souls and were therefore machines incapable of feeling. Their screams were of no greater consequence than an unoiled and squeaking wheel on a hay cart. This complete incapacity for empathy is not unusual in schizoid personalities, who are also prone to sado-masochistic sexual fantasies. It is not implausible that there was a powerfully sadistic motivation at work in his treatment of animals, as indeed there was in the behaviour of another schizoid genius, Marcel Proust, who obtained sexual gratification from, among other things, sticking needles into rats (Painter, 1965). In terms of our neurological model (discussed on pp. 99–103 above), it is as if Descartes' neocortex (his 'cold' brain) were functionally discontinuous with his paleomammalian ('hot' limbic) brain. As a result he lived in his intellect and withdrew from any emotional commitment to the usual events of human life. Hence it was possible for him to define himself metaphysically as nothing more than his own rational thought: *Je pense, donc je suis.*

In addition to being of a schizoid disposition, Descartes seems also to have been somewhat manic-depressive. He described his long morning lie-ins as *tristitia*, saying that when sad he slept a great deal, 'but if joy fills me, I neither eat nor sleep' (*si vero laetitia distendar, nec edo nec dormio*). It seems probable that the day of 'extraordinary enthusiasm' immediately preceding his dream was passed in a hypomanic state. This does not, however, invalidate the insights he gained while thus affected. But it does mean that his apotheosis of his own thinking function was hubristic and that our civilization has been both benefiting and suffering from the consequences of this inflation ever since. His own understanding of his dream did nothing to correct this. On the contrary, it compounded it. It confirmed his sense of *mission* in the quest for true knowledge and convinced him that it would end in success.

Cultural Context When introducing the three-stage procedure (personal, cultural, archetypal) to the analysis of dreams (p. 57 above), I made the point that these stages commonly overlap. This is particularly true when considering the dreams of such towering figures as Freud, Jung, and Descartes, for their contribution to our culture is largely dependent on what life had made of them as people. As Jung put it: 'Even when I am dealing with empirical data I am necessarily speaking about myself' (*CW*4, para. 774). In Descartes' case, his entire philosophical achievement is a rich intellectual expression of his essentially schizoid character. As a result, this section will continue to deal with the personal as well as the cultural context of his life.

Descartes is justly considered to be the father of modern philosophy. Not only was he a major catalyst in the great seventeenth-century reaction against medieval scholasticism, but he made a key contribution to the revolution that occurred during the half century after his death in philosophical and scientific thinking. The idea that seized hold of his imagination on 10 November 1619, of establishing a unitary and universal science that would link together all possible knowledge in one all-embracing system of understanding, was the first recorded anticipation of what has come to be known as the

Theory of Everything. The possibility that this inspired vision might be realizable still excites physicists and philosophers to this day. Under his influence scepticism became the chief scientific virtue. It became the intellectual fashion to doubt everything till it was proved by science, a view that led to the virtual elimination of intuition and feeling as acceptable modes of apperception. Although he explicitly excluded religion from his discourse, he nevertheless changed how people conceived of God and His role in the universe. In place of a creative spirit involving Himself in every detail of the phenomenal world, God retreated into the role of watchmaker, who, having built his cosmic clock, wound up the mechanism and allowed it to tick away untended. Sparrows continued to fall out of the sky, but no one cared. Thus was 'the sacred' divorced from 'the profane', and humanity cast adrift in an insensate universe which automatically performed its gyrations in accordance with mathematical laws.

The impact of René Descartes on our culture is thus hard to exaggerate. His pervasive influence is still apparent in the ways we think about ourselves and the world we live in.

One question which many have raised is why so rational a man as Descartes should be so deeply affected by his dream. Having worked with a number of schizoid patients, I believe the answer lies in the fact that it is only in dreams that people of this disposition can experience what it is to feel involved or committed – to feel *connected* to something that really matters. Dreams give them their only sense of what it is to have a soul (i.e. to be a living, feeling creature with body and 'heart', and not just an efficient intellect).

Schizoid people tend to experience the external world of social relationships and physical objects as unreal, and, as a consequence, they appear cold, distant, unemotional, and uninvolved. This is particularly true of those who have suffered major traumas in child-hood, such as loss of their mother or being sent away from home and family at a tender age. Both these disasters happened to Descartes, with the result that he withdrew into a private world of 'meditation' and intellectual preoccupation. The cruel practice of sending children away to school at an early age has persisted among certain classes in European countries from medieval times to the present, not least in Britain, where it has been customary among the 'gentry' and officer class for many generations. As I have often observed in clinical practice, cutting children off from the security of home and the love of their mother has been an important factor in producing the 'stiff upper lip', the refusal to betray emotion, the polite but aloof formality of 'the officer and gentleman'. The repression of tender emotions is essential if one is to survive in a boarding school at the age of eight. The continuing presence of a warm and loving mother figure confers upon a child the priceless gift which Erik Erikson termed *basic trust* – the secure feeling that mother, world, and life can be trusted and relied upon. For the normally developing child, the mother functions as a 'secure base' from which the child explores the environment, repeatedly scuttling back to her for reassurance that she is still there. It is as if the child is carrying the mother out into the world with him on each exploratory foray and making his connection to the world through her, investing the environment with some of the emotion that he has already accrued in relation to her. We love the world inasmuch as we loved our mother and inasmuch as our mother was *there* for us throughout childhood.

Sorely deprived of these benefits, Descartes not only lacked the capacity to empathize with people or animals but evidently experienced himself as detached from all physical reality, even his own body. As he says in his *Discourse on Method*, 'I am a being whose whole essence or nature is to think, and whose being requires no place and depends on no material thing.' As a consequence, he was able to make a complete distinction between the body and matter (which he called the *res extensa*) and the mind or the soul (the *res cogitans*). This distinction was to prove profoundly influential, and through his publications he was able to bring to completion the divorce between mind and body already established by Christian doctrine. While he admitted that body and mind were sometimes 'intermingled', as when he willed his arm to move and it did so, he insisted that this association was more apparent than real. His followers grappled with this intrinsically unsatisfactory position and one of them, Arnold Geulincx, came up with his solution of the 'two clocks': the body and the mind, he proposed, were like two entirely independent clocks keeping exactly the same time, the difference being that one chimed the hours while the other did not. An observer might persuade himself that the silent clock is implicated in causing the other clock to chime, but he would be mistaken. It is impressive that the causal connection between the mind and the body, which is unquestionably real to most of us, can seem to the schizoid personality little more than a coincidence of timing. It is the position that Gilbert Ryle caricatured as 'the theory of the ghost in the machine'. Much work has been done by contemporary neuroscientists to overcome Descartes' absolute division between the mental and the physical, but this wholly artificial split remains deeply embedded in most people's way of thinking, and psychology is still struggling to get free.

Being cut off from outer reality, the schizoid person doubts the evidence of his senses and adopts a profoundly subjective point of view. This perspective Descartes elevated into a philosophical dogma – his famous 'method of doubt': one should not only doubt everything, but one should doubt it systematically. To accomplish this he reported that he used the device of imagining the interference between himself and reality of a malignant demon 'who has employed all his energies in deceiving me'. In this manner he would, for example, entertain the possibility that 'the sky, earth, colours, shapes, sounds, and all external things are not more than the delusions of dreams . . .'

Such thinking is not uncharacteristic of schizoid people. One of my schizoid patients once told me that whenever he was taken on a train journey as a young child he was convinced that the whole business was a put-up job. The train was not actually travelling from the point of departure to the place of arrival. Instead, gangs of men, cunningly hidden from view, were winding great painted curtains of scenery past the windows so as to create the *illusion* of travel. Descartes was prepared to consider that his malignant demon was getting up to similar tricks. His need to establish *certainty* was as much a psychodynamic necessity for him as a philosophical exercise.

Viewing reality from an intensely subjective, individualistic standpoint, he took the unusual step of writing both his *Discourse on Method* and his *Meditations* in the first person. His method was to make the reader doubt everything and then, slowly, step by step, by logical argument, work towards certainty. Using this procedure, the one philosophical proposition that struck him as being immune from

diabolical doubt was his *thinking*. However great the demon's decep-
tions, Descartes wrote, 'he can never cause me to be nothing so long
as I think I am something'. He concludes: 'I am, I exist . . . I think,
therefore I am.' The only thing that exists beyond all doubt is 'I'.
This is the ultimate schizoid position. It means that his own thought
processes are more certain than matter and *his* thought more certain
than anyone else's. This, one might say without much fear of
contradiction, is hypomanic inflation in a deeply schizoid person.

Archetypal Context   The dream contains a number of archetypal symbols: spirits, sidedness (left and right), wind, the stranger (Monsieur
N., the man in the college quadrangle, and the man interested in
books), the *temenos* (the college, church, quadrangle), fruit (the
melon), good and evil, thunder, and light (the fiery sparks).

Contrary to Freud's assertion, Descartes did in fact record his
associations to some of these symbols and to other aspects of the
dream. For example, he says in his *Private Cogitations* that 'Wind
designates spirit, movement with time, life, light, cognition . . .', he
sees the melon as a symbol 'of the charms of solitude', the dictionary
represents the sum total of all the sciences, and the poems denote
wisdom, enthusiasm, divine inspiration.

To understand the other symbols we have no recourse but to use
the Jungian procedure of *amplification*, examining their significance in
Descartes' life and times as well as their wider manifestations. Consequently, our exposition will have, once more, to include material
from the personal and cultural contexts if we are to comprehend the
manifold references of the dream. We shall take each of the key
symbols in their order of appearance:

Spirits: These appear in the dream in the form of (1) ghosts that
terrify him; (2) evil spirits, which, on his first awakening, he fears,
characteristically for him, are trying to lead him astray; (3) the fiery
sparks that seem to fill his room on his second awakening; and (4)
the unseen hands that seem to play tricks on him, making books
appear and disappear. Jung, who was very interested in spirits, ghosts,
and the like, interpreted them as embodiments of autonomous complexes in the unconscious. Where a culture gave credence to the

actual existence of such manifestations, people were prone to attribute material substance to them. Descartes' experiences on the night of 10 November would suggest that his notion of demons subverting his sense of reality was more than a philosophical device: at the unconscious level, at any rate, he experienced himself as thus afflicted.

Sidedness (left v. right): What commentators on the dream seem to have overlooked is that Descartes fell asleep on his left side and awoke in pain. His first action was to roll over on to his right side. A simple interpretation of this would be that in his dream he was aware of being forcibly held (by dream paralysis) in an uncomfortable leftward posture and that his desire to change this position woke him up. The dream symbolizes his helplessness as a weakness on his right side (because the muscles on the right side of his body that he would need in order to alter his position were paralysed). That previous interpreters have ignored this obvious possibility is probably because the fact of dream paralysis has only recently been widely acknowledged. Although a simple physical explanation would account for Descartes' experience, it would not in itself account for the symbolism associated with it – the ghosts, the fear, the wind, and 'leftness'.

Cross-cultural evidence reveals a remarkable degree of agreement in the meanings that human beings everywhere attribute to the left and to the right. Universally, the right is associated with what is good, sacred, healthy, active, and conscious, and the left with what is evil, profane, sick, passive, and unconscious. These associations are implicit in common usage of the words 'right' and 'left' in many languages.* The general agreement about these distinctions is compatible with what is now known about the different functions of the two sides of the brain (which, because of anatomical cross-over in the organization of the central nervous system, control the opposite sides of the body). The dominant left cerebral hemisphere (which is responsible for the right side of the body, and whose functions are therefore experienced subjectively as attributes of the *right*) is involved in logical, verbal, mathematical and discursive thinking. The right subdominant hemisphere (whose functions are subjectively attributed

*Much of this evidence is summarized in my *Archetype*, pp. 248–50.

to the *left*) is involved in non-logical, non-verbal, non-arithmetic and symbolic processes. In fact, the evidence collected on cerebral lateralization since Roger Sperry began his famous split brain experiments in the 1950s and 60s is broadly in line with Freud's distinction between *primary process* (right hemispheric) thinking, which is relatively unorganized, primitive, magical, and ruled by emotion, and *secondary process* (left hemispheric) thinking, which is logical and develops with the acquisition of language.

In a number of traditions, the left is also associated with the earth, femininity, and the mother, while the right is associated with the heavens, masculinity, and the father.

When we apply this information to the first part of Descartes' dream we see that his fears of the ghosts and the power of the wind deprive him of strength on his right (conscious, rational, intellectual, 'good') side and force him on to his left (unconscious, non-rational, emotional, 'sinful') side. He is ashamed to be seen like this in the street and seeks refuge in the college and the church. This is a salutary experience for a man who has just discovered the basis of all science and is about to inaugurate the Age of Reason. Moreover, he is fearful of falling to the ground (the earth, the mother, the feminine) and is spun round 'three or four times' by the wind. The archetypal symbolism of the figures three and four was of particular interest to Jung, who concluded: 'Four signifies the feminine, motherly, physical; three the masculine, fatherly, spiritual.' As we have already noted in the previous sections, Descartes was to force a lasting separation between the physical and the spiritual, and was never to integrate the 'fourth' − the feminine − in his personal life.

The wind: Descartes' personal association of the wind with spirit, life, light, cognition, is borne out by the archetypal symbolism of wind as the 'pneuma' (the divine spirit 'that bloweth where it listeth'), the *ruach Elohim* (the breath of God). This powerful force has been conjured up by the previous day's realization. The man of the Renaissance, highly conscious of his own individuality, dares to cast off his scholastic cloak and trust in his own thinking. He is at once afflicted by phantoms and by a spiritual force that deprives him of strength on his right side and turns him over to his left. It would seem that an effort at psychic compensation is being made.

The temenos (*college, church, quadrangle*): A *temenos* is a sacred precinct where rituals of transformation and rites of passage are performed. In his dream Descartes seeks refuge in the college quadrangle and the church. Maternally deprived boys commonly feel at home in institutions such as the Army, the Church, the College, which become home to them as well as being a form of mother substitute. Moreover, for the schizoid personality the formalized relationships of institutional life are a reassuring escape – a defence against the more spontaneous and consequently more threatening relationships of normal family and social life. For Descartes the College and the Church were particularly familiar as a result of the eight formative years he spent in the Jesuit College of La Flèche.

Strangers: There are three strangers in the dream: Monsieur N., the man in the college quadrangle, and the man with literary interests. Had one had Descartes in analysis one would have asked him to describe these figures in as much detail as possible and to give all the associations he could muster. This material could also be augmented by getting him to do some active imagination with each of them in turn, establishing their identity and the role they wished to play in his life. Without this information we are, as Freud acknowledged, at something of a disadvantage, and we can only guess what these figures may represent.

The *stranger* is the archetype at the core of the shadow complex, which in dreams embodies those aspects of the dreamer that are still unconscious, either because they are unactualized and unlived or because they have been repressed.

What does the dream tell us about Monsieur N.? Descartes ignores him and leaves him behind. He has a positive attitude to him, however, for he regrets his failure to greet him and wants to go back to make amends. Why did he ignore Monsieur N.? Because he was too preoccupied with the consequences of his intellectual enthusiasm, his struggle with his one-sidedness and the wind. But even so, he feels the need to be on good terms with Monsieur N., presumably because he has some of the qualities that Descartes has 'left behind' and requires if he is to regain his balance and stand upright, like the other men in the quadrangle. His emotional isolation, entrenched scepticism, and intellectual abstraction need the compensation of what Monsieur N. has to offer. What could this be? The capacity to experience emotion, to love, to be committed to life? Without Descartes' associations we cannot know, but clinical experience would incline one to suspect that Monsieur N. is Descartes' positive shadow (i.e. he embodies qualities that Descartes, because of his history, has so far been unable to develop).

As it so happens, the mere attempt to return to Monsieur N. brings about a positive development in the dream, for the reassuring figure in the college quadrangle produces a melon which he wishes to present to Monsieur N. should Descartes succeed in finding him. Dr von Franz argues convincingly that the unknown man in the quadrangle represents that aspect of Descartes which remains securely sheltered within the maternal embrace of the Church. Descartes, for all his practised scepticism in other matters, was to remain a convinced Catholic all his life.

The positive attitude evinced by both this figure and Descartes himself for Monsieur N. suggests that the unlived feeling which is 'left behind' is to some extent sustained by the traditional spirit of the College and the Church. These were the only mother substitutes to which he could relate closely enough to receive some nourishment for this undeveloped part of his personality. The unknown (i.e. unconscious) figure returns in relation to the 'poetic' needs of life in the final sequence of the dream.

The melon: This is the one aspect of the dream on which Freud was prepared to comment: the melon, he said, was a sexual symbol. So it may be, but von Franz's researches have revealed that for Descartes it probably meant a great deal more. She has established, for example. that he would have been aware of both the Biblical and the Manichaean significance of this fruit. It was one of the delights that the children of Israel regretted leaving behind in the land of Egypt: 'We remember the fish, which we did eat in Egypt freely; the cucumbers, the melons, and the leeks, and the onions, and the garlic; But now *our soul is dried away*: there is nothing at all, besides this manna, before our eyes' (Numbers 11.5–6; italics added). The schizoid state is one in which the 'soul is dried away' and the luscious melon is a fitting antidote to this condition. But in psychic terms what does it signify?

There is an interesting etymological relationship between the melon and the apple. The Greek word *mēlo* (= apple) is the origin of the Latin words *melo* and *melonis* from which we and the French both derive the word 'melon'. To distinguish the smaller edible melon from the watermelon the Greeks knew the former as *mēlo-pepon* ('apple-melon'). For a man educated by the Jesuits the symbolism of the apple-melon carried powerful overtones of femininity, sexuality, and evil. This would help to explain why, on first waking from the dream, he spent two hours pondering the question of good and evil in the world.

Dr von Franz also establishes that Descartes was probably aware of the symbolic importance attributed by the Manichaeans (a Gnostic sect persecuted by the Christians) to the melon. To the Manichaeans, the whole meaning and purpose of life was to save the 'germs of light' imprisoned in darkness and to convey them back to the original realm of light. All Manichaean adepts were strictly vegetarian and lived on a diet of plants and fruits which were believed to contain large quantities of these germs of light: among these, cucumbers and melons were especially prized.

The Biblical and the Manichaean symbolism of the apple-melon therefore stresses sexuality, good v. evil and the embryonic possibility of individual consciousness. What is more, it links the melon with the sparks of light seen by Descartes in a hypnopompic vision on awakening from the 'crash of thunder'.

The sexual symbolism of the melon is not only evoked by its suggestive shape but it is also reminiscent of the womb, the fertility of which is symbolized by the profusion of seeds that it contains: it was on account of these that melons were also known as *spermatias*.

Finally, as a sphere, full of seminal possibilities and the capacity for sustaining life, the melon is a symbol of the Self, and when cut open in cross-section it forms a perfect mandala, the archetypal image of totality and completion. That it grows in the shade of the leaves of a ground-growing runner, close to the earth, is a further indication to

Descartes that if he is to live and to individuate he will have to become grounded and caught up in earthly reality. That the fruit comes from a distant, exotic land indicates how far removed is the dreamer's intellectually aspiring ego from his earth-bound Self: there is something 'wholly other' about it. In Jungian terms, the melon carries connotations of the Anima as well as the Self and although Descartes did not understand this, it is perhaps significant that on finally awakening, he resolved to go on a pilgrimage to the Madonna of Loretto, a vow which he eventually honoured. In this dream, the melon is an example of what Jung meant by a transcendent symbol, one capable of uniting previously incompatible or opposite tendencies in the psyche, in this instance between the ego and the unlived Self, particularly its feminine aspect (the Anima).

Good and evil: What were the sins that weighed him down, pulling him over to his left side, of which he repented so sorely? What did Descartes, *le chambriste*, get up to, all those solitary hours he lay in bed? Presumably he was no stranger to erotic fantasies, those devilish manifestations for which Jesuitic teaching prescribed eternal Hell fire. John Cole believes the sexual symbolism of the melon carries not female but male connotations for Descartes, and that his sense of sin was all the more grievous because his secret lust was homosexual. As he points out, 10 November, the night on which the dream was dreamt, was the anniversary of Descartes' first meeting with Isaac Beeckman, with whom there is reason to believe he fell in (unrequited) love. This, and his affair with the Dutch maid, were his only attempts at forming loving relationships, and both ended in failure. Guilt may well have played its part in this as well as schizoid incapacity.

Thunder: Descartes himself interpreted this as a descent upon him from above of 'the spirit of truth'. The mythic and religious overtones of thunder link it with the will or judgement of God, while lightning in dreams is associated with sudden enlightenment and transformation (Jung, *CW*9i, para. 534). Although Descartes hears the thunder, he sees no lightning in his dream: instead, as he wakens, he sees a multitude of fiery sparks glowing in the room.

Light: Light is an archetypal image of consciousness. At one level, Descartes' fiery sparks may be understood as the little dots of light commonly observed in hypnopompic imagery (i.e imagery observed as one wakes up as opposed to hypnagogic images, which are observed as one goes to sleep). But they were evidently of greater significance than this, for they made a deep impression on Descartes: he experienced them as some revelation from on high. In many ways Descartes' 'fiery sparks' resemble the *scintillae* or *oculi piscum* (fishes' eyes) which the alchemist contemporaries of Descartes noted as occurring in the course of the alchemical opus, when the *prima materia* is transformed, yielding many 'small white sparks'. Jung interprets these (in his essay entitled 'The Unconscious as a Multiple Consciousness') as being flickerings of consciousness apparent as unconscious contents grope their way towards awareness. As full ego-consciousness emerges it is surrounded by 'multiple luminosities' which gradually coalesce.

The fiery sparks have also been variously interpreted as manifestations of 'the Anima Catholica', the universal soul identified with the Spirit of God, and as the *'lumen naturale'* described by Paracelsus, the light of nature, 'kindled by the Holy Ghost, and bestowed upon the "inward man"'. Paracelsus believed the natural light to be present in animals and immanent in all nature as the *'luminositas sensus naturae'*. To Jung, such manifestations were all expressions of the teleological goal implicit in all natural forms guiding them towards consciousness. The *scintillae* are images embodying the latent conscious intentions of the archetypes of the collective unconscious.

Descartes experienced the thunderclap and the fiery sparks, like the phantoms and the wind in the earlier sequence, as expressions of a power arising from beyond himself. Like the dream sequences as a whole, they were so overwhelming, that he imagined that they could only have come from on high (*'qu'il s'imagina ne pouvoir être venus que d'enhaut'*).

With these dream events, Descartes knew, something apocalyptic had happened. Something had been revealed to him that had never occurred to him before. A new consciousness was being born and it was taking shape in him. His destiny was to develop his philosophy and in doing this he was accomplishing no less than the will of God.

Through him the *lumen naturale* implicit in all things was to be made manifest in the human mind – or rather in the one human mind of whose existence he, René Descartes, could be certain: his own. The 'natural light', the *res cogitans* in us, comes directly from God: and it was destined to achieve its most lucid manifestation in his thoughts.

Poetry: The poems in the third and final part of the dream speak directly to Descartes' condition. Ausonius was a sceptical poet and his poem 'Quod vitae sectibor iter?' ('What way of life shall I choose?') deals with the futility of social life: on the one hand, 'heavy penalties weigh on the bachelor's life', yet marriage brings man no security 'when the work of Mars claims his blood'. All friendship is to be avoided, for it can lead to the sin for which the Pythagoreans were destroyed. 'Fearing this, on no account cultivate friendship – for this fault Timon was once stoned in Athens.' The poem concludes with a Greek aphorism: 'It is fortunate for a man not to be born, and, if he is, then to die quickly.'

The second poem, 'Est et non' (yes and no), is about doubt and certainty, and about conflict and agreement between men, especially philosophers. How can we be certain that when it is light it must be day? 'For how often does light proceed from a number of torches, or from lightning, that is man's nocturnal light, not daylight.' The poem ends: 'How sad in reality is this life of man, forever swayed by these two words each of one syllable.'

Together these poems sum up his disenchantment with all manifestations of life, save those of the intellect, his wariness of all emotional involvements, and his preoccupation with the need to establish what is real, certain, and beyond doubt. 'Nothing remained for him but the love of truth,' comments Baillet, 'the pursuit of which was to be the occupation of his life from that time on.'

The portraits: This was the time of high achievement in Dutch art, the age of Rembrandt and Frans Hals (who was to paint Descartes' portrait), when the individual personality was studied and celebrated as never before. That there are several portraits in the dream suggests, like the seeds of the melon and the multiple luminosities in the room, that a whole range of previously unimagined possibilities is now becoming available to Descartes. Dr von Franz comments that the first dream symbol of the Self is unitary (the melon) and that this cracks open in the second two dream episodes to reveal that the human personality is inwardly manifold (the seeds, the sparks, the portraits).

Conclusion   If the purpose of dreaming is to promote the individuation of the dreamer, then the Great Dream of René Descartes was both a triumph and a failure. It confirmed his conviction that in his thinking consciousness he possessed an instrument capable of unravelling the mysteries of the universe and discovering the mind of God encoded in the symbols of mathematics. But it failed to bring him down to earth: it did not enable him to mobilize all the potential inherent in the Self to become psychologically and emotionally intact or to participate in life. Moreover, this split in him served, through his great influence, to widen the already developing split between the rational and the non-rational faculties in all educated members of our society.

As a result of Descartes' life, the ego of Western man became stronger, more detached, more determined and more disciplined, thus facilitating the advances and the catastrophes that followed in commercial expansion, planetary exploration, imperial domination, the discoveries of science, the construction of weapons of mass destruction. The little flashes of light that Descartes saw as he awoke from the first part of his dream combined to yield the brilliance of the Enlightenment, and the certainty that thoughts formulated in the language of logic and mathematics possessed a universal validity which could exist beyond the reach of time or history. The torch which Descartes lit and which was to be borne on high during the second half of the seventeenth century by that other schizoid genius, Isaac Newton, resulted from the illumination that Descartes received from one night of dreaming. Thus was the human spirit freed from the darkness of medieval superstition:

> *Nature and Nature's Laws lay hid in Night*
> *God said,* **Let Newton be!** *and all was light.*

Such was the power of the light that Descartes and Newton kindled that it achieved its most dazzling and most dreadful culmination at Hiroshima, and could yet result in the apocalyptic conflagration of our planet. That Descartes' vision has brought us great advantages cannot be denied; its disadvantage is that it dragged us collectively in the schizoid direction. His dream was an attempt to compensate for his social and emotional withdrawal as well as his intellectual hypertrophy, but because he lacked the psychological insight to work on it, its message eluded him, and he took it as a reaffirmation of the mission he had conceived for himself on the previous day's vision of the 'wonderful science'. Our whole culture is still suffering from this dream and his failure to understand it.

13

DREAMING AND THE ART OF CONSCIOUSNESS

What nature leaves imperfect, the art perfects.
Alchemical Maxim

Throughout this book I have argued that beyond the purely personal ego there lies a greater reality which is registered in our dreams. The desire to possess this reality is what has produced analysis: it has also produced religion, mythology, psychology, and art — all attempts to construct mirrors of the Self, to find a cultural route to individuation, and the achievement of 'higher' consciousness. As society became godless and psychology focused on rats, the arts and the rituals of analysis became practically the only means left to celebrate the miracle of living. The unfailing characteristic of great art has been to lead us into the archetypal realm and, through consummate mastery, to reveal the eternal in the transitory, the universal in the particular. In art the Greeks gave us a vessel in which the life of humanity is captured and distilled so as to grant us a glimpse of ultimate reality. The philosopher Ludwig Wittgenstein expressed this perfectly when he said, 'The work of art is the object seen *sub specie aeternitatis*; and the good life is the world seen *sub specie aeternitatis*. This is the connection between art and ethics. The usual way of looking at things sees objects as it were from the midst of them; the view *sub specie aeternitatis* sees them from outside, in such a way that they have the whole world as background.' The dream, as we have approached it, is, like a work of art, an object seen *sub specie aeternitatis*. The dream differs from the work of art in that it is a spontaneous creation which it is in the power of everyone to produce, whereas great art requires an infinite capacity for taking pains, as well as access to the archetypal realm: 'The true work of art,' said Cyril Connolly, 'is one which the seventh wave of genius throws up the beach where the undertow of time cannot drag it back.'

However, there are many valid parallels between dreaming and art. In the first place, both demand the ability to appreciate as well as to create, and both are aspects of the same process – namely, communication. Art, like the dream, is an emotionally loaded form of communication conducted through the use of symbols. Secondly, the artist, no more than the dream-maker, is not someone who merely entertains but a *psychopompos*, a messenger from the gods, with access to a more numinous, more extraordinary world. 'The artist is not a person endowed with free will who seeks his own ends,' wrote Jung, 'but one who allows art to realize its purposes through him. As a human being he may have moods and a will and personal aims, but as an artist he is "man" in a higher sense – he is "collective man" – one who carries and shapes the unconscious psychic life of mankind' (Jung, 1933, p. 189). Thirdly, the arts can perform the same compensatory functions for a whole society as dreams can for an individual member of that society. For this reason artists carry a great cultural responsibility; and it follows that art critics should do their work with the same integrity to which all good analysts aspire. Like myths, works of art are public dreams, and in the past their function has been primarily religious. 'Art,' said Jean Cocteau, 'is not a pastime but a priesthood.'

Seen from this perspective, the supreme function of the great artist is that of the prophet-interpreter – one who receives the archetypal message and who translates it into the language of the present in such a way as to compensate for the deficiencies of the times. Jung described it as follows: 'Recoiling from the unsatisfactory present the yearning of the artist reaches out to that primordial image in the unconscious which is best fitted to compensate the insufficiency and one-sidedness of the spirit of the age.'

The Fall of Icarus

An example of this compensatory aspiration is *The Fall of Icarus* by Pieter Brueghel the Elder, illustrated on the dust-jacket of this book. Now in the Musées des Beaux-Arts in Brussels, it was painted in 1558 and is one of the great icons of our civilization. The mid sixteenth century was a time when human secular ambitions were beginning their inflated ascent to their present manic altitude. We were already well on the way to conquering the elements, and, through a powerful combination of courage, butchery, and scientific ingenuity, to mastering the globe. An era of remarkable achievements has already begun, but what does it amount to, and where will it all end? Brueghel's picture is a meditation on these issues, more crucial for us now than when he painted it. He shows us Icarus, having hubristically over-reached himself by flying too close to the sun, plummeting back into his encounter with Nemesis, the sea – the element from which we all sprang. Meanwhile, the eternal round of human existence proceeds on its timeless course – the fisherman fishes, the shepherd tends his sheep, the ploughman tills the soil, while the sun performs its stately march across God's limitless heaven. Wystan Auden described the scene 380 years later in one of his finest poems:

> In Brueghel's **Icarus,** for instance: how everything turns away
> Quite leisurely from the disaster; the ploughman may
> Have heard the splash, the forsaken cry,
> But for him it was not an important failure; the sun shone
> As it had to on the white legs disappearing into the green
> Water; and the expensive delicate ship that must have seen
> Something amazing, a boy falling out of the sky,
> Had somewhere to get to and sailed calmly on.

This great painting takes an ancient myth and assimilates our modern destiny to its wisdom. The story of man getting above himself and riding for a fall is older far than the tale of Icarus or of Adam's indiscretion. At the dawn of civilization in the city of Kish it was told how the Great Solar Eagle flew heavenwards with King Etna on his back. As they ascend above the highest summit of the world, the King grows fearful: 'Oh, my friend,' he cries, 'do not climb further!' Made aware of the enormity of his achievement, the Eagle loses his nerve, and together they crash to earth.

The mythic theme of man's rise and fall is the allegory of our progress up to the present. It has haunted every generation since, departing from the Garden of Eden, we abandoned our ancestral dependence on the bounty of Nature (the Will of God). Judeo-Christianity portrays this moment as the time when mortality was created. In fact it was the moment when mortality was *recognized*. Stealing fruit from the Tree of Knowledge was like Prometheus' theft of fire – the acquisition of self-conscious independence. God did not expel us from the Garden of Eden, we got sick of it and left. Ever since we have longed to return there, but we can't; for we have burnt most of it down, exploited its resources, and handed the proceeds to the International Monetary Fund.

Rising and Falling

What goes up must come down.
Proverb

Let us amplify Brueghel's painting in the same way as we would a dream – confining ourselves to the cultural and archetypal levels, for we are dealing with a work of art and not a personal dream.

Before the Fall, we adapted to reality more directly than at present through the good offices of the Self, with the result that human communities lived in a state of relative equilibrium with each other and with the physical environment. The ego was present, of course, but had less to say in the proceedings. With the Fall came the discovery of agriculture and the abandonment, in what we Westerners call the Middle East, of the hunter-gatherer existence. Traditional, timeless, 'cool' societies, which had reproduced themselves unchanged over many thousands of years, gave way to dynamic, time-linked, 'hot' societies, which entered the maelstrom of history. At the same time, the ego emerged as a force for Nature to reckon with. For transformation of the primordial mind into the modern mind coincided with a progressive differentiation of the ego from the Self and a 'stretching' of the neuropsychic lines of communication between them (the *ego-Self axis*; Figure 3).

With farming there came a growing awareness of time, but it was not the linear time we live in. It was seasonal, cyclic time: summer to winter and back again; sowing, harvesting, ploughing, sowing again, time moving in circles, time, as Joseph Campbell put it, 'Getting absolutely nowhere.' In a book crammed with insight, Gary Eberle (1995) lists the differences he sees between the primordial and modern

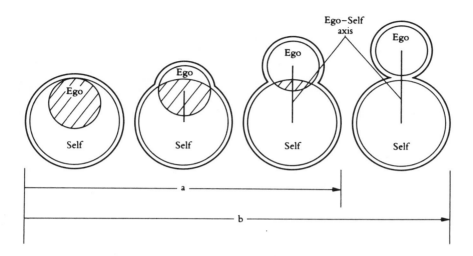

Figure 3. Development of the ego–Self axis from birth to maturity in the primordial mind (a) and the modern mind (b). At first the ego exists only *in potentia* as a component of the Self. Then, as ontological development proceeds, the ego gradually differentiates itself out from the Self. The perpendicular line connecting them represents the ego–Self axis, the vital link which sustains the integrity of the personality. The shaded areas of the ego represent the relative degree of ego–Self identity persisting at stages in the developmental process. (Adapted from Edinger, 1992.)

minds. I have taken the liberty of adapting and extending his list in Table 4.

To the primordial intellect, humanity held a central position in the cosmic order, lived in a state of intimate participation with nature (what Lévy-Bruhl called *participation mystique*), held a rhythmic, circular conception of time, inhabited a reality primarily located in the world of the spirit, accepted moral values as absolute, regarded life as eternal, and believed myth and ritual to be indispensable to the health and vitality of the spirit. By contrast, to the modern intellect, humanity holds a peripheral position in the cosmic order, lives in a state of objective separation from nature, holds a progressive, linear conception of time, inhabits a reality primarily located in the world of matter, accepts moral values as relative, regards life as strictly

Table 4:   Phenomenological differences between primordial and modern
minds.

	PRIMORDIAL MIND	MODERN MIND
Ego-Self axis	short and compact	long and attenuated
Cosmic location	central	peripheral
Relationship to Nature	subjective participation *'participation mystique'*	separation, objectivity
Concept of time	rhythmic and circular	progressive and linear
Reality	the world of the spirit	the world of matter
Moral values	absolute	relative
Life	eternal	finite
Attitude to myth and ritual	essential	futile

finite, and believes myth and ritual to be irrelevant to the require-
ments of modern life.

With increasing separation from the Self the ego lost its innocence
and became heroic, ceased to be earthbound and learned to fly. It has
been flying higher and higher ever since. Intuitively we have known
that Brueghel and the Greeks were right: this is an extremely
hazardous occupation. The Judeo-Christians had good reason to view
man's escape from the primordial ancestral environment as a 'fall',
for they saw it in moralistic terms as a defiance of the Law of God. It
was a fall from grace. The modern secular view is quite contrary: it
sees it as a rise from unconsciousness, an ascent from darkness, while

acknowledging its perils. The danger must always be that we step too far outside the Law of Nature, wilfully play havoc with the principles of homeostasis, stretch the ego–Self axis to breaking point, and get so far out of tune with archetypal realities as to become collectively, cosmically insane. That would be a Fall indeed. Some would say we have already arrived there. I feel we still have some way to go. We are not fallen, but falling. We are like the man who jumped off the Empire State Building and as he passed the fifth floor, was heard to mutter, 'So far, so good!' A modern Icarus.

The point about rising and falling is that growth, development, consciousness need both involution and evolution, depth as well as height. Describing history as 'an epic composed in the mind of God', von Schelling saw it as a drama falling into two main parts: 'first, that which depicts the departure of humanity from its centre up to its furthrest point of alienation from this centre, and secondly, that which depicts the return. It is the story of the *Iliad* and the *Odyssey* reduced to a maxim.' This essentially cyclic rhythm underlying the apparent chaos of events was also understood by Niccolò Machiavelli: '. . . it is ordained by Providence that there should be a continual ebb and flow in the things of this world, as soon as they arrive at their utmost perfection and can ascend no higher, they must of necessity decline . . .' The parallel ebb and flow of sleep and wakefulness sustains the tenuous links of sanity connecting our contemporary to our primordial selves. This is the key phenomenon responsible for human self-awareness and survival and it depends upon the regular systole and diastole of consciousness and dreaming.

Nature's mind

Nature is very consonant and comfortable with herself.
ISAAC NEWTON

When Jung introduced the term 'natural mind' to denote the 'two-million-year-old man that is in all of us', he was coining a metaphor for the age-old dynamic at the core of human existence, there by virtue of our evolutionary heritage as a species. Still active in our dreams and typical adaptive strategies, it goes on struggling to promote our survival in the often alienating conditions of the modern world. When we become ill, disenchanted, or neurotic, it is because its basic needs are being frustrated; when we are happy and most truly alive it is because its basic needs are fulfilled. The two-million-year-old Self represents no less than the will of nature, its intentions worked out through the aeons of evolutionary time, providing a fund of ancient wisdom we neglect at our collective peril.

A central illusion which sustains the modern mind is that it is unprecedented, that modern life is quite unlike anything experienced by human beings in the past. This betrays a degree of mental parochialism which is indeed unprecedented; for no previous culture could have been so blind to the eternal verities of human existence as to believe that the production of a few artefacts – Boeings, telecommunications satellites, and motor cars – could justify the denial of the prevailing influence of the ancestral past. We too easily forget that the human psyche was forged in adversity and is made of durable stuff, that the archetypal capacities of the limbic system have been around for millions of years, their programmes tested by every eventuality that a resourceful and demanding planet could throw at them, and that the entire cerebral architecture has remained totally unchanged since the emergence of our Cro-Magnon kin over a hundred millennia ago.

Since then our brain has not evolved one iota. There has been too little time and it has been too successful – the most adaptable organ ever created. All along it has had exactly the same capacity for consciousness as we had in Eden. What has 'evolved' is no more than the cultural consensus as to how this capacity can be used. *Culture is a memory store existing outside the brain.* The men who devised the first bows and arrows and later painted the caves at Lascaux were perfectly capable of making nuclear missiles and decorating the Sistine Chapel. All they lacked was the cultural back-up, the technical know-how generated, recorded, and passed on by previous generations. Instead of making TV soaps, washing-machines and word-processors, they devoted their genius to religious rituals, narrative poems, fertility dances, songs, and the interpretation of dreams. These, to us, 'primitive' activities were what held them together psychically and socially. If our culture is unprecedented, it is through having abandoned these ancient practices, and therein lies a cause of our contemporary plight.

In the past, all human societies used techniques whose function was to integrate the individual with the collective, the present with the past, the personal conscious mind with the collective unconscious of the species. These rites and ceremonies, with their ritual sacrifices, their elaborate costumes, dances, and chants, have been abolished from our rational, secular society. In so doing, we have abandoned some of the most crucial mechanisms of survival in our repertoire. If we fail to recognize this appalling truth and fail to do anything about it, then it is quite possible that our civilization, and even our species, will be doomed.

Jung understood this: we were spiritually deprived in the modern world because we had lost touch with the natural mind, and its needs were no longer satisfied. The therapy he devised was designed to restore the connection. As he was the first to recognize, the primordial keeps breaking through in our dreams – the sense of being central to all cosmic events, of participating in the phenomena of nature, inhabiting a timeless world of the spirit, or entering a mythic realm where one finds oneself in a rite or ritual such as would never occur in the neon-lit world of today. Unfortunately, Jung's conception of a 'natural mind' is unsatisfactory, even as a metaphor, since there can be no self-contained 'primordial mind' entirely encapsulated within the modern mind and uninfluenced by contemporary events. All mental phenomena are the products of interaction between innate potentials and the facilitating (or frustrating) environment.

Nor is ego-consciousness a faculty that has recently evolved, as Jung (1933), Neumann (1954), Jaynes (1976), and Wilber (1983) in otherwise fascinating books all cheerfully imply. Consciousness has been millions of years in the making. What has happened since the emergence of civilization has been a widening of conscious horizons, an accumulation of technical knowledge, and a strengthening of ego-identity. As this process has continued, the 'primordial' mentality has had to adapt, as the ego separated itself further from the Self, and the individual differentiated out from a total identity with the group.

Growing acknowledgement of the power of individuals to shape cultural history went along with admiration for the charismatic personality able to achieve the highest goals – the hero.

It is no accident that the heroic gods were sun gods, representing the principles of ascent, light, and consciousness. But here again the notions of rising and falling in a rhythmic cycle are incorporated in the myths. Having ascended to the highest point of heaven during the daytime, the hero descends into the depths of the ocean at night, where he does battle with the great sea monster during the hours of darkness and emerges victorious each morning in the East, *Sol Invictus*. 'In this sequence of danger, battle, and victory,' says Neumann, 'the light is the central symbol of the hero's reality. The hero is always a light-bringer and emissary of the light.'

Put in neurological terms, the triumph of the hero is the triumph of the left cerebral hemisphere over the right, and of the forebrain as a whole over the limbic system and the brain stem. The hero myth represents the apotheosis of left hemispheric imperialism. The hero's night sea journey is the nocturnal descent of the conscious ego into the unconscious underworld, and the opening up of elaborate communications between the new and old brains, making possible the busy commerce between them so typical of REM sleep.

The Great Chain of Being

There is a grandeur in this view of life, with its several powers, having been originally breathed by the Creator into a few forms or one; and that, while this planet has gone cycling on according to the fixed law of gravity, from so simple a beginning endless forms most beautiful and most wonderful have been and are being evolved.

CHARLES DARWIN, *The Origin of Species* (1859)

It was Darwin's champion, Thomas Huxley, who first had the insight that the evolution of human consciousness had enabled nature to become conscious of itself. A similar thought struck Jung on a visit to East Africa in 1925. As he stood on a hill looking down on the savannah stretching to the far horizon, watching gigantic herds of gazelle, antelope, gnu, zebra, and warthog grazing and moving forward like slow rivers, 'the cosmic meaning of consciousness' became overwhelmingly clear to him. Without human consciousness to be aware of the scene before him, it would remain in a state of non-being. 'What nature leaves imperfect, the art perfects,' declared the alchemists. Consciousness, Jung now saw, puts the stamp of perfection on the world by giving it objective existence. 'Now I knew what it was, and knew even more: that man is indispensable for the completion of creation; that, in fact, he himself is the second creator of the world, who alone has given to the world its objective existence – without which, unheard, unseen, silently eating, giving birth, dying, heads nodding through hundreds of millions of years, it would have gone on in the profoundest night of non-being down to its unknown end. Human consciousness created objective existence and meaning, and man found his indispensable place in the great process of being (*MDR*, pp. 240–42).

With this insight Jung came to see the journey of personal development towards fuller consciousness as occurring both within a cosmic context and the context of eternity. The psyche, existing *sui generis* as an objective part of nature, is subject to the same laws that govern the universe and is itself the supreme fulfilment of those laws. Through the miracle of consciousness, the human psyche provides the mirror in which Nature sees herself reflected.

In his seventies Jung became interested in the writings of a sixteenth-century alchemist called Gerard Dorn. Dorn believed that the completion of the alchemical *opus* came only with the achievement of a symbolic union of the whole man with the *unus mundus* – the unitary world, the potential world of the first day of Creation, when nothing had yet become differentiated, and everything was still one. The *unus mundus* was, said Jung, 'the eternal Ground of all empirical being, just as the Self is the ground and origin of the individual personality past, present and future' (*CW*16, para. 760). Jung recognized that Dorn was articulating a profound idea at the heart of all religious intuition – the perception of the 'relation or identity of the personal with the suprapersonal Atman, and of the individual tao with the universal tao' (*CW*16, para. 762).

Most of us, I suspect, at some time in our lives discover the perspective that Leibniz called the 'perennial philosophy', some kind of conception of the mysterious precondition of all existence, pervading all reality with a dimly intuited sense of meaning or purpose. The perennial philosophy forms the esoteric core of Hinduism, Buddhism, Taoism, Sufism, and Christian mysticism. Even atheists are touched by it when moved by contemplation of the universe and the laws by which it operates. 'The undevout astronomer,' said Edward Young, 'is mad.'

Refined to a peak of concentrated awareness, contemplation of the Ultimate, the Infinite, the Oneness of All Things is the experience of 'enlightenment' or 'satori', and the great world religions have all devised spiritual disciplines designed to induce this transcendent state of consciousness. Plato described it as leaving the cave of shadows and moving into the Light of Being, while Einstein saw it as 'escaping the delusion of separateness'. Viewed from this transcendent perspective, the whole evolution of life on this planet is the story of the gradual emergence of consciousness and the goal of consciousness is to achieve an ever-heightened awareness of the nature of existence, the Oneness of Everything, the Great Chain of Being.

The Nature of Consciousness

What man knoweth the things of a man,
Save the spirit of man that is in him?
I CORINTHIANS 2.11

While many authorities have written about the 'higher consciousness' achieved by advanced civilizations, and have described the development of consciousness that comes through working with dreams, few have attempted to define what they mean by consciousness and the development of 'higher' forms. It is important, therefore, that we should attempt some description of what these elusive terms may mean, though always with the caveat that we could be missing the main thing.

Central to the concept of consciousness is awareness of oneself as a living individual with a personal identity extending from the past, through the present, into the future. Awareness of the passage of time and of the continuity of personal identity through time goes along with the ability to retain memories and to use them in comprehending the present and anticipating events yet to come. To devise future goals and to work systematically towards their achievement requires conscious resolve to postpone gratification of immediate needs or desires to some time in the future. To focus on a task or an idea long enough to see it through to completion (the 'attention span') also requires a conscious exertion of the will.

Consciousness implies the capacity to recognize and reflect on ideas, sensations, and emotions, to appreciate their implications, to transform them into words, and to form as comprehensive and perceptive an understanding of reality as is possible, given the finite limitations of the human mind-brain. Over all, consciousness is the capacity to monitor what is going on inside and outside oneself, to assess contingencies, to reason about them, and to decide what is best (i.e. most adaptive, most advantageous, most ethical) to do in the circumstances.

Consciousness becomes an art when one deliberately refines one's capacity to experience feelings and sensations in order to celebrate the miracle of existence.

Discussion of how awareness of these manifold capacities can be improved invariably leads us into metaphors of space and vision – e.g. *level* (height and depth), *extent* (breadth), *size* (growth and development), and *complexity* (differentiation, multi-dimensionality). One *heightens* consciousness by adopting a *wider view*, one *views* things on a *higher level*, and so on. The higher and broader the view attained by individual consciousness, the closer it comes to the ultimate achievement of *transcendence*.

Each new stage of an evolutionary process not only transcends but encompasses all the stages that have preceded it. When we become smug about our intellectual achievements we forget how much they depend on the brains of creatures that have gone before us. The slow phylogenetic ascent of consciousness, its lumbering progress through the minds of reptiles, mammals and primates, the record of which is incorporated in our brains as well as in the fossils of our planet, has encouraged some to see the whole course of our evolution mapped out for us – from subconsciousness through selfconsciousness to superconsciousness – claiming that so far 'man is only halfway between the animal and the human being', and that we still have a long way to go. A similar notion is implicit in Kundalini yoga: all higher levels of consciousness exist in us as unrealized potential ('Kundalini energy'), which lies coiled up like a serpent ('serpent power') in the lowest 'chakra' at the base of the spine. The practice of Kundalini yoga is said to awaken the slumbering serpent power so that it may evolve through the Great Chain of Being by ascending from the lowest chakra of material, natural existence, through the mind–brain centre to the seventh and highest chakra of superconsciousness and transcendence.

There is a striking parallel between Kundalini yoga and the 'hierarchy of needs' postulated by Abraham Maslow (1968). According to Maslow there are five levels of need, starting with the basic physiological needs for food, water, and warmth. When these are met the next needs to emerge are concerned with security, safety, and protection. Then comes the need for love, attachment, and belongingness. Satisfaction on this level leads to the emergence of the need for status, respect, and self-esteem. Finally, at the top of the hierarchy, comes the need which demands fulfilment when all the 'lower' needs have been met: the need for *self-actualization* – 'to become everything that one is capable of becoming'. Maslow's first, third, and fourth levels correspond to the first three chakras of Kundalini yoga which, in ascending order, have to do with food, sex, and power. There are also evident parallels with other theoretical orientations described in the course of this book – e.g. love and attachment needs (Freud, Bowlby, and the hedonic mode), esteem and status needs (Adler and the agonic mode), and the need for self-actualization (Jung and the individuation principle). Maslow found that people who were persistent 'self-actualizers' were prone to what he called 'peak experiences' (height again) – akin to mystical awareness, the 'oceanic feeling', a sense of fuller vision extending to apparently limitless horizons. Maslow's descriptions of peak experiences make them sound like an example of Atman-consciousness or an acute episodic awareness of the 'perennial philosophy': there is a loss of identity with the purely personal ego and its replacement by a sense of general identity with everything that exists, that will ever exist, and has ever existed.

How are such desirable states of consciousness achieved? Presumably by the spiritual disciplines that have been devised over the centuries in order to induce them. Some attain them through the practice of transcendental meditation. In my own lifetime, I have only experienced anything approximating such a state in the aftermath of a dream.

Like many people well into the second half of life I often think of death. 'After thirty a man wakes up sad every morning,' wrote Emerson, 'until the day of his death.' In my case it has been a question of going to sleep sad every night. Another day gone from the allocated number. How many left? One morning I awoke knowing that my perspective had changed. I had evidently had a dream in which the whole issue had been presented in a different light. Yet, try as I would, I could remember no details from the dream. All I was left with was the sense that something of significance had changed. What was it? In the absence of the dream there was only one thing I could do – active imagination. I focused on my feeling of change. What was it about? It was about my death. What about it? *It no longer mattered.* Why not? Something else was more important. What was it? *Everything would continue to go on* and *that* mattered far more than my survival or my life as an individual. This brought me feelings of peace and happiness. Why? Because I was released from the problem of mortality. My consciousness no longer felt restricted to my finite existence: it extended into all existence. What then had happened in my dream? *I had received my first intimation of Atman-consciousness.*

As Wilber (1983) has suggested, this is what ritual sacrifice, as it has been practised throughout the world for millennia, was designed to achieve: the sacrifice of identity with ego in favour of an identity with the eternal Ground of all being. The version practised in our culture for the last 2,000 years is the mass: Christ is sacrificed (the lamb), He dies to His personal existence (the Crucifixion), He ascends into Heaven (transcendence) to be united with God, the source and continuation of all existence (Atman-consciousness). By eating the body of Christ (the bread and the wine) one mingles one's identity with His and participates in the mystical transformation from identity with the personal ego to identity with the transpersonal Atman.

To those of us who are not communicants in the Christian Church, the transformative power of the mass is unavailable, but if

333

we are in communion with the unconscious, the transpersonal power of the Self is available to all of us in our dreams. The major difference is that dream transformation is unpredictable: it occurs only when it will. One cannot re-experience it daily or weekly as one might as a believer, by the simple expedient of going to church. But I suspect that many Christians do not experience it either. They participate in the ritual but remain unmoved. As with Hamlet's uncle Claudius, their words fly up, their thoughts remain below. This is what happens when religions reach the end of their vitality. The mystical power falls back to the unconscious from which it came. Icarus once more plunges into the sea.

Whatever Became of the Soul?

Though inland far we be,
Our souls have sight of that immortal sea
Which brought us hither.

WILLIAM WORDSWORTH

Something disastrous begins to happen to societies when they lose faith with their gods. No longer possessing any invisible means of support, their cultural backbone goes soft and crumbles. It is one of the great lessons of history – Babylon, Egypt, Greece, Carthage, Rome ... Without a myth or religion to fill the universe with meaning, it is as if human populations enter a phase of ego-serving futility in which they lose their will to survive. In the present century many commentators have diagnosed this condition in our own society, using such terms as 'death of the soul' (Barrett), 'spiritual bankruptcy' (Eberle), and 'loss of soul' (Jung). 'About a third of my cases,' wrote Jung, 'are not suffering from any clearly definable neurosis, but from the senselessness and aimlessness of their lives. I should not object if this were called the general neurosis of our age' (*CW* 16, para. 83).

Loss of reverence for the great mythic and religious symbols of our culture has coincided with the emergence of social institutions and collective values which alienate us from our archetypal roots. The more secular, materialistic, and compulsively extraverted our civilization becomes, the greater the 'senselessness and aimlessness' of our lives. Respect for traditional institutions – the family, the Church, the government and its ministers, the law and its representatives – goes into irreversible decline, and the fabric of society begins to disintegrate, with increasing crime, political corruption, and public squalor. What is the answer? Not a return to the old ways of the Church, for its symbols are dead and beyond hope of resuscitation. Jung's prescription was the advice to turn inwards – to abandon the exclusively extraverted quest for meaning in the outer world of material objects and, instead, to establish contact with the symbol-forming capacities latent within our own psychic nature. What was needed was hard psychological work to open up our minds to the inner wealth of the unconscious so as to realize in actuality our own capacity for wholeness. Experience had taught him that, in the process, meaning and purpose flood back into one's life.

Jung seems to have believed that if enough individuals did this and developed the higher degree of consciousness attendant upon pursuit of the goal of individuation, a new mythic consensus could arise restoring a sense of meaning and purpose to the collective. To this mythic Renaissance the arts would make an indispensable contribution. Unfortunately, there is little evidence that this is happening. Where dream analysis is practised it remains primarily focused on personal psychodynamics and on issues of personality adjustment, any heightening of consciousness being regarded as an adjunct to the pursuit of those objectives; while the arts have virtually abandoned all spiritual or aesthetic intentions.

Rather than compensating for the disintegrative forces at work in our culture, the arts in the twentieth century have become symptomatic of them. Something similar happens, as we have already noted, in the dreams of depressed patients; instead of compensating the depressed mood the dreams tend to affirm it – until some new archetypal constellation occurs in the collective unconscious, inaugurating the possibility of change.

What has happened to us in the twentieth century can be understood as a culmination of the processes set in train by the Enlightenment and the Age of Reason – both inaugurated by René Descartes' dream and his elevation of the thinking function to such commanding heights that, with the aid of science, it could overlook, command, and eventually topple the Throne of God. The identification of everything crucial in life with the intellect had the inevitable consequence of forcing the human psyche into a soulless rationalism, leading to the emergence of what Herbert Marcuse called 'one-dimensional man'. Accordingly, the arts, reflecting the values of the collective and becoming progressively secular, were stripped of mythic reference and deprived of all spiritual purpose. Growing fat on the corpse of God, the thinking function, triumphant in its extraverted hubris, found apt expression in an art that denied beauty, love, and the human soul. Henceforth, the only place left by Modernist orthodoxy for these despised values would be the subversive world of dreams.

Soul-making

Through experiencing the unconscious I gain soul.
JAMES HILLMAN

Freud's contribution to the spiritual malaise of our century is not to be overlooked. Squinting through his narrow theoretical keyhole at our hidden lechery, he encouraged us to believe that it was always the worst possible explanation of our behaviour that came nearest to the truth. The more perceptive of Freud's disciples acknowledged their complicity in this denigration: 'we were dismayed,' wrote Erik Erikson, 'when we saw our purpose of enlightenment perverted into a widespread fatalism, according to which man is nothing but a multiplication of his parents' faults and an accumulation of his own earlier selves. We must grudgingly admit that even as we were trying to devise, with scientific determinism, a therapy for the few, we were led to promote an ethical disease among the many' (1962). The reductive philosophy, declared Karl Stern, 'is the most widely acclaimed part of psycho-analytic thought. It harmonizes so excellently with a typical petit bourgeois mediocrity, which is associated with contempt for everything spiritual.'

From the standpoint of oneirology, therefore, it should be no cause for regret that the Freudian explanation has failed, for Freud would

336

have done to the art of dreaming what Marcel Duchamp* did to the art of painting, had not Jung come to the rescue. As it was, Freud's influence prevailed through most of the century, augmenting the 'contempt for everything spiritual' that was also the hallmark of Modernism. The 'typically bourgeois' dissociation between cold, abstract intellectualism and hot, unreflective sexuality sustained the split between the thinking and feeling functions, and was later politicized by Herbert Marcuse, who, in the 1960s, identified the superego and the reality principle with the puritanical work ethic and advocated a revolutionary uprising in the service of the pleasure principle and the Id. Marcuse's message was received ecstatically by the young but it did nothing to heal the schizoid wound at the heart of our culture. Ronnie Laing's *The Divided Self*, which purported to be a monograph on schizophrenia, became a runaway best-seller because the public saw that it was describing something that had happened to us all. That was Laing's diagnostic contribution. Jung's contribution was to provide insight into how the Self had become divided and to devise techniques which could prove helpful for its reassembly.

Jung's therapeutic intention was championed after his death by James Hillman, then a startlingly young Director of Studies at the C.G. Jung Institute in Zürich, who published two influential books, *Suicide and the Soul* (1964) and *Insearch* (1967). It was in these that he defined the crucial need of our civilization to be 'soul-making' – a brave suggestion, in view of the deeply unfashionable status of the soul. By soul, Hillman meant a perspective rather than a substance. He conceived the soul as a self-sustaining and *imagining* process on which consciousness rests – 'an unknown component which makes meaning possible, turns events into experiences, is communicated in love, and has a religious concern'. The sense in which he has most frequently used the term in his writings is to designate 'the

---

*In 1914 Duchamp took it upon himself to announce the 'death of art', marking its demise three years later at the Independents' Exhibition in New York with the display of his notorious urinal, to which he gave the ironic title *Fountain*. In fact, this was not a natural death but an assassination, a premeditated attempt to kill off high art for good.

imaginative possibility of our natures, the experiencing through reflective speculation, dream, image and *fantasy* – that mode which recognizes all realities as primarily symbolic or metaphorical' (1975, p. x). The soul is to be equated with the '*poetic basis of mind*', and must be the primary concern of 'depth psychology'. Whereas most religious, psychological, and social aspiration is upwards, Hillman believes our therapeutic orientation should carry us downwards in quest of 'the deeper meanings of the soul'. Depth psychology is summed up for him by a dictum of Heraclitus: 'You could not discover the limits of the soul (*psyche*), even if you traveled every road to do so; such is the depth (*bathun*) of its meaning (*logos*).' For Hillman, the essential point is that 'the dimension of soul is depth (not breadth or height) and the dimension of our soul travel is downward' (p. xi). Psychology, says Hillman, is 'the logos of the soul' and in travelling the soul's labyrinth '*we can never go deep enough*' (1979, p. 25). It is what happens below (*depth, darkness*) that reveals the significance of what happens above (*consciousness, light*).

Hillman reaffirms Jung's insight that anxiety, depression, meaninglessness result from loss of intimacy with the archetypal world: 'the pervading, though masked, depression in our civilization is partly the response of the soul to its lost underworld' (1979, p. 74). Dreamwork provides the ritual necessary for re-establishing the connection by going deep. Our mythic conception of the underworld reaches back in time beyond Dante's *Inferno* to Homer's *Sojourn of the Dead*, the Celtic *Dagda*, the Germanic *Hel*, and the Biblical *Shoel*. The underworld is the realm of death as well as dreams and the abode of the ancestral spirits. In the *Iliad* Homer presents *Hypnos* (Sleep) and *Thanatos* (Death) as twin brothers, and the underworld is ruled by Hades, the shadow side of his brother, Zeus, who rules on Olympus. Assimilated into the Roman Pantheon, Hades became Pluto (*Wealth*).

When we fall asleep at night and enter the REM state, we undertake the hero's descent to visit, on a purely transitory basis, the kingdom of death. Charon conveys us across the Styx, we pass Cerberus and gain admittance to the Empire of Hades/Pluto, the archetypal realm in which time stands still. Soul-making, the creation of psychic wholeness, depends on the interpenetration of these two worlds, for both upperworld and underworld, dayworld and dream-world, stand in intimate relationship to one another. Their mutuality is complete, their interdependence symbiotic in its totality. 'We work on dreams not to strengthen the ego,' says Hillman, ' but *to make psychic reality*, to make life matter through death, to make soul by coagulating and intensifying the imagination' (1979, p. 137).

A crucial function of psychotherapy, as Jung conceived it, is to root one in one's personal myth, to see one's life story against an archetypal background. Or, as Hillman puts it, to transform one's case history into one's soul history. Narrative is the key. The 'once upon a time' quality of myths and fairy tales captivates the narrative longings of the soul and leads it willingly into the timeless realm: *ab illo tempore* − limbic time. In analysis we piece together the story of our lives, work out the dramatic sequence of how we reached this point, what events have shaped us and forged our destiny, and, through amplification, link our story to the transpersonal narratives of humanity, which, when celebrated in myths, scriptures, and the arts, provide a foundation in certainty and a profound sense of connected-ness − to the Self, the collective, the cosmos, and eternity. Thus is the soul reconstructed, the art of consciousness advanced.

The Desire and Pursuit of the Whole

Only connect . . .

E. M. FORSTER

What myths, rituals, and dreams do is integrate the systems of which the mind-brain is composed. What Western culture has achieved is their separation. This is the legacy of René Descartes. Before the Enlightenment, ego, Self, community, and cosmos were experienced as more closely linked because religion *yoked* them together, the world was alive with soul because the imagination put it there: *anima mundi*. I am grateful to Gary Eberle for calling my attention to the fact that the English word *yoke* comes from the same Indo-European root as *yoga* and *religion* from the same Latin root as *ligament*. Dreams, myths, spiritual disciplines, and religious rituals all have the same ligamenting or yoking function. The various *asanas* of *hatha yoga* are specifically designed to tie body, mind, and spirit together. It is not far-fetched to imagine they could have similar neurophysiological consequences – that narrative, ritual, and dreams strengthen ties between the neocortex and the limbic system, yoking them together. If this fantasy is correct, then the hippocampus is the marriage bed in which Ontogeny and Phylogeny perform their *coniunctio*. As is revealed by the *Baghavad Gita*, the purpose of all yogic disciplines is to reunite the ego with Atman/Brahman, the Ground of All Being.

But such techniques are unknown to the great majority of us. Ideologically adrift, with no certainties left, our conscious awareness is fragmented, dissociated, detached. Our collective plight can be understood at a number of levels: in psychological terms, thinking is divorced from feeling, intuiting from sensing, the ego distanced from the Self; in cultural terms, the mass of people is alienated from the artists and the priests and has lost reverence for the great symbols and guiding traditions of our past; in neurological terms, the pathways between neocortex, limbic system, and brain stem are less frequented than hitherto. As the idea of a unique soul in personal relationship to God diminishes in salience, so each of us becomes relativized in the mass, of no account except to ourselves and possibly those who love and depend on us. The more populations increase in size, the more relatively insignificant each of us becomes, until eventually we decline to the status of a statistic. In the arts, Modernism has represented this decline towards meaningless obscurity; Post-Modernism is the record of its accomplishment.

Having jettisoned virtually all cultural manifestations of the unconscious, the only myths left to us are the personal myths we create in our sleep; the only ritual left to us is the intimate ritual of analysis. Unfortunately, devotion to personal myths and intimate rituals, while it promotes integration in the individual psyche, does little to heal the fragmentation of society. The only collective myths are those manufactured by television and the film industry, and the only collective ritual participated in on a daily basis is TV watching, often in solitary isolation. With few praiseworthy exceptions, the myths rehearsed daily on our television screens are devoid of moral or mythic intention, their purpose being merely to divert, pass the time, and make profits for the networks.

'The death of God' coincided with the rise of three secular myths – Darwinism, Marxism, and the Myth of Infinite Progress (the inspiration behind Scientific Materialism). Of these only Darwinism is left intact. A fourth myth, Lovelock's *Gaia* hypothesis (named after the Greek Earth Goddess), has stirred interest among only a handful of intellectuals and has so far failed to achieve the wide currency it deserves, although there are signs that its influence could be spreading.

I realize that in describing Darwinism as a myth I shall offend some biologists. This is not my intention; and if they are offended it can only be because they have become infected with the debased modern conception of myth as an illusion or falsehood. In presenting the world with the idea of evolution through natural selection, Darwin provided us with a secular creation myth which performed the explanatory function of 'how things began' better than any myth before or since. Unfortunately, it performed none of the spiritual or ritual functions of myth. On the contrary, it demythologized the sacred and dethroned the gods, as Darwin feared it would, and left little place in the scheme of things for the life of the soul. This completed the division of psyche from matter inaugurated by Descartes: the cosmos was purged of spirit and perceived as dead. This is Lovelock's point: because we no longer perceive *Gaia* as living we do not realize we are killing her. We have taken Descartes' schizoid scepticism to its ultimate conclusion. What he legitimized was the apotheosis of the intellect sustained by a dictatorship of the left cerebral hemisphere: the only psychic events which have universal and eternal validity are those formulated in the language of logic and mathematics. The sceptical intellect cares only for the profane. Its hostility to the sacred means we can treat the planet and each other the way we do. When nothing is sacred we can use them after any manner we please.

The Sacred Rhizome

The one remains, the many change and pass . . .
PERCY BYSSHE SHELLEY

What needs to be done? There can, I think, be a fair degree of agreement about this. There needs to be a rapprochement and a new

341

synthesis between the modern and the primordial minds, so as to heal the schizoid dissociation between thinking and feeling, between fore-brain and midbrain, between ego and the Self. There needs to be a transpersonal vision, a shift of consciousness away from exclusive identification with the exploitative thinking of the heroic masculine ego in the direction of a more feminine affirmation of what *is* and always has been. There needs to be a reassertion of the collective understanding that we are all parts of one ecological whole and that each of us is responsible for its sustenance. As Alexander Pope expressed it in his *Essay on Man*:

> *All are but parts of one stupendous whole,*
> *Whose body nature is, and God the soul.*

In purely practical terms it is clear that we need to restore some-thing of the primordial balance between our species and all other life on the planet. We need drastically to reduce the world's human population, reverse the rabid destruction of natural habitats and the ecosystem, re-establish the centres of human life in smaller, mutually supportive communities, promote a reverential attitude to all creation, and learn to see ourselves as the servants of nature rather than her mast-ers. Above all, there needs to be a shift in individuational priorities, so that we begin to serve not merely our personal individuation but that of all living things: we need to develop a concept of individuation operating on a planetary scale. Is such a radical alteration in psychic attitudes possible? And if so, how may it be brought about?

If our diagnosis of our condition is correct, and if we know what needs to be done, why should we not go ahead and do it? Here at once we hit the fundamental problem. *To know is not enough.* Knowledge has to be turned into collective action: ego-centred consciousness has to be sacrificed in the service of global consciousness, of Atman consciousness – consciousness that asserts our part of the 'one stupendous whole'. Neither our planet nor our species will survive if their preservation remains merely a scientific or political issue: it has to be a *religious* issue; both planet and species have to be seen as *sacred*. Only then will knowledge be informed with passion, the individual driven by collective energies in quest of a transpersonal wisdom.

At present one can see little sign of the necessary transformation occurring. We have reasons only: we lack the unifying dream. Without a sovereign myth to mobilize our collective resolve and evoke our passionate commitment, we shall do nothing but sit around and chatter about what needs to be done. The twentieth century has effectively demolished the pillars of Christendom, but, as we survey the ruins, no architect with the necessary vision comes tugging at our sleeve. This is not the first time that history has observed a great civilization coming to its end: what is new on this occasion is the very size of the catastrophe and the fact that it is happening to us.

Perhaps the catastrophe will have to take its course before the new myth can arise with enough power to seize our collective imagination. The great and necessary changes of history have all been preceded by disaster. When Buddha's wife, Gopa, tells him of a horrifying dream about a series of terrible accidents, he takes it calmly, telling her that world turmoil is necessary if inner liberation and enlightenment are to occur.

Yet we go on shaping our individual destinies – many of us in greater comfort and contentment than human beings have ever known before – within the context of disaster. For the time being, the human genome survives, and the human spirit struggles to adapt to the cacophonous uncertainties of accelerated change. We each seek reassurance where we can find it – perhaps in Jung's vision of a plant living on its rhizome: 'Its true life is invisible, hidden in the rhizome. The part that appears above ground lasts only a single summer. Then it withers away – an ephemeral apparition. When we think of the unending growth and decaly of life and civilizations, we cannot escape the impression of absolute nullity. Yet I have never lost a sense of something that lives and endures beneath the eternal flux. What we see is the blossom, which passes. The rhizome remains' (*MDR*, p. 18). If our species and our planet are in grave peril, it is purely because of our unconsciousness. Jung's point is that the necessary potential for consciousness exists in us, and may be used by those who learn 'the art of averting their eyes from the blinding light of current opinions and close their ears to the noise of ephemeral slogans'.

To confront our contemporary problems in full consciousness is to summon the collective unconscious to our aid, enabling each of us to contribute our mite to the development of a more embracing, more global consciousness. To those who think in political terms of mass movements, this seems a puny undertaking, the esoteric preoccupation of a mere handful of unusual people. Yet all revolutionary changes are led by individuals who articulate the inchoate perception of a collective need. It cannot be otherwise, for consciousness is not a *collective* phenomenon, except in the sense that we all have it, to a greater or lesser degree. Consciousness both in experience and expression is inescapably individual: each of us carries a single lamp for humanity. When our lamp gutters it makes little difference to the general illumination, as there are so many others to sustain it. In this manner, through millions of flickering lights, some burning with a more brilliant intensity than others, each going out so soon after it has been lit, the cosmos is seen and known, the universe made conscious of itself. God, say the Buddhists, understands himself through the eyes of the many.

When you look at a range of mountains, a vast expanse of sea, or a swallow building its nest, the cosmos is using your eyes and your mind through which to perceive and acknowledge it. There will be moments when you recognize the view as temporary, as being lent to you for your brief sojourn on this planet. But the cosmos, as it makes use of you, 'knows' that it was always thus. At such moments of insight the eternal and the finite are fused. This is the nearest most of us come to an inkling of our Buddha Nature, of Atman or of Tao. For that instant one is vouchsafed a glimpse of the timeless Ground of Being.

Such flashes of enlightenment are fortuitous, however, and many may never know them. The truth is that only by working on dreams and cultivating the liminal state are intimations of transcendence most likely to occur – with a consequent acquisition of the insights and skills necessary for practising the art of consciousness.

14

SCIENCE AND THE SOUL

We should take care not to make the intellect our god; it has, of course, powerful muscles but no personality.

ALBERT EINSTEIN

Half-way through writing the previous chapter, *I dreamt that I was giving a lecture to a multi-racial audience. As I spoke, the realization dawned on me that I was in a dream, and that the lecturer represented my ego and the audience the Self. Part of me spoke the thoughts proceeding in my conscious mind while the rest of me listened attentively. 'The schizoid intellect would like to deny its chthonic origins,' I declared. 'It is a phyletic snob.' I thought to myself: 'This must be non-REM sleep; I'm being too articulate for REM.' I continued in lecturing mode: 'The development of consciousness is a realization of what lies below as well as an aspiration to what is above: it is a gradual unfolding of lower and higher potentiality.' 'That settles it,' I thought: 'Definitely non-REM. Let's go deeper. Let's go for REM. Try flying.' At once I took off and found myself soaring lazily above the Devonshire coast, not far from my house. I noticed that the tide was out. Large stretches of sandy beach were exposed to the sun, and the seaweed was withering. Instead of thrusting my hands downwards as I usually do when 'flying', I was beating my arms rhythmically up and down as if they were wings. The thought occurred to me that I must be a bird, but what kind of bird? 'A liminal bird,' a woman replied from the audience. And what kind of bird is that? I looked down at my legs. They were frog's legs, with enormous webbed feet. 'A fabulous bird,' I thought, 'half avian, half amphibian.' 'It's a shamanbird,' said the voice in the audience.* This so excited me that I woke directly out of the dream and wrote it down.

As my dream so eloquently expressed it, to enter the liminal state through lucid dreaming is to enter an avian-amphibian world, a fabulous world, half conscious (air and light), half unconscious (water and darkness). To go deeper one has to fly. The lesson of the dream, I concluded, was that if the opposites are to find reconciliation in us

345

(between intellect and soul, between the two-million-year-old and the contemporary) then we must cultivate avian-amphibian skills, so as to live in the bielemental world of the *limin*. And the woman in the audience was right: this is, in effect, what shamans have always done. As Mircea Eliade has demonstrated in his masterwork *Shamanism*, che archetypal pattern of shamanic initiation invariably combines descent to the underworld with ascent into the heavens, and the accomplishment of this dual feat both in ritual and in dreams is the necessary precondition of shamanism: 'He who has undergone them has transcended the secular condition of humanity'; that is, he has become holy, sacred, numinous through his encounter with the healer archetype in himself and his consequent ability to constellate it for others. The charismatic power of the shaman depends not only on his ability to fall into a trance but on his ability to fall into a trance *at will* – i.e. he is not the victim of the trance but its master: he controls it. He has the art of *lucid trancing*! He has perfected the skill of voluntary entry to the liminal state. He imparts to all those who encounter him 'that sense of an immortal inhabitant within the individual which is announced in every mystical tradition . . . which [itself] neither dies nor is born, but simply passes back and forth, as it were through a veil, appearing in bodies and departing' (Campbell, 1962). This phenomenon was well understood by the Vedantic tradition, which is the *psychology* of the perennial philosophy: it defined three states of consciousness – waking, sleeping, and dreaming – and a fourth state which transcends and incorporates them all. Could it be that the shaman is the virtuoso of the fourth state?

Why should I have a shamanic dream as I approached the end of this book? In addition to writing the chapter on 'The Art of Consciousness', I had also been revising the chapter on 'Dream Science', and preparing a lecture on neuroscientific and experimental approaches to the study of dreams. I took the dream to be saying I had become too intellectual, too 'left hemispheric' about this: I was in need of a shamanic flight over a much loved part of the world, where the land (consciousness, intellect, science) meets the sea (the unconscious, myth, the soul), each encroaching on and receding from the other with the systole and diastole of the tides. It seemed that the tide had been out too long, for the seaweed was dying. I knew this to be true

346

for our culture, but was it equally true for me? At any event, the dream granted a bird's eye view of the territory I had been covering in the course of writing my book, both metaphorically and literally (the cliffs and beaches I could see from the air are favourite places for me and my dogs when I take a break each day for a walk). What was most striking about the dream was the strength of its feeling: it was numinous, it had religious intensity.

Here my own lack of a religious education could be relevant. As far as I am aware, the shamanbird flying over cliffs bears no relation to Christian iconography, except perhaps the dove indicating the end of the flood to Noah (writing a book is rather like being cast away for an indefinite period on an ark). In the vast majority of cultures, the religious archetype is activated in childhood. To believe in a religion or a myth is to be brought up in it, surrounded by people who share the same belief. To the critical adult, coming upon a religion for the first time, it is literally unbelievable – hence the contempt traditionally manifested by those of one religion towards members of another. In my own case, my parents brought me up with the enlightened liberal intention that I should be allowed to decide on religious matters for myself when I grew up. I therefore received minimal religious instruction as a child. The result? Aesthetic pleasure in religious buildings, art, and ritual; complete scepticism as to the existence of a personal god and the dogma which the priests have erected round Him. Yet in my dream, and during the active imagination that succeeded it, I was clearly having a religious experience: the scene below me, as well as my flight above it, was *sacred*.

Working on the dream, I allowed the idea and feeling of sacredness to return. What was it? The perception of *supreme value*. What is of supreme value to me? Life, consciousness, love, *delight in knowing that I am alive*. Do I need a dream to tell me that? Yes, because I take it for granted. It is a failure of imagination. Lacking a religious community with living rituals to create for me each day the perception of supreme value, the Self produces a dream to do it for me, to wake me up to the sacred dimension, to open me, if only for a few minutes, to the 'divine thrill', the encounter with the *mysterium tremendum et fascinans*.

Occasionally I have received a glimpse of this in Holy places – sometimes in our own Gothic cathedrals, but more reliably in those *temeni* devoid of the banal associations that a moribund Christianity has bestowed on the shrines of its past – those of ancient Greece, Japan, and India. But seldom has it struck me with such impact as in my dream of the shamanbird. In this, I am far from being alone, as I know from the many people who have shared their dreams with me. In the unconscious we remain a primordial creature, *homo religiosus*, approaching the mystery of existence in quest of a religious understanding.

The writer J. B. Priestley had such a dream during a period when he was working hard on his plays about Time: 'I think it left a deeper impression upon my mind than any experience I had ever known before, awake or in dreams, and said more to me about this life than any book I have ever read,' he wrote. The dream was as follows:

I dreamt I was standing at the top of a very high tower, alone, looking down upon myriads of birds all flying in one direction; every kind of bird was there, all the birds of the world. It was a noble sight, this vast aerial river of birds. But now in some mysterious fashion the gear was changed and time speeded up, so that I saw generations of birds, watched them break their shells, flutter into life, mate, weaken, falter and die. Wings grew only to crumble; bodies were sleek, and then, in a flash, bled and shrivelled; and death struck everywhere at every second. What was the use of all this blind struggle towards life, this eager trying of wings, this hurried mating, this flight and surge, all this gigantic meaningless effort? As I stared down, seeming to see every creature's ignoble little history almost at a glance, I felt sick at heart. It would be better if not one of them, if not one of us, had been born, if the struggle ceased for ever. I stood on my tower, still alone, desperately unhappy, but now the gear was changed again, and time went faster still, and it was rushing by at such a rate, that the birds could not show any movement, but were like an enormous plain sown with feathers. But along this plain, flickering through the bodies themselves, there now passed a sort of white flame, trembling, dancing, then hurrying on; and as soon as I saw it I knew that this white flame was life itself, the very quintessence of being; and then it came to me, in a rocket burst of ecstasy, that nothing mattered, nothing could ever matter, because nothing else was real but this quivering and hurrying lambency of being. Birds, men and creatures not yet shaped and coloured, all were of no account except so far as this flame of life travelled through them. It left nothing to mourn over behind it; what I had thought was tragedy was mere emptiness or a shadow show; for now all real feeling was caught and purified and danced on ecstatically with the white flame

348

of life. I had never before felt such deep happiness as I knew at the end of my dream of the tower and the birds, and if I have not kept that happiness with me, as an inner atmosphere and a sanctuary for the heart, that is because I am a weak and foolish man who allows this mad world to come in destroying every green shoot of wisdom. Nevertheless, I have not been quite the same man since. A dream had come through the multitude of business (Priestley, 1947, pp. 304–6).

With such a dream, one becomes, in Karlfried Durkheim's phrase, transparent to transcendence. One shares the mythic view of those American Indians who believed that every individual plant, animal, and human being was the carrier of *orenda* (soul), and that animals shared with us the knowledge that the life energy implicit in each individual soul survives death, for it is transcendent of purely temporal existence. Thus the cycle of life can proceed on its uninterrupted course, all creatures living off each other, life living on life, yet allowing all life to continue: the *uroborus*! So it is that the bison can enter into a contract with man to return each year to the same place to be hunted, and surrender willingly to being slaughtered and eaten. The energy that flickers in each individual part of existence contributes its mite to the Great Chain of Being, and then returns to its source. The plant and the rhizome again.

To work with dreams of this kind is to understand that we are moved by energies that we do not control. That is a religious understanding. Such energies are experienced as 'divine' because they come from the biological ground of all being: we do not create them, they create us. Rituals, whether public or private, whether religious or analytic, canalize these energies: in a ritual something transcendent to the intentions of the individual takes over; personal will is sacrificed to the will of the collective as constellated in its myth; the ego becomes to the Self as the moved to the mover.

The most exciting place to be is, as in my dream, the border zone between the known and the unknown – because it is full of realizable possibilities; one never knows what is going to happen next. The most creative policy is to be open to these events, never to force them into conformity with some already established dogma, but to let them develop and see where they lead. This is as true of science as it is in the analysis of dreams. Scientists, alas, do not always see it this way. Their dedication to theoretical parsimony and experimental rigour encourages them to neglect a holistic approach to the phenomena they are studying in favour of an attitude of uncompromising reductionism. Accordingly, they can assert that dreams are the meaningless by-products of neurochemical processes. In this they suffer from a kind of hysterical blindness which is no less severe than that afflicting analysts who maintain that brain research is irrelevant to their practice. It leads to the stalemate of the mindless v. the brainless. The probability is that all theories of dreams that are incompatible with the neuroscience of the twenty-first century will fade into obscurity and will find about as much practical application in psychology as the phlogiston theory in modern chemistry. If analytic theories cease to be verifiable by objective data and confirmed by discoveries in related disciplines, then members of the different schools of analysis will be reduced to the status of a querulous peasantry squabbling round a village pump.

Fortunately there is no inherent conflict between the scientific and analytic approaches to dreams, any more than there is an inherent conflict between science and the soul. Conflict occurs only when scientists become arrogant and when analysts cling to outdated beliefs. Psychology, like religion, has to accommodate to the discoveries of the present, while science has to accommodate to archetypal needs persisting from the past. If Judeo–Christian belief systems have collapsed, it is not because they are 'unscientific' but because they are 4,000 years out of date – their roots being established in Sumerian mythology. A myth incompatible with the cosmology of today will perish – as will a psychology of dreaming incompatible with our neurophysiological understanding of the brain.

Dream Ecology

Man has been endowed with reason, with the power to create, so that he can add to what he's been given. But up to now he hasn't been a creator, only a destroyer. Forests keep disappearing, rivers dry up, wildlife's become extinct, the climate's ruined and the land grows poorer and uglier every day.
ANTON CHEKHOV, *Uncle Vanya* (1900)

A patient dreamt that *he found himself in a back garden full of human faeces, polystyrene hamburger boxes, and dirty plastic bags. He surveyed the scene with feelings of profound desolation. Surely, he thought to himself, I am worthy of something better than this.*

Working on the dream, he felt that it symbolized the mess he was making of his life. But as we worked on it together, we came to see that it was also an allegory of the mess we are collectively making of our planet. His life was in a mess because of his ruthless singlemindedness: he placed professional ambition above concern for his family, his friends, his community, and himself. Our planet is in a mess because collectively we share the patient's tunnel vision. Surely, we are worthy of something better than this.

In active imagination after the dream, he was able to find a gate leading out of the garden into a landscape of hills, trees, rivers and birds, and, as he walked about in it in his inner vision, he began to feel hope and happiness returning.

Part of his problem had been his education. Ambitious parents had encouraged him to do well in the sciences at school, put him through technical college, and enabled him to become an architect. He was successful. To him a client would come with a commission to build a structure. This my patient would see as a series of 'problems' to be 'solved'. The result was that he made buildings that were efficient, but which lacked aesthetic merit – like much of the architecture that had disfigured our cities since the Second World War. In this regard, his educational history was fairly typical of our times, for it laid stress on the development of left hemispheric functions at the expense of those of the right. This is in marked contrast to the ancient view of education, which granted as much attention to music, the dance, athletics, and the arts as to the training of the intellect, the goal being to develop the *whole* human being, body and soul, in the service of a greater wisdom transcending both the Promethean and Epimethean demands of human nature.

A television series that has been running for over four decades now, called *Seven-Up*, follows a group of people from different social backgrounds from the age of seven, through fourteen, twenty-one, twenty-eight, thirty-five, and so on. With few exceptions, their personalities were at their richest and most vital at the age of seven, before Western educational practices and Western values had begun to exert their narrowing and deadening influences. It was not the evident intention of the programme makers to demonstrate this tragic process of attrition, but to the sensitive viewer the evidence is apparent. The two-million-year-old Self, still resplendent with imaginative vitality in playground and classroom in all the subjects at seven years of age, gradually shrivels up as the series unfolds. One glimpses the perplexity of this primordial survivor in their eyes, which seem filled with a fatalistic acceptance of what is lost and what might have been. 'What is happening to us,' they seem to ask, 'what are we doing with our lives?' It is as if they are bewildered by the world they find themselves inhabiting and want to know why things are not as they ought to be. What do they expect? Perhaps the two-million-year-old in them is wondering why we no longer tell the myths, beat the drums, chant the epics, paint the hunt, share our dreams, sing paeans to the gods, propitiate the demons tempting us to destruction. Bravely, they rehearse cheerful platitudes for the camera; but there is a background sense that something is wrong, something incomprehensible, something sad and pregnant with foreboding.

The survival of cultures, as well as genes, dictates that each generation must integrate old wisdom with new knowledge. This was the function of myths, ritual, initiation rites, and religion, as it still is the function of dreams. Myth provides a people with its unifying metaphor, its narrative sense of owning a place in the story of creation. Religion provides us with a code of behaviour, regulating how we treat each other and the living world around us. The trouble with the present century is that we have not only lost our myth but have forgotten our manners. Too readily we overlook the simple truth that we are here as temporary guests of our Mother, Nature, and that, like spoiled children, we have abused her hospitality. She has made us a beautiful nest and we have fouled it. But her indulgence is not inexhaustible. Already she gives signs of growing restive, implying that we have overstayed our welcome, and she is contemplating means of getting rid of us. If we wish to stay on we must learn to mend our ways. Instead of behaving like hooligans, we need to show some deference and humility. This is the message of Lovelock's *Gaia* myth. Greater consciousness is the key, but it has to be *mythic* consciousness, informed with the intuitive wisdom of the dreaming mind as well as the factual knowledge of left-hemispheric consciousness.

Since dreams have contributed to some of the most important developments in scientific and philosophical thinking, it is not unreasonable to suggest that they could be of assistance to us in our present planetary pickle. Our ecological circumstances reflect our spiritual condition, and in the course of the next century our thinking about ourselves as a species will have to undergo a revolution so profound as to make all previous revolutions seem like minor reorganizations of a parish fête. New versions of old strategies are urgently required – and that is precisely what dreams evolved to provide.

To work on dreams, therefore, is not a petty form of self-indulgence, but a spiritual ritual of cultural and ecological significance: the more conscious we become as individuals, the more hope there is for our tiny portion of the universe. In Celia Green's classic work on *Lucid Dreams* (1968), she suggests that lucid dreaming is 'the last frontier' of human psychology. In this she could be right in that cultivation of this capacity would enable each of us in our own way to become shamanic, truly at home in the bielemental world of the *limin*. But I feel we must also heed Liam Hudson's (1985) warning that dreams are our 'last wilderness', to be protected with the same fervour as the rain forests, the ozone layer, and the whale. As the only natural oases of spiritual vitality left to us, dreams are among our most precious possessions, and we must stand up to those who would diminish the value that we place on them.

Through science and technology we have achieved remarkable things in the material world, but our capacities for consciousness and development of the personality have only just begun to be explored. The scientists will further elucidate the neurological basis of consciousness, but what will continue to matter to us and to our planet is what we do with the consciousness that we have. In this application of nature's supreme achievement, our dreams will always have an indispensable role to perform.

Bibliography

Note: In the text the author/date system of reference is used with the following exceptions:

CW   *Collected Works* (Jung)
MDR *Memories, Dreams, Reflections* (Jung)
SE   *Standard Edition* (Freud)

Adler, A. (1927), *The Practice and Theory of Individual Psychology*, Harcourt, New York.

Altshuller, G. S. (1984), *Creativity as an Exact Science: The Theory of the Solution of Inventive Problems* (trans. A. Williams), Gordon & Breach, New York.

Ansbacher, H. and L. (1956), *The Individual Psychology of Alfred Adler*, Basic Books, New York.

Aserinsky, E. and Kleitman, N. (1953), 'Regularly occurring periods of eye motility, and concomitant phenomena, during sleep', *Science*, 118, 273–4.

Auden, W. H. (1976), *Collected Poems*, ed. Edward Mendelson, Faber & Faber, London.

Bailey, K. (1987), *Human Paleopsychology: Applications to Aggression and Pathological Processes*, Lawrence Erlbaum Associates, Hillsdale, N.J.

Baillet, Adrien (1691), *La Vie de M. Descartes*, Paris.

Balling, J. D. and Falk, J. H. (1982), 'Development of visual preference for natural environments', *Environment and Behavior*, 14, 5–28.

Barrett, William (1987), *Death of the Soul: From Descartes to the Computers*, Anchor Books, Garden City, N.J.

Bartlett, F. C. (1932), *Remembering*, Cambridge University Press, Cambridge.

de Becker, Raymond (1968), *The Understanding of Dreams or the Machinations of the Night*, George Allen & Unwin, London.

Beebe, John (1992), *Integrity in Depth*, Texas A&M University Press, College Station.

Bennet, E. A. (1982), *Meetings with Jung*, Anchor, London.

de Bono, E. (1969), *The Mechanism of Mind*, Simon & Schuster, New York.

Bosnak, Robert (1988), *A Little Course in Dreams*, Shambhala, Boston & Shaftesbury.

Boss, Medard (1957), *The Analysis of Dreams*, Rider, London.

Bowlby, John (1969), *Attachment and Loss, Volume 1 : Attachment*, Hogarth Press and Institute of Psycho-Analysis, London.

Bruner, Jerome (1990), *Acts of Meaning*, Harvard University Press, Harvard.

Burton, Robert (1961), *The Anatomy of Melancholy*, Dent, London.

Campbell, Joseph (1949), *The Hero with a Thousand Faces*, Pantheon, New York.

Campbell, Joseph (1959), *The Masks of God, Volume 1, Primitive Mythology*, Viking, New York.

Campbell, Joseph (1962), *The Masks of God, Volume 2, Oriental Mythology*, Viking, New York.

Carotenuto, Aldo (1984), *A Secret Symmetry*, Routledge & Kegan Paul, London.

Cawson, Frank (1995), *The Monsters in the Mind*, Book Guild, London.

Chance, M. R. A. (ed.) (1988), *Social Fabrics of the Mind*, Lawrence Erlbaum Associates, Hove and London.

Chomsky, Noam (1965), *Aspects of the Theory of Syntax*, MIT Press, Cambridge, Mass.

Cirlot, J. E. (1971), *A Dictionary of Symbols*, Routledge & Kegan Paul, London.

Cole, John R. (1992), *The Olympian Dreams and Youthful Rebellion of René Descartes*, University of Illinois Press, Urbana and Chicago.

Cosmides, L. (1985), *Deduction of Darwinian Algorithms? An explanation of the 'elusive' content effect on the wason selection task*, doctoral dissertation, Department of Psychology and Social Relations, Harvard University. Quoted by Walters, S. (1993).

Crawford, C. B. and Anderson, J. L. (1989), 'Sociobiology: An Environmentalist Discipline?' *American Psychologist*, 44 (12), 1449–59.

Crick, F. H. C. and Mitchison, G. (1983), 'The Function of Dream Sleep', *Nature*, 304, 111–14.

Darwin, Charles (1871), *The Descent of Man and Selection in Relation to Sex*, John Murray, London.

Deikman, Arthur (1971), 'Bimodial Consciousness', *Archives of General Psychiatry*, 125, 481–9.

Diamond, Jared (1991), *The Rise and Fall of the Third Chimpanzee*, Vintage, London.

Eberle, Gary (1995), *The Geography of Nowhere: Finding One's Self in the Post Modern World*, Sheed & Ward, Kansas City, MO.

Edelman, Gerald (1989), *The Remembered Present: A Biological Theory of Consciousness*, Basic Books, New York.

Edinger, E. F. (1992), *Ego and Archetype*, Shambhala, Boston and London.

355

van Eeden, F. (1913), 'A study of dreams', *Proceedings of the Society for Psychical Research*, 26, 431–61.

Eliade, Mircea (1964), *Shamanism*, Pantheon, New York.

Ellenberger, Henri (1970), *The Discovery of the Unconscious*, Basic Books, New York.

Ellis, Havelock (1899), 'The stuff that dreams are made of', *Popular Science Monthly*, 54, 721.

Erikson, E. H. (1959), *Identity and the Life Cycle*, Psychological Issues, Volume I, Number 1, Monograph 1, International Universities Press, New York.

Erikson, Erik (1954), 'The Dream Specimen of Psychoanalysis', in *Psychoanalytic Psychiatry and Psychology*, ed. R. Knight and C. Friedman, International Universities Press, New York.

Erikson, E. H. (1962), *Young Man Luther: A Study in Psychoanalysis and History*, Norton, New York.

Evans, Christopher (1983), *Landscapes of the Night: How and Why We Dream*, ed. Peter Evans, Viking, New York.

Feinstein, A. David (1979), 'Personal mythology as a paradigm for a holistic public psychology', *American Journal of Orthopsychiatry*, 49 (2), 198–217.

Fest, Joachim C. (1983), *Hitler*, Penguin Books, London.

Firestone, R. W. (1986), 'The "inner" voice of suicide', *Psychotherapy*, 23, 439–44.

Flanders, Sara (ed.) (1993), *The Dream Discourse Today*, New Library of Psychoanalysis, 17, Routledge and The Institute of Psycho-Analysis, London.

Flor-Henry, P. (1976), 'Lateralized temporal-limbic dysfunction and psychopathology', *Annals of the New York Academy of Sciences*, Vol. 380, 777–97.

Fodor, J. A. (1985), 'Précis of the modularity of mind (plus peer commentary)', *Behavioral and Brain Sciences*, 8, 1–42.

Fontana, David (1990), *Dreamlife: Understanding and Using Your Dreams*, Element Books, Shaftesbury, Dorset.

Fox, O. (1962), *Astral Projection*, University Books, New Hyde Park, New York.

Fox, Robin (1975), 'Primate Kin and Human Kinship', *Biosocial Anthropology*, ed. R. Fox, pp. 9–35, Malaby Press, London.

Foulkes, David (1978), *A Grammar of Dreams*, Basic Books, New York.

von Franz, Marie-Louise (1968), 'The Dream of Descartes', trans. Andrea Dykes and Elizabeth Welsh, *Timeless Documents of the Soul*, Northwestern University Press, Evanston.

French, Thomas and Fromm, Erika (1964), *Dream Interpretation*, Basic Books, New York.

Freud, Sigmund (1900; 1976), *The Interpretation of Dreams*, Pelican Books, London.

Freud, Sigmund (1933), 'New Introductory Lectures on Psycho-Analysis', *Standard Edition*, 22, 3–182.

Freud, Sigmund (1966), *Project for a Scientific Psychology*, ed. and trans. J. Strachey, Hogarth Press, London. (Original work published in 1895.)

The Freud/Jung Letters: The correspondence between Sigmund Freud and C. G. Jung (1974), ed. William McGuire, trans. Ralph Manheim and R. F. C. Hull, Princeton University Press, New Jersey.

Freud, Sigmund (1985), *The Complete Letters of Sigmund Freud to Wilhelm Fliess*, ed. Jeffrey Masson, Harvard University Press, Harvard, Connecticut.

Fromm, Erich (1951), *The Forgotten Language*, Grove Press, New York.

Gachenbach, J. (ed.) (1987), *Sleep and Dreams: A Sourcebook*, Garland, New York.

Gardner, Howard (1985), *Frames of Mind*, Paladin, London.

Garfield, P. (1975), 'Psychological Concomitants of the Lucid Dream State', *Sleep Research*, 4, 184.

Garfield, Patricia (1976), *Creative Dreaming*, Ballantine Books, New York.

Gerard, R. W. (1955), 'The Biological Basis of Imagination', in *The Creative Process*, ed. B. Ghiselin (pp. 226–51), New American Library, New York.

Gilbert, Paul (1989), *Human Nature and Suffering*, Lawrence Erlbaum Associates, Hove and London.

Green, Celia (1968), *Lucid Dreams*, Hamish Hamilton, London.

Griffith, R. M., Miyagi, O., and Tago, A. (1958), 'The universality of typical dreams: Japanese versus Americans', *American Anthropologist*, 60: 1173–8.

Guilford, J. P. (1977), *Way Beyond the IQ*, Creative Education Foundation, New York.

Hadamard, J. (1945), *The Psychology of Invention in the Mathematical Field*, Princeton University Press, Princeton, New Jersey.

Hall, C. S. (1966), *The Meaning of Dreams*, McGraw-Hill, New York.

Hall, Calvin S. and Nordby, Vernon J. (1972), *The Individual and His Dreams*, New American Library, New York.

Hall, Calvin, and Domhoff, Bill (1963), 'A Ubiquitous Sex Difference in Dreams', *Journal of Abnormal and Social Psychology*, Vol. 66, No. 3, 278–80.

Hall, James A. (1991), *Patterns of Dreaming: Jungian Techniques in Theory and Practice*, Shambhala, Boston and London.

357

Henry, J. P. (1977), 'Comment' (on 'The Cerebral Hemispheres in Analytical Psychology' by Rossi), *Journal of Analytical Psychology*, 22, 52–7.

Hildebrandt, F. W. (1875), *Der Traum und seine Verwertung für's Leben*, Leipzig.

Hillman, James (1964), *Suicide and the Soul*, Hodder & Stoughton, London.

Hillman, James (1967), *Insearch*, Hodder & Stoughton, London.

Hillman, James (1975), *Re-Visioning Psychology*, Harper & Row, New York.

Hillman, James (1979), *The Dream and the Underworld*, Harper & Row, New York.

Hobson, J. Allan (1988), *The Dreaming Brain*, Basic Books, New York.

Horton, R. (1961), 'Destiny and the Unconscious in West Africa', *Africa*, 31, 110–16.

Hudson, Liam (1985), *Night Life: The Interpretation of Dreams*, Weidenfeld & Nicolson, London.

Hunt, Harry T. (1989), *The Multiplicity of Dreams: Memory, Imagination and Consciousness*, Yale University Press, New Haven and London.

Inglis, Brian (1987), *The Unknown Guest*, Chatto & Windus, London.

Jacobi, Jolande (ed.) (1953), *Psychological Reflections: An Anthology of the Writings of C. G. Jung*, Routledge & Kegan Paul, London.

Jaynes, J. (1976), *The Origin of Consciousness in the Breakdown of the Bi-cameral Mind*, Houghton Mifflin, Boston.

Johnson, Robert A. (1986), *Inner Work*, Harper Collins, New York.

Jones, Ernest (1955), *The Life and Work of Sigmund Freud*, Vol. 2, The Hogarth Press, London.

Jouvet, Michel (1967), 'The States of Sleep', *Scientific American*, 216, 62–72.

Jouvet, Michel (1975), 'The Function of Dreaming: A Neurophysiologist's Point of View', in *Handbook of Psychobiology*, ed. M. S. Gazzaniga and C. Blakemore, Academic Press, New York.

Jung, C. G. The majority of quotations in the text are taken either from *The Collected Works of C. G. Jung* (1953–78), ed. H. Read, M. Fordham and G. Adler and published in London by Routledge, in New York by Pantheon Books (1953–60) and the Bollingen Foundation (1961–7) and in Princeton, New Jersey by Princeton University Press (1967–78), or from *Memories, Dreams, Reflections* (1963), published in London by Routledge & Kegan Paul and in New York by Random House. Sources of quotations from *The Collected Works* are indicated by the volume number followed by the number of the paragraph from which the quotation is taken, e.g. *CW*10, para. 441. Quotations from *Memories, Dreams, Reflections* are indicated by the page number thus: *MDR*, p. 111.

Jung. C. G., *Nietzsche's Zarathustra, notes of the seminar given in 1934–39 by C. G. Jung*, ed. James L. Jarrett in two parts, Princeton University Press, 1988, and Routledge, 1989.

Jung, C. G. (1930), *Visions Seminar I*, lecture notes of Mary Foote, C. G. Jung Institute, Zürich.

Jung, C. G. (1933), *Modern Man in Search of a Soul*, Kegan Paul, London.

Kaplan, Stephen (1992), 'Environmental Preference in a Knowledge-Seeking, Knowledge-Using Organism', in *The Adapted Mind*, ed. Jerome H. Barkow, Leda Cosmides, and John Tooby, Oxford University Press, New York and Oxford.

Kaplan-Williams, Strephon (1990), *Dreamwork*, Element Books, Shaftesbury, Dorset.

Katz, Mark and Shapiro, Colin M. (1993), 'Dreams and Mental Illness', *British Medical Journal*, Vol. 306, pp. 993–5.

Klein, M., Heimann, P., Isaacs, S., and Riviere, J. (1952), *Developments in Psycho-Analysis*, Hogarth Press, London.

Kluger, H. Y. (1975), 'Archetypal dreams and "everyday" dreams', *Israel Annals of Psychiatry*, 13, 6–47.

Koestler, Arthur (1964), *The Act of Creation*, Macmillan, New York.

Krippner, Stanley and Dillard, Joseph (1988), *Dreamworking: How to Use Your Dreams for Creative Problem-Solving*, Bearly, Buffalo, N.Y.

Kugler, Paul (1982), *The Alchemy of Discourse: An Archetypal Approach to Language*, Bucknell University Press, Lewisburg, Pa.

Kuiken, D. (1987), 'Dreams and Self-Knowledge', in *Sleep and Dreams: A Sourcebook*, ed. J. Gachenbach, Garland, New York.

LaBerge, Stephen (1985), *Lucid Dreaming*, Ballantine Books, New York.

Laing R. D. (1960), *The Divided Self: A Study of Sanity and Madness*, Tavistock Publications, London.

Langer, Susanne (1967), *Mind: An Essay on Human Feeling*, Johns Hopkins Press, Baltimore.

Loewi, Otto (1960), 'An Autobiographical Sketch', *Perspectives in Biology and Medicine*, Autumn number, pp. 3–25.

Lovelock, James (1987), 'Gaia: A Model for Planetary and Cellular Dynamics', in *Gaia: A Way of Knowing: Political Implications of the New Biology*, ed. William Irwin Thompson, Lindisfarne Press, Great Barrington, Mass.

Lévi-Strauss, Claude (1967), *Structural Anthropology*, Anchor, Garden City, N.Y.

Lévi-Strauss, Claude (1968), *The Savage Mind*, University of Chicago Press, Chicago.

Lowy, Samuel (1942), *Foundations of Dream Interpretation*, Kegan Paul, Trench & Trubner, London.
MacKenzie, Norman (1965), *Dreams and Dreaming*, Vanguard Press, New York.
MacLean, P. D. (1973), *A Triune Concept of the Brain and Behavior*, ed. T. J. Boag and D. Campbell, University of Toronto Press.
MacLean, P. D. (1975), 'Brain Mechanisms of Primal Sexual Functions and Related Behavior', in *Sexual Behavior, Pharmacology and Biochemistry*, ed. M. Sandler and G. L. Gessa, Raven, New York.
MacLean, P. D. (1976), 'Sensory and Perceptive Factors in Emotional Function of the Triune Brain', in *Biological Foundations of Psychiatry*, ed. R. G. Grenell and S. Gabay (Vol. 1, pp. 177–98), Raven, New York.
Mallon, Brenda (1989), *Children Dreaming*, Penguin, London.
Marcuse, Herbert (1964), *One Dimensional Man*, Routledge & Kegan Paul, London.
Maslow, Abraham (1968), *Towards a Psychology of Being*, Van Nostrand, Princeton.
Mattoon, Mary Anne (1984), *Understanding Dreams*, Spring Publications, Dallas, Texas.
Murdock, G. P. (1945), 'The Common Denominator of Culture', in *The Science of Man in the World Crisis*, ed. R. Linton, Cambridge University Press, New York.
Murphy, Gardner (1958), *Human Potentialities*, Basic Books, New York.
Murphy, Michael and White, Rhea (1978), *The Psychic Side of Sports*, Addison-Wesley, Redding, Mass.
Neumann, Erich (1954), *The Origins and History of Consciousness*, Pantheon, New York.
Niederland, W. G. (1957), 'The Earliest Dreams of a Young Child', *The Psycho-Analytic Study of the Child*, 12, 190–208.
Orians, Gordon H., and Heerwagen, Judith H. (1992), 'Evolved Responses to Landscapes', *The Adapted Mind: Evolutionary Psychology and the Generation of Culture*, ed. Jerome H. Barkow, Leda Cosmides, and John Tooby, Oxford University Press, New York and Oxford.
Ornstein, R. (1986), *Multimind: A New Way of Looking at Human Behavior*, Macmillan, London.
Otto, Rudolf (1950), *The Idea of the Holy*, Oxford University Press.
Painter, George D. (1965), *Marcel Proust: A Biography*, Chatto & Windus, London.
Perls, Frederick S. (1992), *Gestalt Therapy Verbatim*, The Gestalt Journal, Highland, N.Y.

Piaget, Jean (1962), *Play, Dreams, and Imitation in Childhood*, Norton, New York.

Pribram, Carl H. (1969), *Brain and Behaviour*, Lawrence Erlbaum Associates, Hove.

Priestley, J. B. (1947), *Rain Upon Godshill*, Heinemann, London.

Rosen, David H. (1993), *Transforming Depression: A Jungian Approach Using Creative Expression*, Putnam, New York.

Rosenberg, John (1963), *The Darkening Glass*, Routledge & Kegan Paul, London.

Rossi, E. L. (1972), *Dreams and the Growth of Personality*, Pergamon, New York.

Rycroft, Charles (1979), *The Innocence of Dreams*, Hogarth Press, London.

Ryle, Gilbert (1976), *The Concept of Mind*, Penguin, London.

Sagan, Carl (1977), *The Dragons of Eden*, Hodder & Stoughton, London.

Saint-Denys, Hervey de (1982), *Dreams and How to Guide Them*, Duckworth, London (first published in 1867 as *Les Rêves et les moyens de les diriger*).

Samuels, Andrew (1985), *Jung and the Post-Jungians*, Routledge & Kegan Paul, London.

Schopenhauer, A. (1862), 'Versuch über das Geisterschen und Was Damit Zusammenhängt', in *Parerga und Paralipomena* (Essay 5), Vol. 1: 313, second edition, Berlin (first edition, 1851, Leipzig).

Schubert, G. H. von (1814), *Die Symbolik des Traums*, Bamberg.

Schwartz, G. E., Davidson, R. J., and Maer, F. (1975), 'Right Hemisphere Lateralization for Emotion in the Human Brain: Interactions with Cognition', *Science*, 190, 286–8.

Sharpe, Ella Freeman (1937), *Dream Analysis*, Hogarth Press, London (reprinted 1978).

Sperry, R. W. (1968), 'Hemisphere Disconnection and Unity in Conscious Awareness', *American Psychologist*, 23, 723–33.

States, Bert O. (1988), *The Rhetoric of Dreams*, Cornell University Press.

Stevens, Anthony (1982), *Archetype: A Natural History of the Self*, Routledge & Kegan Paul, London: William Morrow & Co., New York.

Stevens, Anthony (1993), *The Two Million-Year-Old Self*, Texas A. & M. University Press, College Station.

Stevens, Anthony (1994), *Jung*, Oxford University Press, Oxford.

Taylor, Jeremy (1983), *Dream Work: Techniques for Discovering the Creative Power in Dreams*, Paulist Press, Ramsey, N.J.

Taylor, Jeremy (1992), *Where People Fly and Water Runs Uphill*, Warner Books, New York.

Tinbergen, Niko (1951), *The Study of Instinct*, Oxford University Press, Oxford.

Turner, Frederick and Poppel, Ernst (1983), 'The Neural Lyre: Poetic Meter, the Brain and Time', *Poetry*, August, pp. 277–309.

Ullman, Montague (1958), 'Hypotheses on the Biological Roots of the Dream', *Journal of Clinical and Experimental Psychopathology*, 19, 128–33.

Ullman, Montague (1962), 'Dreaming, Life Style and Physiology: A Comment on Adler's View of the Dream', *Journal of Individual Psychology*, 18, 18–25.

Ullman, Montague and Zimmerman, Nan (1983), *Working with Dreams*, Hutchinson, London.

Walters, Sally (1993), *Archetypes and Algorithms: Evolutionary Psychology and Carl Jung's Theory of the Collective Unconscious*, unpublished paper received from the Department of Psychology, Simon Fraser University, Burnaby, B.C., Canada V5A 1S6.

Wenegrat, Brant (1984), *Sociobiology and Mental Disorder*, Addison-Wesley Publishing Company, Menlo Park, California.

Whitmont, Edward C. (1990), 'On Dreams and Dreaming', in *Dreams in Analysis*, ed. Nathan Schwartz-Salant and Murray Stein, Chiron Publications, Wilmette, Illinois.

Whyte, L. L. (1979), *The Unconscious Before Freud*, Julian Freedman, London.

Wilber, Ken (1983), *Up From Eden: A Transpersonal View of Human Evolution*, Routledge & Kegan Paul, London.

Wilson, E. O. (1978), *On Human Nature*, Harvard University Press, Cambridge, Massachusetts and London.

Winnicott, D. W. (1977), *The Maturational Process and the Facilitating Environment*, International University Press, New York.

Winson, J. (1985), *Brain and Psyche*, Vintage Books, New York.

Winson, J. (1990), 'The Meaning of Dreams', *Scientific American*, November, pp. 42–8.

Glossary

agonic mode: an affect state characteristic of hierarchically organized social groups where **agonistic behaviour** (i.e conflict behaviour, such as attack, withdrawal, dominance, or submission) is inhibited.

algorithms: genetically acquired learning mechanisms which organize experience into adaptive patterns specific to certain typical activities, such as mate selection, predator avoidance, site selection, and so on.

amnesia: inability to remember.

analytical psychologist: an analyst who subscribes to the theories and who practises the therapeutic techniques devised by C. G. Jung. To be distinguished from **psychiatrist, psychoanalyst, psychologist**, and **psychotherapist** (q.v.).

anima: the contrasexual complex in the male.

animus: the contrasexual complex in the female.

archetypes: innate neuropsychic centres possessing the capacity to initiate, control and mediate the common behavioural characteristics and typical experiences of all human beings irrespective of race, culture, or creed. Archetypes are the components of the **collective unconscious** (q.v.).

collective unconscious: term introduced by C. G. Jung to designate the **phylogenetic psyche** (i.e. those aspects of the psyche which are inherited and common to all humanity).

complex: a group of interconnected ideas and feelings which exert a dynamic effect on conscious experience and on behaviour. Complexes are to the **personal unconscious** (the **ontogenetic psyche**) what **archetypes** are to the **collective unconscious** (the **phylogenetic psyche**). Both components are inextricably linked in the sense that complexes are 'personations' of archetypes.

coniunctio oppositorum: an alchemical term for the conjunction or union of opposites in the creation of new possibilities.

denial: a mechanism of ego-defence whereby a painful experience or an aspect of **the Self** is denied and disowned.

EEG: the electro-encephalograph, which measures and records differences in electrical potential between different parts of the brain.

ego: the part of the personality which one consciously recognizes as 'I' or 'me'.

363

environment of evolutionary adaptedness (EEA): the **ancestral environment** in which our species evolved and in which it has lived out 99 per cent of its existence.

ethogram: a diagrammatic representation of an animal's total behavioural repertoire, the **biogrammer** of a species.

ethology: the study of the behaviour of organisms living in their natural habitats.

Gestalt: German word meaning *form, pattern*, or *configuration*; used in psychology to designate an integrated whole that is greater than the sum of its parts.

hedonic mode: an affect state associated with affiliative social behaviour and the absence of **agonic tensions** or **agonistic behaviour** (q.v.).

homeostasis: the maintenance of constancy or dynamic balance between opposing physiological or psychic systems.

hypnagogia: images or hallucinations experienced during the drowsy state just before falling asleep (**hypnagogic** phenomena) or just after waking (**hypnapompic** phenomena).

id: Latin for 'it'; used by Freud's translators for '*das Es*'. 'We approach the id with analogies: we call it a chaos, a cauldron full of seething excitations . . . it is filled with energy reaching it from the instincts, but it has no organization, produces no collective will, but only a striving to bring about the satisfaction of instinctual needs subject to the observance of the pleasure-principle' (Freud, 1933).

individuation: term used by Jung to designate the process of personality development which leads to the fullest possible actualization of **the Self** (q.v.). 'Individuation means becoming a single, homogeneous being, and, in so far as "individuality" embraces our innermost, last, and incomparable uniqueness, it also implies becoming one's own self. We could, therefore, translate individuation as "coming to selfhood" or "self-realization"' (*CW*7, para. 266).

libido: term used by analysts of all schools to designate a hypothetical form of mental energy. It was originally conceived by Freud as energy derived from the sexual instinct; Jung rejected this as unduly narrow, preferring to conceive libido as general psychic energy which could be expressed in a great variety of forms, of which sexuality was one.

limbic system: part of the old mammalian brain, consisting of the hippocampus, hypothalamus, thalamus, and pituitary gland. The limbic system is involved in memory storage, the mediation of basic archetypal patterns of behaviour and experience, and the maintenance of **homeostasis** (q.v.).

liminality: derived from the Latin *limin*, meaning threshold or doorway:

used in psychology to refer to the threshold between conscious and unconscious levels of experience; hence, *sub*liminal, referring to psychic processes occurring below the threshold of consciousness. In falling asleep and in waking up one crosses and recrosses this threshold; in experiencing **hypnagogia** (q.v.) one straddles it.

lucid dreaming: the state of being consciously aware that one is dreaming while continuing to be in the dream.

mandala: Sanskrit word for 'magic circle', a geometric figure incorporating both a circle and a square, divided up into four (or multiples of four) segments radiating from the centre. The mandala stands as a symbol for the wholeness of **the Self** (q.v.), the deity, and the cosmos.

neocortex: this is the cerebral cortex, the new mammalian brain, responsible for cognition and sophisticated perceptual processes as distinct from the instinctive and affective behaviour patterns mediated by the old mammalian brain and the reptilian brain.

neurotransmitters: chemicals responsible for the transmission of nervous impulses throughout the central nervous system.

numinosity: term introduced into psychology by Jung, who borrowed it from the German theologian Rudolf Otto. Otto used it to describe what he regarded as the fundamental experience common to all religions – namely, the sense of awe and exaltation generated by the feeling of being in the presence of the Creator, an experience which Otto designated the *mysterium tremendum et fascinans*.

objective psyche: Jung sometimes referred to the **collective unconscious** (q.v.) as the objective psyche in order to stress its conaturality with all existence: it is as *real* and as *existent* as anything in nature. This is why fundamental natural laws, like the principles of adaptation, homeostasis, and growth, apply to the psyche just as surely as to any other biological phenomenon.

ontogeny: the development of the individual, as opposed to **phylogeny**, which refers to the development of the species.

orienting response: this was termed by Pavlov the 'what is it?' reflex. It serves to focus an animal's attention when it is presented with a stimulus. The orienting response is commonly associated with increased heart rate and other signs of arousal, which have the function of preparing the animal for an emergency reaction.

participation mystique: term borrowed by Jung from the anthropologist Lévy-Brühl to describe the psychic state in which a subject experiences a sense of identification with an object. In modern psychoanalytic terminology the phenomenon is known as **projective identification**.

persona: the mask worn by an actor in classical times; Jung used the term to describe the 'packaging' with which we present ourselves to the world. The persona is 'a functional complex that comes into existence for reasons of adaptation or personal convenience, but is by no means identical with the individuality' (*CW*6, para. 801).

phylogeny: the developmental history of the species, as opposed to **ontogeny**, the developmental history of the individual.

pleasure principle: Freud conceived the psyche in infancy as being motivated entirely by the desire to experience pleasure and avoid pain; only later, when the ego had developed, was the pleasure principle modified by the **reality principle** (q.v.). In Freud's view the pleasure principle operated throughout life as a built-in propensity to keep instinctual tensions at a minimal level.

polysemy: multiple meanings.

projection: the unconscious process by which aspects of **the Self**, or feelings or ideas associated with those aspects, are experienced as if they were located in some one or some thing external to oneself. Projection commonly functions in association with another ego-defence mechanism, **denial** (q.v.), in that one denies the existence in oneself of the beliefs, motives, or intentions that one attributes to the person, animal, or thing on to whom or which one projects them.

psyche: the totality of all mental processes, unconscious as well as conscious; as opposed to **mind**, which is conventionally applied to conscious processes only. 'The psyche is not of today,' wrote Jung; 'its ancestry goes back many millions of years. Individual consciousness is only the flower and the fruit of a season, sprung from the perennial rhizome beneath the earth . . .' (*CW*5, p. xxiv).

psychiatrist: a medically qualified practitioner who specializes in the treatment of mental illness. Only a small minority of psychiatrists are also analysts.

psychoanalyst: an analyst who subscribes to the theories and who practises the therapeutic techniques devised by Sigmund Freud.

psychologist: a pure scientist who studies all behaviour, normal and abnormal, human and animal.

psychotherapist: a generic term for therapists who use their own minds to treat the minds of others, with or without reference to unconscious processes or using the techniques of any particular school of analysis.

reality principle: term used by Freud to designate the constraints imposed as a result of environmental circumstances on fulfilment of the **pleasure principle** (q.v.). Freud believed that the reality principle developed in the course of **ontogeny** (q.v.), whereas the pleasure principle was innate and present at birth.

REM sleep: rapid eye movement sleep, which is reliably associated with the experience of dreams and with characteristic physiological changes in the body of the dreamer.

repression: the defence mechanism by which an impulse or psychic component unacceptable to the **superego** (q.v.) is rendered unconscious.

the Self: term introduced by Jung for the dynamic nucleus at the core of the personality responsible for the process of **individuation** (q.v.); the Self incorporates the entire archetypal potential of the unconscious psyche.

set: the adoption of an attentive attitude to a task with a specific goal in view.

shadow: Jung's term for the aspect of **the Self** (q.v.) which remains unconscious because it is repressed by the **superego** (q.v.) or unactivated because of deficiencies in the life experience of the individual.

soul: the animating principle in the human organism; used in the present work synonymously with **psyche** (q.v.).

superego: term introduced by Freud to designate the inner moral authority or ethical complex which monitors individual behaviour in such a way as to make it acceptable first to the parents and later to society. In the Jungian literature it is referred to as the **moral complex**.

sympathetic nervous system: the part of the autonomic nervous system that enables an organism to act in an emergency. Its activity has the effect of accelerating the heart rate, increasing blood supply to the muscles, dilating the air passages to the lungs, reducing intestinal activity, etc., thus preparing the individual to respond to an imagined or actual threat with appropriate physical activity – the so-called 'flight or fight response'.

transcendent function: Jung's term for the mutual influence which is exerted between the **ego** (q.v.) and **the Self** (q.v.) in the course of personality development and individuation (q.v.).

unus mundus: the 'unitary world', the eternal ground of all empirical being.

uroborus: ancient symbol of a serpent bent in a circle and biting its own tail; it incorporates the notion of self-regeneration, the eternal cycle of nature, and the food chain, as well as standing as an image of the primordial **Self** (q.v.) out of which ego-consciousness is born.

INDEX

abreaction, 33
abyss, 123
active imagination, 17, 76, 123, 143,
    191, 236–46, 270–71, 287, 290,
    351
Adam, 187, 321
adaptation, 125, 131, 139, 267
    as function of the Self, 206
Adler, Alfred, 31–2, 69–70, 158, 332
Aeneid, 125
Aeschylus, 241
affective script, 163
aggression, 104, 108
    see also agonistic behaviour
agonic mode, 69, 105–6, 332
agonistic behaviour, 101
agriculture, discovery of, 181
alchemy, 59, 171–2, 276
The Alchemy of Discourse, 147
Alexander, 41, 293
algorithms, 127
All-Sinn, 30
Altshuller, G.S., 280
Alzheimer's disease, 94–5
Amerindians, 13
Amfortas, 60
amygdala, 101
analysis, as a dialectical procedure, 195
analytical psychology, 32, 127
    classical school, 190
    developmental school, 82
The Anatomy of Melancholy, 88
ancestral environment, 127, 185
    see also environment of
      evolutionary adaptedness

Anderson, J.L., 127
androgyne, 30
anger, 102, 106
anima, 2, 142, 214–17, 314
anima mundi, 339
animal magnetism, 32
animism, 13, 172, 181, 268
animus, 214–17
Anna O., 33, 35–6
Ansbacher, H. and L., 70
anthropology, 3–4, 9–13, 128
Anthropos, 142
anxiety dreams, 47–8, 212, 253–6
Apollo, 188
apple, 161
Archetype: A Natural History of the Self,
    2, 126, 309n.
archetypes, 4, 17, 52
    activation (constellation) of, 132–7,
      164
    as archaic heritage, 130
    archetype-as-such, 126, 145
    biological basis of, 80, 103–8, 126–9
    and Darwinian algorithms, 127
    as fundamental psychological
      concepts, 130
    hypothesis of, 107, 125–30, 153
    as innate repertoires of adaptation,
      126
    and neuroscience, 107–8, 114
    parallel concepts to, 128–9
    as 'patterns of behaviour', 80, 103–6
    unconscious functioning of, 144
archetypes, manifestations of:
    archetypal dreams, 106–7

mental illness, 167–70
mentalism, 84
Mercury, 177, 187
Merlin, 59–61
Mesmer, Franz Anton, 32
method of doubt, 307
metric pulse, 155
Miller, Miss Frank, 119–21
mind, primordial and modern, 323–4,
    327, 342
  natural, 325–8
  poetic basis of, 338
Mitchison, Graeme, 85, 96, 98
Mithras, 186
Miyagi, O., 248
Modernism, 337, 340
Mohammed, 23, 24, 292
monotremes, 96, 144
monsters, 107, 117, 187–8, 258
morality, 226
morphogenic resonance, 30
The Moth and the Sun, 119
mother
  see under archetype and complex
mountain, 122–3
Mozart, Wolfgang Amadeus, 278, 285
Müller, Johannes, 83
multiple luminosities, 316
multiple personality, 133–4, 136, 142
The Multiplicity of Dreams, 88
Murdock, George, 130
Murphy, Gardner, 279–81
Murphy, Michael, 289
mutation, 161
mysticism, 220, 330
myth, 328, 334, 340–42, 347, 352

natural selection, 109, 127, 184, 341
nature mysticism, 13
Naturphilosophie, 30
nemesis, 265, 321
neocortex, 95, 188, 340
Neumann, Erich, 172–4, 327, 328

neural Darwinism, 109–12
neuronal gating, 95
neurosis, 210
neurotransmitters, 95
Newton, Isaac, 317, 325
Niederland, W.G., 106
Nietzsche, Friedrich, 31–2, 70
nightmares, 47–8, 253–6
night sea journey, 328
nigredo, 161
Nineveh, 8
Ninsun, 8–9
Nirvana principle, 64
Nordby, Vernon J., 72–3, 104, 247–8
Norris, John, 29
Novalis, Friedrich von Hardenberg,
    166
NREM sleep, 90–91
numinosity, 12, 131, 220, 238, 346–7

object relations, 82
Occam's razor, 88
oceanic feeling, 332
Odin, 294
Odyssey, 18, 325
Oldfield, Carolus, 1–4
Olds, James, 99
Olympica, 298
On Divination, 22
On Dreams, 19
Oneirocritica, 8, 25–7
oneirology, 3–4, 11–12, 83
oneiromancy, 12
On Prophecy in Sleep, 19
On Psychic Energy, 179
On Sleep and Waking, 19
On the Making of Man, 28
ontogeny, 89, 136
Orage, A.R., 1
orenda, 349
Orians, Gordon, 266
orientation response, 101

3:00